THE COMPL
PRO FOOTBALL

1988
14TH EDITION
THE COMPLETE HANDBOOK OF
PRO FOOTBALL

EDITED BY ZANDER HOLLANDER

AN ASSOCIATED FEATURES BOOK

A SIGNET BOOK
NEW AMERICAN LIBRARY

ACKNOWLEDGMENTS

In baseball, basketball and hockey, turnovers in managers or coaches—a seemingly constant game of musical chairs—are the norm in-season and out. But for coaching stability, no league can compare with the NFL. Certainly not this year. There are only two new head coaches in the NFL—Green Bay's Lindy Infante and the Los Angeles Raiders' Mike Shanahan. The new season also marks the birth of the Phoenix (nèe St. Louis) Cardinals, the first NFL franchise shift since Baltimore became Indianapolis in 1984.

For the 14th edition of *The Complete Handbook of Pro Football,* we acknowledge contributing editor Eric Compton, the writers on the contents page and David Kaplan, Rich Rossiter, Linda Spain, Westchester Book Composition, Dot Gordineer of Libra Graphics, Elias Sports Bureau, Pete Abitante, Dick Maxwell, Roger Goodell, Joe Browne, Jim Heffernan, Rich Mauch and the NFL team publicists.

Zander Hollander

PHOTO CREDITS: Cover—Focus on Sports; back cover—Mickey Palmer/Focus on Sports. Inside photos—George Gojkovich, Ira Golden, Vic Milton, Mitch Reibel, Wide World, Armstrong Tire, Capital Cities/ABC, UPI and the NFL and college team photographers.

SIGNET, SIGNET CLASSIC, MENTOR, ONYX, PLUME, MERIDIAN AND NAL BOOKS are published by NAL PENGUIN, 1633 Broadway, New York, New York 10019

First Printing, August 1988

1 2 3 4 5 6 7 8 9

PRINTED IN THE UNITED STATES OF AMERICA

CONTENTS

Here's Dierdorf!
Who's Madden?...............By Bernie Miklascz 6

Bo Jackson and the Impossible
Dream...Or Is It?...........By Bob Nightengale 16

The Super Saga of
Doug Williams..................By George Willis 24

San Francisco's Brimming
Bowl of Rice.................. By Dwight Chapin 34

Inside the AFC ....By Milt Northrop 42

Buffalo Bills 44   Los Angeles Raiders......112
Cincinnati Bengals.........54   Miami Dolphins...........120
Cleveland Browns 64   New England Patriots.....128
Denver Broncos 75   New York Jets............137
Houston Oilers 85   Pittsburgh Steelers 145
Indianapolis Colts..........94   San Diego Chargers......153
Kansas City Chiefs 103   Seattle Seahawks 161

Inside the NFC ....By Marty Hurney 170

Atlanta Falcons...........172   New Orleans Saints 234
Chicago Bears 181   New York Giants.........243
Dallas Cowboys..........190   Philadelphia Eagles......252
Detroit Lions 200   Phoenix Cardinals 261
Green Bay Packers.......208   San Francisco 49ers.....270
Los Angeles Rams 216   Tampa Bay Buccaneers...279
Minnesota Vikings 225   Washington Redskins....288

NFL Statistics 298
NFL Standings: 1921-1987 324
NFL Draft 346
NFL Schedule 362
NFL TV Schedule.....................................367

Editor's Note: The material herein includes trades and rosters up to final printing deadline.

HERE'S DIERDORF!
WHO'S MADDEN?

By BERNIE MIKLASCZ

How would John Madden describe Dan Dierdorf? Probably something like this:

Big guy. Takes up a lot of room in the booth. Big voice. Boom. Lets you know what he thinks. Viewers like this guy. He's a funny guy. You'd like to have a few beers with him. Even the TV critics like him.

In 1987 some of the TV critics loved Dierdorf more than Madden, who for several years has been the unchallenged king of football analysts. But now that reign may be coming to an end.

ABC's Dan Dierdorf, who shot up to No. 2 like a bullet in his first season on "Monday Night Football." Wants to be No. 1. Wants Madden's title belt. Since both are sizable former offensive linemen, it should fit.

"I want to be the top football analyst in the country," said Dierdorf. "If I didn't want that distinction, I wouldn't have gone into this business."

Last season Dierdorf made Al Michaels and Frank Gifford move over and promptly saved MNF from boredom, if not eventual extinction. Proving that there was room for a third person in the booth, even a former All-Pro tackle who stands 6-foot-3 and weighs 300 pounds, Dierdorf grabbed a tired, slumping MNF package by the throat and shook it up.

The customary 50 million people who regularly tune into MNF suddenly sat up in their arm chairs. They took notice of this giant belly-laugh of a man with walrus mustache.

Unlike a string of predecessors who failed to reach out and touch viewers, Dierdorf had something to say, and stated it loudly. Dierdorf, who likes to talk, filled the booth with an ample supply of fresh air.

Bernie Miklascz, who spent the last three seasons writing pro football for the St. Louis Post-Dispatch, *now covers the Dallas Cowboys for the* Dallas Morning News.

The ABC crew: Dan Dierdorf, Frank Gifford, Al Michaels.

"Dan is such a special talent," says ABC play-by-play man Al Michaels, "that you could throw him in the booth with anybody and the presentation would snap, crackle and pop. From the first time I met him, I knew we would click."

Dierdorf's first year was such a smash success that ABC ripped up his three-year contract during Super Bowl week and signed him through 1992 at a salary of $900,000 a year.

Then, a few days later, on Super Sunday, Dierdorf helped keep the broadcast peppy even though Washington led, 35-10, at the half and went on to defeat Denver in a 42-10 rout.

"Dierdorf was as much an MVP as Doug Williams," one reviewer wrote.

It was a perfect way to end a near-perfect debut season.

Before his arrival, the second-longest-running prime-time program on network TV clearly needed a wake-up call. Ratings were down. ABC was losing money on it. Previous tinkering had failed to stop the slide. It was a sad deterioration for a show that once had been a national event. For three hours each Monday night, millions crammed into saloons and the next-door neighbor's house as well as their own living rooms to watch. This form of pack worship became a new American tradition.

Those were the good old days. Before Howard Cosell became bitter. Before Don Meredith became stale. Before Alex Karras landed a starring role in a bad sitcom. Before a series of dull combinations—O.J. Simpson and Joe Namath with Gifford; then Gifford with Michaels in a two-man format—that sent snoozing football fans into bed.

Had MNF been an extended flash fad, destined to go the way of the hula hoop and the Nehru jacket?

"The Monday Night vehicle was a comet," Dierdorf said. "Its initial success was unprecedented. It was a comet that just appeared and exploded. It made people like Cosell a big star. Sports fans wanted prime-time football. And here it was.

"Nothing could maintain that kind of energy. It was inevitable that it would eventually slow down. But I don't think anyone at ABC was prepared for the decline. They tried a number of things, but it seemed like nothing would work."

Enter Dierdorf, who came to the network after aggressive recruiting by Dennis Swanson, president of ABC Sports. Dierdorf, now 38, had joined rival CBS in 1985 after a successful internship at radio station KMOX in St. Louis, where he played 12 seasons with the Cardinals.

After a season of play-by-play duties with a variety of partners, Dierdorf was shifted to the more comfortable role of analyst. Paired with Dick Stockton, Dierdorf caught on with his rollicking style and the team quickly became CBS' No. 2 unit.

"Dan garnered immediate respect and attention within our industry," Michaels said. "Except for Madden, it became obvious that Dan was superior to anyone out there. Everybody was talking about him."

CBS had an option to retain Dierdorf for 1987, with an increase in pay. But the network never got Dierdorf to sign the contract, which apparently got lost in someone's filing cabinet. Swanson took advantage of the administrative blunder to swoop in for the steal.

"I couldn't say no to ABC," Dierdorf said. "CBS was great. CBS gave me a start. But how could anyone turn down the chance to become a part of the most visible weekly football broadcast?"

Dierdorf also realized that the top analyst's chair at CBS would still be filled by the ample Madden. "As long as he would be there, he'd be No. 1 and I'd have been No. 2," Dierdorf said.

Dierdorf in his heyday with the St. Louis Cardinals.

Who is this guy? Dierdorf as a collegian at Michigan.

"That wasn't sour grapes; that was the reality. John deserves that status because he's excellent. But if I was going to move ahead in my career, I had to literally move."

Even though Dierdorf's potential was as enormous as his frame, his hiring by ABC carried some risk. "I never had to worry about walking through airports because no one knew me," he said. "I was not a household name. I had never scored a touchdown. I was just an old lineman with some things to say about football. I don't think I had much marquee value. I will always be grateful to Dennis Swanson for having the courage to do what he did. He made the decision based on my skills as a broadcaster, not my name value or sex appeal."

There were some early bumps. Dierdorf, Michaels and Gifford got off to a somewhat sluggish start in the preseason. Michaels had to play the role of traffic cop to keep the flow of conversation going between three voices.

"It was frustrating at first," Dierdorf said. "It was difficult not being able to say something when you wanted to say it. I'd see something on the replay and I'd have a point to make and Frank would be talking. You'd have to keep quiet. Then there also were times, I'm certain, when Frank had something to say and I was running my mouth."

Gifford presented another problem. He had been yanked from play-by-play responsibilities and moved to commentary in 1986 when Michaels joined MNF. So in 1987 Gifford had to share air-time with Dierdorf.

That the mistake-prone Gifford had been regularly lambasted by critics made the situation even more sensitive because most viewed Dierdorf's entry as the first step in Gifford's exit.

"It was, at first, a touchy situation," Michaels said. "Frank had been part of the Monday Night package almost from Day One. I think Dan and I had to move carefully, out of respect to Frank. That was fairly easy, because the three of us like each other. We have fun away from the booth, so it's only natural that we would have a good time in the booth. You can't hide animosity. If there's some bad feeling, eventually it will surface on the air.

"But it was never a problem, really. Frank enjoyed Dan's work as much as anybody. It didn't take Frank long to realize why Dan was brought in. It wasn't a matter of ABC deciding to put just any third man in the booth. It wasn't a reflection on anyone else. It was a matter of making room for a special talent. Frank accepted Dan because he knew that Dan was going to make our presentation better. And that's what all of us want—to restore the high quality of Monday Night Football."

What makes Dierdorf so special?

1. Obviously, he understands football. But so did Johnny Unitas and Jim Brown, two NFL greats who were among dozens of former stars to fizzle under the bright TV lights.

"Knowledge is only one part of it," Michaels said. "Dan understands what it takes to communicate. He understands television and what works."

2. Dierdorf is spontaneous.

"This isn't a science," Dierdorf said. "You can't write a book to show how it's done. When something happens on the field and you have a split-second to react, you can't turn to a cue-card for your lines. I don't have a bag of tricks. I don't have a routine or a schtick. Something happens and I just react. I go into a game with very little outside information. I don't want to rehash something that's already been said or written about a player. I don't want to say the same things each week. I don't want to copy-cat Madden or someone else. I just want to react to that moment when something happens on the field."

As Michaels learned, Dierdorf's reaction time doesn't lose any speed away from the booth. "We were in Denver last year, and after the game I made a bet with [broadcaster] Jack Buck about the World Series," Michaels said. "Jack put up his $150 and gave it to Dan to hold. They told me to give my $150 to Dan, who would forward the money to the winner. I insisted that I was good for the money. I'd just give it to Jack if I lost the bet. To Dan, this would not do.

"This is all taking place in the lobby of a hotel. Next thing I know, Dierdorf has picked me up, turned me upside down and is shaking the contents of my pockets out of my pants. Bills, coins, credit cards are frying all over the place. I'm hanging in mid-air, at the mercy of this huge man. People are horrified for me. Dan is just having fun."

Buck, a St. Louis institution who served as the voice of the football Cardinals, recalls Dierdorf's first game as a color analyst for KMOX. "This is right after he retired," Buck said. "I noticed Dan getting edgy before kickoff. They play the national anthem. Smoke was coming out of his ears. He's breathing heavy. He's still feeling those emotions that trigger a player moments before this violence begins. I thought he was going to smack me."

Working for CBS in 1986, Dierdorf spotted former President Richard Nixon at a New York Giants' game. Dierdorf, who'd once met Nixon at an impromptu meeting in a Philadelphia restaurant, hopped out of the booth and interviewed him. It was a high moment in an otherwise dull game.

3. The affable Dierdorf has a sense of humor that appeals to all levels of fans.

His deep laughter is contagious. He does, indeed, come across as the kind of guy you'd share a six-pack with. You'd offer him your pretzels, your nachos, the bean dip.

"Here's this big guy, crammed into an ill-fitting blazer in some small booth in the cold, having a lot of fun talking about football," Michaels described. "Viewers relate to him. There's no 'Holier than thou' aspect to him."

Dierdorf can go from a serious dissection of a just-completed play in one breath to sharp-edged wisecrack in the next. You don't know what he'll say. That's the Dierdorf personality.

As a player with the Cardinals, he was a serious, often somber, team leader. "The most intense individual I've ever seen," said former Cardinal quarterback Jim Hart, now a partner of Dierdorf's in five St. Louis restaurants.

But in the locker room, Dierdorf and linemate Conrad Dobler led the team in practical jokes and salty, irreverent behavior.

"Football is a serious business," Dierdorf said. "And part of me will always treat it that way. I played the game a long time. I see how players sweat and bleed on the field. I've seen them cry when they can no longer perform. I had a knee ripped up. I know the pain.

"But I always was the kind of player who could bring a light touch to a serious situation. I'd find a way to juggle seriousness with off-the-wall behavior. I still try to do that in broadcasting."

4. Dierdorf, unlike Gifford, isn't afraid to criticize.

He jumped on New England's Stanley Morgan for dropping a pass in a game last season. He complained about the inhumane way that injured Miami center Dwight Stephenson was carted off the field. He blasted Denver cornerback Mark Haynes in the Super Bowl for making a half-hearted effort at a possible interception.

"I'm sure that I'm not well loved in the Haynes household," Dierdorf said. "But I just can't tolerate someone who doesn't give his best."

And Dierdorf, unlike Namath, learned something important: constant criticism can become tiresome, redundant. It must be meaningful or credibility erodes.

"You have to be careful," he said. "If criticism becomes too routine, it just loses its effectiveness."

5. Despite a brilliant career in which he captured All-Pro honors six times, Dierdorf isn't the typical, one-dimensional ex-jock with a microphone.

He polished his broadcasting skills during his long apprenticeship in St. Louis. A workaholic, he hosted a two-hour talk show five nights a week, arguing with callers about everything from indoor soccer to Ozzie Smith. He did color commentary on a variety of games: Cardinal pro football, University of Missouri football and St. Louis Blues' hockey.

"It used to drive me right over the edge when people would see me, a former athlete in a booth, and put that 'jockcaster' stamp on me," he said. "I think I worked hard to achieve something in this business. I just happened to be a pro athlete. I paid my dues. When my chance came, I was ready because of my training in radio, not because I played pro football."

In 1985-86, Dierdorf nearly overtrained. In addition to his regular radio work, he began anchoring a nightly sportcast on a St. Louis TV station. On the weekends, he was off to work for

All-Everywhere John Madden at Armstrong Super Bowl fete.

CBS. Monday mornings, he did an NFL highlight segment for a CBS news program. Then he'd check in on his restaurants. Then he'd tape local TV commercials for a home builder and a car dealer.

Too much.

"I met Dan for dinner one night after he was wrapping up a typical week and he looked very worn," said Dan's wife, Debbie. "He had bags under his eyes. He was exhausted. I worried for him. I reminded him that it had been something like five weeks since the last time he had dinner with the family."

Dierdorf responds: "I didn't even realize it. I was just caught up in this routine. I knew I had to cut back."

The ABC contract enabled Dierdorf to refocus his career. Although he still hosts an occasional talk show for KMOX, he no longer feels the need to hold a microphone seven days a week. On most nights, except for Mondays during the football season, of course, he can be found at home with Debbie and his four children.

But shouldn't he be cashing in on his new success? Madison Avenue is calling, but Dierdorf isn't answering. He has no desire to out-Madden Madden, who has become something of a one-man advertising blitz.

Dierdorf has purposely refrained from endorsing products and writing his autobiography. "You do too much of that," he said without naming Madden, "and pretty soon you become over-exposed. You get old with the viewers in a hurry because they see you too much. By the time the game comes around, the person at home is saying, 'Oh no, here's that guy again.'"

Of comparisons between him and Madden, Dierdorf said, "John seeks the limelight. I don't. John is a conglomerate. I'm not. John has a routine. And if I started saying 'boom, biff and bam' during games, I'd sound stupid. I respect John, but I'm not trying to be like John."

Dierdorf wants to maintain a low profile because he believes it will keep his image fresh, thus prolonging his appeal. That he still keeps his home in St. Louis is a source of amazement to some network types, who expected Dierdorf to be under some palm tree in Palm Springs by now.

But it's all part of a Dierdorf plan. This reluctant celebrity wants to remain an Everyman in touch with his roots and the people he speaks to. Born and raised in Canton, Ohio, he's maintained his small-town values.

"I'm not a shy person," he said. "But I'm happy in my little circle of life. I make plenty of money. We live a great life. I don't want to make commercials. I'd rather use the time to be with the family, or play golf. Why should I write a book? Do I really have anything that's interesting to say? No, unless I sling mud at somebody to sell the book or spill some secrets. That would be violating a sacred trust, hurting people I played ball with. It's not worth it to me.

"I'm able to live my life the way I want to. I'm not greedy. When we go on vacation, you won't see the Dierdorfs in Paris. We go to the Lake of the Ozarks, which is this big lake in the middle of Missouri. We just jump off the back of a boat and float around. How's that for glamor?"

It won't make "Lifestyles of the Rich and Famous." But Dierdorf doesn't need that. Remember, he's already the star of a prime-time TV show, one that he may have saved.

Bo Jackson And The Impossible Dream... Or Is It?

By BOB NIGHTENGALE

It was seven years ago, back in Bo Jackson's junior year in high school, historians will note, when the controversy all began.

It was a time, curiously enough, when only Jackson's three older brothers believed he was making a mistake.

Nowadays, it seems like the whole nation has an opinion on whether Jackson should be playing football or baseball.

Yes, even in high school—when the only people who ever heard of Edward Vincent Jackson outside his hometown of Bessmer, Ala., were football and baseball scouts—Jackson couldn't make up his mind which sport to play. He was a pitcher in baseball, and would hit 20 home runs in 25 games. He was a track star, and eventually set the Alabama prep decathlon record. Football, strangely enough, might have been his worst sport. He was rated only the fourth-best halfback in the state.

So long before the Los Angeles Raiders and Kansas City Royals would begin their tug-of-war over his services, Jackson's family tried to convince him to stop this foolishness, and stick to one sport.

"They said I wouldn't succeed in three sports, that I should stick with one and stop trying to impress my friends and people in the community," Jackson said. "I told them I was going to do it, that it was none of their business what I did."

Today, Jackson says it's still no one's business what he does. He's tired of hearing people say that he can't excel while playing in the major leagues during the spring and summer, and the National Football League in the fall and winter.

"Everyone asks, 'When will I give this up and pick one

Bob Nightengale covers Bo Jackson and the Royals for the Kansas City Times *and he has followed Jackson as a Raider.*

Bo Jackson surveys the present—and the future.

Jackson fouls one, but can he connect for career in the bigs?

sport?'" Jackson said. "Well, right now I feel I have the God-given ability to display talents in both sports, and I'm going to do that.

"Criticism doesn't bother me. Everybody gets criticized. Tammy Bakker gets criticized for wearing too much makeup. Rich people get criticized for having too much money.

"No one will live my life for me. The Royals know that. The Raiders know that. But there's going to be a time when I'm going to give up a sport. I know that. I never meant to be a dual-sport athlete for the rest of my life. If I did that, by the time I was 35, I'd feel like a 50-year-old man.

"So I'll tell you now, and I want this to sink in: baseball's what I will make a career out of, not football. Football is the sport I'll give up first. The only question is when. I don't know. Right now, I'm just taking this one day at a time."

Even the Royals, who have been assured by Jackson that he'll never quit the game of baseball, hardly are basing their long-term plans around him.

"Who knows what will happen?" Royals' co-owner Avron Fogelman said. "I've been surprised so many times by what Bo says and does that I'm no longer surprised. The first night I met Bo, for instance, he said he wanted to play baseball for the Royals and give up football. I haven't been surprised by anything since."

Neither has anyone who's been in contact with Jackson.

Jackson opened his bag of surprises with his response after he was offered $220,000 out of high school to sign with the New York Yankees.

The money seemed unreal to Jackson. After all, he was one of 10 children living under the same roof, and his mother had to make ends meet by working as a domestic. You just don't scoff at almost a quarter-million dollars, folks in Bessmer said, when you're on a free-lunch program.

"I never even came close to signing with them," Jackson said. "I never let them talk to me. I didn't want any part of it.

"I figured, now what would an 18-year-old kid do with a quarter-million dollars right out of high school? I'd never seen that much money in my life, never seen a quarter of that much money in my life. And I'd be moving from a small town, where the tallest building is a 10-room courthouse, to New York.

"I said, 'No way,' simply because I had a scholarship to college, and I could play football, baseball and track at the same time. Plus, I could get my degree. So it was like I could get four things for the price of one, and I excelled at all four."

Of course, if given the time, Jackson undoubtedly could have excelled in even more sports. His high-school football coach, George Atchison, says that Jackson was an excellent swimmer and loved to high-dive. He frequently would stop by Atchison's tennis class, pick up a racket and beat everyone on the varsity. And although he never lifted weights, Jackson could bench-press 400 pounds if he wanted to.

Actually, Jackson has indicated that his favorite sport is track and field. As a schoolboy, and at Auburn in his freshman and sophmore seasons, he was an outstanding sprinter. At McAdory High he excelled in field events as well. He won the state decathlon crown with a record performance in 1982 without even competing in the final event—the mile run.

"I can remember his senior year in high school when we went

to the state track meet," said Atchison. "The state record in the triple jump was 44 feet. Bo had jumped 44 during the season, but this was the state meet. Well, with only one jump left, a kid from Fayette goes 47-8. Everybody in the stands is saying, 'Oh, that record will never be broken. That's over three feet longer than the old record.'

"Bo had one jump left. I'm sitting there with my assistant coach, and Bo goes after this kid—and he goes 48-8¼. And I mean, you knew when he was sitting in the pit he had broken it. That's what I mean. Had that kid jumped 48 feet, Bo might have gone 49.

"I saw Bo his senior year in high school high-jump 6-9 indoors. He still holds the indoor record."

Bo won the Heisman Trophy in 1985 as the nation's top collegian in football. Yet Atchison noted, "When he was at Auburn, we never really felt like he'd turned it loose. A lot of times, it looked like he was holding back, as far as making cuts and doing little things that we'd seen him do in high school.

"I don't know if Bo has ever played to his potential. That sounds crazy, a guy who's gone to L.A. and has gotten over 200 yards rushing in a game as a rookie. But he only does what he has to do."

It's safe to say that the 6-1, 222-pound Jackson didn't do research in the football and baseball encyclopedias to make a case for his playing both sports as a professional.

Only a handful of athletes have combined the two—and the results have been far from memorable in both sports, if in one.

Jim Thorpe, the Sac and Fox Indian called "the greatest athlete in the world" by Sweden's King Gustav V at the 1912 Olympics, starred for the Canton Bulldogs and other teams in the NFL's early years. Starting in 1913, for parts of six seasons in which he was an outfielder for the New York Giants, Reds and Boston Braves, he compiled a .252 batting average. In his final season, 1919, he hit .327 with the Giants and Braves. They said he couldn't hit the curve.

It's little known, but Papa Bear George Halas appeared in 12 games with the New York Yankees in 1919. An outfielder, he batted .091. The storied coach and owner was a Bear end for 10 years, starting in 1920.

Ace Parker was a colorful quarterback for the Brooklyn Dodgers (yes, they were in the NFL) from 1937-41 and with the Boston Yanks (so were they) in 1945. But over the 1936-37 seasons he played infield for the Philadelphia Athletics. He batted .179 in 94 games.

Carroll Hardy played halfback for the 49ers in 1955 before

The celebrated Jim Thorpe did it all.

launching a baseball career as an outfielder from 1958-67 with the Indians, Red Sox, Astros and Twins. He batted .225 lifetime.

Tom Brown played first and the outfield for the Washington Senators in 1963, batting .147 in 61 games. His future was not in baseball. So from 1964-68 he was a halfback with the Green Bay Packers, finishing up with the Redskins in 1969.

History be damned. Bo Jackson responded with a "yea" when Al Davis, the Raiders' general, lured him with a pro football

Bo ran wild in MNF game against Seattle.

challenge and a five-year, $7.4-million contract in 1987.

"Bo has never left a challenge unfulfilled," said Richard Woods, Jackson's attorney. "It excites him, sets his adrenaline going."

Football, Jackson had initially claimed, was a sport already conquered once he won the Heisman. But, after getting his chance with the Royals, he'd heard talk that he didn't go into the NFL because he was afraid of the contact and violence, or afraid of simply being mediocre, or even a failure.

"I wanted to shut some people's mouths," he said.

He did so on an electrifying Monday night (Nov. 30) last season when he rushed for 221 yards on 18 carries against Seattle, including a 91-yard run that proved to be the longest of the year in the NFL. He wound up his short season with 554 yards on 81 carries, a 6.8-yard average, and four touchdowns.

"There's no question he's a Hall of Fame back," said former Raider halfback Clem Daniels, who held the team's single-game rushing record of 200 yards until Jackson ran over Brian Bosworth and past everyone else. "They come along every 20 years, one like him."

Raiders' cornerback Lester Hayes said: "Bo is God's gift to halfbacks. He's unreal. He's a step beyond stupendous. He was destined to be a football player."

Well, maybe so, if it just wasn't for this game that's played with a white, round ball with funny red stitching.

"He's the finest athlete and prospect of our time, maybe ever," said Art Stewart, Royals' scouting director. "I mean, there have been others, but never anyone with the overall talent, never anyone who combined the speed of a Willie Wilson, the arm of a Roberto Clemente, and the power of a Mickey Mantle."

Jackson displayed his baseball talents in the majors in 1987 after just 89 collegiate games and 79 in the pros when he hit 18 homers and drove in 45 runs while batting .254 at the All-Star break. Yet, after making his announcement on July 11 that he would play football in the offseason, the fans, as well as some of his teammates, turned on him. He hit just .188 after the All-Star break, and was benched much of the last two months. He was .245 for the season.

It was expected that Jackson would have to start the '88 season in the minors, replaced by Gary Thurman. Well, he arrived a week before the rest of his position teammates in spring training, worked harder than anyone, and wound up once again as the Royals' starting left fielder.

Jackson is in the final year of a three year, $1,0666-million baseball contract. How he fares in the '88 baseball season will be critical to his two-sport plan. Clearly, off his pro debut in football he can make it as a Raider.

Money, he agrees, is not a factor."I've never seen a paycheck, and I never want to see a paycheck," he says. "I wouldn't know what to do with that money. The only thing I have are two credit cards with me. Whenever I see something I want, I charge it. I don't want to be known as a guy who cares about all that, a guy who carries a pocketful of money. I'm not that type of person."

The Royals may help Jackson make up his mind by issuing an ultimatum to choose a sport. Avron Fogelman hints that he will speak with Jackson after the baseball season and have him "decide if he wants to be a baseball player or not."

Jackson, in the meantime, will keep the sports world guessing.

"I really don't know if anyone is having a better time than I'm having now," he said. "Right now, I feel like I'm sitting on top of the world. So I won't decide until I have to."

Bo Jackson would have it no other way.

THE SUPER SAGA
OF
DOUG WILLIAMS

By GEORGE WILLIS

On Feb. 13, 1988, nearly 40,000 people lined the main street of tiny Zachary, La., hoping for a glimpse of the latest American hero. He happened to be their own native son, Doug Williams, the Super Bowl's Most Valuable Player and living proof that nice guys don't always finish last.

Two weeks earlier, his Washington Redskins won Super Bowl XXII in San Diego with a surprisingly one-sided 42-10 victory over the Denver Broncos. In the process, Williams won the heart of America by overcoming personal tragedy and setbacks to lead his team to football's most coveted prize. It was the most pleasant story of the 1987 football season, complete with a storybook ending.

Throughout his moment in the sun, Williams repeatedly praised his hometown of Zachary, a tiny rural community about 15 miles north of Baton Rouge. "If you want to know about Doug Williams, go to Zachary," he told reporters a day after the Redskins defeated the Vikings, 17-10, for the NFC championship.

Now it was time for Zachary to pay tribute to him. So, the good folks threw the biggest celebration next to Mardi Gras that southern Louisiana has ever seen. First there was a parade down Main Street followed by a ceremony at the local high school. "Never in my wildest dreams did I think the Super Bowl MVP would be Doug Williams," the 32-year-old Redskin quarterback told the crowd. "It's a great feeling."

Williams was an interesting story before the Super Bowl, having overcome the tragic death of his first wife, a bitter split from

George Willis of Newsday *visited Doug Williams' hometown and was an eyewitness to the MVP's Super Bowl exploits.*

Doug Williams uncorks MVP performance in Super Bowl XXII.

the Tampa Bay Bucs, and two obscure seasons in the USFL to go from backup to starter with the Redskins. But after a fabulous Super Bowl, the one-time forgotten man became a national celebrity.

How fabulous was Williams in Super Bowl XXII? This fabulous:

• Posted a record 340 yards passing, 228 of which came in the second quarter when the Redskins scored a record 35 points.

• Had a record-tying four touchdown passes, all of which came in the second quarter on throws of 80, 27, 50 and 8 yards.

• Engineered a comeback from a 10-0 deficit—the biggest comeback in Super Bowl history—after shaking off a first-quarter knee injury that would momentarily take him out of the game and would later require surgery.

Instantly, everyone wanted a piece of Williams. *Sports Illustrated* and *People* did feature stories. Walt Disney produced a quick commercial. Wheaties put Williams and the Redskins on

After the ball was over...

their boxes, and an appearance on the "Oprah Winfrey Show" was scheduled for March.

Eddie Sapir, Williams' agent, estimated his client easily could make $500,000 during the offseason promoting everything from "soup to nuts" if he wanted. But Williams prefers the quiet of Zachary to the bustle of Madison Avenue. "I'm not going on tour," he declared. "I might make some visits to some charity organizations, banquets or something like that. But I'm not going to be hopping on a plane every other day."

And you know what? He didn't. Before undergoing arthroscopic surgery on his left knee March 10, Williams made few personal appearances. The majority of his time was spent as he said it would be, "doing things around the house."

"He's really a momma's boy at heart," said Doug's youngest brother Mike, who played three years in the Canadian Football League. "He likes the pure and simple life. Anything complicated and he doesn't want to deal with it."

The ground work for Williams' growth into athletic excellence began in Zachary, where the eight children of Laura and Robert Williams spent most of their free time playing sports in the front yard of their home off Plank Road. Back then, Doug didn't dream of winning the Super Bowl. Baseball was his game.

A star pitcher in Little League and later in American Legion, Williams looked as if he would follow in the footsteps of his oldest brother Robert Jr., who pitched his way to the Class AA level of the Cleveland Indians' organization before an arm injury ended a promising career. "Everybody once thought that I would be the superstar of the family," said Robert, 46. "When I hurt my arm, then I started grooming Doug to be the superstar."

Robert, now the director of middle schools for east Baton Rouge, was coaching a junior high football team when he forced Doug to play quarterback and middle linebacker. "It was either play football or be whipped," Doug recalled. He played.

Also the varsity basketball coach, Robert made Doug the ballboy and would often pull his brother aside after practices and grill him on the fundamentals.

"He was always my toughest coach," said Doug, who led Chaneyville High in scoring for three straight years. "I wouldn't have been in the Super Bowl if it weren't for Robert."

By his senior year, Williams had established himself as a top football prospect. He passed for 1,800 yards and 22 touchdowns his senior year. But because black quarterbacks were a rarity among major college teams in the South, only Mississippi Valley State and Southern University offered scholarships.

Grambling was a late entry, thanks to Robert. A Grambling

alumnus, he contacted Eddie Robinson, who later telephoned Doug to offer him a scholarship. "I accepted," Doug said, "without meeting him [Robinson] in person."

A few weeks later, after watching Williams pitch in an American Legion game, an LSU coach was so impressed that he offered a baseball scholarship.

"It's too late," Robert told the coach. "He's going to Grambling."

By the time Williams had finished his college career, he was first-team Kodak All-America, the first black quarterback to receive such an honor. But his years at the predominantly black school weren't all sunshine. After redshirting his first year, Williams was the third-string quarterback at the start of his freshman season. Disappointed, he contemplated transferring to another school. But he got his chance in the fifth game of the season and led the Tigers to a 21-0 win over Tennessee State. Needless to say, he remained the starter for the remainder of his career.

In those 3½ seasons at Grambling he passed for 8,411 yards and 93 touchdowns. He finished fourth in the 1977 Heisman Trophy balloting (Earl Campbell of Texas won the award), was voted MVP of the East-West Shrine All-Star Game and played in the Senior Bowl.

That winter he met Joe Gibbs, a little known offensive coordinator with the Tampa Bay Bucs. Gibbs was sent to Louisiana to do a personality check on Williams, whom the Bucs were considering drafting in the first round. There was no question about his talent. "We wanted to find out about his personality and football mind," Gibbs recalled.

During that one-day visit, Gibbs followed Williams to a Monroe, La., high school where he was student-teaching. Later, they had lunch at McDonald's, followed by a blackboard session where Gibbs sketched out some plays and situations and asked for Williams' opinions.

Upon his return, Gibbs filed a glowing report calling Williams "a top-caliber prospect. I was sold on him playing for the Bucs."

Two months later, Tampa Bay selected the Grambling star in the first round (17th overall), the first black quarterback to be drafted that early. (Gibbs would leave the Bucs after Williams' rookie year to join the Chargers' staff in San Diego, but the mutual respect they gained for one another that season laid the foundation for a world championship nearly 10 years later.)

When Williams arrived for training camp his rookie season, Bucs coach John McKay called him "the future of the franchise" and immediately made him the starting quarterback. At first, the alliance was everything the Bucs would want.

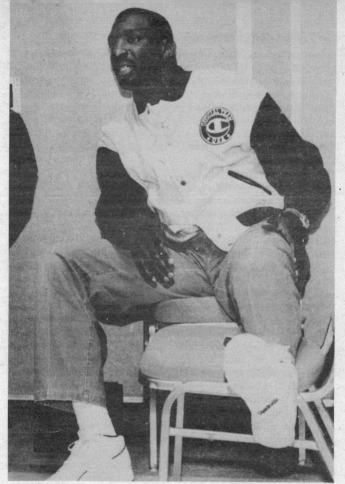

The damaged knee required surgery in the offseason.

In five years, Williams led the Bucs to three playoff appearances and the NFC championship game in 1979. Though he didn't always look pretty (he completed just 47 percent of his passes and never made the Pro Bowl), Williams and the Bucs appeared headed toward a consistent level of competitiveness.

"He may not have had good numbers, but he was definitely a winner," said Jimmie Giles, a former Buc tight end.

Despite their success, the Tampa fans had a love-hate relationship with Williams throughout his 33-31 record as a starter.

During the good times, he was called hero. But when things went bad, the Tampa fans could be vicious. Once after a 1981 playoff loss to Dallas, someone sent him a beautifully wrapped package. Inside was a rotten watermelon with the note: "If it wasn't for your black ass, Tampa Bay would have won."

Still, Williams was fond of Tampa and never intended to leave the team when his contract came up for renewal after the 1982 season. His salary of $125,000 that year ranked 46th among 83 NFL quarterbacks. With a new wife and baby to care for, he sought the security of a lucrative contract. Publicly he asked for $875,000, but was willing to settle for $600,000 a year for three years. The Bucs stood firm at $400,000.

The negotiations quickly got messy. Verbal exchanges in the media got nasty. Bridges were burned.

In the midst of the negotiations, Williams suffered a personal tragedy. His wife of less than a year, Janice, died eight days after surgery for a brain tumor. Their daughter, Ashely Monique, was 11 weeks old. Janice was 26.

"They began dating during his freshman year at Grambling when he was just a long, lanky, big-eyed country boy," Mike Williams said. "He trusted her more than anyone else in the whole world. Her death left him on an island. I don't think he'll be that close to anybody again."

Family and friends did what they could to ease the pain. But even they had trouble measuring how much he was hurting. "He doesn't talk about things that trouble him," said his mother, Laura. "You've got to know him to see it. I could see it. I knew he was hurting."

While Williams grieved, the Bucs grew impatient and in June 1983 they traded a first-round draft pick to Cincinnati for Jack Thompson, a backup quarterback. That August, a frustrated Williams signed a five-year, $3-million contract with the Oklahoma Outlaws of the USFL.

In two seasons (1984-85) at Oklahoma and Arizona, Williams completed 51.3 percent of his passes for 6,737 yards and 36 touchdowns. He also underwent his third knee operation.

When the USFL folded in August 1986, he made it known to the NFL that his services were available. Amazingly, only one team was interested: the Redskins. Gibbs and Washington general manager Bobby Beathard agreed that Williams was the best available backup for Jay Schroeder, who had established himself as the club's starting quarterback.

The Redskins made it clear he wouldn't be the starter and asked Williams if he could handle the role mentally. With no other options available, Williams said he could.

Doug did his fling at Tampa Bay.

In 1986, he threw only one pass—it was incomplete—while Schroeder enjoyed a Pro Bowl season. And it didn't appear the next season would be any different.

They were different in one respect, however. Before the '87 training camp, Williams married Lisa Robinson, who co-produced the Redskins' "12th Man" video.

But until Schroeder suffered a shoulder injury in the opener against Philadelphia, and had to leave the game, Williams seemed destined for backup duty. In the first of three relief appearances and two starts he would make during the regular season, Williams led the Redskins to a 34-24 victory.

Schroeder reclaimed his job after the players' strike and remained the starter until he was pulled from a Nov. 15 game against the Lions after repeatedly overthrowing open receivers. Williams entered in relief and led the Redskins to a 20-13 win.

But just when the starting job appeared to be his, Williams pulled a ligament in his back during practice and sat out a game with the Giants Nov. 29. Schroeder earned his job back by passing for 331 yards and three touchdowns in a 23-19 win.

That week Williams was speaking to a group of writers when tears formed in his eyes. "It's not because I wasn't starting," he said later, "but because of a lifetime of frustrations."

But fate made one more turn towards Williams' way. In the regular-season finale at Minnesota, Schroeder lost his touch and confidence, prompting Gibbs to put in Williams, who came off the bench to rally his team to a 27-24 victory. A few days later, Gibbs announced Williams would be his team's starting quarterback for the playoffs.

When the Redskins beat the Vikings for the NFC championship, Williams became part of pro football history. He would be the first black quarterback to start a Super Bowl, something the 2,000 reporters who covered the event would never let him forget.

For two weeks, he carried Black America on his shoulders, or so you would have thought. Each day he was questioned again and again about the significance of his achievement.

Did he feel honored? Did he feel like a pioneer? Will this make it easier for other black quarterbacks to be accepted in the NFL? And the one question from a well-meaning Mississippi reporter, "How long have you been a black quarterback?"

Williams answered as cordially and carefully as he could. "I just happen to be a Redskin, a quarterback and a black," he repeated. "I'm just trying to deal with the football game. After the game—black, white, green or yellow—we'll deal with that then."

A week after the Super Bowl, Williams was critical of the enormous attention given to his blackness. "Most people made it seem like the Redskins were more like the Ringling Brothers circus," he said. "You know how when the circus comes to town, they've got the fat man, the man with the two heads and everything else. Everybody came to San Diego to look at the Washington Redskins with a black quarterback and nobody gave us a chance to win the football game."

Only time will tell what Williams' performance will mean for future black quarterbacks, but at least one man considers it a meaningful step. "I think the NFL has finally removed the stigma of a black man playing quarterback in this league," said Grambling coach Eddie Robinson. "Now I hope they remove the stigma of a black being a head coach."

While future black quarterbacks will still have to prove themselves, Williams entered the 1988 training camp as the unquestioned starter. "It'll be just like old times," he said. "That's what I've been most of my career."

The surgery to his knee in March should, if anything, give him the kind of mobility he had earlier in his career. Bone chips and other fragments were removed from the knee, which was expected to be at full strength by training camp.

Williams is to make $500,000 this season in the final year of his three-year contract. And despite his season-ending success, he won't push the Redskins for a more lucrative deal. "I'm not going to ask for more money," he said, knowing Schroeder will make $900,000 this year. "If they think I deserve having my contract renegotiated, the Redskins will come to me."

Along with presenting Williams with an $18,000 sports car and a trophy for being named the Super Bowl MVP, Subaru offered to make a $10,000 donation to the charity of his choice. He selected the Arthritis Foundation and asked that the check be given in the name of his father, Robert Williams Sr., 65, who had been crippled with rheumatoid arthritis the past 20 years. In 1983, he had his left leg amputated just above the knee and was not among the 15 family members who journeyed to San Diego —at Doug's expense—for the game.

"It was tough on him because he'd always been an active individual who liked to hunt and fish and do all those things," Doug said. "Now here's a guy losing his leg and he's not going to be able to do those things being confined to a wheelchair.

"We were worried about him for a while. He didn't eat. But somewhere along the line, he realized you can live without anything but life. He went on and started doing the things the doctor wanted him to do. Now mentally, he's a lot stronger than he was. It helps when you watch someone in your family go through those things and are able to survive. That's why I look at myself and say, 'No matter what happens to me, I've got it a heck of a lot better than other people.'"

And it's getting better.

SAN FRANCISCO'S BRIMMING BOWL OF RICE

By DWIGHT CHAPIN

Jerry Rice was asked in a television interview not long ago how he would cover Jerry Rice, if he were a defensive back.

Rice, who enjoys self-analysis about as much as he would fancy having small spikes driven under his fingernails, fidgeted, squirmed and smiled self-consciously for several seconds. Just when it looked as if his silence might extend into the next commercial, Rice said, "Nothing comes to mind."

It is a view he shares with most of his fellow NFL players, particularly the defensive backs.

Rice had an astounding 22 touchdown receptions in an even more astounding 12 games during the NFL's strike-shortened 1987 season, topping Mark Clayton's record by four. He set another league mark with at least one TD catch in 13 straight games (including one in 1986). And he had 23 total touchdowns and a league-high 138 points.

His coach, Bill Walsh of the San Francisco 49ers, says, "He's the single most dominating player in the game today."

Coach Mike Ditka of the Chicago Bears says, "You're not going to stop him. He's going to make the big play somewhere."

There's no question that Rice, who won nearly 30 postseason awards for his spectacular play, is a star—maybe the NFL's brightest young star at 25. It wasn't just what he did on the way to becoming virtually everybody's NFL Player of the Year, it was how he did it. Rice seemed to be operating in a different world —a private world—much of the time. No matter the quality of

Dwight Chapin, formerly of the Los Angeles Times, *has been a cityside columnist and sportswriter for the* San Francisco Examiner *for nearly a decade.*

No argument. Jerry Rice was NFL Player of the Year.

the opposition during the regular season, he would fake and glide past defenders with those long, flowing strides and that deceptive speed . . . then, the terry-cloth towel in his waistband streaming behind him, he'd catch almost everything Joe Montana and Steve Young threw, with huge, sure hands.

As it was happening, he knew it was a special season. "I'd watch myself on game films and I think, 'Hey, that's not me; that's not real,'" he said.

But those who had watched Rice closely since he joined the

49ers as a No. 1 draft choice out of tiny Mississippi Valley State in Itta Bena, Miss., three seasons ago, were not particularly surprised.

At the start of his professional career veteran 49er wide receiver Dwight Clark took one look at him and said, "He's a natural."

And, also from the beginning, he's had a lot of blue-collar worker in him.

"He's a really good student of the game," says 49er receivers coach Dennis Green. "He studies everything—defenses, players he'll be going against, types of coverages. Everything. He's never going to take it easy. I've never seen him run a half-speed pattern. There's never a pass he considers routine. When the ball is in the air, he thinks it's his."

"Jerry wants to be the best," says 49ers defensive back Tim McKyer. "He works very hard, plus he has all the necessary skills. Put it all together and it spells awesome."

The work ethic that drives Jerry Rice stems from his boyhood as one of eight children in Crawford, Miss., population just over 500, and his father, Joe, a bricklayer.

"He took me out with him several times on jobs," Rice says. "We'd go out at five in the morning and come back after the sun went down. I learned the meaning of hard work, but I also learned, from the first day, that I didn't want to lay bricks for a living."

Joe Rice says that Jerry handled bricks better than any assistant he ever had, however, and at one time Jerry thought of becoming an auto mechanic (he majored in mechanics at Mississippi Valley State before switching to electronics).

"I've always been good with my hands," he says.

He might never have played football, however, if he hadn't decided to play hooky from B.L. Moor High School one day when he was a sophomore. He was sneaking down a hall when the assistant principal came up from behind and scared the stuffing out of him. Rice dashed away. The principal was so amazed by how swiftly he moved that he sent Rice a message the following day: "Go see the football coach. He needs your speed."

"I really had no interest in playing," Rice says. "I know this might sound strange since I was skipping school that day but I was mostly into the books then. At the very first workout, though, I found out I could play. I was catching the ball good and I said to myself, 'Wow, I didn't know I had this in me.'"

The toughness—he isn't afraid to lay a block on an opponent when the occasion dictates it—and discipline that have become so much a part of his game and his mind-set surfaced soon after.

"A lot of times I didn't have transportation to and from practice," he says. "I had to run five or six miles to practice and then another five or six miles to get home."

He survived well enough to attract a small amount of attention for his high-school play, but the big colleges didn't come calling.

Rice wanted to go to Mississippi State but ended up at Mississippi Valley State, which was the only school that sent a coach to see him. Still, he was able to look at things practically.

"It was a way to get a free college education," he says.

By the time he was a college junior, his teammates had nicknamed him "World" (as in All-World), and he knew he had a shot at being a professional.

"But the self-doubt about whether I'd make it was always in my mind," he says. "One of my older brothers, Tom, who had played at Jackson State, didn't make it in the pros."

The major reason Rice wanted to play for money, he says, was to give something back to his parents, Joe and Eddie B.

"If Tom had been successful in the pros, he would have built them a house," Rice says. "I was the last shot in our family to do that. In 1986, I saw to it that they got a new home, in Starkville."

Despite almost constant double-teaming by opponents, the 6-2, 200-pound Rice exceeded 1,000 receiving yards three straight years in the Phi Hook 'Em, Juke' Em passing attack of Mississippi Valley State, had more than 100 receptions each of the last two seasons and scored 28 TDs as a senior, when he was a Division 1-AA All-American.

"Playing in our offense, Jerry saw everything, and I mean everything, so he was much better prepared for pro football than most receivers," Delta Devils' coach Archie Cooley said after his senior season. "He saw all kinds of coverages designed to stop him and ran patterns from every position—outside, the slot, from the backfield. There's very little he can't do. It's just a routine job for him to get open."

Paul Hackett noticed. Hackett, then a 49er assistant coach, was in charge of scouting college receivers for the team in 1985.

"The day I sent Bill Walsh film of Jerry he just raved," says Hackett, now a Dallas Cowboys' assistant. "He said, 'This guy looks great. He's a John Jefferson with more speed. But I don't think we have a chance to get him.'"

They did get him, however, by "trading up" to 16th place in the first round of the 1985 NFL draft.

That July, Rice signed a five-year contract estimated to be worth about $1.8 million, including a signing bonus of approximately $365,000 (he now is trying to renegotiate the contract).

The early raves from Clark and others notwithstanding, there was more than a bit of trouble just ahead for Rice. He had considerable difficulty holding onto passes, dropping a dozen in his rookie season.

"I couldn't understand it," he says. "I'd never done that before, and I really got down on myself. I wore gloves for awhile thinking they would help. But I realized it wasn't my hands that were the problem, it was my confidence."

Rice was helped through this time of trial by Clark and wide receiver Freddie Solomon, a notably unselfish man, considering Rice was out to take his job.

"There was no animosity with Freddie," he says. "He took me under his wing and we became the best of friends. The main thing he did was to tell me to stop worrying about running and just catch the ball."

Thus assured, Rice went from stone hands to gold fingers.

On Dec. 10, 1985, against the Rams, he caught 10 passes for 241 yards, setting a 49ers' record and coming within 15 yards of breaking the NFL record for receiving yardage by a rookie.

"I knew then I was on my way," he says.

Rice ended the season with 53 catches for 972 yards and three TDs, and was chosen UPI's NFC Rookie of the Year.

He drove himself through a rigorous conditioning program, and, in 1986, he caught everything in sight, 86 receptions. He broke three team records and tied three others, and his 1,570 receiving yards were the third best for one season in league history behind Charley Hennigan's 1,746 and Lance Alworth's 1,602. He was selected NFL Player of the Year by *Sports Illustrated* and started in the Pro Bowl.

But in the NFC playoff semifinal against the Giants, Rice fumbled the ball away to New York after catching a Montana pass that would have been the game's first touchdown. The 49ers eventually lost, 49-3, so the bobble probably made little difference, but it dogged him all that winter and spring.

Again, he worked harder and with even more dedication— "He has an opinion, and it's correct, that the harder he works the better he'll be," says Green—and that led to the magic of '87.

Some think deception is more important to Rice's game than speed. He and his five brothers used to chase their neighbors' horses over seven acres of farmland when they were boys and Rice developed plenty of moves.

But he bristles a bit when you question whether he can run as fast as other top NFL receivers. Most rivals agree that whatever his clockings, he has wondrous football speed.

"I understand that Rice doesn't run under a 4.5 or 4.6 40," says Ram defensive end Gary Jeter. "But he's one of those guys

Nobody ever caught more TD passes (22) in a season.

who runs a 4.2 or 4.1 when he's going for the ball. He seems to accelerate when everybody else slows down."

"When the ball is in the air," 49er quarterback Young says, "Jerry is the world's fastest human."

Rice himself says, "If I get side to side with a defender and Montana or Young puts up the ball, I'm confident I can get the separation and make the catch."

Montana, in particular, is due some of the credit for Rice's emergence as one of the game's elite.

"We have a good chemistry going," Rice says. "I know where his passes are going to be, so I just have to make sure I get to the right spot at the right time."

Many of the connections have come after Montana has called

audibles at the line of scrimmage.

"Once Joe starts audibilizing, I just smile," says Rice, who was captured grinning in several photographs last season, "because I know there will be one-on-one coverage and I'll be open."

In some ways, Jerry Rice is an extrovert.

Last season he wore the inscription "Flash 80" on his trademark towel, until league officials, ever conscious of conformity, told him to stop. After touchdowns, he does an end-zone dance called the Cabbage Patch. He drives a Jaguar with "World80" plates, favors flamboyant clothes out of *Gentleman's Quarterly* and sports a frou-frou haircut that had led teammates to nickname him "Fifi" and "6-7" (6-2 worth of body topped by five inches of hair). He's so concerned about his appearance that his wife, Jackie, says, "He spends more time in front of the mirror than I do."

His teammates have harassed him a lot about his hair—"If you got Wiffle Balls and a club, it would make a helluva tee," says guard Randy Cross—and his mother wishes he'd choose a more conservative look, but he has no plans to do that, maybe because the current coiffure is good for business at the beauty salon he owns in Mississippi.

"Everybody there has a Jerry Rice cut," he says.

On the field, Rice leads by example. "I try to inspire the other players," he says.

And because he's aware he also has become a role model for kids and wants to present the proper image, he's polishing his public speaking, which still shows traces of his ethnic roots, with the help of voice coach Sylvester Jackson, a San Francisco radio personality.

"I've tried to help him be more conscious of getting his thoughts together, of what he's saying and how he looks," says Jackson. "We have a lot of work to do, but Jerry will continue to grow, just as he has a football player. He has a down-home quality that's very special."

There's still plenty of the introvert in Jerry Rice. He hasn't completely overcome the shyness that made him shun the spotlight when he arrived in San Francisco and for some time afterward.

"I was overwhelmed at first," he says. "I got off the plane, saw all those cameras and was shocked. I had never been exposed to that kind of attention."

He had to venture out a lot this last offseason, to pick up all the awards and honors, and he dutifully made all the stops. But, clearly, he's much happier at home in his Redwood Shores, Cal., condominium with Jackie and year-old daughter Jaqui (he plans to build a home soon and bring out his family from Mississippi).

"I'm a quiet person and I like my privacy," Rice says. "I've only been to San Francisco a few times because I don't like the traffic."

The whole football world is watching him now but he seems unlikely to change much.

"I do think he's more polished, more mature, more worldly than he used to be, but he's still rather modest and shy," says his agent, Jim Steiner of Sports Management Group in St. Louis. "You just wouldn't think, dealing with Jerry on a day-to-day basis, that he's the superstar he is. He doesn't have the huge ego.

"He won't have any trouble handling the attention because he doesn't seek it out, or thrive on it. It's not his first priority. His first priority is football."

So, while there are some off-the-field things in the works— Rice is thinking of opening a Bay Area restaurant and developing a "Flash 80" merchandise line of several products—he's much more interested in improving his blocking and his pass routes and pursuing perfection.

"I really love the game of football," he says. "I'm still like a little kid. That gives me the drive to be successful. This is all really like a dream come true for me."

It might seem that he could never improve on his numbers of 1987, that it was a once-in-a-lifetime season, but he doesn't seem to think so.

"I could have stopped in 1986, after the kind of season I had then, and just said, 'This is it, I don't need to do anything else.' But I'm trying to get better every year. So there's more to come."

As if he needed it, Jerry Rice has another little bit of incentive going into this season.

The brilliance of '87, in his mind, was tarnished by what happened in the 49ers' 36-24 NFC semifinal loss to the Minnesota Vikings.

Rice, who played with a partial shoulder separation that forced him to miss several days of practice before the game, was held to just three catches for 28 yards and no touchdowns, and was up-staged by the Vikings' Anthony Carter.

"I was really fatigued," he says. "I don't like to miss practice. It throws my timing off. I wasn't the real Jerry Rice in that game."

The real Jerry Rice, of course, is the one that Rice himself, after considerable deliberation, implies nobody can cover, the one who could continue to set the NFL on its ear until he doesn't have enough hair left to style.

INSIDE THE AFC

By MILT NORTHROP

PREDICTED ORDER OF FINISH

EAST	CENTRAL	WEST
Buffalo	Cleveland	Seattle
New England	Houston	Denver
Miami	Pittsburgh	Kansas City
New York Jets	Cincinnati	L.A. Raiders
Indianapolis		San Diego

AFC Champion: Cleveland

Reflecting on the apparent disparity between the AFC and NFC, New England's Raymond Berry and the Jets' Joe Walton contend that the AFC has to play more physical football. Miami's Don Shula, the Colts' Ron Meyer and Buffalo's Marv Levy disagree.

Yet there's no getting away from the fact that the AFC has sent what are basically speed and finesse teams to face the NFC champions in the last four Super Bowls. Result: four straight NFC victories by a combined 165-56 score.

So the emphasis in the AFC these days is to muscle up and imitate the Bears, Giants and Redskins. As it happens, among the AFC entries with the best chance of getting to Super Bowl XXIII are some of its most physical teams—the Browns, the Oilers, the Bills and the Seahawks. All have to be considered among favorites for the playoffs.

The AFC East produced the tightest race in the NFL in '87. But things might not be as tight this year because there is a growing consensus that Buffalo, with young defensive stars

---

Milt Northrop of the Buffalo Evening News *has been the Bills' beat man and overall NFL observer since 1980.*

Bruce Smith, Cornelius Bennett and Shane Conlin, and quarter-back Jim Kelly, is ready to take charge of the division.

New England, however, still may have the most talented and deepest team in the conference. If rookie running back John Stephens can replace Tony Collins and a rebuilt offensive line can get the Pats' running game back to where it was in 1985, they will be tough to beat.

As long as Miami has Marino, the Marks Brothers and Shula, the Dolphins will be dangerous, especially with second-year dynamo Troy Stradford. The Colts, defending AFC-East champs, face a potential quarterback problem, but they still have AFC rushing champion Eric Dickerson. The Jets are retooling the offensive line and the defense.

Cleveland missed going to the Super Bowl in heart-breaking losses to Denver in the last two conference championship games. They just might get to the Super Bowl behind crafty quarterback Bernie Kosar, but their spavined veterans have to hold up.

No team in the AFC is more physical than Houston, a wild-card entrant in '87. The Oilers are still learning how to win. After four disappointing finishes, the suspicion is that Cincinnati's talent is overrated, while the Steelers can't overcome their quarterback deficiencies.

Denver is haunted by its two dismal Super Bowl performances. Dan Reeves went for size and strength in the draft, but the Broncos are still built around quarterback John Elway and his swift receivers.

If the Broncos slip at all, Seattle will be nipping at their heels as long as running back Curt Warner is healthy. The Raiders conceded they were getting tattered from age and collected three first-round draft picks, headed by Notre Dame Heisman winner Tim Brown. But they have quarterback problems that will give new coach Mike Shanahan an immediate baptism.

Kansas City must claw its way back. San Diego hopes former Steeler Mark Malone can do a reasonable Dan Fouts impersonation.

When all is said and done, the playoff teams will be Buffalo, Cleveland, Houston, Seattle and Denver. Look for Kosar to cooly guide Cleveland past Seattle for the AFC crown and then it's on to the Super Bowl in Miami.

BUFFALO BILLS

TEAM DIRECTORY: Pres.: Ralph Wilson; GM/VP-Administration: Bill Polian; Dir. Pro Personnel: Bob Ferguson; Dir. Media Rel.: Dave Senko; Dir. Pub. and Community Rel.: Denny Lynch; Head Coach: Marv Levy. Home field: Rich Stadium (80,290). Colors: Scarlet red, royal blue and white.

SCOUTING REPORT

OFFENSE: The Bills were the only team in the NFL without a run, pass or return play of at least 50 yards long last season. Their longest offensive play was a 47-yard pass completion. Ball control is nice, but so is a home run every once in a while. Even without a dominating running back, the Bills averaged four yards per rush in a 7-8 season.

After Greg Bell was traded, the running-back job fell to Robb Riddick and third-down specialist Ronnie Harmon. When Riddick was lost, it hurt, "We need an every-down running back, a blood-in-the-mud halfback," coach Marv Levy says.

The Bills think they discovered a blood-in-the-mud fullback in Jamie Mueller, who moved into the starting lineup in the second game and averaged 4.3 yards per carry. Jim Kelly's development in his second season pleased the Bills' staff even though he went belly-up in the last two games. To make matters worse, Kelly's offseason sore right elbow set off alarm bells in Orchard Park.

Kelly's main targets, wideouts Andre Reed and Chris Burkett, finished second and tied for third, respectively, in the AFC in total receptions. Yet, the cry among the cognoscenti in Buffalo is that Kelly needs a speed receiver to go to. The offensive line is not dominating. One tackle, Will Wolford, belongs back at guard. The other, Joe Devlin, is 34. They could be beaten out.

DEFENSE: "We've gone from being a very weak defensive team to at least a respectable one," Levy says in what may be a classic understatement.

Buffalo introduced five new starters into its defense in 1987, a major overhaul. Most notable was outside linebacker Cornelius Bennett, who joined the team at midseason and had an immediate impact, not only with his own play but by freeing another rookie, Shane Conlan, to move from outside, where he played well, to inside, where he was outstanding. Bennett compiled 8½ sacks and 59 tackles in just eight games and won raves from everyone for his attitude and performance.

Besides that, young defensive end Bruce Smith established

Mighty young LBs: Shane Conlan (58), Cornelius Bennett.

himself as an All-Pro. Smith had 12 sacks and took a back seat only to Philadelphia's Reggie White among NFL defensive ends in 1987.

KICKING GAME: Punter John Kidd finished the season strong, despite punting in the trickiest weather conditions in the NFL. He averaged 39.0, dropping 20 of his 67 kicks inside the 20. Scott Norwood hit 10 of 15 field goals (3-5 in the 40s) but his short kickoffs leave him open to a challenge. Coverage excellent on punts and kickoffs, but the Bills are missing return threat of their own.

THE ROOKIES: Oklahoma State's Thurman Thomas ran for 1,613 yards and 18 touchdowns as a senior but pros shied away because of his junior-year knee injury. By gambling, though, the Bills may have gained the every-down back they need. Also added 4.3 speed with WR Bernard Ford (81 catches) from Central Florida. Kicker Kirk Roach hit 7 of 11 FG tries from beyond

BILLS VETERAN ROSTER

HEAD COACH—Marv Levy, Assistant Coaches—Walt Corey, Ted Cottrell, Bruce DeHaven, Chuck Dickerson, Rusty Jones, Chuck Lester, Ted Marchibroda, Elijah Pitts, Jim Ringo, Dick Roach, Ted Tollner.

No.	Name	Pos.	Ht.	Wt.	NFL Exp.	College
—	Beecher, Willie	K	5-10	170	2	Utah State
55	Bennett, Cornelius	LB	6-2	235	2	Alabama
50	Bentley, Ray	LB	6-2	245	3	Central Michigan
81	Broughton, Walter	WR	5-10	180	3	Jacksonville State
85	Burkett, Chris	WR	6-4	210	4	Jackson State
29	Burroughs, Derrick	CB	6-1	180	4	Memphis State
61	Burton, Leonard	T	6-3	275	3	South Carolina
80	Butler, Jerry	WR	6-0	178	8	Clemson
35	Byrum, Carl	RB	6-0	235	3	Miss. Valley State
69	Christy, Greg	G	6-4	285	2	Pittsburgh
58	Conlan, Shane	LB	6-3	230	2	Penn State
21	Davis, Wayne	CB	5-11	175	4	Indiana State
70	Devlin, Joe	T	6-5	280	12	Iowa
45	Drane, Dwight	S	6-2	205	3	Oklahoma
—	Fox, Chas	WR-KR	5-11	190	2	Furman
59	Frerotte, Mitch	G	6-3	280	2	Penn State
53	Furjanic, Tony	LB	6-1	228	3	Notre Dame
99	Garner, Hal	LB	6-4	235	3	Utah State
8	Gelbaugh, Stan	QB	6-3	207	2	Maryland
75	Hamby, Mike	DE	6-4	270	2	Utah State
33	Harmon, Ronnie	RB	5-11	192	3	Iowa
71	Hellestrae, Dale	T	6-5	275	3	Southern Methodist
67	Hull, Kent	C	6-4	275	3	Mississippi State
—	Jackson, Kirby	CB	5-10	180	2	Mississippi State
48	Johnson, Lawrence	S	5-11	202	8	Wisconsin
86	Johnson, Trumaine	WR	6-1	196	4	Grambling State
52	Kaiser, John	LB	6-3	227	5	Arizona
12	Kelly, Jim	QB	6-3	215	3	Miami
38	Kelso, Mark	S	5-11	177	3	William & Mary
4	Kidd, John	P	6-3	208	5	Northwestern
63	Lingner, Adam	C	6-4	260	6	Illinois
95	McNanie, Sean	DE	6-5	270	5	San Diego State
54	Marve, Eugene	LB	6-2	240	7	Saginaw Valley State
74	Mesner, Bruce	NT	6-5	280	2	Maryland
88	Metzelaars, Pete	TE	6-7	243	7	Wabash
25	Mitchell, Roland	CB-KR	5-11	180	2	Texas Tech
39	Mueller, Jamie	RB	6-1	225	2	Benedictine College
11	Norwood, Scott	K	6-0	207	4	James Madison
37	Odomes, Nate	CB-KR	5-9	188	2	Wisconsin
27	Pitts, Ron	CB-S	5-10	175	3	UCLA
57	Pike, Mark	LB	6-4	257	2	Georgia Tech
30	Porter, Kerry	RB	6-1	210	2	Washington State
26	Porter, Ricky	RB	5-10	210	4	Slippery Rock State
79	Prater, Dean	DE	6-4	260	7	Oklahoma State
97	Radecic, Scott	LB	6-3	242	5	Penn State
83	Reed, Andre	WR	6-0	190	4	Kutztown State
14	Reich, Frank	QB	6-3	208	4	Maryland
40	Riddick, Robb	RB	6-0	195	7	Millersville State
51	Ritcher, Jim	G	6-3	265	9	North Carolina State
87	Rolle, Don (Butch)	TE	6-3	242	3	Michigan State
42	Roquemore, Durwood	S	6-1	190	4	Texas A&I
—	Sampson, Clint	WR	5-11	183	5	San Diego State
96	Seals, Leon	DE	6-4	265	2	Jackson State
76	Smerlas, Fred	NT	6-3	280	10	Boston College
78	Smith, Bruce	DE	6-4	285	4	Virginia Tech
56	Talley, Darryl	LB	6-4	227	6	West Virginia
89	Tasker, Steve	WR-KR	5-9	185	4	Northwestern
62	Traynowicz, Mark	G	6-5	280	4	Nebraska
—	Vital, Lionel	RB	5-9	195	2	Nicholls State
65	Vogler, Tim	G	6-3	285	10	Ohio State
73	Wolford, Will	T	6-5	276	3	Vanderbilt

TOP DRAFT CHOICES

Rd.	Name	Sel. No.	Pos.	Ht.	Wt.	College
2	Thomas, Thurman	40	RB	5-10	194	Oklahoma State
3	Ford, Bernard	66	WR	5-9	168	Central Florida
5	Gadson, Zeke	123	DB	6-0	205	Pittsburgh
5	Roach, Kirk	135	K	6-1½	223	Western Carolina
6	Murray, Dan	150	LB	6-2	240	East Stroudsburg

50 and kicked off to the end zone consistently at Western Carolina. "Ball just explodes off his foot," says scout A.J. Smith.

OUTLOOK: Assuming Kelly is healthy, offense will be potent enough, but could use some additional weapons. With Smith, Bennett and Conlan making big plays, this could be the next dominant defense in the NFL. Some growing to do, but a definite threat to win division.

BILL PROFILES

JIM KELLY 28 6-3 215   Quarterback

Bills believe strapping quarterback eventually can take them to the Super Bowl, despite the flop he took in next-to-last week of season against New England...Buffalo went into Pats' game in AFC-East driver's seat, but lost at home as Kelly completed only 13 of 31 in windstorm and couldn't get Bills into end zone from 16 and 11 yards away...First truly bad game for Kelly as a Bill...Second NFL season was comparable to his first. In 1986 Kelly completed 59.4 percent for 22 TDs and 17 interceptions and 83.3 rating points. In 12 games last season numbers were 59.7, 19, 11, 83.8...In first game after players' strike, he completed 18 of 23 for 244 yards after intermission as Bills erased a 20-3 deficit and took a 34-31 overtime victory in Miami...Named to 1988 AFC Pro Bowl team when Dan Marino could not participate and ended up scoring game's only touchdown...Starred at University of Miami...Born Feb. 14, 1960, in East Brady, Pa.

BRUCE SMITH 25 6-4 285   Defensive End

When Big Bruce sets his mind to something he usually does it...Upset over failing to make Pro Bowl after 1986 season, he came back to Buffalo in top shape and determined to earn respect and recognition. Wound up collecting numerous All-Pro honors...Went to Pro Bowl vowing he would not hold anything back, and he didn't. Was voted the game's Most Valuable Player...Led Bills with 12 sacks from right end position despite being double-teamed and held most of season.

Sack total tied him for fourth in NFL... Tremendous explosion off the ball and agility for huge man... Put on awesome display in shutout of Miami. Threw Troy Stradford for loss and on next play he went over and through Dwight Stephenson to wrap up Dan Marino for sack... Virginia Tech product was born June 18, 1963, in Norfolk, Va.

CORNELIUS BENNETT 23 6-2 235   Outside Linebacker

Came to Bills at midseason in blockbuster trade which sent Eric Dickerson from Rams to Colts and made immediate impact... Playing mainly on passing downs in his NFL debut against Denver, he was credited with four tackles, a sack and three quarterback pressures as Buffalo upset the AFC champions... In their first four games, the Bills had eight sacks. After Bennett arrived they had 22 in the next eight... In 20 games going back to the start of the 1986 season, Buffalo intercepted only 12 passes and recovered only 11 fumbles. With Bennett in lineup the last eight games of 1987 they picked off 12 passes and captured nine fumbles... Coach Marv Levy calls him best practice player he's had in 35 years of coaching... He's not bad in games, either... Awesome performance in last regular-season game at Philadelphia: 17 tackles, four sacks and forced three fumbles... Finished season with 8½ sacks... Born Aug. 25, 1965, in Birmingham, Ala... Was No. 2 pick overall in 1987 draft, out of Alabama.

JOE DEVLIN 34 6-5 280   Offensive Tackle

Buffalo's oldest player but still team's best-conditioned and most-dedicated professional ... Although he'd prefer to remain in background and quietly do his job, he responded to need and stepped forward to assume leadership role on a young team, especially during the 1987 players' strike when he and veteran defensive tackle Fred Smerlas held Bills together... Rarely misses an assignment and has gone through last two seasons without a holding or illegal use of hands penalty... Teammates outspoken in their complaints after Devlin again received hardly any consideration from peers for Pro Bowl... Changed weight-lifting regimen to bulk up be-

fore 1986 season and now plays at about 280 instead of 265 . . .
Avid outdoorsman and there's good deer hunting only 10 minutes
or so from Rich Stadium . . . Born Feb. 23, 1954, in Phoenixville,
Pa. . . . Attended Iowa.

SHANE CONLAN 24 6-3 230   Inside Linebacker

Led Bills in tackles, first time a rookie has
done so since another Shane (Nelson) did it in
1977 . . . Moved from outside to inside when
Bennett arrived and did not miss a beat . . .
Even made AP's second team All-Pro, which
is amazing when you consider he played only
seven full games at ILB . . . Bills' defensive
staff loves his instinctive play and the leverage
he gets in punishing ball-carriers . . . Difficult to block and keep
blocked . . . Often pops up from the turf to make the tackle . . .
Ranged to other side of field to save possible touchdowns on
couple of occasions last season . . . With Bruce Smith and Cornelius Bennett, is expected to provide cornerstone for a dominating
Buffalo defense . . . Born April 3, 1964, in Olean, N.Y. . . . Grew
up in Frewsburg, N.Y., about 60 miles from Buffalo . . . Father is
an investigator for New York State Police.

ROBB RIDDICK 31 6-0 195   Running Back

Two seasons ago Bills' followers doubted he
would survive final cut . . . Instead he became
one of most valuable of Bills and his loss was
felt when he suffered broken collarbone and
missed final seven games last year . . . Leading
league in touchdowns when he was injured
and finished as Bills' leading touchdown pro-
ducer with eight (five rushing, three
receiving) . . . Buffalo's hardest running halfback, he also contributed as receiver, return man and on special teams . . . Played part
of '86 season with broken hand in cast and still led team in
rushing yards (632) and tied for second in receptions with 49 . . .
In previous five years with the team, he carried ball only 10 times
for 50 yards and caught 26 passes for 319 . . . Played college ball
at Millersville (Pa.) University . . . Younger brother Louis was
frosh running back and safety at Pitt last fall . . . Once took offseason job selling life insurance door to door . . . Born April 26,
1957, in Quakertown, Pa.

ANDRE REED 24 6-0 190   Wide Receiver

One of Bills' two talented, yet overlooked young wide receivers...Third in AFC behind Al Toon and Steve Largent with 57 receptions, giving him 158 in three pro seasons and a 13-plus average per catch...Five TD catches led Bills...Best receiving games in 1987 came in losses to Redskins (8 catches, 108 yards) and Raiders (7-153)...Caught at least three balls in 12 games he played and has a reception in last 20 games he's played...Born Jan. 29, 1964, in Philadelphia, where he spent part of his youth, but now lives in Allentown, Pa., where he attended Louis E. Dieruff High...Was quarterback in high school and played at little Kutztown (Pa.) University...Despite small-college background, he earned starting slot in rookie training camp in 1985 and finished season with 48 receptions.

CHRIS BURKETT 26 6-4 210   Wide Receiver

Long-legged, gliding receiver with deceptive speed...Improved once he built upper body strength and learned techniques to avoid getting jammed at line of scrimmage...Tied for fourth in AFC with 54 receptions in 1987 as he blossomed under tutoring of former Southern Cal coach Ted Tollner...Averaged 13.7 yards per catch...In 1986 averaged dazzling 22.9 as he took in scoring bombs of 84 and 75 yards from Jim Kelly ...Shoulder and elbow injuries slowed his development first two years but he started all 12 games last fall...Had successive games of 115 and 130 yards in receiving yards in major victories against Oilers and Dolphins...Only drawback is occasional lack of maturity...Sometimes loses concentration in reacting to cheap shots and taunting of opposing cornerbacks...Born Aug. 21, 1962, in Laurel, Miss...Went to Jackson State.

RONNIE HARMON 24 5-11 192   Running Back

Figured to be third-down specialist and change-of-pace man at running back...Then Greg Bell was traded and Robb Riddick was injured, so he handled most of duty as running back and rushed for 485 yards to lead the Bills...Also caught 56 passes (tied for fourth in AFC) for 477 yards...Was a controversial first-round selection when Bills picked him out of Iowa in 1986 . . . Fans and media thought team had more critical needs at other positions . . . However, Harmon proved to be a handy man to have around last season . . . Brother Derrick played at Cornell and for the 49ers. Younger brother Kevin completed eligibility as running back at Iowa last season . . . Bills would like to see more North-South running from Harmon, who has habit of going off on his own in effort to turn big play . . . Gives Buffalo a deep threat out of backfield, which helps make up for lack of it at tight end . . . Born May 7, 1964, in Queens, N.Y.

STEVE TASKER 26 5-9 185   **WR-KR**

Made Pro Bowl on the strength of his special-teams play . . . Bills claimed him on procedural waivers late in 1986 season when Oilers tried to sneak him on active roster . . . Marv Levy, always on lookout for special-teams standouts, quickly grabbed him . . . Came to Bills with reputation as kickoff-return man (26.3 average with Houston in 1985) but he's proven even more valuable as coverage man on punts and kickoffs and as rusher on punts and field goals . . . Blocked punt for safety against Denver and partially blocked three other punts during season . . . Second on squad in special-teams tackles with 20 in 12 games and forced three fumbles . . . Attended college and was fraternity brother of Bills' punter John Kidd at Northwestern . . . Became a Wildcat after spending two years at Dodge City Community College in his native Kansas . . . Amazes teammates with distance of his golf drives and power he generates as a batter in softball . . . Born April 10, 1962, in Smith Center, Kan.

COACH MARV LEVY:

Well-organized and decisive, he got Bills back on track despite major roster overhaul and presence of five new defensive starters, three of them rookies . . . He and staff adjusted well to midseason trade for Cornelius Bennett and didn't panic when injuries to running back Robb Riddick and offensive tackle Will Wolford threatened to ruin promising season . . . Phi Beta Kappa graduate of Coe

College with master's degree in English history from Harvard, but he's no egghead...Intelligent, soft-spoken, witty but down to earth...Works closely with special teams, where he has hands-on approach and Buffalo showed major improvements in coverage, kick-blocking and kick protection in his first full season...First season as head coach of Chiefs he ran wing-T offense because of quarterback and defensive problems...It created false stereotype of him as three-yards-and-a-cloud-of-dust devotee...Actually, he favors a balanced attack...Ability to deal with media probably stems from lessons learned as broadcast analyst when he was away from coaching...Bills hired him to be their 10th head coach after Hank Bullough was dismissed Nov. 3, 1986...Led Bills to 2-5 mark the remainder of '86...Team went 7-8 and challenged for AFC-East title last year...Owns 40-55 NFL head-coaching record, but he has taken over two teams at low ebb...Went to Kansas City after a 2-12 season in 1977 and Chiefs made steady improvement, 4-12, 7-9, 8-8, 9-7, until 1982 players' strike tore them apart and led to his firing... Was head coach at New Mexico, California and William & Mary ...Was an assistant under Jerry Williams with the Eagles and under George Allen with Rams and Redskins...Won two Grey Cups in five seasons as head coach of Montreal Alouettes (1973-77) and coached Chicago Blitz in USFL in 1984...Born Aug. 3, 1928 in Chicago.

LONGEST PLAY

The Boston Patriots, always a Buffalo nemesis in the 1960s, again were breathing down the necks of the Bills this day on Nov. 7, 1965, at Boston's Fenway Park. The Patriots had narrowed Buffalo's lead to 13-7 on a short touchdown run by J.D. Garrett. This time, Boston's comeback hopes ended suddenly and dramatically.

Defensive back Charley Warner of the Bills gathered in Gino Cappelletti's kickoff two yards deep in the end zone and took it back 102 yards to break the game open. Buffalo won, 23-7. It was one of two kickoffs Warner returned for touchdowns in Buffalo's second straight AFL championship season.

Thirteen years later (Sept. 24, 1978) Curtis Brown of the Bills equalled Warner's feat, bringing a Toni Linhart kickoff back against the Baltimore Colts in Buffalo's Rich Stadium. It came in a 24-17 Buffalo victory, the Bills' first under new coach Chuck Knox.

INDIVIDUAL BILL RECORDS

Rushing

Most Yards Game:	273	O. J. Simpson, vs Detroit, 1976
Season:	2,003	O. J. Simpson, 1973
Career:	10,183	O. J. Simpson, 1969-77

Passing

Most TD Passes Game:	5	Joe Ferguson, vs N.Y. Jets, 1979
Season:	26	Joe Ferguson, 1983
Career:	181	Joe Ferguson, 1973-84

Receiving

Most TD Passes Game:	4	Jerry Butler, vs N.Y. Jets, 1979
Season:	10	Elbert Dubenion, 1964
Career:	35	Elbert Dubenion, 1960-67

Scoring

Most Points Game:	30	Cookie Gilchrist, vs N.Y. Jets, 1963
Season:	138	O. J. Simpson, 1975
Career:	420	O. J. Simpson, 1969-77
Most TDs Game:	5	Cookie Gilchrist, vs N.Y. Jets, 1963
Season:	23	O. J. Simpson, 1975
Career:	70	O. J. Simpson, 1969-1977

CINCINNATI BENGALS

TEAM DIRECTORY: Chairman: Austin E. Knowlton; Pres.: John Sawyer; VP/GM: Paul Brown; Asst. GM: Michael Brown; Dir. Player Personnel: Pete Brown; Dir. Pub. Rel.: Allan Heim; Bus. Mgr.: Bill Connelly; Head Coach: Sam Wyche. Home field: Riverfront Stadium (59,754). Colors: Orange, black and white.

SCOUTING REPORT

OFFENSE: Somehow the Bengals managed to finish with a dismal 4-11 record last season despite an offense that ranked fifth in the NFL (and a defense that was eighth). It sounds impossible.

Cincinnati is counting on quarterback Boomer Esiason to come back with a big season and hopes that James Brooks will return to the level of his sensational '86 season. It may be asking for too much. The multitalented Brooks may no longer be able to fill the role of heavy-duty running back and the Bengals' offensive line may have seen its better days.

Esiason threw 19 interceptions. When the offensive line had to protect him in losses to Pittsburgh and New Orleans, it allowed five and six sacks, respectively.

Eddie Brown led Cincinnati with 44 catches but averaged only 13.9 per catch. Cris Collinsworth battled injuries and caught only 31 passes. When so many offensive players have below-par seasons, the tendency is to sit back and wait for them to return to form.

DEFENSE: Cincinnati outgained its opponents by a wide margin, almost 700 yards, which is incredible when you look at the won-lost record. What was missing was big plays. The Bengals had 40 sacks, but only 14 interceptions and recovered just 12 fumbles. Also they gave up 24 TD passes and allowed opponents to complete 58.6 percent of their passes.

Nose tackle Tim Krumrie was the Bengals' only Pro Bowl performer. The Bengals are looking for improved second-year performances from Jason Buck and Skip McClendon at ends. Reggie Williams, in his 13th season, leads the linebacker group. The Bengals believe they may have a future All-Pro in huge strong safety David Fulcher.

KICKING GAME: Jim Breech, one of the most unflappable and accurate field-goal kickers in pro football, hit 24 of 30 and was 18 of 19 inside 40 yards. Punter Scott Fulhage, picked up as a free agent, beat out drafted Greg Horne and averaged 41.7.

Boomer Esiason led AFC in pass yardage, but had 19 INTs.

BENGALS VETERAN ROSTER

HEAD COACH—Sam Wyche. Assistant Coaches—Jim Anderson, Bruce Coslet, Bill Johnson, Dick LeBeau, Jim McNally, Dick Selcer, Mike Stock, Bill Urbanik, Kim Wood.

No.	Name	Pos.	Ht.	Wt.	NFL Exp.	College
61	Aronson, Doug	G	6-3	290	2	San Diego State
35	Barber, Chris	S	6-0	187	2	North Carolina A&T
53	Barker, Leo	LB	6-2	227	5	New Mexico State
24	Billups, Lewis	CB	5-11	190	3	North Alabama
74	Blados, Brian	G	6-5	295	5	North Carolina
55	Brady, Ed	LB	6-2	235	5	Illinois
3	Breech, Jim	K	5-6	161	10	California
21	Brooks, James	RB	5-10	182	8	Auburn
81	Brown, Eddie	WR	6-0	185	4	Miami
99	Buck, Jason	DE	6-5	264	2	Brigham Young
27	Bussey, Barney	S	6-0	195	3	South Carolina
80	Collinsworth, Cris	WR	6-6	192	8	Florida
93	Deayala, Kiki	LB	6-1	225	3	Texas
67	Douglas, David	T	6-4	280	3	Tennessee
73	Edwards, Eddie	DE	6-5	256	12	Miami
7	Esiason, Boomer	QB	6-4	220	5	Maryland
33	Fulcher, David	S	6-3	228	3	Arizona State
17	Fulhage, Scott	P	5-11	191	2	Kansas State
71	Hammerstein, Mike	DE	6-4	270	3	Michigan
89	Hillary, Ira	WR	5-11	190	2	South Carolina
82	Holman, Rodney	TE	6-3	238	7	Tulane
20	Horton, Ray	CB	5-11	190	6	Washington
92	Inglis, Tim	LB	6-3	232	2	Toledo
37	Jackson, Robert	S	5-10	186	7	Central Michigan
36	Jennings, Stanford	RB	6-1	205	5	Furman
30	Johnson, Bill	RB	6-2	230	4	Arkansas State
84	Kattus, Eric	TE	6-5	235	3	Michigan
58	Kelly, Joe	LB	6-2	227	3	Washington
90	King, Emanuel	LB	6-4	251	4	Alabama
28	Kinnebrew, Larry	RB	6-1	251	9	Tennessee State
64	Kozerski, Bruce	G	6-4	275	5	Holy Cross
69	Krumrie, Tim	NT	6-2	262	6	Wisconsin
52	Manos, Sam	C	6-3	265	2	Marshall
88	Martin, Mike	WR	5-10	186	6	Illinois
72	McClendon, Skip	DE	6-6	270	2	Arizona State
85	McGee, Tim	WR	5-10	175	3	Tennessee
47	Meehan, Greg	WR	6-0	191	2	Bowling Green
65	Montoya, Max	G	6-5	275	10	UCLA
78	Muñoz, Anthony	T	6-6	278	9	Southern California
12	Norseth, Mike	QB	6-2	200	2	Kansas
75	Reimers, Bruce	T	6-7	280	5	Iowa State
46	Rice, Dan	RB	6-1	241	2	Michigan
87	Riggs, Jim	TE	6-5	245	2	Clemson
50	Rimington, Dave	C	6-3	288	6	Nebraska
15	Schonert, Turk	QB	6-1	196	9	Stanford
70	Skow, Jim	DE	6-3	250	3	Nebraska
25	Smith, Daryl	CB	5-9	185	2	North Alabama
22	Thomas, Eric	CB	5-11	175	2	Tulane
63	Walter, Joe	T	6-6	290	4	Texas Tech
51	White, Leon	LB	6-2	236	3	Brigham Young
41	Wilcots, Solomon	CB	5-11	180	2	Colorado
57	Williams, Reggie	LB	6-0	228	13	Dartmouth
—	Wilson, Stanley	RB	5-10	210	4	Oklahoma
49	Wright, Dana	RB	6-1	219	2	Findlay College
91	Zander, Carl	LB	6-2	235	4	Tennessee

TOP DRAFT CHOICES

Rd.	Name	Sel. No.	Pos.	Ht.	Wt.	College
1	Dixon, Rickey	5	S	5-10	184	Oklahoma
2	Woods, Elbert (Ickey)	31	FB	5-11	211	Nevada-Las Vegas
3	Walker, Kevin	57	LB	6-2	230	Maryland
4	Grant, David	84	DT	6-3	270	West Virginia
5	Wester, Herb	114	OT	6-7	300	Iowa

Mike Martin (9.9 average) turned in good punt-return work, but kickoff returns were below par. Coverage on kicks and punts was good.

THE ROOKIES: The Ricky and Ickey Show. Ricky Dixon was rated the only blue-chip cornerback prospect in the draft and the Bengals got him on the fifth pick. He also figures at free safety, a problem spot. Elbert (Ickey) Woods of Nevada-Las Vegas is a typical Bengal fullback and could unseat inconsistent Larry Kinnebrew.

OUTLOOK: After chasing the Steelers and Browns home for three years, the Bengals collapsed last season. Now they have the Browns AND the Oilers to worry about. Their key players are getting older and some are overrated. It may be no accident that Cincinnati dipped badly. Another season out of the money may convince Paul and Mike Brown that it's time for an overhaul.

BENGAL PROFILES

BOOMER ESIASON 27 6-4 220   Quarterback

His 1987 season considered somewhat of a disappointment despite impressive 3,321 passing yards in only 12 games to lead AFC... However, completion percentage was down to 54.5 and he threw more interceptions (19) than touchdown passes (16)... TD-INT ration was 24-17 the year before... Part of problem may be that Bengals played from behind much of season as team lost eight of 10 poststrike games... Five interceptions came on last-gasp drives, three occurring on last or next-to-last play of game... His concentration may have been affected by strike and angry fan reaction... Outspoken union advocate and very involved in strike as player rep and team leader ... When Bengals went sour after return of regulars, fans made Boomer their scapegoat. Was booed even in games when he threw for 350 and 400 yards... Took over as starting quarterback in third game of 1985 season, his second in the NFL... Had choice between college football and pro baseball offers after he was 15-0 as a pitcher in high school, and decided on Maryland football... Was Bengals' second-round pick in 1984... Given name is Norman... Born April 17, 1961, in East Islip, N.Y.

EDDIE BROWN 25 6-0 185   Wide Receiver

Fell short of 50-catch plateau after seasons with 53 and 58 receptions but led Bengals with 44 grabs, including three for touchdowns... Thumb tendon problem plagued him again last season and caused some erratic play. Made some tough catches and dropped some easy ones as a result... Only the fifth Bengal to catch 50 or more passes in a season and he has done it twice in three NFL seasons... First-round pick in 1985 out of the University of Miami... Was 13th player selected... Teams with Cris Collinsworth to give Bengals diversified passing attack... Before going to Miami as a defensive backfield candidate he attended Navarro Junior College in Texas... Born Dec. 18, 1962, in Miami.

ANTHONY MUNOZ 30 6-8 278   Offensive Tackle

Offensive line coach Jim McNally calls Munoz the "most athletic" of all the offensive linemen in the NFL... Bengals used to count Munoz Pancakes, the number of opponents he flattened with his blocks... Munoz Tortillas have become rarer as size of defensive linemen he faces increases, but he dominates opponents with technique now where he used to do it with sheer size and power... Born Aug. 19, 1958, in Ontario, Cal., and lives in Cincinnati area... Played in seven successive Pro Bowls 1982-88... Caught fourth touchdown pass of his pro career as tackle-eligible receiver last season. Now has seven career receptions... Graduate of USC.

CRIS COLLINSWORTH 29 6-5 192   Wide Receiver

Averaged more than 60 receptions his first six NFL seasons but had only 31 receptions in 1987, the first year he failed to catch a touchdown pass... Pro scouts had questioned whether his slim frame would hold up in NFL but until last season he seldom missed a game ... "That's what I take pride in as much as anything," Collinsworth says... In 1986, however, he started only six of 12 regular-season games because of cracked ribs and sprained foot... Around Bengals they say painful rib injuries would have put most players on sideline for season, but Collinsworth toughed it out despite fact team was obviously going nowhere. He missed four games outright... Last time he was absent was next-to-last game of 1984 season ...Began college career as quarterback at University of Florida ...Went to high school in Titusville, Fla., but was born in Dayton, Ohio, Jan. 27, 1959.

RODNEY HOLMAN 28 6-3 238   **Tight End**

This Rodney doesn't get a lot of respect either but he should...His 15.9-yard reception average last season is remarkable for a tight end...Caught 28, three for touchdowns despite ankle and knee problems on different legs which nagged him all season...Doesn't get the notice some other AFC tight ends receive but former Tulane star has turned in excellent production in Bengal passing attack which likes to spread the wealth...Considered all-around player who is a good blocker...Became starter in 1985...Seven of his 38 receptions that season went for touchdowns....Caught 40 passes in 1986, when he averaged 14.3 per catch...When he left college at Tulane he was Green Wave's all-time reception leader with 133... Born April 20, 1960, in Ypsilanti, Mich.

JAMES BROOKS 29 5-10 182   **Running Back**

Versatile man fell off badly in 1987 after brilliant 1986 season when he ran for 1,087 yards and a 5.3 average and caught 47 passes for 686 more...He was voted Bengals' MVP that year and was named to several All-AFC teams...Struggled through the last eight weeks of '87 with nagging ankle injury... Ran for only 290 yards and caught 22 passes for 272...Some wonder if he would not be better off playing a more limited role now that he may be past peak years for a running back...Acquired in a 1984 trade from San Diego in exchange for fullback Pete Johnson...One in a series of star running backs who came out of Auburn in last 10 years—Joe Cribbs, William Andrews, Lionel James, Bo Jackson and Brent Fullwood...Born Dec. 28, 1958, in Warner Robbins, Ga.

TIM KRUMRIE 28 6-2 262   Nose Tackle

It's unusual when a nose tackle leads the team in tackles, but Krumrie has done it for the last three years...Credited with 88 tackles in 1987 as well as 3½ sacks...Made first appearance in Pro Bowl after last season as replacement for injured Bob Golic of the Browns...Some say Krumrie belonged there ahead of Golic anyway and should have gone in 1986 as well...Was only a 10th-round draft choice out of Wisconsin in 1983...Selected mostly because of his attitude and hustle..."I was 6-2, ran the 40-yard dash in about five seconds and weighed about 245 when I first reported to the Bengals' minicamp after I was drafted," Krumrie says...It's his relentless, keep-on-coming approach which has helped make him All-Pro...A wrestler in college, he thrives in close quarters in middle-of-line action...Born May 20, 1960, in Eau Claire, Wis., where he makes his offseason home.

LEWIS BILLUPS 24 5-11 190   Cornerback

Won a starting job as a rookie in 1986 after he was drafted in the second round from North Alabama, a Division II school...Bengals filled half the jobs in their secondary in that draft because that's the year they also landed strong safety David Fulcher...Small-college background didn't prevent him from being selected to play in Senior Bowl...Bengals' scouts regarded him as best cover man coming out of college...Has one career sack but is still looking for first NFL interception...Always wears the enemy T-shirt on the day of the game because, he says, it helps him keep his mind on the game...Born Oct. 10, 1963, in Tampa, Fla.

EMANUEL KING 25 6-4 251   Outside Linebacker

Former first-round draft pick from Alabama won starting job in 1986 and led Bengals with nine sacks from his outside linebacker position...Had four sacks last season...Offseason speculation had Bengals going to a more multiple defensive look from their 3-4 base with King's combination of size and speed placing him in a number of roles either

as linebacker or as outside rusher from down lineman's position
...A gifted athlete who has worked hard to increase his strength
since coming to Bengals...Remained in Cincinnati and took
part in team's offseason weight program and it has paid
dividends...Was a two-time All-State basketball player in high
school...Born Aug. 15,1963, in Leroy, Ala.

DAVID FULCHER 23 6-3 228   Safety

Was the Ironhead Heyward of the 1986 draft
when he came out of Arizona State a year
early...Had flunked out of school and passed
up opportunity to regain eligibility...Instead
he opted for the draft and NFL let him in...
Circumstances surrounding his draft entry
caught many NFL teams by surprise or raised
some doubts and he lasted until third round
...Now the consensus is that the Bengals made a steal...Not
the greatest in coverage but is like extra linebacker against the
run because of his size and knack for being around the ball...
Fourth among Bengals in tackles with 49...Registered three
sacks and had three interceptions...Bengals toying with idea of
shifting him to free safety to make room in lineup at strong safety
for Leonard Bell or Barney Bussey...All-Pacific 10 for three
seasons as a Sun Devil...Born Sept. 28, 1964, in Los Angeles
...Was basketball and baseball (catcher) standout at Fremont
High in L.A.

DAVE RIMINGTON 28 6-3 288   Center

First two-time Outland Trophy winner in history when he played at Nebraska and won
award given to outstanding lineman in college
football, 1981 and 1982...Injuries plagued
former No. 1 pick most of 1987...One problem may have been that an offseason elbow
surgery prevented him from going through his
usual weight-lifting routine...When healthy
can be dominating run-blocker...One of players who must re-
bound big if the Bengals are to turn it around...One of line of
Nebraska linemen who have come to the NFL, starting with Mick
Tingelhoff and later Mark Traynowicz (Bills), Dean Steinkuhler
(Oilers) and Bill Lewis (Raiders)...Born May 22, 1960, in
Omaha, Neb.

COACH SAM WYCHE: Bengals barely missed playoffs his
 first two seasons, then finished two games be-
hind AFC-Central champion Cleveland in
1986, but roof fell in during 4-11 1987
campaign ... To almost everyone's surprise,
though, he was invited back to serve out final
year of five-year contract with Bengals ...
Series of late-game tactical blunders in 1987
cost games and gave second-guessers a field
day. Most notorious was in 27-26 loss to visiting 49ers second
week of season. Leading by six points, Wyche tried to use up
final six seconds with fourth-down running play rather than punting from deep in own territory. It left Niners two seconds to go 25
yards for winning touchdown ... During strike games Bengals
were leading San Diego, 9-0, when Wyche passed up 40-yard
field-goal try. Chargers came back for 10-9 victory. In three-point
loss to Pittsburgh, rather than spike ball to stop clock Bengals
tried to hurry field-goal unit on field with clock running. There
was mass confusion and they never got kick off. Result: 23-20
loss to Steelers ... Mishaps tarnished reputation of man considered one of most innovative and bright young head coaches in
NFL ... As free-agent quarterback who had played at Furman
University and then briefly for Wheeling Ironmen of Continental
Football League, he earned roster place with expansion Cincinnati team in 1968 ... Saw most action of checkered NFL playing
career in 1969, when he completed 54 of 108 for 838 yards and
seven touchdowns in seven games for Bengals ... First pro
coaching experience came under Bill Walsh with 49ers in 1979-
82 ... Became head coach at Indiana in 1983 and returned to
Bengals in 1984 ... Born Jan. 5, 1945, in Atlanta ... Brother
Bubba played at Tennessee and in CFL and WFL.

LONGEST PLAY

Willie Shelby was only a rookie, but the running back from
Alabama provided the impetus that sent the Bengals on to a 45-24
victory over the Browns in Cleveland Stadium on Oct. 3, 1976.

The Browns had just scored in the first quarter to tie the game
at 7-7, but Shelby fielded Don Cockroft's kickoff three yards
short of the goal line and took it back 97 yards for the longest
play in Bengal history. Cincinnati soon moved to a 24-7 lead, but
after the Browns had closed to 31-24 in the fourth period, Ken

Anderson threw his fourth touchdown pass of the game and Boobie Clark ran it in for another TD to close out the victory.

Anderson was 19 for 27, but it was Shelby's return which stunned the Browns.

INDIVIDUAL BENGAL RECORDS

Rushing

Most Yards Game:	163	James Brooks, vs New England, 1986	
Season:	1,087	James Brooks, 1986	
Career:	5,421	Pete Johnson, 1977-83	

Passing

Most TD Passes Game:	5	Boomer Esiason, vs N.Y. Jets, 1986	
Season:	29	Ken Anderson, 1981	
Career:	196	Ken Anderson, 1971-85	

Receiving

Most TD Passes Game:	3	Bob Trumpy, vs Houston, 1969	
	3	Isaac Curtis, vs Cleveland, 1973	
	3	Isaac Curtis, vs Baltimore, 1979	
Season:	10	Isaac Curtis, 1974	
Career:	53	Isaac Curtis, 1973-83	

Scoring

Most Points Game:	24	Larry Kinnebrew, vs Houston, 1984	
Season:	115	Jim Breech, 1981	
Career:	713	Jim Breech, 1981-87	
Most TDs Game:	4	Larry Kinnebrew, vs Houston, 1984	
Season:	16	Pete Johnson, 1981	
Career:	70	Pete Johnson, 1977-83	

CLEVELAND BROWNS

TEAM DIRECTORY: Owner/Pres.: Art Modell; Exec. VP-Legal Administration: James Bailey; VP-Football Operations: Ernie Accorsi; Dir. Player Relations: Ricky Feacher; Dir. Player Personnel: Chip Falivene; VP-Pub. Rel.: Kevin Byrne; Head Coach: Marty Schottenheimer. Home field: Cleveland Stadium (80,098). Colors: Seal brown, orange and white.

SCOUTING REPORT

OFFENSE: In just two seasons the Browns' offense took on a look which suits their young quarterback, Bernie Kosar. Dink, a pass here. Dink, another pass there. A run inside the tackles and watch out for Webster Slaughter or Reggie Langhorne sneaking deep. Kosar sees all, knows all and is full of surprises. Most important: he doesn't make mistakes and he doesn't—won't— take sacks.

Boring as the Browns' style is, it's going to be that way for a long time because Bernie is going to be around a long while. He's only 24, even though he plays like 34. "We knew we had a special person all along," says coach Marty Schottenheimer, "but he has captured everyone's confidence with his ability to win in any circumstance."

Although they don't run like they did in 1985 when Kevin Mack and Earnest Byner both went over 1,000 yards, Schottenheimer says he's gratified because "we showed an ability to run the ball when we had to."

The Browns like their receiving threesome of Slaughter, Langhorne and Brian Brennan, but there has to be some concern at tight end because the great Ozzie Newsome has slowed up considerably.

Cleveland's no-name offensive line has had to overcome injuries each of the last two seasons. "They consistently win the battle in the trenches," Schotzy says of the group led by right tackle Cody Risien and center Mike Baab.

DEFENSE: It's mostly an odd collection of castoffs and rejects, and it's perhaps the main reason the Browns have failed to get to the Super Bowl the last two seasons. It's the defensive line. Despite two All-Pro cornerbacks who stick to receivers like glue, the Browns had to struggle to get 34 sacks last season. The team leader in sacks was 36-year-old Carl Hairston with eight.

Cleveland's linebacking is steady, though a shade overrated. Cornerbacks Frank Minnifield and Hanford Dixon make the de-

Bernie Kosar had AFC's highest rating and completion pct.

fense work and set the physical tone with their intimidation. Denver made the Browns' journeymen safeties look bad in the AFC title game last year.

KICKING GAME: A major headache. Veteran Matt Bahr had to be brought back because rookie draft pick Jeff Jaeger couldn't handle the pressure (8 for 15 in the 30s and 40s). Houston castoff Lee Johnson ended up as the punter. Not championship-caliber kicking. The return game with Gerald (Ice Cube) McNeil (11.4 on punt returns) and Glen Young (22.9 on kickoffs) was excellent, as was kick coverage.

BROWNS VETERAN ROSTER

HEAD COACH—Marty Schottenheimer. Assistant Coaches—Dave Adolph, Ray Braun, Bill Cowher, Richard Mann, Howard Mudd, Jim Pendry, Tom Pratt, Dave Redding, Kurt Schottenheimer, Marc Trestman, Darvin Wallis.

No.	Name	Pos.	Ht.	Wt.	NFL Exp.	College
61	Baab, Mike	C	6-4	270	7	Texas
9	Bahr, Matt	K	5-10	175	10	Penn State
60	Baker, Al	DE	6-6	270	11	Colorado State
43	Baker, Tony	RB	5-10	175	2	East Carolina
39	Bellinger, Rodney	CB	5-8	189	4	Miami
77	Bolden, Rickey	T	6-6	280	5	Southern Methodist
75	Bosley, Keith	T	6-5	302	2	Eastern Kentucky
36	Braggs, Stephen	CB-S	5-9	173	2	Texas
86	Brennan, Brian	WR	5-9	178	5	Boston College
44	Byner, Earnest	RB	5-10	215	5	East Carolina
96	Camp, Reggie	DE	6-4	280	6	California
91	Clancy, Sam	DE	6-7	260	5	Pittsburgh
47	Crawford, Mike	RB	5-10	215	2	Arizona State
18	Danielson, Gary	QB	6-2	196	11	Purdue
29	Dixon, Hanford	CB	5-11	186	8	Southern Mississippi
26	Dudley, Brian	S	6-1	180	2	Bethune-Cookman
24	Ellis, Ray	S	6-1	196	8	Ohio State
74	Farren, Paul	T-G	6-5	280	6	Boston University
69	Fike, Dan	G	6-7	280	4	Florida
28	Fontenot, Herman	RB	6-0	206	4	Louisiana State
79	Golic, Bob	NT	6-2	270	9	Notre Dame
56	Grayson, David	LB	6-2	229	2	Fresno State
53	Griggs, Anthony	LB	6-3	230	7	Ohio State
27	Gross, Al	S	6-3	195	6	Arizona
94	Guilbeau, Rusty	LB	6-4	235	6	McNeese State
78	Hairston, Carl	DE	6-4	260	13	Maryland East. Shore
65	Haley, Darryl	T-G	6-4	280	5	Utah
23	Harper, Mark	CB	5-9	174	3	Alcorn State
48	Hoggard, D.D.	CB	6-0	188	3	North Carolina State
38	Horn, Alvin	S	5-11	185	2	Nevada-Las Vegas
8	Jaeger, Jeff	K	5-11	189	2	Washington
51	Johnson, Eddie	LB	6-1	225	8	Louisville
11	Johnson, Lee	P	6-2	198	4	Brigham Young
59	Johnson, Mike	LB	6-1	228	3	Virginia Tech
95	Jones, Marlon	DE	6-4	260	2	Central State (Ohio)
54	Junkin, Mike	LB	6-3	238	2	Duke
19	Kosar, Bernie	QB	6-5	219	4	Miami
88	Langhorne, Reggie	WR	6-2	195	4	Elizabeth City State
84	Mack, Kevin	RB	6-0	225	4	Clemson
42	Manoa, Tim	RB	6-1	227	2	Penn State
57	Matthews, Clay	LB	6-2	235	11	Southern California
89	McNeil, Gerald	WR-KR	5-7	147	3	Baylor
52	Miller, Nick	LB	6-2	238	2	Arkansas
31	Minnifield, Frank	CB	5-9	180	5	Louisville
82	Newsome, Ozzie	TE	6-2	232	11	Alabama
10	Pagel, Mike	QB	6-2	206	7	Arizona State
72	Puzzuoli, Dave	NT	6-3	260	6	Pittsburgh
73	Rakoczy, Gregg	T	6-6	290	2	Miami
63	Risien, Cody	T	6-7	280	9	Texas A&M
37	Rockins, Chris	S	6-0	195	5	Oklahoma State
98	Rusinek, Mike	NT	6-3	250	2	California
50	Sanford, Lucius	LB	6-2	216	11	Georgia Tech
99	Sims, Darryl	DE	6-3	282	4	Wisconsin
84	Slaughter, Webster	WR	6-0	170	3	San Diego State
—	Stouffer, Kelly	QB	6-3	214	1	Colorado State
38	Swarn, George	RB	5-10	205	2	Miami (Ohio)
50	Telfke, Mike	C	6-4	255	2	Akron
81	Tennell, Derek	TE	6-5	245	2	UCLA
87	Tucker, Travis	TE	6-3	240	4	So. Connecticut State
5	Watson, Louis	WR	5-11	173	2	Miss. Valley State
6	Watson, Remi	WR	6-0	174	2	Bethune-Cookman
85	Weathers, Clarence	WR	5-9	170	6	Delaware State
70	Williams, Larry	G	6-5	290	3	Notre Dame
64	Winters, Frank	C	6-3	290	2	Western Illinois
22	Wright, Felix	S	6-2	190	4	Drake
83	Young, Glen	WR-KR	6-2	205	5	Mississippi State

TOP DRAFT CHOICES

Rd.	Name	Sel. No.	Pos.	Ht.	Wt.	College
1	Charlton, Clifford	21	LB	6-2	232	Florida
2	Perry, Michael Dean	50	DT	6-1	271	Clemson
3	Waiters, Van	77	LB	6-3½	230	Indiana
4	Blaylock, Anthony	104	DB	5-10	184	Winston-Salem State
7	Gash, Thane	188	DB	5-11	205	E. Tennessee State

THE ROOKIES: "The thing you have to do to continue to be a very good football team is not get old in any area all at once," said Schottenheimer as Browns drafted heavily for defense, selecting Florida's blitzing OLB Clifford Charlton, Clemson tackle Michael Dean Perry and Indiana OLB Van Waiters early. It means Mike Junkin goes inside and some veteran LBs are in trouble.

OUTLOOK: The Browns had the AFC title in their grasp each of the last two seasons and let it get away. Now, with Houston coming on fast, the Browns (10-5 last year) may not even be the best team in their division, let alone conference. Big questions on the defensive line and kicking game have to be addressed. However, one thing is certain: owner Art Modell and GM Ernie Accorsi will keep tinkering until they get a Super Bowl team.

BROWN PROFILES

BERNIE KOSAR 24 6-5 219   Quarterback

 Won't be 25 until Nov. 25 but already has started 37 NFL regular-season games (Browns are 20-8 in games he's started last two seasons) and has played in five postseason games, including two AFC championships... Not classic thrower or very athletic in his movements but he's smart and finds a way to get the job done... Completed 16 of 22 for 256 yards, three TDs and no interceptions in Browns' second-half rally in AFC championship game at Denver... Needs to throw 332 passes this season to qualify for NFL's all-time passing list (a player needs 1500 attempts to qualify). His lifetime rating of 84.6 after three seasons would place him fifth among all-time quarterbacks... Completed 62 percent, threw for 22 TDs and had only nine intercepted for a league-leading 2.3 interception rate as he ranked second to 49ers' Joe Montana in overall QB ratings with 95.4 mark. Montana was at 102.1... They say he doesn't move well in pocket but was sacked only 22 times despite fact that injuries upset Browns' offensive line. "It's so frustrating with a guy like Kosar," says Raiders' defensive end Howie Long. "He's not even looking at you, but he can tell you're there and the pass is gone."... Taking law courses at Case Western Reserve in offseason... Will be reunited with his University of

Miami quarterback coach, Marc Trestman, who joins Browns' staff as an assistant from the Vikings... Born Nov. 25, 1963, in Boardman, Ohio... Selected by Browns in first round of 1985 supplemental draft.

FRANK MINNIFIELD 28 5-9 180   Cornerback

One half of the Browns' super cornerback duo with Hanford Dixon... Starter in the Pro Bowl and named first-team All-Pro by UPI, *The Sporting News*, *Pro Football Weekly*, and *Football News*... Despite size, is aggressive and feisty... Throws opposing receivers off with his talk but backs up the yapping with his toughness and ability to cover... Led Browns with 13 passes defensed... That included four interceptions... Began career in the USFL with George Allen's Chicago Blitz in 1983, then moved on to Arizona Wranglers in 1984 and played in league championship game... Undrafted in NFL because of his early signing with Blitz... Came to Browns in fall of 1984 as free agent... It took him just four games to win left cornerback job after reporting late... Made Pro Bowl first time in 1986... Was walk-on in college at University of Louisville but ended up starting three seasons at cornerback and led nation in kickoff returns with 30.4 average as a junior with Cardinals and had 14.6 career punt-return average... Born Jan. 1, 1960, in Lexington, Ky.

HANFORD DIXON 29 5-11 186   Cornerback

Originator of "Dogs Defense" nickname, he one of those mainly responsible for putting some bite as well as bark in the Browns' defense... Reputation among receivers around league is that on first pass in Dixon's area he will give you something extra just to discourage you on next visit... Matches that kind of aggressiveness and toughness with ability... Was starter for second year in a row in Pro Bowl and almost everybody's first team All-Pro... Intercepted three passes to give him 23 in his career, which began in 1981 when he was Cleveland's first-round selection. Was 22nd player selected that year, out of Southern Mississippi, but the fifth defensive back to go behind Kenny Easley, Ronnie Lott, Dennis Smith and Ted

Watts . . . Never has missed regular-season or postseason game as a Brown . . . Has played in 101 straight regular-season games . . . In fact, the only start he's missed since his rookie season was in 1983, when an equipment problem caused him to miss first play of Detroit game . . . Born Christmas Day, 1958, in Mobile, Ala.

WEBSTER SLAUGHTER 23 6-0 170   Wide Receiver

Pencil-thin receiver from San Diego State developing into big-play man . . . Averaged 17.1 yards on 47 receptions, seven of which went for touchdowns . . . Averaging almost 16 yards per catch in his career . . . Explosive. Took a short slant throw from Bernie Kosar against Buffalo blitz and when defender fell off his tackle, Slaughter was gone in a flash. It was Browns' longest scoring play of season (54 yards) . . . With exception of last year's strike games, has started all 28 games since he joined Browns and has at least one reception in each . . . Second-round pick in 1986 and broke in with 40 receptions, including 36-yard overtime reception to beat Pittsburgh . . . Eighty-two receptions in senior year broke San Diego State record, which is notable because Aztecs sent Haven Moses and Gary Garrison, among others, to the pros . . . Did not play football until senior year at Franklin High in Stockton, Cal., which is also alma mater of Browns' safety Al Gross . . . Born Oct. 19, 1964, in Stockton, Cal.

OZZIE NEWSOME 32 6-2 232   Tight End

Just when we all thought the Wizard of Oz was slowing up, he goes out and catches six in Browns' season finale and adds five more in playoffs, including some key receptions in victory over Colts . . . Entering his 11th NFL season, he has 575 career catches for 7,073 yards, tops among all-time tight ends . . . A catch in Browns' opener would extend his reception streak to 128 games, second-longest in pro football history . . . Production has dropped considerably—from career highs of 89 in both 1983 and 1984 to 39 in 1986 and 34 in 1987 . . . Currently the ninth-leading receiver of all time in NFL . . . Late Bear Bryant, his coach at Alabama, once called Ozzie "the best end I ever coached." ... Some thought he might be thinking of retirement but Ozzie is determined to come back, saying: "My plans are to be in training camp when it opens. Why? Three reasons: First, I'm a lot healthier now than I was at this time a year ago, when I was still getting over those ankle and shoulder injuries. Second, I still want to play and I still love the game. And third, I've got the thirst for the Super Bowl. I think the third time can be the charm." ... Born March 16, 1956, in Muscle Shoals, Ala.

KEVIN MACK 26 6-0 225   Running Back

It's taken him just three seasons, but Mack already is the sixth-leading rusher in Browns' history with 2,504 yards ... Ran 201 times for 735 yards to lead the Browns last year and also had a career-high 32 receptions for 223 yards ... When Mack has run for 90 yards or more, the Browns are 15-0 ... Played in second Pro Bowl last season. First made it in 1985 when he ran for 1,104 yards in first season with Browns after coming from Los Angeles Express in USFL ... Cleveland selected him with a first-round pick obtained from Chicago in 1984 supplemental draft ... Leading rusher at Clemson in 1983, when he led Tigers to Atlantic Coast Conference crown with 9-1-1 record ... Once ran a 9.5 100-yard dash as high-school track star ... Born Aug. 9, 1962, in Kings Mountain, N.C.

CODY RISIEN 31 6-7 280   Offensive Tackle

This towering former Texas A&M captain is no Aggie joke ... He made the AFC Pro Bowl team for second year in a row last year ... At 31, he's senior member of the Cleveland offensive line of Ricky Bolden, Paul Farren, Mike Baab and Dan Fike backed by Larry Williams and Gregg Rakoczy. Only member of this unheralded group over 30 ... "They find a way to get it done," is what Marty Schottenheimer says of his OL ... Personable Risien came to Browns as seventh-round pick in 1979 and played in all 16 games, including last 10 as starter at left guard ... Moved to right tackle the next season and has started every game since with the exception of entire 1984 season, which he missed because of knee injury in final preseason game ... Born March 22, 1957, in Cypress, Tex.

EARNEST BYNER 25 5-10 215   **Running Back**

It's unfortunate that one of most respected players on the team became goat of Browns' playoff loss at Denver when he fumbled as he apparently was going into the end zone for go-ahead touchdown with 1:12 left in the game ... Says coach Marty Schottenheimer: "You can talk about the fumble all you want, but anyone who blames the loss on that doesn't know anything about football. Earnest is our heart and soul on offense. Without him, we don't even make the playoffs." ... One of most respected players among his teammates because of his work habits and his dedication to team goals ... In 1985, Byner (1,002) and Mack (1,104) became only the third pair of backs on the same team to each rush for 1,000 yards ... Earnest, though, has taken on a more diversified role. Did run for 432 yards last season, but often was set out as wide receiver and led Browns with 52 receptions for 552 yards ... Came to Cleveland as 10th-round pick in 1984 and immediately attracted attention. He was one of eight East Carolina players drafted that year ... Began rookie season mostly as special-teams player but by end of year was an integral part of offense and finished as third-leading rusher with 426 yards ... Born Sept. 15, 1962, in Milledgeville, Ga.

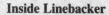

MIKE JOHNSON 25 6-1 228   **Inside Linebacker**

Another of the former USFL stars who have helped the Browns extend their string of AFC-Central titles to three in a row ... Cleveland obtained his rights with its second first-round pick in the 1984 NFL supplemental draft ... Played in two USFL championship games with the Philadelphia/Baltimore Stars ... Joined Browns in 1986 and led team in special-teams tackles ... Defensive coaches realized they had to find a place for him in starting lineup. He ended up starting 10 of 11 games he played at right inside linebacker last season and led team in total tackles with 98 ... Also had two sacks, broke up one pass, caused three fumbles and recovered another ... Played on same Virginia Tech team that produced Bruce Smith (Bills) and Jesse Penn (Cowboys) ... Studied architecture in college ... Born Nov. 26, 1962, in Southport, N.C.

FELIX WRIGHT 29 6-2 190   Free Safety

This free agent from the Canadian Football League broke into the Browns' starting secondary as the free safety the last seven games of last season and it will be difficult to move him out...Shared team lead in interceptions (four) with Frank Minnifield. Even though he started only seven games in his first three seasons in NFL, he has nine career interceptions ...Spent first two seasons with Browns as nickle back and special-teams player...Had two blocks and one partially blocked punt in 1986...Brief tryout with Houston Oilers in 1982 before heading north for three seasons with Hamilton Tiger Cats of CFL...A four-year starter at Drake, he never missed a game with Bulldogs and was defensive MVP as senior...Owns restaurant in Joplin, Mo., called "The Wright Place."...Comes from athletic family. Brother Joe played basketball at Kansas State. Brother Charles played defensive back at Tulsa and sister Wilma Jean was scholastic track standout...Born June 22, 1959, in Carthage, Mo.

COACH MARTY SCHOTTENHEIMER: He's more than a coach with a big name. He's now a big-name coach...In three-plus seasons as head coach Schottzy is 34-21 and his Browns have won last three AFC-Central titles...Browns' owner Art Modell once boldly predicted that Schottenheimer will be "the next great coach in football." Of course, Modell hired him, but Marty may be on his way to proving his owner

right...Predecessor Sam Rutigliano had pizazz and a gift of gab. Marty isn't as glib but his steadfast, deliberate and determined approach is producing better results..."I'm a goal-oriented person," he says...The Browns' goal remains to get to the Super Bowl after coming so close twice in AFC championship-game losses to Denver...Has shown ability to make major adjustments in his planning...His first full season, Browns were run-oriented team. In 1986, they opened things up a bit with Bernie Kosar and by hiring Lindy Infante...Last year, Browns incorporated some Bear-type defenses and more four-man fronts into their base 3-4...Now he has to adjust to loss of Infante, who took head-coaching job at Green Bay...Was Browns' defensive coordinator before taking head job in middle of '84 season. Much of his defensive philosophy stems from Denver's Joe Collier, who coached Marty with Buffalo Bills in '60s and encouraged him to get back into football after spending 2½ years in business in early '70s . . . Born Sept. 23, 1943, in Canonsburg, Pa . . . Was All-American linebacker at Pitt.

LONGEST PLAY

The Browns were holding a slim one-game lead over the surprising New York Giants in the Century Division of the NFL as they took the field at Cleveland Stadium on Nov. 26, 1967, against Washington. The Redskins were struggling toward a 5-6-3 season but were dangerous because of quarterback Sonny Jurgensen, who was on his way to throwing 31 touchdown passes for the season.

Rookie defensive back Carl Ward saved the Browns' bacon this day. His 104-yard kickoff return provided the difference in a wild 42-37 Cleveland victory. Meanwhile, the Giants were winning, 44-7, over Philadelphia to keep pace. Cleveland defeated the Giants the next week to virtually wrap up the division, but was routed, 52-14, by Dallas in the Eastern Conference playoff, sending the Cowboys on to their Ice Bowl game against the Packers for the NFL championship.

INDIVIDUAL BROWN RECORDS

Rushing

Most Yards Game:	237	Jim Brown, vs Los Angeles, 1957	
	237	Jim Brown, vs Philadelphia, 1961	
Season:	1,863	Jim Brown, 1963	
Career:	12,312	Jim Brown, 1957-65	

Passing

Most TD Passes Game:	5	Frank Ryan, vs N.Y. Giants, 1964	
	5	Bill Nelsen, vs Dallas, 1969	
	5	Brian Sipe, vs Pittsburgh, 1979	
Season:	30	Brian Sipe, 1980	
Career:	154	Brian Sipe, 1974-83	

Receiving

Most TD Passes Game:	3	Mac Speedie, vs Chicago, 1951
	3	Darrell Brewster, vs N.Y. Giants, 1953
	3	Ray Renfro, vs Pittsburgh, 1959
	3	Gary Collins, vs Philadelphia, 1963
	3	Reggie Rucker, vs N.Y. Jets, 1976
	3	Larry Poole, vs Pittsburgh, 1977
	3	Calvin Hill, vs Baltimore, 1978
Season:	13	Gary Collins, 1963
Career:	70	Gary Collins, 1962-71

Scoring

Most Points Game:	36	Dub Jones, vs Chicago Bears, 1951
Season:	126	Jim Brown, 1965
Career:	1,349	Lou Groza, 1950-59, 1961-67
Most TDs Game:	6	Dub Jones, vs Chicago Bears, 1951
Season:	21	Jim Brown, 1965
Career:	126	Jim Brown, 1957-65

DENVER BRONCOS

TEAM DIRECTORY: Owner: Patrick D. Bowlen; GM: John Beake; Dir. Media Rel.: Jim Saccomano; Head Coach: Dan Reeves. Home field: Mile High Stadium (76,273). Colors: Orange, blue and white.

SCOUTING REPORT

OFFENSE: Denver led the AFC in total yardage in '87 but learned in another Super Bowl that, as brilliant as he is, John Elway can't do it alone. And, as explosive as the Broncos' passing game is with Elway throwing to the Three Amigos, Vance Johnson, Mark Jackson and Ricky Nattiel, their running game is just as pedestrian—despite solid Sammy Winder. But the arrival of Tony Dorsett from Dallas will add some dash.

John Elway: Still seeking a Super Bowl ring.

The longest running play for Denver during its 10-4-1 regular season was only 29 yards. Denver averaged only 3.9 yards per running play. The Broncos' offensive line simply can't blow people off the line, which is one reason Denver has to throw so many different offensive looks at its opponents.

To make matters worse, the Broncos will have to look for replacements for veteran center Bill Bryan and tackle Dave Studdard, who was injured in the Super Bowl loss to the Washington Redskins.

DEFENSE: Joe Collier's defense was badly embarrassed in the second half of the AFC championship game and the first half of the Super Bowl, when it gave up 65 points over four consecutive quarters.

Critics say that unless the defensive signal-callers are guessing right with blitzes, overshifts and stunts, the Broncos aren't physically strong enough to stand up and take on an offense.

A key area of concern is in the secondary. Mark Haynes came on to be the Broncos' best cornerback but Denver missed Louis Wright, as they did handyman Mike Harden, cornerback, strong safety and free safety who couldn't play in the AFC title game and Super Bowl. Dennis Smith and Tony Lilly were up-and-down performers at safety.

Rulon Jones continues as a standout at defensive end. Karl Mecklenburg leads the linebackers along with Jim Ryan and an improving Ricky Hunley. Opponents found ways to beat Simon Fletcher, a former defensive end who doesn't operate well in open space.

KICKING GAME: Kicker Rich Karlis hit 18 of 25 and his career percentage of .726 is fifth-best in NFL history. He was 4-7 in the 40s. Punter Mike Horan averaged 41.1, not good in Denver's rarified air, and he allowed 34 returns for a 12.5 average and also had two blocked in the Buffalo game. K.C. Clark averaged 12.9 on punt returns and Ken Bell had a healthy 21.5 kickoff-return average. Denver's special teams were just average on coverage.

THE ROOKIES: The Broncos didn't bulk up on defense with 260-pound nose tackle Ted Gregory of Syracuse. They did, however, add 6-6, 311-pound offensive tackle Gerald Perry of Southern U., who weighed 212 entering college and 235 as sophomore. "Then, whoom," Perry says, "it was all over after that." Teammates called him "Ice Truck," he says, "because I was the coolest big man they had ever seen."

BRONCOS VETERAN ROSTER

HEAD COACH—Dan Reeves. Assistant Coaches—Marvin Bass, Rubin Carter, Joe Collier, Mo Forte, Chan Gailey, George Henshaw, Stan Jones, Larry Kennan, Pete Mangurian, Al Miller, Myrel Moore, Mike Nolan, Charlie Waters, Charlie West.

No.	Name	Pos.	Ht.	Wt.	NFL Exp.	College
86	Andrews, Mitch	TE	6-2	239	2	Louisiana State
35	Bell, Ken	RB	5-10	190	3	Boston College
54	Bishop, Keith	C-G	6-3	265	8	Baylor
24	Boddie, Tony	RB	5-11	198	2	Montana State
65	Bowyer, Walt	DE	6-4	260	4	Arizona State
34	Braxton, Tyrone	S	5-11	174	2	North Dakota State
56	Brooks, Michael	LB	6-1	235	2	Louisiana State
64	Bryan, Billy	C	6-2	255	12	Duke
95	Bryan, Steve	NT	6-2	256	2	Oklahoma
28	Castille, Jeremiah	CB-S	5-10	175	6	Alabama
27	Clark, Kevin	S	5-10	185	2	San Jose State
69	Colorito, Tony	NT	6-5	260	2	Southern California
55	Dennison, Rick	LB	6-3	220	7	Colorado State
—	Dorsett, Tony	RB	5-11	188	12	Pittsburgh
7	Elway, John	QB	6-3	210	6	Stanford
73	Fletcher, Simon	DE-LB	6-5	240	4	Houston
62	Freeman, Mike	G	6-3	256	4	Arizona
90	Gilbert, Freddie	DE	6-4	275	3	Georgia
83	Graddy, Sam	WR	5-10	165	2	Tennessee
31	Harden, Mike	CB-S	6-1	192	9	Michigan
36	Haynes, Mark	CB	5-11	195	9	Colorado
78	Hood, Winford	G	6-3	265	5	Georgia
2	Horan, Mike	P	5-11	190	5	Long Beach State
79	Humphries, Stefan	G	6-3	268	5	Michigan
98	Hunley, Ricky	LB	6-2	238	5	Arizona
80	Jackson, Mark	WR	5-9	174	3	Purdue
82	Johnson, Vance	WR	5-11	174	4	Arizona
20	Jones, Daryll	S	6-0	193	3	Georgia
75	Jones, Rulon	DE	6-6	260	9	Utah State
12	Karcher, Ken	QB	6-3	205	2	Tulane
3	Karlis, Rich	K	6-0	180	7	Cincinnati
72	Kartz, Keith	T	6-4	270	2	California
88	Kay, Clarence	TE	6-2	237	5	Georgia
97	Klostermann, Bruce	LB	6-4	225	2	South Dakota State
71	Kragen, Greg	NT	6-3	245	4	Utah State
8	Kubiak, Gary	QB	6-0	192	6	Texas A&M
33	Lang, Gene	RB	5-10	196	5	Louisiana State
76	Lanier, Ken	T	6-3	269	8	Florida State
68	Lee, Larry	G-C	6-2	263	7	UCLA
22	Lilly, Tony	S	6-0	199	5	Florida
59	Lucas, Tim	LB	6-3	230	2	California
29	Marshall, Warren	RB	6-0	216	2	James Madison
85	Massie, Rick	WR	6-1	190	2	Kentucky
77	Mecklenburg, Karl	DE-LB	6-3	230	6	Minnesota
46	Micho, Bobby	RB	6-3	235	4	Texas
89	Mobley, Orson	TE	6-5	256	3	Salem
51	Munford, Marc	LB	6-2	231	2	Nebraska
84	Nattiel, Ricky	WR	5-9	180	2	Florida
38	Plummer, Bruce	CB	6-1	197	2	Mississippi State
74	Remsberg, Dan	T	6-6	275	3	Abilene Christian
48	Robbins, Randy	S	6-2	189	5	Arizona
50	Ryan, Jim	LB	6-1	225	10	William & Mary
30	Sewell, Steve	RB	6-3	210	4	Oklahoma
49	Smith, Dennis	S	6-3	200	8	Southern California
70	Studdard, Dave	T	6-4	260	10	Texas
61	Townsend, Andre	DE-NT	6-3	265	5	Mississippi
81	Watson, Steve	WR	6-4	195	10	Temple
47	Willhite, Gerald	RB	5-10	200	7	San Jose State
45	Wilson, Steve	CB	5-10	195	10	Howard
23	Winder, Sammy	RB	5-11	203	7	Southern Mississippi

TOP DRAFT CHOICES

Rd.	Name	Sel. No.	Pos.	Ht.	Wt.	College
1	Gregory, Ted	26	DT	6-1	260	Syracuse
2	Perry, Gerald	45	OT	6-6	311	Southern
3	Guidry, Kevin	79	DB	6-0	176	LSU
5	Ervin, Corris	136	CB	5-11	173	Central Florida
7	Frank, Garry	192	C	6-2	289	Mississippi State

OUTLOOK: The Broncos were humbled and you have to wonder if their time has come and gone. Clever, resourceful coaching as much as anything has gotten Denver to the title game twice. Coaching can only carry you so far and the Broncos may need some more football talent.

BRONCO PROFILES

JOHN ELWAY 28 6-3 210   **Quarterback**

"If he's not the Most Valuable Player in the NFL, I don't know who is," says Denver coach Dan Reeves...Indeed, the Associated Press named him the Most Valuable Player in the NFL in 1987...Many handicappers expected him to single-handedly win Super Bowl XXII for the Broncos but he didn't...That's about all the former Stanford star has failed to accomplish for the Broncos in his five seasons...Now has a 48-23-1 (.676) record as starting quarterback in NFL...In last four seasons has directed his team to more regular-season victories (42) than any other quarterback...Completed 54.6 percent for 19 touchdowns with 12 interceptions in 1987, throwing for 3,198 yards in 12 games...Marked the third season in a row he's thrown for more than 3,000 and has taken the Broncos to the Super Bowl twice...Continues to mature as a quarterback who can read and understand opposing coverages and stay cool in pocket...Still has ability to scramble and either buy time for big play or run for good yardage...Now has 1,197 career rushing yards in NFL...AFC starter for second year in a row in Pro Bowl...Has thrown for 85 touchdowns in his career...Born June 28, 1960, in Port Angeles, Wash....Selected by Baltimore Colts as No. 1 overall in 1983 draft, then was traded to Broncos.

VANCE JOHNSON 25 5-11 174   **Wide Receiver**

One of Denver's speedy and gifted Three Amigos receiving corps, Vance enjoyed his best NFL season in 1987 when he caught 42 passes for 16.3-yard average and seven touchdowns. That was despite missing almost two games because of dislocated shoulder...Had games of 116, 96, 95, 87, 88 and 86 yards during season and scored a touchdown by reception in six straight games...Was second-round draft pick in

1985 out of Arizona, where he played tailback . . . In 1983 scored 13 touchdowns for Wildcats, 10 by rushing . . . Won 1982 NCAA long-jump championship with a 26-11½ effort and also captured 1984 Pacific 10 Conference long-jump title in 1984 . . . Just missed (by half inch) making 1984 U.S. Olympic team as long-jumper. Majored in commercial art in college. Is an accomplished artist specializing in acrylics, with particular interest in women's faces . . . Makes home in Tucson, Ariz., where he attended high school . . . Born March 13, 1963, in Trenton, N.J.

KEITH BISHOP 31 6-3 265   Guard

Only offensive lineman in history of Denver franchise to be named to Pro Bowl and he has been selected twice—1986, 1987 . . . Earned the respect of his peers in NFL but is relatively anonymous to most NFL fans . . . A starter in Bronco line since 1983 . . . Also serves as Denver's long snapper and coaches consider him the best in the NFL at that specialty . . . Named team's Most Inspirational Player, the only Bronco besides Tom Jackson to have ever received the honor . . . Drafted by Broncos in sixth round in 1980 out of Baylor, but began his college career at Nebraska, where he played for two seasons . . . Born March 10, 1957, in LaJolla, Cal., but went to high school in Midland, Tex., and now makes his home in Englewood, Colo.

CLARENCE KAY 27 6-2 237   Tight End

After spending part of 1986 season undergoing treatment for substance abuse, the bulky former Georgia bulldog came back last year to turn in his most productive NFL season . . . Has become a major offensive weapon for the Broncos . . . Caught career-high 31 passes for 14.2 yards average, impressive for a tight end . . . Now has 91 receptions in four seasons . . . Always considered a fine blocker, the improvement in his receiving has been gratifying development for Denver staff . . . Plays on-line tight end for a team that often employs a second tight end as move man or H-back . . . Caught 51 passes for 740 yards and six touchdowns during career at Georgia, where he played in two Sugar Bowls and one Cotton Bowl . . . Was only a seventh-round draft pick in 1984 . . . Born and raised in Seneca, S.C. . . . Once high-jumped 6-8 at Seneca High.

MARK JACKSON 25 5-9 174   Wide Receiver

When two Cleveland Browns failed to tackle Jackson after he took a short pass from John Elway in the AFC championship game, it was Adios Amigo. Jackson took it 80 yards to give the Broncos a 28-10 lead early in the third quarter . . . It was just a sample of this former Purdue Boilermaker's explosiveness . . . Earned a starting berth after a strong showing in training camp and in preseason . . . Overlooked in 1986 NFL draft until sixth round despite 47 catches for 15.6-yard average in senior season at Purdue . . . Quickly became game-breaking reciever for Broncos, taking in 38 passes for 19.4-yard average as a rookie . . . Caught 26 for 16.8 last season . . . His best game was against Seattle when he gained a career-high 85 yards, including one reception of 47 yards . . . His career average per catch of 18.3 is second-best in team history . . . Born July 23, 1963, in Chicago, but grew up in Terre Haute, Ind.

RULON JONES 30 6-6 260   Defensive End

This rangy Utah native should become Broncos' career sack leader sometime this season . . . In eight NFL seasons, Rulon has 68½ sacks for Denver. Barney Chavous owns the franchise record with 72 . . . Set Broncos' single season record of 13½ sacks in 1986, when Denver won the first of its two successive AFC championships. Had seven sacks in 1987, six in final seven games of season . . . Durable performer who missed only one game in his four seasons at Utah State and just four games (knee injury in 1983) since he joined the Broncos as a second-round draft choice in 1980 . . . A true son of the West, he likes to hunt and fish and his hobbies include painting Western art and sculpting . . . Born March 25, 1958, in Salt Lake City.

RICKY NATTIEL 22 5-9 180   Wide Receiver

Shocked Super Bowl XXII crowd in San Diego by burning Redskins for 56-yard touchdown bomb on the first play of the game . . . Turned out to be Denver's only TD but may be an omen of headaches facing AFC secondaries once Ricky gets established . . . Numero 3 of the Three Amigos joined Broncos as first-round draft choice out of University of Florida in 1987 . . . By the end of rookie season had become a force to be reckoned with . . . Had 21 receptions for 516 yards, a 25.9 average, and two TDs in last seven games while playing with broken bone and a broken thumb on his left hand . . . In all, caught 31 passes for 20.3-yard average, best average ever for a Denver rookie . . . Also was used as punt-return man . . . Was an option quarterback in high school in Newberry, Fla., where he ran for 15 TDs as a senior and passed for three scores . . . Finished college career as sixth-leading receiver in Gators' history with 117 receptions . . . Born Jan. 25, 1966, in Gainesville, Fla.

SAMMY WINDER 29 5-11 203   Running Back

When Nick Nicolau, who used to coach the Denver running backs, calls Sammy "a garbage runner" he means it as a compliment. "Give him just a crack and he's going to gain five yards," Nicolau says. "Not a big hole, just a crack. When there's a big hole any back in the NFL can gain five yards." . . . The knock against Winder is that he isn't explosive or flashy enough, but Winder has methodically run for 700 yards or more the last five seasons. He's led the Broncos in rushing the last six seasons and twice has played for the AFC in the Pro Bowl . . . Sammy's so blue-collar ordinary he's interesting in an era when athletes try to out-do each other with flash . . . When he picks up the newspaper in the morning he turns to classified section first, looking for bargains in heavy equipment. Already owns two dump trucks and often drives his Kenworth cab to Bronco practices . . . Intends to get into contracting business after his football days are over . . . Played at Southern Mississippi with NFL stars Hanford Dixon and Louis Lipps . . . Makes his home in Jackson, Miss. . . . Born July 15, 1959, in Madison, Miss.

KARL MECKLENBURG 27 6-3 230   Linebacker

The television cameras are gone and everybody is yawning by the time the 12th round of the NFL college draft comes around every year. The 12th and final round of the draft, though, is where the Broncos found Mecklenburg in 1983 . . . All he's done is make the AFC Pro Bowl team each of the last three years and this wild-card performer has become the key to Denver's multiple-look defenses . . . Has 38½ sacks in five seasons, including 13 in 1985 . . . Listed as inside linebacker on depth chart but could turn up at any of the defensive line or linebacker positions when the ball is snapped . . . Did not become a starter for the Broncos until late in 1985 . . . Was voted team's defensive MVP for 1987 . . . Mother is former deputy secretary of the Department of Health, Education and Welfare . . . Has raised a quarter of a million dollars for Denver's Mercy Hospital with "For Mercy's Sack, Sack 'Em" program, which he initiated . . . Born Sept. 1, 1960, in Edina, Minn. . . . Holds degree in biology from Minnesota and is an accomplished guitarist.

MARK HAYNES 29 5-11 195   Cornerback

Former New York Giants' All-Pro replaced retired Louis Wright as starter at left corner and re-established his reputation as one of the top cornerbacks in the NFL . . . Was a three-time Pro Bowl selection as a Giant (1982, 1983 and 1984) . . . Had seven interceptions for New York in 1985 . . . Held out in 1985 in contract dispute before rejoining team for final six games . . . Traded to Denver on draft day 1986, but was hampered by injuries most of season . . . Intercepted three passes for Broncos in 1987 and now has 16 for his career . . . Returned a William Perry fumble 24 yards for a touchdown in Monday night victory over the Chicago Bears last Nov. 16 . . . Giants made him a first-round pick in 1981 out of the University of Colorado . . . Returned an interception 97 yards for Colorado in 1977 game against Army . . . Unanimous All-American selection in 1979 and twice made All-Big Eight team . . . Born in Nov. 6, 1958, in Kansas City, Kans.

COACH DAN REEVES: He was the youngest coach in the NFL

when he took over the Denver Broncos in 1981 at age 37. Hard to believe, but Handsome Dan became a grandfather in March. That helped make up for a second disappointing showing in the Super Bowl . . . Challenge facing Reeves in his eighth season in Denver is how to deal with "Super Bowl burnout." The Broncos have gone twice and lost . . . The feeling is that Reeves will find a way to deal with it because he's handled just about every other problem thrown his way . . . His record as a head coach is 66-37-1 in regular-season games. Since 1981 only three NFL coaches, Joe Gibbs, Bill Walsh and Don Shula, have posted more victories than Reeves . . . Four times Reeves-coached Denver teams failed to make the playoffs and two that didn't went 10-6 in 1981 and 11-5 in 1985 . . . There was a lot of hysteria in Denver, especially over the Broncos' poor defensive showing against Redskins in Super Bowl XXII. Reeves won't panic. "It's embarrassing, but all of a sudden we didn't become a bad team in one game. And all of a sudden, we didn't win all the games we won because we didn't have a defense," he says . . . A quarterback in college at South Carolina, he made the Dallas Cowboys in 1965 as a free-agent running back and stayed around eight seasons as an all-purpose back . . . He finished his career as the Cowboys' fifth all-time leading rusher with 1,990 yards and 25 touchdowns . . . He also caught 129 passes for 1,693 yards and 17 touchdowns . . . He was a coach his last three seasons with Cowboys. He left the game for one year (1973) then returned as a Dallas assistant and stayed until he got the Denver job in 1981 . . . Born Jan. 19, 1944, in Americus, Ga.

LONGEST PLAY

The Broncos fell far short of being an American Football League power in the 1960s. They were suffering through another dreadful campaign in 1966. They were 0-3 and coach Mac Speedie already had been fired, replaced by Ray Malavasi, when Houston came to Mile High Stadium on Oct. 2.

Up to then, the high point of the Denver season had been an 88-yard kickoff return by Goldie Sellers for the Broncos' only points in a 45-7 loss to the Oilers on opening day.

Sellers did it to the Oilers again in Denver, but this time his scoring kickoff return, 100 yards, was a factor. The Broncos overcame five touchdown passes by George Blanda and won, 40-38, on Gary Kroner's fourth field goal of the game with 27 seconds left.

INDIVIDUAL BRONCO RECORDS

Rushing

Most Yards Game:	183	Otis Armstrong, vs Houston, 1974	
Season:	1,407	Otis Armstrong, 1974	
Career:	6,323	Floyd Little, 1967-75	

Passing

Most TD Passes Game:	5	Frank Tripucka, vs Buffalo, 1962	
	5	John Elway, vs Minnesota, 1984	
Season:	24	Frank Tripucka, 1960	
Career:	85	John Elway, 1983-87	

Receiving

Most TD Passes Game:	3	Lionel Taylor, vs Buffalo, 1960	
	3	Bob Scarpitto, vs Buffalo, 1966	
	3	Haven Moses, vs Houston, 1973	
	3	Steve Watson, vs Baltimore, 1981	
Season:	13	Steve Watson, 1981	
Career:	44	Lionel Taylor, 1960-66	
	44	Haven Moses, 1972-81	

Scoring

Most Points Game:	21	Gene Mingo, vs Los Angeles, 1960
Season:	137	Gene Mingo, 1962
Career:	736	Jim Turner, 1971-79
Most TDs Game:	3	Lionel Taylor, vs Buffalo, 1960
	3	Don Stone, vs San Diego, 1962
	3	Bob Scarpitto, vs Buffalo, 1966
	3	Floyd Little, vs Minnesota, 1972
	3	Floyd Little, vs Cincinnati, 1973
	3	Haven Moses, vs Houston, 1973
	3	Otis Armstrong, vs Houston, 1974
	3	Jon Keyworth, vs Kansas City, 1974
	3	Steve Watson, vs Baltimore, 1981
	3	Gerald Willhite, vs Dallas, 1986
	3	Gerald Willhite, vs Kansas City, 1986
Season:	13	Floyd Little, 1972
	13	Floyd Little, 1973
	13	Steve Watson, 1981
Career:	54	Floyd Little, 1967-75

HOUSTON OILERS

TEAM DIRECTORY: Pres./Owner K.S. (Bud) Adams Jr,; Exec. VP/GM: Ladd Herzeg; VP/Player Personnel: Mike Holovak; Dir. Administration: Rick Nichols; Dir. Media Rel.: Chip Namias; Dir. Pub. Rel.: Gregg Stengel; Head Coach: Jerry Glanville. Home field: Astrodome (50,452). Colors: Scarlet, Columbia blue and white.

SCOUTING REPORT

OFFENSE: It's gonna take points, a whole lot of points, to beat these Oilers. They seem to have all the offensive weapons on line to make a concerted run at the Browns for the AFC-Central title. To start with, there is quarterback Warren Moon and the most

Warren Moon got respect as Oilers made divisional playoffs.

explosive pair of receivers in the AFC, Drew Hill and Ernest Givins.

At running back Houston has Mike Rozier, who was good for 957 yards, and fullback Alonzo Highsmith, who signed when the season was well underway and was just starting to make a contribution when it ended.

Up front is a solid blocking line led by Mike Munchak, who some rate the best guard in the NFL, tackle Dean Steinkuhler and guard Bruce Matthews. Backing up Munchak and Matthews is former Rams' All-Pro Kent Hill.

DEFENSE: This is where the Oilers must get more consistent. They lost games when the offense scored 30 and 27 points and needed to tally into the 30s to get by Atlanta and Cincinnati. Of course, part of the reason Houston gives up big plays is coach Jerry Glanville's gambling blitzing style. For all their all-out pressure, the Oilers came up with only 35 sacks last season.

Houston corners Patrick Allen and Steve Brown held up fairly well and safety Keith Bostic intercepted six passes, but a cover man is needed at nickel back. The linebacking could be upgraded, too. More speed is needed.

The Oilers allowed 4.1 yards per rushing play in 1987.

KICKING GAME: Kicker Tony Zendejas hit 20 of 26 field-goal tries, including 8 of 12 between 40 and 49 yards. The Oilers waived punter (and kickoff man) Lee Johnson late in the season, then they picked up former Cleveland punter Jeff Gossett. Johnson, ironically, ended up punting for the Browns. Oilers' special teams have to be improved. They averaged only 6.7 and 18.3 on punt and kickoff returns while yielding 10.6 and 20.6.

THE ROOKIES: Instead of defensive speed, Houston took Michigan State's durable RB Lorenzo White with Mike Rozier and Allen Pinkett already there. There's a message somewhere. "He's not a breakaway back," says personnel director Mike Holovak, "but maybe used less often, we'll get that out of him, too. You're going to see one helluva football player." Another ex-Spartan, Greg Montgomery, should solve punting woes.

OUTLOOK: The Oilers (9-6 in '87) have most of the ingredients for a division champion. They have to fill in around the edges, add speed and special-teams players. Developing an attitude they can beat the Browns is important, too. The Browns handled them, 40-7, in their Astrodome showdown. It was the only home game Houston's regular team lost last season, but it was a big one.

OILERS VETERAN ROSTER

HEAD COACH—Jerry Glanville, Assistant Coaches—Kim Helton, Milt Jackson, June Jones, Floyd Reese, Nick Saban, Ray Sherman, Doug Shively, Richard Smith.

No.	Name	Pos.	Ht.	Wt.	NFL Exp.	College
29	Allen, Patrick	CB	5-10	180	5	Utah State
36	Birdsong, Craig	S	6-2	217	2	North Texas State
25	Bostic, Keith	S	6-1	223	6	Michigan
24	Brown, Steve	CB	5-11	187	6	Oregon
38	Bryant, Domingo	S	6-4	175	2	Texas A&M
71	Byrd, Richard	DE	6-4	265	4	Southern Mississippi
90	Caston, Toby	LB	6-1	235	2	Louisiana State
79	Childress, Ray	DE	6-6	276	4	Texas A&M
98	Cooks, Rayford	DE	6-3	245	2	North Texas State
77	Davis, Bruce	T	6-6	280	10	UCLA
73	Davis, John	T-G	6-4	304	2	Georgia Tech
31	Donaldson, Jeffy	S	6-0	194	5	Colorado
82	Drewrey, Willie	WR-KR	5-7	164	4	West Virginia
80	Duncan, Curtis	WR-KR	5-11	184	2	Northwestern
21	Eason, Bo	S	6-2	205	5	California-Davis
51	Fairs, Eric	LB	6-3	238	3	Memphis State
95	Fuller, William	DE	6-3	260	3	North Carolina
81	Givins, Ernest	WR	5-9	172	3	Louisville
8	Gossett, Jeff	P	6-2	200	7	Eastern Illinois
59	Grimsley, John	LB	6-2	236	5	Kentucky
83	Harris, Leonard	WR	5-8	165	3	Texas Tech
32	Highsmith, Alonzo	RB	6-1	235	2	Miami
85	Hill, Drew	WR	5-9	170	9	Georgia Tech
49	James, Arrike	TE	6-4	238	2	Delta State
84	Jeffires, Haywood	WR	6-2	198	2	North Carolina State
22	Johnson, Kenny	S	5-10	175	9	Mississippi State
23	Johnson, Richard	CB	6-1	190	4	Wisconsin
57	Johnson, Walter	LB	6-0	241	2	Louisiana Tech
—	Jones, Sean	DE	6-7	265	5	Northeastern
93	Lyles, Robert	LB	6-1	223	5	Texas Christian
78	Maggs, Don	T-G	6-5	277	2	Tulane
94	Martin, Charles	NT	6-4	280	5	Livingston
74	Matthews, Bruce	T-G	6-5	280	6	Southern California
26	McMillian, Audrey	CB	6-0	190	4	Houston
91	Meads, Johnny	LB	6-2	230	5	Nicholls State
1	Moon, Warren	QB	6-3	210	5	Washington
63	Munchak, Mike	G	6-3	280	7	Penn State
89	Parks, Jeff	TE	6-4	240	3	Auburn
10	Pease, Brent	QB	6-2	200	2	Montana
52	Pennison, Jay	C	6-1	275	3	Nicholls State
20	Pinkett, Allen	RB	5-9	185	3	Notre Dame
30	Rozier, Mike	RB	5-10	211	4	Nebraska
53	Seale, Eugene	LB	5-10	250	2	Lamar
54	Smith, Al	LB	6-1	230	2	Utah State
99	Smith, Doug	NT	6-5	282	4	Auburn
70	Steinkuhler, Dean	T-G	6-3	278	5	Nebraska
33	Tillman, Spencer	RB	5-11	206	2	Oklahoma
45	Valentine, Ira	RB	6-0	212	2	Texas A&M
35	Wallace, Ray	RB	6-0	220	3	Purdue
69	Williams, Doug	T-G	6-5	288	3	Texas A&M
87	Williams, Jamie	TE	6-4	245	6	Nebraska
7	Zendejas, Tony	K	5-8	165	3	Nevada-Reno

TOP DRAFT CHOICES

Rd.	Name	Sel. No.	Pos.	Ht.	Wt.	College
1	White, Lorenzo	22	RB	5-10	213	Michigan State
2	Jones, Quintin	48	CB	5-11	188	Pittsburgh
3	Montgomery, Greg	72	P	6-3	219	Michigan State
5	Dishman, Cris	125	DB	6-0	173	Purdue
5	Verhulst, Chris	130	TE	6-2	227	Cal State-Chico

OILER PROFILES

WARREN MOON 31 6-3 210   Quarterback

Winner in college (Rose Bowl) and in the Canadian League (five Grey Cup titles with Edmonton), but the NFL jury was out on former University of Washington star until he guided the Oilers to wild-card spot and victory over Seattle in opening round last season . . . Now the question: Can Moon be consistent enough to take the Oilers deeper into the playoffs? . . . His 21 TD passes (fourth in the AFC) was the most by an Oiler since George Blanda tossed 24 in 1963 . . . Finished 10th in AFC passing standings with 74.2 points mainly because his completion rate was only 50.0 and his interception rate was 4.9. However, he has a strong arm to hit his speed receivers deep and still has good mobility in pocket . . . Very active in many causes, including Special Olympics . . . He's really Harold Warren Moon, born Nov. 18, 1956, in Los Angeles.

MIKE ROZIER 27 5-10 211   Running Back

Third year with Oilers most productive yet in the NFL for the former Heisman Trophy winner from Nebraska and earned him first trip to Pro Bowl . . . Finished fourth in the league with 957 yards rushing. Rushing average of 4.2 in 1987 a considerable improvement over the 3.5 and 3.3 marks of his first two seasons . . . Also caught 27 passes for 7.1-yard average . . . Missed last three games of 1986 with knee ligament damage which required arthroscopic surgery but started 11 of 12 regular games in 1987, missing only loss to Niners . . . Rushed for 792 yards and caught 32 passes as rookie with Pittsburgh Maulers of USFL in 1984, then gained 1,361 yards and scored 12 TDs rushing and caught 50 passes in 18 games for Jacksonville Bulls in 1985 before jumping to NFL and debuting that fall . . . Houston had tabbed him in 1984 supplemental draft . . . Played three seasons at Nebraska after transferring from Coffeyville, Kans. Junior College. Averaged an amazing 7.1 yards, scored 49 touchdowns and gained 4,780 yards as Cornhusker . . . Born March 1, 1961, in Camden, N.J.

DREW HILL 31 5-9 170 Wide Receiver

Perhaps the bargain player of the last 10 years. First, the L.A. Rams got him in the 12th round of the 1979 draft as basically a kick-returner (he averaged 30.0 yards to lead nation for Georgia Tech as a senior). Then Oilers acquired him for seventh- and fourth-round draft picks ... After catching 60 passes, including 10 for TDs in five seasons for the Rams, has nabbed 178 for 3,270 yards and 20 TDs for Houston ... In 1987 just missed third straight 1,000-yard season in receiving, catching 49 for 989 (20.2 average) and six TDs ... Was fifth in NFL in receiving yards ... Has started 44 straight games for Houston not counting last year's strike weeks ... Born Oct. 5, 1956, in Newnan, Ga.

MIKE MUNCHAK 28 6-3 280 Guard

Voted as starter with Denver's Keith Bishop in last Pro Bowl, his second starting selection and third appearance ... Might have gone in 1986, too, but sprained knee ligaments in sixth game knocked him out of action. Received injury trying to block Bears' Refrigerator Perry, one of few losing battles former Penn State star has fought ... Scrapped with Bills' Bruce Smith in Buffalo last year. Smith got tossed. Munchak escaped because official called wrong number for his ejection ... First-round pick of Oilers in 1982 and won starting job in camp but broken ankle caused him to miss five games ... Was fullback and defensive end in high school ... Born March 5, 1960, in Scranton, Pa.

ERNEST GIVINS 23 5-9 192 Wide Receiver

One of brightest young receivers in football ... Broke in in 1986 with 61 catches for 1,062 yards, only ninth rookie in NFL history to have 1,000-yard season ... Led team with 53 receptions for 933 yards and six TDs in 1987 ... Six 100-yard receiving games so far in career, including three last season ... Caught 3 for 126 in loss to Cleveland, including 83-

yarder that did not go for score . . . Brilliant return man, runner and receiver at Louisville, where he played two seasons, one under Howard Schnellenberger . . . As senior, accounted for 34 percent of total offense . . . Returned kickoffs 94 and 93 yards for TDs in college . . . Played two seasons at Northeast Oklahoma Junior College . . . Born Sept. 3, 1964, in St. Petersburg, Fla.

RAY CHILDRESS 25 6-6 276   **Defensive End**

First pick in 1985 draft was tossup between him and another defensive end, Bruce Smith. Buffalo took Smith but Oilers are happy with Childress, who has 15½ sacks in three seasons . . . Has now started 44 straight games (except for '87 strike) since joining Houston . . . Extremely active left end who usually faces strong side of formation. Stepped right in as rookie and was second on team in tackles and was second again in 1986 . . . Was first defensive player taken in first round by Oilers since Robert Brazile in 1975 . . . Played at Texas A&M, where he broke into starting lineup midway through freshman season. Majored in building construction in his Aggie days and owns a construction business in Dallas. Majoring in destruction in NFL . . . Born Oct. 20, 1962, in Memphis, Tenn.

ALONZO HIGHSMITH 23 6-1 235   **Fullback**

No. 1 pick of 1987 did not sign with Oilers until Week 9 of season, ended up starting at fullback last three regular games and two playoff encounters . . . Best game was 12-carries, 74-yard performance in wild-card playoff against Seattle . . . Underwent offseason arthroscopic knee surgery, but is expected to be ready to blossom in first full pro season . . . Originally attended University of Miami as defensive end/linebacker but was converted to fullback as freshman and ran for 1,873 yards in four-year career . . . Also caught 92 passes . . . Father Walter is offensive coordinator at Florida A&M, where he once played. Dad spent 13 seasons as offensive lineman in NFL and CFL, including 1972 campaign with Oilers . . . Born Feb. 26, 1965, in Bartow, Fla.

KEITH BOSTIC 27 6-1 223   Strong Safety

"He has as much ability at that position as anybody in the league," Jerry Glanville once proclaimed... Bostic lived up to it last season, making Pro Bowl for first time after brilliant season in which he had 46 tackles, three sacks, six interceptions, forced three fumbles and recovered one and broke up 14 passes... Shared AFC lead in interceptions with two others... Now has started 72 consecutive regular games... Attended Pioneer High School in Ann Arbor then went on to University of Michigan, where he had 10 career interceptions... Very physical player, which is what Glanville preaches... Likes to windsurf and play basketball and is said to be best player on Oilers' cage squad... Born Jan. 17, 1961, in Ann Arbor, Mich.

JAMIE WILLIAMS 28 6-4 245   Tight End

Caught only 13 passes in 1987 compared to career high of 41 for Oilers in 1984, but many argue he had his best season... Still, he equaled his career high with three touchdown grabs... Considered one of best blocking tight ends in AFC... Was second tight end selected in 1983 draft when Giants made him their third-round pick... New York waived him at final cut... Became property of two other teams before season was over. Played four games with Cardinals, was released and signed with Tampa Bay, which also cut him... Claimed on waivers by Oilers from Bucs prior to 1984 season and has started every regular game for Houston since... Takes acting and piano classes during offseason in Houston... Born Feb. 25, 1960, in Vero Beach, Fla., but went to high school in Davenport, Iowa.

STEVE BROWN 28 5-11 187   Cornerback

Serious actor on and off the field. A member of Screen Actors Guild, he appeared in 1984 episode of "Miami Vice," in which sister Olivia Brown is featured in regular cast... Third-round pick in 1983 from Oregon, where he was outstanding kick-returner. Averaged 23.9 for career on kickoffs and led Pac-10 with 10.3 punt-return average as senior...

Appeared in all 16 games as rookie with Oilers, averaging 23.6 on kickoffs (second-best in AFC). It included 93-yarder for score against Cleveland... Became starter at left corner in second pro season... Now has 11 career interceptions but his forte is playing very physically against the run... Born March 20, 1960, in Sacramento, Cal.

COACH JERRY GLANVILLE: The Man in Black did something nobody dared to do back in the 70s: Get 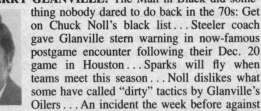 on Chuck Noll's black list... Steeler coach gave Glanville stern warning in now-famous postgame encounter following their Dec. 20 game in Houston... Sparks will fly when teams meet this season... Noll dislikes what some have called "dirty" tactics by Glanville's Oilers... An incident the week before against New Orleans also was cited in building a case against Houston ... Glanville does teach a gambling, aggressive style of football ... Oilers use blitz tactics similar to old Atlanta "Grits Blitz" of a few years ago when Glanville was on Falcon staff... He also likes secondary hitters who make receivers pay the price... Despite playoff season, questionable play-calling which led to rout by Denver in playoffs puts him on hot seat in '88... Has to be only man born in Detroit (Oct. 14, 1941) and who was educated in Ohio, Montana and Michigan who speaks fluent Dixie, drawl and all... Was Oilers' defensive coordinator in 1984, then took over as head coach last two games of 1985 season when Hugh Campbell was fired.

LONGEST PLAY

Ken Hall was a legendary high-school football player in Texas, but he never lived up to all the acclaim during his college days at Texas A&M or in his pro career. Hall, however, did have one big moment in the pro spotlight. It came in New York's Polo Grounds on Oct. 23, 1960.

In a wild game that was typical of the early AFL years, Hall returned a Bill Shockley kickoff 104 yards for a touchdown in the Oilers' 42-28 victory over the Titans. It still is the longest play in the history of the Houston franchise.

INDIVIDUAL OILER RECORDS

Rushing

Most Yards Game:	216	Billy Cannon, vs N.Y. Jets, 1961	
Season:	1,934	Earl Campbell, 1980	
Career:	8,574	Earl Campbell, 1978-84	

Passing

Most TD Passes Game:	7	George Blanda, vs N.Y. Jets, 1961
Season:	36	George Blanda, 1961
Career:	165	George Blanda, 1960-66

Receiving

Most TD Passes Game:	3	Bill Groman, vs N.Y. Jets, 1960
	3	Bill Groman, vs N.Y. Jets, 1961
	3	Billy Cannon, vs N.Y. Jets, 1961
	3	Charlie Hennigan, vs San Diego, 1961
	3	Charlie Hennigan, vs Buffalo, 1963
	3	Charles Frazier, vs Denver, 1966 (twice)
	3	Dave Casper, vs Pittsburgh, 1981
Season:	17	Bill Groman, 1961
Career:	51	Charlie Hennigan, 1960-66

Scoring

Most Points Game:	30	Billy Cannon, vs N.Y. Jets, 1961
Season:	115	George Blanda, 1960
Career:	596	George Blanda, 1960-66
Most TDs Game:	5	Billy Cannon, vs N.Y. Jets, 1961
Season:	19	Earl Campbell, 1979
Career:	73	Earl Campbell, 1978-84

INDIANAPOLIS COLTS

TEAM DIRECTORY: Pres./Treas.: Robert Irsay; VP/GM: Jim Irsay; VP/Gen. Counsel: Michael Chernoff; Dir. Player Personnel: Jack Bushofsky; Dir. Pub. Rel.: Craig Kelley; Head Coach: Ron Meyer. Home field: Hoosier Dome (60,127). Colors: Royal blue and white.

SCOUTING REPORT

OFFENSE: The Colts have Eric Dickerson, a one-man ball-control offense. They also have Albert Bentley, a productive, sturdy back and they may get yet another premier runner if Randy McMillan is fully recovered from injuries suffered when struck by a car in the spring of 1987. All that suits Ron Meyer fine, but he would like to see his team (9-6 last year) add another dimension as it goes after a second AFC-East championship.

"We need to be able to hit a home run," Meyer says. "We need to be able to strike with the long ball better."

To do that the Colts will have to add some deep speed to their wide receiver corps. Bill Brooks is a talented young receiver who can get open downfield, but steady Matt Bouza is strictly a possession man.

Of course, the Colts should worry first about their quarterbacking. They don't know if Gary Hogeboom will be sufficiently recovered from shoulder surgery to play effectively. If not, the job could fall into the lap of Jack Trudeau for the third year in a row. Former Charger backup Mark Herrmann will also get a look.

Nothing wrong with the Indianapolis offensive line, which, Meyer says, "can be as dominating as Washington's."

Even if the Colts add a game-breaker, it will only give them a change of pace, not a meat-and-potatoes pitch. Meyer is still a conservative coach and Dickerson is a weapon any run-minded coach is happy to have.

DEFENSE: Indy's defense played well enough to win the division last season, holding three of the last four opponents to seven points or less. And they've added nose tackle Joe Klecko, the 34-year-old former Jet who has made the Pro Bowl four times.

The Colts can still use another corner who can cover man-for-man to go with their crack linebacking corps of Johnie Cooks and Duane Bickett, Cliff Odom and Barry Krauss, defensive ends Donnell Thompson and Jon Hand and underrated corner Eugene Daniel.

Ex-Ram Eric Dickerson wound up as NFL's No. 2 rusher.

Colt opponents ran for only 3.9 yards per attempt and completed just 49.9 of their passes while Indy rang up 39 sacks, including eight by Bickett. The Indy defense is always under pressure not to let the game get out of hand because the Colts lack the striking power to score quickly. That's something Meyer wants to remedy.

KICKING GAME: Kicker Dean Biasucci made the AFC Pro Bowl team after hitting 24 of 27 field-goal tries. Punter Rohn Stark's abilities always have been overrated. Until last season (40.0), his raw average was always gaudy, but every season he allowed a high percent of returns. Once again, in 1987, opponents averaged in double figures on returns of his punts. Bentley averaged a healthy 22.7 on kickoff returns. Brooks was secure in handling punts but averaged only 6.2 per return.

THE ROOKIES: The Colts spent the offseason signing graybeards such as Klecko, Billy (White Shoes) Johnson and Ray Ellis because they didn't draft until the third round. Then, they

COLTS VETERAN ROSTER

HEAD COACH—Ron Meyer. Assistant Coaches—John Becker, Greg Briner, Leon Burtnett, George Catavolos, George Hill, Tom Lovat, John Marshall, Chip Myers, Keith Rowen, Rick Venturi, Tom Zupancic.

No.	Name	Pos.	Ht.	Wt.	NFL Exp.	College
57	Ahrens, Dave	LB	6-4	249	8	Wisconsin
78	Armstrong, Harvey	NT	6-3	268	6	Southern Methodist
35	Banks, Chuck	RB	6-1	227	3	West Virginia Tech
81	Beach, Pat	TE	6-4	252	6	Washington State
87	Bellini, Mark	WR	5-11	185	2	Brigham Young
20	Bentley, Albert	RB	5-11	214	4	Miami
4	Biasucci, Dean	K	6-0	191	4	Western Carolina
50	Bickett, Duane	LB	6-5	243	4	Southern California
85	Bouza, Matt	WR	6-3	212	7	California
84	Boyer, Mark	TE	6-4	242	4	Southern California
88	Brandes, John	TE	6-2	237	2	Cameron
—	Breeden, Louis	CB	5-11	185	11	N.C. Central
80	Brooks, Bill	WR	6-0	191	3	Boston University
74	Brotzki, Bob	T	6-5	293	3	Syracuse
68	Broughton, Willie	DE	6-5	281	3	Miami
72	Call, Kevin	T	6-7	302	5	Colorado State
31	Coleman, Leonard	S	6-2	202	4	Vanderbilt
98	Cooks, Johnie	LB	6-4	252	7	Mississippi State
38	Daniel, Eugene	CB	5-11	178	5	Louisiana State
72	Darby, Byron	DE	6-4	260	6	Southern California
29	Dickerson, Eric	RB	6-3	217	6	Southern Methodist
69	Dixon, Randy	T	6-3	293	2	Pittsburgh
53	Donaldson, Ray	C	6-3	288	9	Georgia
25	Glasgow, Nesby	S	5-10	187	10	Washington
37	Goode, Chris	CB-S	6-0	193	2	Alabama
51	Hancock, Kevin	LB	6-2	225	2	Baylor
78	Hand, Jon	DE	6-7	298	3	Alabama
—	Herrmann, Mark	QB	6-4	207	8	Purdue
75	Hinton, Chris	G	6-4	295	6	Northwestern
7	Hogeboom, Gary	QB	6-4	208	9	Central Michigan
21	Holt, John	CB	5-10	179	8	West Texas State
58	James, June	LB	6-1	236	3	Texas
94	Kellar, Scott	NT	6-3	279	3	Northern Illinois
55	Krauss, Barry	LB	6-3	268	10	Alabama
59	Lowry, Orlando	LB	6-4	236	4	Ohio State
49	McCloskey, Mike	TE	6-5	246	4	Penn State
32	McMillan, Randy	RB	6-0	220	7	Pittsburgh
86	Murray, Walter	WR	6-4	202	3	Hawaii
14	Nugent, Terry	QB	6-4	214	3	Colorado State
93	Odom, Cliff	LB	6-2	245	8	Texas-Arlington
65	Patten, Joel	T	6-7	307	3	Duke
43	Perryman, Jim	CB-S	6-0	187	3	Millikin
39	Prior, Mike	CB-S	6-0	200	3	Illinois State
47	Robinson, Freddie	CB-S	6-1	191	2	Alabama
13	Salisbury, Sean	B	6-5	215	3	Southern California
76	Sally, Jerome	NT	6-3	270	3	Missouri
83	Sherwin, Tim	TE	6-5	252	8	Boston College
66	Solt, Ron	G	6-3	285	5	Maryland
3	Stark, Rohn	P	6-3	204	7	Florida State
26	Swoope, Craig	CB-S	6-1	200	3	Illinois
99	Thompson, Donnell	DE	6-4	275	8	North Carolina
62	Thorp, Don	DT-DE	6-4	260	3	Illinois
10	Trudeau, Jack	B	6-3	213	3	Illinois
42	Tullis, Willie	CB	5-11	195	8	Troy State
64	Utt, Ben	G	6-6	286	7	Georgia Tech
48	Walczak, Mark	TE	6-6	246	2	Arizona
34	Wonsley, George	RB	5-10	219	5	Mississippi State
—	Woodard, Ken	LB	6-4	227	7	Tuskegee Institute
27	Wright, Terry	CB-S	6-0	195	2	Temple

TOP DRAFT CHOICES

Rd.	Name	Sel. No.	Pos.	Ht.	Wt.	College
3	Chandler, Chris	76	QB	6-3	215	Washington
4	Ball, Michael	102	S	6-0	211	Southern
5	Baylor, John	129	CB	6-0	192	Southern Mississippi
9	Herrod, Jeff	243	LB	6-1	241	Mississippi
10	Alston, O'Brien	270	LB	6-6	239	Maryland

selected Washington quarterback Chris Chandler, infuriating holdover Trudeau. "By drafting another young quarterback, it makes me wonder just what my future is here or if I even have one," Trudeau moaned.

OUTLOOK: A running game and solid defense gives the Colts the ingredients to win another division title, but they may have a quarterback problem. Even if the Colts don't repeat, their days of being doormats are over. Meyer will keep them solid and in the hunt.

COLT PROFILES

ERIC DICKERSON 27 6-3 217   Running Back

Second-leading rusher in NFL in 1987 with 1,288 yards for Rams and Colts...Earned fourth Pro Bowl selection as starter... Ironically, was dethroned as rushing champion by Charles White, who succeeded him as Rams' starter...Went from L.A. to Indy in blockbuster trade which found Colts giving up Nos. 1 and 2 draft picks in 1988, No. 2 in 1989, running back Owen Gill as well as turning over rights to their No. 1 pick in 1987, Cornelius Bennett, to Buffalo...Had led NFL in rushing in three of his five seasons...Career totals are now 8,256 yards rushing for 4.7-yard average, 61 rushing touchdowns, 136 receptions for 1,045 yards...Has 44 career 100-yard games, including three 200-yard efforts in regular season. His 248 yards Jan. 1, 1986, against Dallas is single-game rushing record for playoffs...Holder of single-season NFL rushing record of 2,105. Two other season performances (1,821 in 1986 and 1,808 in 1983) rank among NFL's top ten...Originally recruited to SMU by his present head coach, Ron Meyer...Born Sept. 2, 1960, in Sealy, Tex.

DUANE BICKETT 25 6-5 243   Outside Linebacker

Earned starting assignment for AFC in Pro Bowl after one of finest seasons of any linebacker...Led team with 113 tackles and eight sacks. Also broke up three passes, forced two fumbles and recovered two. Credited with pressuring quarterback 10 times in addition to sack total...Has started all 44 games he has played in career since Colts made him No. 1

pick in 1985 . . . Once caught 47 passes as tight end at Glendale (Cal.) High, where he also led basketball team to CIF championship. However, made switch to linebacker at USC . . . Holds degree in business accounting from USC where he attained 3.67 grade-point average . . . Made 16 tackles in victory at New England and preserved 9-7 upset at Cleveland by batting down Bernie Kosar pass late in fourth quarter . . . Born Dec. 1, 1962, in Los Angeles.

BILL BROOKS 24 6-0 191   Wide Receiver

Represents about only reliable deep threat Colts can muster. Fourth-round draft pick from Boston University led Indy with 51 catches for 722 yards and three touchdowns after 65-catch season as a rookie in 1986 . . . Caught six for 146 against Bengals in opener, including 52-yarder from Jack Trudeau for his longest reception of season . . . Also handled Colts' punt-return duties. Returned 22 for 6.2-yard average . . . Now has caught a pass in all 28 regular-season games he has played in NFL . . . Had 228 career receptions for 3,579 yards and 32 touchdowns at Boston U . . . Was highest draft pick from his school since 49ers selected defensive back Bruce Taylor in first round in 1970 . . . Born April 6, 1964, in Boston.

RAY DONALDSON 30 6-3 288   Center

If it weren't for presence of Dwight Stephenson and Mike Webster in same conference, he might be perennial All-Pro choice. Earned starting Pro Bowl slot for AFC after last season . . . His chance for acclaim suffered in Colts' losing years, but now is getting overdue recognition . . . Playing streak of 107 games and 91 starts ended by last year's players' strike . . . "Chris Hinton is our most talented lineman but Ray is our most valuable player," says Ron Meyer . . . Born May 18, 1958, in Rome, Ga.

CHRIS HINTON 27 6-4 295   Offensive Tackle

Was first rookie offensive lineman in NFL history to make Pro Bowl when he was selected at right guard in 1983 . . . He's been back four times since but as left tackle . . . Only time he missed was when he fractured his ankle in 1984 . . . One big reason Colts sliced sacks-allowed total from 53 in 1986 to 24 in 1987 . . . Obtained by Colts in deal that sent draft rights to John Elway to Denver . . . Originally a linebacker and tight end at Northwestern University before he was switched to offensive left tackle as a senior. Bulked up for new position without losing 4.8 speed and quickly caught attention of scouts . . . Holds degree in sociology . . . Was also a wrestler at Phillips High in Chicago . . . Born July 31, 1961, in Chicago.

BARRY KRAUSS 31 6-3 268   Inside Linebacker

One of many NFL players who have had to make courageous and tedious rehabilitation from major knee surgery. Returned from reconstructive surgery and started 11 of 12 games he played in 1987 . . . Suffered injury during Week 4 of 1986 season against Jets and faced extensive rehab . . . Weight dropped from 255 to 215 . . . Colts were hoping to get limited use from him in '87. Instead he ended up as third-leading tackler on team with 104 tackles . . . Recorded 16 tackles against Dolphins in triumphant return to starting lineup Sept. 20 . . . Entering 10th season with Colts but remains inspiration despite eight losing seasons before playoff visit at last in 1987 . . . Remembered for his meet-you-at-the-top-of-the-pile stop on Penn State's Matt Suhey to preserve Alabama's national championship victory in 1979 Sugar Bowl game . . . Should be blessed with Luck o' the Irish. Born March 17, 1957, in Pompano Beach, Fla.

DEAN BIASUCCI 26 6-0 191   Kicker

Hottest kicker in NFL last season when he hit 24 of 27 field goals, including 7 of 9 from 40 and out . . . Only two kickers in NFL history have kicked for a higher percentage than his .889 mark. They were Mark Moseley, 20 for 21 in 1982, and Jan Stenerud of Green Bay, 22 of 24 in 1981 . . . This is his second go-round with Colts. Signed as free agent in Week 2 of 1984 season as kickoff specialist after having been cut by Atlanta. Took over placekicking when Raul Allegre was 3-5 on field-goal tries, with both misses from 50 or longer . . . Colts waived him during camp in 1985 but brought him back in 1986 and he beat out Allegre for job . . . Now is 40 for 57 in career field goals . . . Finished college career at Western Carolina as leading scorer in Southern Conference history with 280 points on 57 of 93 field goals and 109 of 113 extra points . . . Born July 25, 1962, in Niagara Falls, N.Y.

JACK TRUDEAU 25 6-3 213   Quarterback

Leads Colts' quarterback derby because Gary Hogeboom is coming off shoulder surgery, but Trudeau is bothered because Ron Meyer drafted U. of Washington QB Chris Chandler ... "I wish they'd make a commitment to me and obviously they haven't," said Trudeau ... Ex-Illinois standout started eight of 10 games he played in '87, completing 55.9 percent of his passes ... His TD-INT ratio was an even 6-6 ... Those aren't All-Pro numbers, but Trudeau has matured into a solid performer ... He guided the Colts to three victories in final four games to wrap up the division title and completed 21 of 33 passes for 251 yards and two TDs in playoff loss at Cleveland ... Born Sept. 9, 1962, in Forest Lake, Minn.

JOHNIE COOKS 29 6-4 252   Outside Linebacker

Ron Meyer thinks Cooks and Duane Bickett are finest pair of outside linebackers in NFL ... His 1987 season got off to slow and painful start. Missed first two games after suffering torn retina when poked in left eye during pre-season finale at Tampa Bay ... Then came NFL strike. Did start final 10 games and finished with 47 tackles and five sacks ... Was second player selected in 1982 draft ... Lettered four seasons and was leading tackler three of those at Mississippi State ... It took a while before he found his niche in Colts' defense. Started as right outside backer as rookie, then moved inside. Even spent a brief stint at right defensive end in 1984 before finding home at left outside ... Born Nov. 23, 1958, in Leland, Miss.

JON HAND 24 6-7 298   Defensive End

Towering former No. 1 pick blocked a punt and a field goal in 1987 ... Posted steady season and led defensive linemen on team with 67 tackles ... Had two sacks and three quarterback pressures. Colts are looking for more than that from former Alabama star ... Favorite athlete is former Colt Bubba Smith. Once served as stand-in for Bubba in movie "Stroker Ace" ... Majored in criminal justice at Alabama. Colts hope havoc he wreaks as pass-rusher will soon be criminal, too ... Was basketball standout and state shot-put champion in high school ... Born Nov. 13, 1963, in Sycalauga, Ala.

COACH RON MEYER: This former walk-on defensive back at Purdue has proven himself a winner wherever he's coached . . . It didn't take him long to turn Colts around without major influx of new talent . . . Guided Indy to AFC-East title upset in 1987, franchise's first winning season since 1977 team went 10-4 and won AFC East . . . Meyer had 27-8 record in three seasons at Nevada-Las Vegas . . . Took over at SMU in 1976 and his last team there went 10-1 in 1981 . . . Hired by the Patriots in 1982, he became the first coach in NFL history to be fired in the midst of a winning season . . . The Patriots released Meyer at midseason in 1984 when his record was 5-3, and a lot of veterans who didn't like his disciplinary code rejoiced . . . His overall mark with the Pats was 18-15 . . . Was player agent in years between firing by Pats and hiring by Colts near end of '86 season . . . Indy has solid base for future, especially if Gary Hogeboom comes back from shoulder injury . . . "We're proud of last season," Meyer says, "but there is an unquentionable thirst still there that needs to be satisfied." . . . Born Feb. 17, 1941, in Westerville, Ohio.

LONGEST PLAY

Claude (Buddy) Young was an exciting 5-4, 180-pounder who had starred in track and football at the University of Illinois and had broken into pro football with the New York Yankees of the All-America Football Conference.

Now it was Nov. 15, 1953, and he was with the new Baltimore Colts, who had rejoined the NFL. They were playing the Eagles at Philadelphia's Connie Mack Stadium.

Buddy was nearing the end of his career, but on this Sunday he was the waterbug ball-carrier of his younger days for at least one play. He returned a Vic Sears kickoff 104 yards in the 45-14 loss to the Eagles.

He later became the NFL's director of player relations and died tragically five years ago in a Texas auto crash.

INDIVIDUAL COLT RECORDS

Rushing

Most Yards Game:	198	Norm Bulaich, vs N.Y. Jets, 1971
Season:	1,200	Lydell Mitchell, 1976
Career:	5,487	Lydell Mitchell, 1972-77

Passing

Most TD Passes Game:		5	Gary Cuozzo, vs Minnesota, 1965
		5	Gary Hogeboom, vs Buffalo, 1987
	Season:	32	John Unitas, 1959
	Career:	287	John Unitas, 1956-72

Receiving

Most TD Passes Game:		3	Jim Mutscheller, vs Green Bay, 1957
		3	Raymond Berry, vs Dallas, 1960
		3	Raymond Berry, vs Green Bay, 1960
		3	Jimmy Orr, vs Washington, 1962
		3	Jimmy Orr, vs Los Angeles, 1964
		3	Roger Carr, vs Cincinnati, 1976
	Season:	14	Raymond Berry, 1959
	Career:	68	Raymond Berry, 1955-67

Scoring

Most Points Game:		24	Lenny Moore, vs Chicago, 1958
		24	Lenny Moore, vs Los Angeles, 1960
		24	Lenny Moore, vs Minnesota, 1961
		24	Lydell Mitchell, vs Buffalo, 1975
	Season:	120	Lenny Moore, 1964
	Career:	678	Lenny Moore, 1956-67
Most TDs Game:		4	Lenny Moore, vs Chicago, 1958
		4	Lenny Moore, vs Los Angeles, 1960
		4	Lenny Moore, vs Minnesota, 1961
		4	Lydell Mitchell, vs Buffalo, 1975
	Season:	20	Lenny Moore, 1964
	Career:	113	Lenny Moore, 1956-67

KANSAS CITY CHIEFS

TEAM DIRECTORY: Owner: Lamar Hunt; Pres.: Jack Steadman; VP/GM: Jim Schaaf; VP-Administration: Don Steadman; Player Personnel Dir.: Whitey Dovell; Dir. Pub. Rel.: Gary Heise; Head Coach: Frank Gansz. Home field: Arrowhead Stadium (78,094). Colors: Red and gold.

SCOUTING REPORT

OFFENSE: When the Chiefs' defense slumped in midseason and the bounces stopped coming their way, what had been viewed as a challenger for the AFC-West title flopped to a 4-11 season. Kansas City sank on the weight of its own offense.

Dino Hackett made it two in row as Chiefs' top tackler.

Sure, the Chiefs got an impressive rookie season from their tank of a fullback, Christian Okoye, a Pro Bowl season from Carlos Carson and a workmanlike performance from quarterback Bill Kenney, but they were in the bottom half of the league in offensive statistics. The much-touted dream offensive line allowed too many sacks on the immobile Kenney.

Kansas City gave up on former No. 1 pick Todd Blackledge, trading him to Pittsburgh. In comes veteran journeyman Steve DeBerg to contend with Kenney for the QB job. Actually, if the KC defense had played to par in 1987, the offense might have been good enough to produce a winning season. The Chiefs averaged 4.3 yards per running play and Kenney's quarterback rating was a healthy 85.8, fourth in the AFC.

DEFENSE: The touted Chiefs' defense allowed 116 points during a three-game stretch interrupted by the players' strike. Its failings was one reason the KC regulars dropped six straight games and fell from playoff contention early.

Opponents averaged 4.4 per run, hammering the Chiefs for 2,333 yards. They also completed 57.6 percent and bombed KC for 25 touchdowns. Despite standouts such as Pro Bowl nose tackle Bill Maas, linebacker Dino Hackett, Pro Bowl cornerback Albert Lewis, and standout safeties Deron Cherry, another Pro Bowler, and Lloyd Burruss, the defense has holes to fill.

Judging by efforts to trade him in the offseason, the Chiefs were not happy with the play of veteran defensive end Art Still. So No. 1 pick Neil Smith of Nebraska will get a chance to start. Aside from Hackett, the linebacking corps lacks speed and mobility.

KICKING GAME: The AFC's best kicker in the '80s, Nick Lowery had a good season again, hitting 19 of 23. Kelly Goodburn finally made the Chiefs' roster as the punter. He averaged 40.9 and had a 32.4 net average, taking over after Lewis Colbert injured his back. Paul Palmer led the AFC with his 24.3 kickoff-return average. He brought two back for touchdowns. Tiny rookie Michael Clemons averaged 8.5 on punt returns. The Chiefs' famed coverage teams went in the tank, yielding 10.3 on punt returns and 23.0 on kickoffs. Special teams put KC in the playoffs the season before, but weren't good enough in '87.

THE ROOKIES: The Chiefs were so eager to get the 6-4, 262-pound Smith they gave up a second-round pick to the Lions to ensure they'd get him. He's a good pass-rusher and can play the

CHIEFS VETERAN ROSTER

HEAD COACH—Frank Gansz. Assistant Coaches—Ed Beckman, Tom Bettis, Dave Brazil, J.D. Helm, C.T. Hewgley, Don Lawrence, Billie Matthews, Carl Mauck, Rod Rust, George Sefcik, Richard Wood.

No.	Name	Pos.	Ht.	Wt.	NFL Exp.	College
61	Adickes, Mark	G	6-4	270	3	Baylor
76	Alt, John	T	6-7	290	5	Iowa
91	Baldinger, Gary	NT-DE	6-3	265	3	Wake Forest
77	Baldinger, Rich	G-T	6-4	285	7	Wake Forest
58	Baugh, Tom	C	6-3	274	3	Southern Illinois
99	Bell, Mike	DE	6-4	260	8	Colorado State
34	Burruss, Lloyd	S	6-0	209	8	Maryland
88	Carson, Carlos	WR	5-11	188	9	Louisiana State
20	Cherry, Deron	S	5-11	193	8	Rutgers
46	Clemons, Michael	RB-KR	505	166	2	William & Mary
22	Cocroft, Sherman	S-CB	6-1	192	4	San Jose State
54	Cofield, Tim	LB	6-2	245	3	Elizabeth City State
81	Colbert, Darrell	WR	5-10	174	2	Texas Southern
5	Colbert, Lewis	P	5-11	179	2	Auburn
55	Cooper, Louis	LB	6-2	240	4	Western Carolina
—	DeBerg, Steve	QB	6-3	210	12	San Jose State
50	Del Rio, Jack	LB	6-4	238	4	Southern California
51	Donnalley, Rick	C	6-2	260	7	North Carolina
75	Eatman, Irv	T	6-7	293	3	UCLA
40	Fields, Jitter	CB-S-KR	5-9	180	3	Texas
2	Goodburn, Kelly	P	6-2	195	2	Emporia State
98	Griffin, Leonard	DE	6-4	258	3	Grambling
56	Hackett, Dino	LB	6-3	228	3	Appalachian State
57	Harrell, James	LB	6-2	240	9	Florida
86	Harry, Emile	WR	5-11	175	2	Stanford
64	Harvey, James	G	6-3	265	2	Jackson State
—	Hawkins, Andy	LB	6-2	230	7	Texas A&I
85	Hayes, Jonathan	TE	6-5	240	3	Iowa
44	Heard, Herman	RB	5-10	182	5	Southern Colorado
23	Hill, Greg	CB	6-1	197	6	Oklahoma State
93	Holle, Eric	NT	6-5	265	5	Texas
53	Howard, Todd	LB	6-2	235	2	Texas A&M
81	Jones, Rod	TE	6-4	242	2	Washington
73	Jozwiak, Brian	G	6-5	310	3	West Virginia
80	Keel, Mark	TE	6-4	228	2	Arizona
9	Kenney, Bill	QB	6-4	207	10	Northern Colorado
74	Koch, Pete	DE	6-6	265	5	Maryland
29	Lewis, Albert	CB	6-2	192	6	Grambling
8	Lowery, Nick	K	6-4	189	9	Dartmouth
72	Lutz, David	T	6-6	290	6	Georgia Tech
63	Maas, Bill	NT	6-5	268	5	Pittsburgh
89	Marshall, Henry	WR	6-2	216	13	Missouri
32	Moriarty, Larry	RB	6-1	237	6	Notre Dame
35	Okoye, Christian	RB	6-1	253	2	Azusa Pacific
83	Paige, Stephone	WR	6-2	185	6	Fresno State
26	Palmer, Paul	RB-KR	5-9	184	2	Temple
43	Parker, Robert	RB	6-1	190	2	Brigham Young
96	Pearson, Aaron	LB	6-0	240	3	Mississippi State
24	Pearson, J.C.	CB	5-11	183	3	Washington
31	Ross, Kevin	CB	5-9	182	5	Temple
10	Seurer, Frank	QB	6-1	195	3	Kansas
97	Snipes, Angelo	LB	6-0	215	3	West Georgia
67	Still, Art	DE	6-7	255	11	Kentucky
38	Thomas, Carlton	CB	6-0	195	2	Elizabeth City State
62	Tupper, Jeff	NT	6-5	269	3	Oklahoma
98	Walker, John	DE-NT	6-6	270	2	Nebraska-Omaha
70	Woodard, Ray	DE	6-6	290	2	Texas

TOP DRAFT CHOICES

Rd.	Name	Sel. No.	Pos.	Ht.	Wt.	College
1	Smith, Neil	2	DE	6-4	262	Nebraska
3	Porter, Kevin	59	S	5-10	210	Auburn
4	Ambrose, J.R.	96	WR	6-0	188	Mississippi
6	Saxon, James	139	RB	5-11	205	San Jose State
7	Stedman, Troy	170	LB	6-3	235	Washburn

run. Auburn's Kevin Porter, a third-rounder, joins an already strong secondary as a safety.

OUTLOOK: Chiefs won three of last five and one of the losses was in overtime, showing that they shouldn't be overlooked in '88. KC forced 49 turnovers and made the playoffs in 1986. Without the help of cheap scores, though, the Chiefs were far from a playoff team in '87 and may not be in '88 as Frank Gansz embarks on his second year as head coach.

CHIEF PROFILES

STEVE DeBERG 34 6-3 210   Quarterback

Trade in early spring brought NFL journeyman from Tampa Bay to his fifth NFL stop... Originally a 10th-round draft choice of Dallas in 1977, was claimed on waivers by 49ers and spent five weeks on San Francisco's active roster... Next 10 seasons were spent with Niners, Denver and then Bucs... Always made way for a stellar replacement—Joe Montana, John Elway and Vinny Testaverde... In K.C. he gets to battle veteran Bill Kenney. He also gets to throw to talented receivers Carlos Carson and Stephone Paige... Attended Fullerton Junior College before San Jose State... The quarterback nobody seems to want to keep has thrown for 19,582 yards in his career with 116 TD passes and 139 interceptions... Led NFL with 347 completions with 49ers in 1979... Born Jan. 19, 1954, in Oakland, Cal.

DERON CHERRY 28 5-11 193   Free Safety

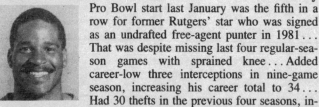

Pro Bowl start last January was the fifth in a row for former Rutgers' star who was signed as an undrafted free-agent punter in 1981... That was despite missing last four regular-season games with sprained knee... Added career-low three interceptions in nine-game season, increasing his career total to 34... Had 30 thefts in the previous four seasons, including AFC-leading nine in 1986... Was strong safety and punter in college. When it became apparent he wouldn't beat out Chiefs' incumbent punter Bob Grupp in 1981, he turned his attention to defense and eventually made team after final cutdown ... Articulate team leader... Biology major at Rutgers...

Donates money to Cystic Fibrosis for every tackle he makes...
Born Sept. 12, 1959, in Riverside, N.J.

CARLOS CARSON 29 5-11 188   Wide Receiver

Led team with 55 receptions for 1,044 yards
(19.0 average) and nine TDs...First Chief
ever to have three 1,000-yard receiving seasons. Had 1,351 in '83 when he had a career-
high 80 receptions and 1,078 in '84...Earned
second Pro Bowl appearance last season...Is
now fourth on Chiefs' career receptions list
with 299 and third in receiving yards (5,554)
...A distinct deep threat. Eighteen of his catches went for 20
yards or more in this era of the junk pass...Caught 89 passes
during his career at LSU. Set an NCAA record in '77 when he
caught six consecutive touchdown passes, including five in one
game...Born Dec. 28, 1958, in Lake Worth, Fla.

DINO HACKETT 24 6-3 228   Inside Linebacker

Chiefs' leading tackler for the second straight
season, collecting 103 to follow 140-tackle
rookie season...This was despite being hampered by neck and shoulder injuries and missing one game...Second-round pick (35th
overall) in 1986 draft out of Appalachian State
in Boone, N.C....Very intense and active
...Teammates voted him Mack Lee Hill
Award as the top rookie in his first season...Full name is Barry
Dean Hackett...Older brother Joey played tight end for Denver
after three years in USFL...Holds degree in criminal justice
from Appalachian...Born June 28, 1964, in Greensboro, N.C.

MIKE BELL 31 6-4 260   Defensive End

Returned to the Chiefs after 1½ year absence
which included a four-month prison term on
drug charges and led team with 6½ sacks,
starting 12 games at right end...Often brilliant during career when injuries and other
problems don't get in the way...Second
player selected in 1979 college draft but
missed five games with knee injury. Played
only two games in 1980 because of torn bicep and injuries cur-
tailed his seasons in '82 and '84...Had team-leading 13½ sacks
in 1984 despite late-season knee injury. It was good enough to
earn him Pro Bowl spot...Played at Colorado State University

along with twin brother Mark, who was tight end in NFL with Seattle and Colts... Born Aug. 30, 1957, in Wichita, Kan.

BILL MAAS 26 6-5 268   Defensive Tackle

Considered the reigning AFC nose tackle after second straight selection to Pro Bowl... Registered six sacks, forced three fumbles, scored first NFL TD by returning a punt six yards for a score vs. Pittsburgh and blocked a field goal at Cincinnati which was returned for a touchdown... Started 11 games, missing one because of ankle injury... A No. 1 pick out of Pitt in 1984 when he was first defensive lineman selected and fifth player overall... Had immediate impact when he joined Chiefs in 1984 as team set franchise record with 50 sacks... Plays with relentless, aggressive style... Born March 2, 1962, in Newtown Square, Pa.

LLOYD BURRUSS 30 6-0 209   Strong Safety

Went without an interception for first time in his six-year career with Chiefs, but still is considered one of AFC's best at his position... Went on injured reserve last week of season with knee sprain after playing in first 11 regular games. Still finished as team's fifth-leading tackle with 45... Was Pro Bowl choice in 1986... Seventeen career interceptions, including five in '86 when he returned three for TDs. Also scored on a blocked punt against Pittsburgh in regular-season finale which helped clinch playoff berth... Had three interceptions (all in one quarter), including record-tying two for touchdowns against San Diego that year... Born Oct. 31, 1957, in Charlottesville, Va.... Third-round pick out of Maryland in 1981.

ALBERT LEWIS 27 6-2 192   Cornerback

Ironically, he finally earned Pro Bowl berth in season when he intercepted just one pass after picking off 20 in first four seasons... That included eight in 1985, when he shared AFC leadership with Eugene Daniel of Colts... A special-teams demon as well. Blocked four punts during 1986 regular season and also tackled punter once for loss... Tall and lanky, he can smother receivers... At career peak, may be best performer now of crack KC secondary which some think is league's best . . . Was All-Southwestern Athletic Conference selection at Grambling before Chiefs drafted him in third round in 1983 . . . Born Oct. 6, 1960, in Mansfield, La.

STEPHONE PAIGE 26 6-2 185   Wide Receiver

Enjoyed the best receiving game in NFL history when he caught eight for 209 yards in season finale in 1985. So what if it was against San Diego? . . . Second on Chiefs with 43 catches for 707 yards and four touchdowns in '87 . . . Now has at least 30 catches, 500 yards and five TDs in all five NFL seasons . . . His 198 career receptions tie him with Fred Arbanas for sixth on all-time KC list . . . Amazingly, he joined Chiefs as undrafted free agent out of Fresno State in 1983 . . . Overshadowed in college by teammate Henry Ellard, drafted in second round by Rams that year . . . Born Oct. 15, 1961, in Slidell, La., but grew up in Long Beach, Cal.

CHRISTIAN OKOYE 27 6-1 253   Fullback

Huge and talented native of Nigeria was top rusher among NFL rookies last season with 660 yards on 157 carries . . . Broke in with 105-yard game against San Diego . . . Also team's third-leading receiver with 24 catches . . . Scored record four touchdowns in 1987 Senior Bowl game . . . Just four years of organized football behind him . . . Came to Azusu-Pacific in 1982 to compete in school's national championship track program and helped lead A-P to four more NAIA titles . . . African record-holder and champion in discus throw and some say he could have been world class if he had concentrated on it . . . Timed in 4.46 for 40 . . . Ran for 6.8-yard average in college as team went 19-3-3 during his career . . . Born Aug. 16, 1961, in Enugu, Nigeria . . . Nickname is "Cho Cho."

COACH FRANK GANSZ: Was the rookie head coach in over

his head last season? Chiefs, who made playoffs with 10-6 record under John Mackovic, finished 4-11 under Gansz's leadership . . . KC turned to its highly-successful special-teams coach after player dissatisfaction over Mackovic surfaced as club was about to reward him with new contract . . . New coach started giving impassioned pep talks in August. Chiefs were super-psyched for exhibitions and flat when it counted . . . It didn't help with revelations in Kansas City media that Gansz's military exploits as a pilot and his playing career at Naval Academy had been exaggerated in press guide biographies and he had done little to set the record straight . . . It was awkward and embarrassing for Gansz and a distraction for team . . . Conducted a thorough evaluation of what went wrong with promising KC team. It was supposed to include a study of his own performance. "We'll look at what I'm doing, how I'm doing," Gansz said. "And I want an objective evaluation, not something from my mother." . . . He can afford to be objective because he has three seasons remaining on four-year contract . . . Born Nov. 22, 1938, in Altoona, Pa.

Carlos Carson broke loose for 1,044 receiving yards.

LONGEST PLAY

They called him "Super Gnat." Noland Smith was only 5-6 and weighed just 164 pounds. He was one of pro football's first return specialists. Chiefs' coach Hank Stram selected Smith in the sixth-round draft pick of the 1967 college draft primarily as a kick-returner. Indeed he led the Chiefs in returns in two of the three seasons he spent with the team.

Smith had only one return for a touchdown during his Kansas City career, but it was a beauty. It went for 106 yards in the regular-season finale at Denver on Dec. 17, 1967, in a 38-24 Chiefs' victory.

INDIVIDUAL CHIEF RECORDS

Rushing

Most Yards Game:	193	Joe Delaney, vs Houston, 1981
Season:	1,121	Joe Delaney, 1981
Career:	4,451	Ed Podolak, 1969-77

Passing

Most TD Passes Game:	6	Len Dawson, vs Denver, 1964
Season:	30	Len Dawson, 1964
Career:	237	Len Dawson, 1962-75

Receiving

Most TD Passes Game:	4	Frank Jackson, vs San Diego, 1964
Season:	12	Chris Burford, 1962
Career:	57	Otis Taylor, 1965-75

Scoring

Most Points Game:	30	Abner Haynes, vs Oakland, 1961
Season:	129	Jan Stenerud, 1968
Career:	1,231	Jan Stenerud, 1967-79
Most TDs Game:	5	Abner Haynes, vs Oakland, 1961
Season:	19	Abner Haynes, 1962
Career:	60	Otis Taylor, 1965-75

LOS ANGELES RAIDERS

TEAM DIRECTORY: Managing Gen. Partner: Al Davis; Exec. Asst.: Al LoCasale; Senior Administrators: Irv Kaze, John Herrera, Mike Ornstein; Bus. Mgr.: Ken LaRue; Special Projects: John Herrera; Publications: Steve Hartman; Head Coach: Mike Shanahan. Home field: Los Angeles Memorial Coliseum (92,487). Colors: Silver and black.

SCOUTING REPORT

OFFENSE: New coach Mike Shanahan will try to blend the multiple look with the deep passing game which has been the Raider trademark. Versatile and speedy Tim Brown, the 1987 Heisman Trophy winner from Notre Dame, fits right into that scheme.

If indeed he left voluntarily, Tom Flores knew when to get out. Shanahan takes over a 5-10 team in the throes of rebuilding its offensive line; a team with a standout wide receiver in James Lofton, who is 32; a team with one quality running back, Marcus Allen, until hobbyist Bo Jackson returns from the American League baseball wars.

The sudden release of Marc Wilson leaves only Rusty Hilger, Vince Evans and Jim Plunkett (yes, he was still there at press time) on the QB roster.

Shanahan's coaching gets a severe test right off the bat, trying to hold together an offense that is in transition. Having Bo full time would change things quickly, however.

DEFENSE: The ability of cornerbacks to cover man-for-man has been a key ingredient in the Raiders' defensive scheme. Now, the team seems in sad shape at the corners unless 34-year-old Mike Haynes can defy the aging process. Nothing wrong with the pass rush that recorded 53 sacks despite an off year from nose tackle Bill Pickel. New blood is badly needed at linebacker. Only one starter, tough guy Matt Millen, who is very limited in ability, is younger than 31.

End Howie Long and safeties Stacy Toran and Vann McElroy are the only bright spots and some think Long is losing some of his zest for the game because of all his outside interests.

KICKING GAME: Stan Talley, who replaced the great Ray Guy, may have been the AFC's most effective punter despite 40.7 gross average. His net was 34.4. Chris Bahr may have had it as kicker. He was only 3-10 between 40 and 49 yards. Return game

Howie Long has made Pro Bowl five times in seven years.

was steady. Vance Mueller averaged 21.8 on kickoff returns and Chris Woods returned punts for a 7.3 mark. Coverage teams performed well.

THE ROOKIES: The Raiders drafted earlier and more often in the first round than they have in years and came up with a mixed bag. Brown, the No. 1 pick, is destined for stardom, but CB Terry McDaniel of Tennessee comes with a surgical shoulder and DE Scott Davis once quit Illinois because of football "burnout." Heavy draft activity was concession to need for major reshuffling.

OUTLOOK: It's never wise to count the Raiders out, but they have a ton of questions, such as: What to do about quarterback? Did Al Davis wait too long to start rebuilding the defensive and offensive lines? How much do Lofton and Todd Christensen have

RAIDER VETERAN ROSTER

HEAD COACH—Mike Shanahan. Assistant Coaches—Willie Brown, Alex Gibbs, Sam Gruniesen, Earl Leggett, Nick Nicolau, Terry Robiskie, Pete Rodriguez, Joe Scannella, Art Shell, Charlie Sumner, Tom Walsh, Jimmy Warren.

No.	Name	Pos.	Ht.	Wt.	NFL Exp.	College
44	Adams, Stefon	S	5-10	185	3	East Carolina
32	Allen, Marcus	RB	6-2	205	7	Southern California
33	Anderson, Eddie	S	6-1	200	3	Fort Valley State
10	Bahr, Chris	K	5-10	170	13	Penn State
56	Barnes, Jeff	LB	6-2	230	12	California
—	Bennett, Barry	DE	6-4	260	11	Concordia
—	Black, Mel	LB	6-2	225	3	Eastern Illinois
82	Branton, Gene	TE	6-5	245	2	Texas Southern
95	Buczkowski, Bob	DE	6-5	270	2	Pittsburgh
—	Carter, Russell	CB	6-2	195	5	Southern Methodist
46	Christensen, Todd	TE	6-3	230	10	Brigham Young
78	Clay, John	T	6-5	295	2	Missouri
45	Davis, James	S	6-0	195	7	Southern
—	Doig, Steve	LB	6-2	240	5	New Hampshire
11	Evans, Vince	QB	6-2	200	9	Southern California
21	Fellows, Ron	CB	6-0	175	8	Missouri
86	Fernandez, Mervyn	WR	6-3	200	2	San Jose State
63	Gesek, John	C-G	6-5	275	2	Cal State-Sacramento
73	Hannah, Charley	G	6-5	265	12	Alabama
27	Hawkins, Frank	RB	5-9	210	7	Nevada-Reno
37	Hayes, Lester	CB	6-0	200	11	Texas A&M
22	Haynes, Mike	CB	6-2	190	13	Arizona State
84	Hester, Jessie	WR	5-11	170	4	Florida State
12	Hilger, Rusty	QB	6-4	205	4	Oklahoma State
76	Holloway, Brian	T	6-7	285	8	Stanford
34	Jackson, Bo	RB	6-1	220	2	Auburn
74	Jordan, Shelby	T	6-7	285	12	Washington, Mo.
87	Junkin, Trey	TE	6-2	230	6	Louisiana Tech
59	Kimmel, Jamie	LB	6-3	235	3	Syracuse
52	King, Linden	LB	6-4	250	11	Colorado State
40	Lee, Zeph	RB	6-3	210	2	Southern California
51	Lewis, Bill	G-C	6-7	275	3	Nebraska
80	Lofton, James	WR	6-3	195	11	Stanford
75	Long, Howie	DE	6-5	265	8	Villanova
60	Marsh, Curt	G	6-5	275	5	Washington
53	Martin, Rod	LB	6-2	225	12	Southern California
65	Marvin, Mickey	G	6-4	270	11	Tennessee
26	McElroy, Vann	S	6-2	195	7	Baylor
54	McKenzie, Reggie	LB	6-1	235	4	Tennessee
20	McLemore, Chris	RB	6-1	230	2	Arizona
55	Millen, Matt	LB	6-2	245	9	Penn State
64	Miraldi, Dean	G	6-6	280	5	Utah
72	Mosebar, Don	C	6-6	275	6	Southern California
42	Mueller, Vance	RB	6-0	210	3	Occidental
81	Parker, Andy	TE	6-5	245	5	Utah
71	Pickel, Bill	DT	6-5	260	6	Rutgers
16	Plunkett, Jim	QB	6-2	225	17	Stanford
77	Riehm, Chris	G	6-6	275	2	Ohio State
57	Robinson, Jerry	LB	6-2	225	10	UCLA
—	Schubert, Eric	K	5-8	185	3	Pittsburgh
43	Seale, Sam	CB	5-9	185	5	Western State (Colo.)
35	Smith, Steve	RB	6-1	235	2	Penn State
39	Strachan, Steve	RB	6-1	220	4	Boston College
—	Sullivan, John	S	6-1	190	2	California
5	Talley, Stan	P	6-5	220	2	Texas Christian
61	Tautolo, John	T	6-4	280	4	UCLA
96	Taylor, Malcolm	DT	6-6	280	5	Tennessee State
30	Toran, Stacey	S	6-2	200	5	Notre Dame
93	Townsend, Greg	DE	6-3	250	6	Texas Christian
48	Washington, Lionel	CB	6-0	185	6	Tulane
67	Wheeler, Dwight	G-C	6-3	280	8	Tennessee State
68	Wilkerson, Bruce	G	6-5	280	2	Tennessee
85	Williams, Dokie	WR	5-11	180	6	UCLA
98	Willis, Mitch	DT	6-8	275	4	Southern Methodist
90	Wise, Mike	DE	6-7	265	2	California-Davis
88	Woods, Chris	WR	5-11	190	2	Auburn
66	Wright, Steve	T	6-6	270	6	Northern Iowa

TOP DRAFT CHOICES

Rd.	Name	Sel. No.	Pos.	Ht.	Wt.	College
1	Tim Brown	6	WR	6-0	195	Notre Dame
1	Terry McDaniel	9	CB	5-10	170	Tennessee
1	Scott Davis	25	DE	6-7	268	Illinois
4	Tim Rother	90	DE	6-7	270	Nebraska
5	Dennis Price	131	CB	6-2	174	UCLA

left? Perhaps the Raiders could sneak into second, but they are more likely to settle to the bottom of the division.

RAIDER PROFILES

MARCUS ALLEN 28 6-2 205   Running Back

Will pull down $1 million in salary this year and still appears in his prime even though his stats are relatively down... After three straight 1,000-yard rushing seasons through 1985, he fell to 759 in '86 and 754 last year when he led Raider rushers and had 51 receptions... Is first back to lead team in receptions since fullback Hewritt Dixon in 1967 ... Has topped team in rushing six straight years and has carried ball more times than any back in Raider history (1,489)... Has scored 70 NFL touchdowns... Won 1981 Heisman Trophy at USC... Showed not only his versatility but his class when he moved to fullback-type role in Raider backfield to make room for Bo Jackson... Born March 26, 1960, in San Diego.

JAMES LOFTON 32 6-3 195   Wide Receiver

Only 41 receptions, his fewest since short 1982 season, but had 21.5 average per catch, best in the AFC, and caught five for touchdowns... Still can be among more dangerous NFL receivers... Was one of only four Raider offensive players to start all 12 non-strike games... Traded by Green Bay April 13, 1987, to Raiders for third-round pick in '87 and a conditional pick in '88 draft after he caught 530 passes for 9,656 yards in career with Packers... Best year was 1981 when he caught 71 for 1,294 yards and eight TDs... Seven times made Pro Bowl... Is now No. 10 receiver in NFL history with 571 receptions and ranks fourth all-time with 10,536 yards... Besides football, competed in track as world class long-jumper at Stanford... Born July 5, 1956, in Fort Ord, Cal.

MARC WILSON 31 6-6 205   Quarterback

Much-maligned by Los Angeles fans but he finished '87 campaign with 84.6 rating, fifth among AFC quarterbacks... Had some impressive late-season performances and may be No. 1 man in 1988... Completed 57.1 percent and had only eight interceptions as he threw for 2,070 yards and 12 touchdowns... It was his first extended NFL season with positive

TD-INT ratio . . . May benefit from change in team passing philosophy under new coach Mike Shanahan . . . Raiders won't be so long-ball macho but will use more deception in formations and take the short and intermediate pass . . . When Raiders lose to Seattle or have an off year it's always painful for him to go back home to Woodinville, Wash., and listen to gloating Seahawk fans . . . That's why late season 37–14 rout of Seahawks in Kingdome was so pleasing to him . . . Passed for 7,637 yards during career at Brigham Young . . . Born Feb. 15, 1957, in Bremerton, Wash.

DON MOSEBAR 26 6-6 275   Center

Only third regular starting center in Raiders' history, following Jim Otto and Dave Dalby . . . Was offensive tackle at Southern Cal . . . One of only four Raider offensive players and only offensive lineman to start all 12 non-strike games last season . . . Besides having good size, is regarded as excellent technique blocker . . . First-round selection in 1983 when he was the 26th player selected . . . Born Sept. 11, 1961, in Yakima, Wash.

JOHN CLAY 24 6-5 295   Offensive Tackle

Bears look of the classic Raider tackle . . . Started as rookie but injuries slowed his development . . . Still, Raiders haven't seen anything to doubt the wisdom of making him their No. 1 draft pick in 1987 . . . Was a consensus All-America at Missouri and a finalist for Outland and Lombardi trophies . . . Majored in commercial recreation . . . Figures to assume right tackle spot held down for so many seasons by Henry Lawrence . . . Born May 1, 1964, in St. Louis.

TODD CHRISTENSEN 32 6-3 230   Tight End

One of only two Raiders to go to Pro Bowl last January (fifth straight visit) even though his 47 catches in 12 games was well off his 95 catches in 16 games the season before . . . Raised his Raider career total to 446 catches, third-highest in club history. Only Fred Biletnikoff (589) and Cliff Branch (501) have more. Not bad for free-agent pickup who failed to make it as running back with Cowboys and Giants . . . His success is one of larger embarrassments for Cowboys and

their sophisticated talent-hunting system... Started four years at
running back for BYU but also caught 152 passes, 15 for touchdowns, and led team in receiving three seasons... Glib and in-
sightful commentator on the football scene and life in
general... Born Aug. 3, 1956, in Bellefonte, Pa.

BO JACKSON 25 6-1 220   Running Back

It took him only one Monday Night game in
Seattle on national television to capture the
imagination of fans across the country...
Destroyed the Seahawks with 221 yards
rushing... If Raiders ever get Bo full time,
they could return to NFL elite very quickly
... Finished season with 554 yards in just
81 carries for 6.8-yard average (two TDs) and
caught 16 passes for 136 yards (two TDs)... Week after Seattle
game, Bills were so nervous about Jackson getting away on
sweeps they mounted little pass rush on Marc Wilson, and he
picked them apart. That's kind of effect Bo can have on every
opponent if he gives up baseball with the Kansas City Royals...
Was 1985 Heisman Trophy winner at Auburn when he rushed for
1,786 yards and 17 touchdowns... Was outstanding as well in
track and baseball... Born Nov. 30, 1962, in Bessemer, Ala.

STACEY TORAN 26 6-2 200   Strong Safety

Was fifth-leading tackler with 65 and intercepted three passes in fourth pro season...
Became starter in 1985 and now has opened in
37 straight games for the Silver and Black...
Very aggressive, with good size and range...
Except for strike, has not missed a league
game since coming to NFL as Raiders' sixth-
round choice out of Notre Dame in 1984...
Returned an interception 76 yards against Jets in 1985... Born
Nov. 10, 1961, in Indianapolis, where he also starred in basketball at Broad Ripple High.

HOWIE LONG 28 6-5 265   Defensive End

Returned to Pro Bowl for fifth time after 1987
season, but it was not one of his best... Had
only four sacks after totalling 54½ in first six
NFL seasons... Still, nobody dare say he's
slipping. Not with the strength, quickness and
intensity he brings to his position... Had 13
sacks in 1983, including five in one game
against Redskins... Making name for himself

off the field with weekly spot on Home Box Office "Inside the NFL" show . . . Was second-round pick out of Villanova in 1981 . . . Born Jan. 6, 1960, in Somerville, Mass. . . . Grew up on mean streets of Charlestown, Mass., near Boston, where he learned to handle himself . . . Was a collegiate boxing champion.

VANN McELROY 28 6-2 195   Free Safety

His 80 tackles were second only to veteran linebacker Jerry Robinson and he also led Raiders in interceptions with four . . . Second year in a row he led team in interceptions . . . Started all 12 regular games in 1987 . . . Was Pro Bowl selection in 1983 and 1984 . . . Has 25 interceptions in 79 NFL regular-season games . . . Once drafted as pitcher by baseball's Montreal Expos . . . All-American defensive back as senior at Baylor in 1981 . . . Was all-star quarterback at Uvalde High in Texas. Born Jan. 13, 1960, in Birmingham, Ala.

COACH MIKE SHANAHAN: After four seasons as the offen-

sive coordinator for the Denver Broncos, he becomes youngest head coach in NFL at 35 . . . His selection ended long-anticipated crowning of successor to Tom Flores by Al Davis, "The Genius." . . . "As I went into his character, as I went into his background as I searched him out through the players at Denver, the coaches at Denver and everywhere he had been, I found no flaws," Davis said . . . A boy wonder in the profession, he began coaching as a junior in college at Eastern Illinois. A reserve quarterback, he was hit so hard in practice one day he had to have a kidney removed, ending his playing days . . . First coaching job was on Barry Switzer's staff at Oklahoma. Also coached under Joe Salem at Minnesota and Northern Arizona, Charley Pell at Florida and Darrell Mudra at Eastern Illinois . . . Born Aug. 22, 1952, in Oak Park, Ill.

LONGEST PLAY

George Halas owned many National Football League records as coach of the Chicago Bears, but one he set as a player endured for 49 years. That was Halas' NFL record for the longest fumble return, 98 yards. It was broken by Jack Tatum of the Oakland Raiders at Green Bay on Sept. 24, 1972.

Tatum returned MacArthur Lane's fumble of a pitchout 104 yards for a touchdown that helped provide the Raiders with a 20-14 victory. It was a controversial play.

"I don't want to make a big thing of it, but the rules seem to back me up," coach Dan Devine of the Packers said after the game as he read aloud a rule that says a muffed lateral cannot be advanced by the defending team. Game officials ruled, however, that Lane had possession of ball long enough that it was a fumble, not a muffed lateral. Fumbles, of course, can be advanced.

On Oct. 25, 1979, Ira Matthews of the Raiders returned a kickoff 104 yards against the Chargers at Oakland-Alameda County Coliseum in a 45-22 Oakland victory.

INDIVIDUAL RAIDER RECORDS

Rushing

Most Yards Game:	221	Bo Jackson, vs Seattle, 1987
Season:	1,759	Marcus Allen, 1985
Career:	6,151	Marcus Allen, 1982-87

Passing

Most TD Passes Game:	6	Tom Flores, vs Houston, 1963
	6	Daryle Lamonica, vs Buffalo, 1969
Season:	34	Daryle Lamonica, 1969
Career:	150	Ken Stabler, 1970-79

Receiving

Most TD Passes Game:	4	Art Powell, vs Houston, 1963
Season:	16	Art Powell, 1963
Career:	76	Fred Biletnikoff, 1965-78

Scoring

Most Points Game:	24	Art Powell, vs Houston, 1963
	24	Marcus Allen, vs San Diego, 1984
Season:	117	George Blanda, 1968
Career:	863	George Blanda, 1967-75
Most TDs Game:	4	Art Powell, vs Houston, 1963
	4	Marcus Allen, vs San Diego, 1984
Season:	18	Marcus Allen, 1984
Career:	77	Fred Biletnikoff, 1965-78

MIAMI DOLPHINS

TEAM DIRECTORY: Pres.: Joseph Robbie; Head Coach: Don Shula; Dir. Pro Scouting: Charley Winner; Dir. Player Personnel: Chuck Connor; Dir. Publicity: Eddie White. Home field: Joe Robbie Stadium (75,000). Colors: Aqua and orange.

SCOUTING REPORT

OFFENSE: If Dan Marino and the Marks Brothers, Mark Duper and Mark Clayton, weren't enough to make AFC East defensive coordinators lose sleep, the Dolphins went out last year and added perhaps the most dangerous back in rookie Troy Stradford. The quick-silver back led the Fish in both rushing and receiving and personally destroyed the Cowboys with 169 yards rushing and 83 more receiving. He rendered Lorenzo Hampton, the bright prospect of the season before, virtually useless by season's end, although coach Don Shula has not given up on Hampton.

Still, the Dolphins (8-7 in '87) are not a complete offensive team. Their fullback play is spotty. Woody Bennett is steady but drab. Ron Davenport is talented but inconsistent. Miami's tight ends, Bruce Hardy and Dan Johnson, had off years.

The offensive line? Center Dwight Stephenson comes off serious knee surgery and may miss the start of the season. Left guard Roy Foster is trying to bounce back from a mediocre season. LT Jon Giesler has had knee problems. Right side occupants, Tom Toth and Ron Lee, are journeymen.

The skill positions are Miami's strength. Marino continues to roll on at a pace that will eclipse most pro football career passing records.

DEFENSE: Despite new faces and improvements, Miami's defense was among the league's worst statistically. The Dolphins registered only 21 sacks and had just 16 pass interceptions. They allowed rushing yards at a 4.4-yard-per-crack pace and opponents completed 59.7 percent.

But lean and mobile John Bosa, their No. 1 draft pick in '87, stepped right in at right end. Another rookie, rangy Rick Graf, apparently has taken over Bob Brudzinski's outside linebacker spot. Inside backers John Offerdahl and Jackie Shipp look solid and Mark Brown will play the other outside spot unless Hugh Green comes back from knee problems.

Miami's secondary is getting shaky, though. The Dolphins really haven't added a top-caliber defensive back in the last five years and may start to feel the pinch there. Veteran safety Glenn

Dan Marino led the AFC in TD passes and completions.

Blackwood is coming off knee surgery. The other safety, Bob Brown, is a hitter and tries to intimidate but can't cover.

KICKING GAME: Both punter Reggie Roby and kicker Fuad Reveiz missed games with injuries. Roby punted only 32 times for a 42.8 average. Opponents brought back his boomers for only a 5.4-yard average return. Reveiz made nine of his 11 field-goal tries with both misses coming within the 40s. Miami averaged only 17.6 on kickoff returns and Scott Schwedes (8.5) had some horrible games handling punts.

THE ROOKIES: Eric Kumerow went to Ohio State as a quarterback candidate and started three years as OLB. Now, the Dolphins are gambling he can play as a standup defensive end in NFL. Shula believes this rangy Kim Bokamper-type will become a standout pass-rusher with added strength. Second pick Jarvis Williams of Florida probably will start because of safety weakness.

DOLPHINS VETERAN ROSTER

HEAD COACH—Don Shula. Assistant Coaches—Tom Olivadotti, Mel Phillips, John Sanduksy, Larry Seiple, Dan Sekanovich, David Shula, Chuck Studley, Carl Taseff, Junior Wade, Mike Westoff.

No.	Name	Pos.	Ht.	Wt.	NFL Exp.	College
86	Banks, Fred	WR	5-10	180	3	Liberty
—	Bennett, Charles	DE	6-5	255	2	Louisiana
34	Bennett, Woody	RB	6-2	244	10	Miami
75	Betters, Doug	DE	6-7	265	11	Nevada-Reno
47	Blackwood, Glenn	S	6-0	190	10	Texas
97	Bosa, John	DE	6-4	263	2	Boston College
43	Brown, Bud	S	6-0	194	5	Southern Mississippi
51	Brown, Mark	LB	6-2	235	6	Purdue
59	Brudzinski, Bob	LB	6-4	233	12	Ohio State
—	Caterbone, Mike	WR-KR	5-11	180	2	Franklin and Marshall
—	Cesario, Sal	T-G	6-4	255	2	Cal Poly-SLO
83	Clayton, Mark	WR	5-9	175	6	Louisville
98	Cline, Jackie	NT	6-4	276	2	Alabama
67	Conlin, Chris	G-C	6-4	290	2	Penn State
30	Davenport, Ron	RB	6-2	230	4	Louisville
65	Dellenbach, Jeff	T-C	6-6	280	4	Wisconsin
74	Dennis, Mark	T	6-6	291	2	Illinois
85	Duper, Mark	WR	5-9	187	7	NW Louisiana
—	Flaherty, Tom	LB	6-3	227	2	Northwestern
61	Foster, Roy	G	6-4	275	7	Southern California
53	Frye, David	LB	6-2	227	6	Purdue
79	Giesler, Jon	T	6-5	265	10	Michigan
66	Gilmore, Jim	G	6-5	275	3	Ohio State
58	Graf, Rick	LB	6-5	239	2	Wisconsin
55	Green, Hugh	LB	6-2	225	8	Pittsburgh
71	Gruber, Bob	T	6-5	280	2	Pittsburgh
—	Halloran, Shawn	QB	6-4	215	2	Boston College
27	Hampton, Lorenzo	RB	6-0	203	4	Florida
84	Hardy, Bruce	TE	6-5	234	11	Arizona State
29	Hobley, Liffort	S	6-0	199	3	Louisiana State
—	Holloway, Steve	TE	6-3	235	2	Tennessee State
—	Hunley, Lamonte	LB	6-1	240	3	Arizona
17	Jaworski, Ron	QB	6-1	195	14	Youngstown State
11	Jensen, Jim	WR-RB	6-4	215	8	Boston University
87	Johnson, Dan	TE	6-3	245	6	Iowa State
—	Jordan, Kenneth	LB	6-2	235	2	Tuskegee
49	Judson, William	CB	6-2	190	7	South Carolina State
—	Kehoe, Scott	T	6-4	282	2	Illinois
—	King, Bruce	RB	6-1	219	4	Purdue
54	Kolic, Larry	LB	6-1	238	2	Ohio State
69	Lambrecht, Mike	NT	6-1	271	2	St. Cloud State
44	Lankford, Paul	CB	6-2	184	7	Penn State
72	Lee, Ronnie	T	6-4	265	10	Baylor
99	Little, George	DE-NT	6-4	270	2	Iowa
13	Marino, Dan	QB	6-4	214	6	Pittsburgh
78	Marrone, Doug	G-C	6-5	269	2	Syracuse
28	McNeal, Don	CB	5-11	192	8	Alabama
—	Middleton, Frank	RB	5-11	205	4	Florida A&M
52	Nicolas, Scott	LB	6-3	226	7	Miami
56	Offerdahl, John	LB	6-2	232	3	Western Michigan
82	Pruitt, James	WR	6-2	199	3	Cal State-Fullerton
7	Reveiz, Fuad	K	5-11	217	4	Tennessee
4	Roby, Reggie	P	6-2	242	6	Iowa
—	Schankweiler, Scott	LB	6-0	225	2	Maryland
81	Schwedes, Scott	WR-KR	6-0	174	2	Syracuse
—	Scott, Chris	DE	6-4	250	4	Purdue
50	Shipp, Jackie	LB	6-2	236	5	Oklahoma
—	Simpson, Travis	C-G	6-2	265	2	Oklahoma
25	Smith, Mike	CB	6-0	175	2	Texas-El Paso
70	Sochia, Brian	NT	6-3	274	6	NW Oklahoma State
57	Stephenson, Dwight	C	6-2	258	9	Alabama
23	Stradford, Troy	RB	5-9	191	2	Boston College
10	Strock, Don	QB	6-5	225	15	Virginia Tech
24	Thompson, Reyna	CB	5-11	194	3	Baylor
76	Toth, Tom	G	6-5	275	3	Western Michigan
95	Turner, T.J.	DE	6-4	275	3	Houston
—	Warren, Vince	WR	6-0	180	2	San Diego State
—	Watters, Scott	LB	6-3	230	2	Wittenberg
—	Wimberly, Derek	DE	6-4	265	2	Purdue

TOP DRAFT CHOICES

Rd.	Name	Sel. No.	Pos.	Ht.	Wt.	College
1	Eric Kumerow	16	DE	6-6	249	Ohio State
2	Jarvis Williams	42	S	5-11	193	Florida
3	Ferrell Edmunds	73	TE	6-5	243	Maryland
4	Greg Johnson	99	G	6-4	339	Oklahoma
5	Rodney Thomas	126	CB	5-10	197	Brigham Young

OUTLOOK: Anybody can win the AFC-East, including the Dolphins, but something has to be done about the defense. It won't get Miami very far in the playoffs in the event Shula can get his team there. With Marino and all that offensive talent, the Dolphins seemed to have fallen into the Air Coryell syndrome. As long as points come cheap, they go cheap, too.

DOLPHIN PROFILES

DAN MARINO 26 6-4 214   Quarterback

The NFL's all-time top-ranked passer with a 94.1 career rating. Stats read: 71 games, 69 starts, 2,494 attempts, 1,512 completions, 19,422 yards, .606 completion percentage, 168 touchdowns, 80 interceptions . . . Voted to Pro Bowl but did not play. Went in the hospital for his annual "oil change," surgery on his knee. Still, has started 60 of the last 63 games played by Dolphins. Exceptions were three 1987 strike games . . . Streak of 30 consecutive games with at least one touchdown pass ended when Dolphins were shut out at Buffalo Nov. 29 . . . Finished 1987 as second-ranked QB in AFC and fourth overall in NFL with 89.2 rating . . . Most productive game came in victory over Redskins when he led late drive for winning TD . . . Pitt grad has thrown TD pass against every other NFL foe except Minnesota and New York Giants, whom he has never faced in regular season . . . Born Sept. 15, 1961, in Pittsburgh.

TROY STRADFORD 23 5-9 191   Running Back

Named NFL's Offensive Rookie of Year by Associated Press. His play was brightest development in otherwise disappointing Miami season . . . Led team in both rushing (619 yards, 4.3 average) and receiving (48, 9.5 average). Also returned 14 kickoffs for 18.4-yard average . . . Fourth-round pick from Boston College in 1987 did not become a starter until Week 12 . . . Had Lorenzo Hampton virtually glued to Dolphin bench by end of season . . . Put on brilliant display in 20-14 victory at Dallas when he ran for 169 yards and caught six passes for 83 more . . . All-time leading rusher at BC with 3,504 yards . . . Born Sept. 11, 1964, in Elizabeth, N.J.

JOHN OFFERDAHL 24 6-2 232   Inside Linebacker

Played only last nine games due to preseason bicep injury but still finished second on team in tackles with 67 . . . A starter in Pro Bowl as a rookie, out of Western Michigan, he was named as backup after 1987 season . . . A late second-round pick in '86, he made major impact, leading team in tackles with 135 . . . Sharp enough to call Miami's defensive signals even as a rookie . . . Started every game in four seasons as a collegian . . . Once had 24 tackles (15 solos) against Central Michigan . . . Majored in biomedicine and spent offseason after his rookie season taking classes at University of Miami to finish up work on undergraduate degree . . . Born Aug. 17, 1964, in Wisconsin Rapids, Wis.

DWIGHT STEPHENSON 30 6-2 258   Center

Considered by many the most gifted center in NFL . . . Against 4-3 defenses is agile enough to get outside and help double-team rushing ends. Against 3-4 is able to cover area inside the tackles and pick off any traffic coming through . . . Now faces uphill battle to resume career after tearing anterior cruciate and lateral collateral ligaments in his left knee when he took a blind-side hit from former Alabama teammate Marty Lyons of Jets last Dec. 7 . . . Selected for sixth straight year to play in Pro Bowl and for the second year in a row forced to miss it because of injury . . . Became full-time starter in 12th game of 1981 season. Then started 80 games in a row before last season's strike . . . Born Nov. 20, 1957, in Murfreesboro, N.C. . . . A second-round choice in 1980 out of Alabama, where Bear Bryant called him "the greatest center I have ever coached."

ROY FOSTER 28 6-4 275   Guard

Follows in tradition of great Miami guards (Larry Little, Bob Kuechenberg and Ed Newman) coached by veteran offensive line coach John Sandusky . . . Replaced Kuechenberg as starter in 1984 . . . Was Pro Bowl choice in 1985 and 1986, but missed out last year . . . Miami's first-round pick in 1982 out of USC . . . Blocked for Heisman Trophy winners Charles White and Marcus Allen in college. Was three-year starter at guard . . . Born May 24, 1960, in Los Angeles, but completed high school in Shawnee Mission, Kan.

JACKIE SHIPP 26 6-2 236   Inside Linebacker

Silenced many of his critics with his best season as a pro, leading Dolphins with 79 tackles ... Up to then had been considered somewhat of a flop after Miami picked him in first round of 1984 ... Didn't win a starting job until 1985, when he was involved in 83 tackles ... Limited experience in pass coverage hindered development ... Four-year letterman at Oklahoma, where he led team in tackles last three seasons and called defensive signals ... Father is head of student corrections and minority relations at Oklahoma State. Mother is state's administrator for vocational schools ... Proud to be an Okie from Muskogee, where he was born March 19, 1962.

JOHN BOSA 24 6-4 263   Defensive End

Showed in his rookie year that he will be a player, but will he rush the passer? ... Led Dolphins' defensive linemen in tackles with 50 but had only three sacks. Started all 12 regular games despite reporting the week of final preseason game ... Three-year starter at Boston College, where he played mostly left tackle. Dolphins projected him as defensive end in their 3-4 and made him first-round pick in 1987 draft ... Was red-shirted as freshman in 1982. Took masters in business administration courses while completing his eligibility in fifth year at BC ... Born Jan. 10, 1964, in Keene, N.H.

MARK DUPER 29 5-9 187   Wide Receiver

Midseason rib injury hampered him. During stretch of six weeks, missed one game entirely and caught only six passes for 99 yards. Not the production Dolphins have come to expect from owner of team record for career 100-yard receiving games (21) ... In three of the other six games last season Duper went over 100, including a career-high nine receptions for 123 at New England and 6-170-3TD performance in victory over Washington ... Of 33 catches in '87, eight went for touchdowns and average per catch was 18.1 ... Surprise second-round draftee in 1982 because he had played only two seasons at Northwestern Louisiana State ... Broke into lineup in '83 in a wild 38-35 overtime loss to Buffalo as he enjoyed the second-best receiving day in Dolphins' history with 202 yards on seven catches (68- and

48-yard TDs)...Now has career totals of 257 receptions for 4,869 yards and 40 TDs, including a pair of 85-yard scoring catches...Born Jan. 25, 1959, in Pineville, La.

MARK CLAYTON 27 5-9 175   Wide Receiver

No longer holds NFL record for touchdowns in season. His mark of 18 set in 1984 was broken by 49ers' Jerry Rice, who had 22... Since 1984 he's had 39 TD catches in four seasons...Second on team with 46 catches in 1987 and scored seven TDs...Caught only six passes as rookie in 1983 but contributed as punt returner, bringing back 41 for 9.6 average, including a 60-yard TD...Caught passes worth 2,004 yards in four seasons at Louisville, where he averaged 20.9 yards a catch...Born April 8, 1961, in Indianapolis.

WILLIAM JUDSON 29 6-2 190   Cornerback

Voted the Dolphins' outstanding defensive back for four straight seasons, but did not have his best year in 1987...Still Miami's most accomplished corner...Has 18 career interceptions...Was eighth-round draft choice in 1981 out of South Carolina State. Was senior co-captain of team that went 10-1 and was NCAA Division 1-AA playoff semifinalist...Graduated magna cum laude in business administration...Once intercepted three passes and threw two touchdown passes in same high school game for Sylvan Hills High in Atlanta...Born March 26, 1959, in Detroit.

COACH DON SHULA: No doubt about his Hall of Fame

credentials...Career regular-season mark is 255-101-6 for 25 seasons. Counting playoffs, it's 272-114-6. He's only 33 behind George Halas' all-time victory total of 325...This fierce competitor won't rest on past laurels, though. Especially after finishing out of playoffs for second straight season... Dolphins can expect turnover in personnel with several veterans who haven't produced lately...Defensive ranking, 26th for second year in row, rankles Shula...Manages to maintain unusual stability among key members of coaching staff...Son David, one of five Shula offspring, is Dolphins' assistant head coach...Has taken six teams to Super Bowl and won twice . . . Played running back at John Carroll and seven years in NFL as defensive back for Browns, Colts and Redskins . . . Born Jan. 4, 1930, in Painesville, Ohio.

LONGEST PLAY

It was Sept. 14, 1969, and the Dolphins were playing the opener of their fourth season and unveiling rookie running back Mercury Morris to go along with Larry Csonka and Jim Kiick.

Morris debuted in grand style, returning a kickoff 105 yards against the Bengals in the University of Cincinnati's Nippert Stadium. But the Dolphins lost, 27-21, and went on to a 3-10-1 season. Owner Joe Robbie was so disappointed he fired George Wilson as head coach and thus began the Don Shula era.

One undefeated season, two Super Bowl championships and five Super Bowl appearances later, Shula is still at the Miami helm.

Morris, meanwhile, has not been so fortunate. He spent time in prison for drug dealing in 1980s, but was released in 1987.

INDIVIDUAL DOLPHIN RECORDS

Rushing

Most Yards Game:	197	Mercury Morris, vs New England, 1973
Season:	1,258	Delvin Williams, 1978
Career:	6,737	Larry Csonka, 1968-74, 1979

Passing

Most TD Passes Game:	6	Bob Griese, vs St. Louis, 1977
	6	Dan Marino, vs N.Y. Jets, 1986
Season:	48	Dan Marino, 1984
Career:	192	Bob Griese, 1967-80

Receiving

Most TD Passes Game:	4	Paul Warfield, vs Detroit, 1973
Season:	18	Mark Clayton, 1984
Career:	74	Nat Moore, 1974-86

Scoring

Most Points Game:	24	Paul Warfield, vs Detroit, 1973
Season:	117	Garo Yepremian, 1971
Career:	830	Garo Yepremian, 1970-78
Most TDs Game:	4	Paul Warfield, vs Detroit, 1973
Season:	18	Mark Clayton, 1984
Career:	75	Nat Moore, 1974-86

NEW ENGLAND PATRIOTS

TEAM DIRECTORY: Pres.: William Sullivan Jr.; VP: Bucko Kilroy; GM: Patrick J. Sullivan; Dir. Pub. Rel. and Sales: Dave Wintergrass; Dir. Publicity: Jim Greenidge; Head Coach: Raymond Berry. Home field: Sullivan Stadium (60,794). Colors: Red, white and blue.

SCOUTING REPORT

OFFENSE: The Pats' offense really got rolling only three times last season and once was a 42-20 romp over the listless, demoralized Jets. With all the talent the Pats supposedly have on their attack unit they shouldn't rely on their defense as much as they do, but they do. It's not terrifically imaginative, but for the most part it works.

Steve Grogan carried most of the quarterbacking burden with Tony Eason out with injuries again. Grogan gets the most out of the offense, but he's 34. The Pats will be minus team-leading

Garin Veris (plus Andre Tippett) make case for the defense.

rusher Tony Collins, waived following drug-related problems. But they have Reggie Dupard, who finished with a flourish in '87. Bob Perryman and Mosi Tatupu also made contributions and Craig James and Robert Weathers are coming back from injuries. Still, New England averaged only a dreadful 3.5 yards per rush. First-round draft pick John Stephens, a fast, rugged 217-pounder out of Northwest Louisiana, could improve that average.

Pats have depth at receiver, but if hamstring problems that plagued 33-year-old Stanley Morgan return, they will be missing an accomplished deep receiver. Irving Fryar and Starring have been brilliant but inconsistent. Cedric Jones is consistent but not brilliant.

The task of rebuilding the offensive line began last year when Danny Villa and Bruce Armstrong took over at tackle. Trevor Matich moved in at center and Sean Farrell was acquired to play left guard.

DEFENSE: Still the strong point of Raymond Berry's team. Bulwarked by perennial Pro Bowler Andre Tippett at linebacker and Garin Veris at defensive end, the Pats are tough to crack. However, there are some holes to fill. Steve Nelson retired and Don Blackmon, the outside backer opposite Tippett, is a question mark because of neck problems.

The Pats do get back Raymond Clayborn at cornerback and Roland James at strong safety. Both missed good portions of '87 with knee injuries. Clayborn, 33, may soon give way to Ernest Gibson. Ronnie Lippett on the other side has developed into a standout corner.

KICKING GAME: Kicker Tony Franklin fizzled (15-26 on field-goal tries) after his brilliant '86 season and was only 9-18 between 30 and 49 yards. Punter Rich Camarillo did not have on of his best years either. The Pats covered punts and kicks well, and Fryar averaged 9.7 on punt returns. Stephen Starring was less than sensational (19.3) on kickoff returns.

THE ROOKIES: The Pats have a deep corps of RBs, yet selected Stephens, who could turn out to be their most complete back. "The value of a big running back that can do everything is just too great to pass up," said Dick Steinberg, New England's player development director. Second pick Vincent Brown of Mississippi Valley State eyes ILB spot vacated by retiring Nelson.

OUTLOOK: New England (8-7 in '87) still has the best personnel and one of the most solid lineups in the AFC East. It should

PATRIOTS VETERAN ROSTER

HEAD COACH—Raymond Berry. Assistant Coaches—Dean Brittenham, Jimmy Carr, Bobby Grier, Ray Hamilton, Rod Humenuik, Harold Jackson, Eddie Khayat, John Polonchek, Dante Scarnecchia, Don Shinnick, Les Steckel.

No.	Name	Pos.	Ht.	Wt.	NFL Exp.	College
78	Armstrong, Bruce	T	6-4	284	2	Louisville
28	Bowman, Jim	S	6-2	210	4	Central Michigan
58	Brock, Pete	C	6-5	275	13	Colorado
3	Camarillo, Rich	P	5-11	185	8	Washington
26	Clayborn, Raymond	CB	6-0	186	12	Texas
40	Davis, Elgin	RB	5-10	192	2	Central Florida
87	Dawson, Lin	TE	6-3	240	7	North Carolina State
21	Dupard, Reggie	RB	5-11	205	3	Southern Methodist
11	Eason, Tony	QB	6-4	212	6	Illinois
66	Fairchild, Paul	G-C	6-4	270	5	Kansas
62	Farrell, Sean	G	6-3	260	7	Penn State
2	Flutie, Doug	QB	5-10	175	3	Boston College
49	Francis, Russ	TE	6-6	242	13	Oregon
1	Franklin, Tony	K	5-8	182	10	Texas A&M
80	Fryar, Irving	WR	6-0	200	5	Nebraska
48	Gadbois, Dennis	WR	6-1	183	2	Boston University
43	Gibson, Ernest	CB	5-10	185	5	Furman
14	Grogan, Steve	QB	6-4	210	14	Kansas State
35	Hansen, Bruce	RB	6-1	225	2	Brigham Young
97	Hodge, Milford	NT	6-3	278	3	Washington State
41	Holmes, Darryl	S	6-2	190	2	Fort Valley State
32	James, Craig	RB	6-0	215	4	Southern Methodist
38	James, Roland	S	6-2	191	9	Tennessee
83	Jones, Cedric	WR	6-1	184	7	Duke
93	Jordan, Tim	LB	6-3	226	2	Wisconsin
17	Linne, Larry	WR	6-1	185	2	Texas-El Paso
42	Lippett, Ronnie	CB	5-11	180	6	Miami
31	Marion, Fred	S	6-2	191	7	Miami
64	Matich, Trevor	C	6-4	270	4	Brigham Young
48	McCabe, Jerry	LB	6-1	225	2	Holy Cross
50	McGrew, Lawrence	LB	6-5	233	8	Southern California
23	McSwain, Rod	CB	6-1	198	5	Clemson
67	Moore, Steve	T	6-5	305	6	Tennessee State
86	Morgan, Stanley	WR	5-11	181	12	Tennessee
75	Morriss, Guy	C-G	6-4	260	16	Texas Christian
34	Perryman, Bob	RB	6-1	233	2	Michigan
70	Plunkett, Art	T	6-8	282	7	Nevada-Las Vegas
22	Profit, Eugene	CB	5-10	175	3	Yale
12	Ramsey, Tom	QB	6-1	189	4	UCLA
52	Rembert, Johnny	LB	6-3	234	6	Clemson
95	Reynolds, Ed	LB	6-5	242	6	Virginia
65	Ruth, Mike	NT	6-1	266	2	Boston College
88	Scott, Willie	TE	6-4	245	8	South Carolina
77	Sims, Kenneth	DE	6-5	271	7	Texas
81	Starring, Stephen	WR	5-10	172	6	McNeese State
30	Tatupu, Mosi	RB	6-0	227	11	Southern Methodist
56	Tippett, Andre	LB	6-3	241	7	Iowa
60	Veris, Garin	DE	6-4	255	4	Stanford
73	Villa, Danny	T	6-5	305	2	Arizona State
24	Weathers, Robert	RB	6-2	225	6	Arizona State
—	Wilburn, Steve	DE	6-4	266	2	Lincoln College
96	Williams, Brent	DE	6-3	278	3	Toledo
82	Williams, Derwin	WR	6-1	185	4	New Mexico
54	Williams, Ed	LB	6-4	244	5	Texas
90	Williams, Toby	NT	6-4	270	6	Nebraska
61	Wooten, Ron	G	6-4	273	7	North Carolina

TOP DRAFT CHOICES

Rd.	Name	Sel. No.	Pos.	Ht.	Wt.	College
1	John Stephens	17	RB	5-11	216	NW Louisiana
2	Vincent Brown	43	LB	6-1	245	Miss. Valley State
3	Tom Rehder	69	T	6-6	270	Notre Dame
4	Tim Goad	87	DT	6-2	270	North Carolina
4	Sammy Martin	97	WR	5-11	175	LSU
4	Teddy Garcia	100	K	5-10	180	NE Louisiana

be a top contender. However, the offense has to break out once in a while. And many of the veterans are reaching the age where you either lose it fast or nagging injuries become more difficult to overcome.

PATRIOT PROFILES

ANDRE TIPPETT 28 6-3 241   **Outside Linebacker**

Re-signed to six-year contract for reported $4.5 million in April after rumors that Niners were readying major contract pitch to him... Player the Pats' defense could least afford to lose... Selected AFC's Linebacker of the Year in vote of running backs and quarterbacks last year after coming back from 1986 knee injury ... Has made four Pro Bowls in last four seasons and was selected as starter last three... Fourth on team in tackles with 83 (53 primary hits)... Registered 12½ sacks, tying him with Bears' Richard Dent for second in NFL... Also credited with four passes broken up, three fumble recoveries... Returned fumble 29 yards for TD against Jets... Also blocked Oilers' field-goal try which was returned 71 yards for a score by Raymond Clayborn... Second-round pick out of Iowa in 1983 ... Holds second-degree black belt in karate... Born Dec. 27, 1959, in Birmingham, Ala.

GARIN VERIS 25 6-4 255   **Defensive End**

Some wondered if he was too light for heavy-duty action in NFL as defensive lineman, but his savvy, quickness and athletic ability have served him well... Had 49 tackles in second season as full-time starter at right end... Second on team with seven sacks after leading with 11 the season before. Also had 10 in 1985, his rookie year... Broke up two passes and forced two fumbles in '87... Second-rounder out of Stanford in '84... Superbly gifted athlete, in addition to football he threw shot 64-8¾ and discus 191-4 in high school, played basketball and was pitcher-third baseman in baseball... Born Feb. 27, 1963, in Chillicothe, Ohio.

STEVE GROGAN 35 6-4 210   Quarterback

Pats were 1-4 in games he didn't play. Left shoulder sprain suffered in third period of overtime loss to Dallas and absence in subsequent losses to Philadelphia and Denver may have cost division title... Came back to lead late-season wins over Jets, Bills and Dolphins ...Suffered through numerous head and shoulder injuries during season... Completed 57.8 percent of his passes... Entering 14th season as a pro. Holds numerous club career records—pass attempts (3,100), completions (1,629), passing yardage (23,740) and passing touchdowns (165)... Shared team MVP award with linebacker Andre Tippett... Not only does he call his own plays, but also makes calls when Tony Eason, Doug Flutie or Tom Ramsey is on field as Pats' QB... Born July 24, 1953, in San Antonio, Tex.

STANLEY MORGAN 33 5-11 181   Wide Receiver

Missed nearly all of team's final four games with hamstring problems, but still caught 40 passes for 16.8 average and was selected to Pro Bowl for third time in career... Was fourth in AFC in receptions when injured... Showing no signs of slowing up... Going into 12th season... One of nine players in NFL who have caught passes for 9,000 yards or more and is third among actives behind Steve Largent and James Lofton... Pats' career leader in receptions (475), reception yards (9,364) and touchdown receptions (60)... Born Feb. 17, 1955, in Easley, S.C.... Spends offseason in Germantown, Tenn., where he and his wife own a dress shop.

IRVING FRYAR 25 6-0 200   Wide Receiver

Problems off the field have clouded his career, but moments of brilliance in four seasons with Pats show what this 1983 first overall draft pick out of Nebraska is capable of... Was third on team in receptions with 31 catches for 467 yards (15.1 average), led the team in touchdown receptions with five... Career totals are 124 receptions in 56 regular-season games with 19 touchdowns. Best season was 1986, when he

caught 43 in 14 games for 17.1 average . . . Led NFL with 14.1-
yard punt-return average and brought two back for touchdowns in
1985 . . . Was receiver at New Jersey's Rancocas Valley Regional
High, same school that produced the Harris brothers, Franco,
Giuseppe and Pete . . . Born Sept. 9, 1962, in Mount Holly, N.J.

RONNIE LIPPETT 27 5-11 180   Cornerback

May have supplanted Raymond Clayborn as
Pats' No. 1 corner in 1987 . . . Started all 12
games on left side and scored touchdowns on
his first two interceptions of season . . . Had
three pickoffs for 103 yards, a 45-yard run-
back against Indianapolis and another for 20 in
season opener against Miami . . . Had career-
high eight interceptions in 1986, second in
AFC and third in NFL . . . "Ronnie Lippett has developed into
one of the best cornerbacks in the league," says Raymond Berry
. . . Only an eighth-round draft pick in 1983 out of the University
of Miami, but moved into lineup immediately . . . Born Dec. 10,
1960, in Melbourne, Fla.

SEAN FARRELL 28 6-3 260   Offensive Guard

Pats gave up three draft choices to Tampa Bay
in 1987 to obtain this former first-round pick
and begin rebuilding offensive line . . .
Seventh-year pro was not able to perform at
his best because of severe shoulder problem. It
was corrected with offseason surgery. "We
haven't had a chance to see the real Sean Farrell yet," said coach Raymond Berry . . . Pats
using him at left guard, where Jonn Hannah once held forth.
With Bucs he played right guard and also some stints at both left
and right tackle . . . Father Donald is general surgeon who played
football at Columbia . . . Penn State went 28-8 in his three seasons
as offensive starter . . . Runnerup to Dave Rimington of Nebraska
for 1981 Outland Trophy . . . Born May 25, 1960, in Southamp-
ton, N.Y.

REGGIE DUPARD 24 5-11 205   Running Back

This 1986 first-round pick's NFL debut was delayed a bit, but when he began to get extensive action last year it proved that the Pats have an embarrassment of riches at running back... Was only able to pick up 39 yards on 15 carries as rookie because he spent all but final six weeks on injured reserve with turf toe... Spent nearly two months of 1987 on IR with hip problem but came on strong at finish, gaining 286 yards on 75 carries the last four weeks of season, including 91-yard output against Jets... Alternated with Jeff Atkins as tailback at SMU but managed to lead Southwest Conference with 1,278 yards rushing in 1985. Played behind Eric Dickerson and Craig James as Mustang frosh in 1982... Born Oct. 30, 1963, in New Orleans, La.

CRAIG JAMES 27 6-0 215   Running Back

Team's rushing leader in 1984, 1985 and 1986, he's coming back from knee surgery... Played only two games in 1987, carrying ball only four times for 19 yards... Ran for 1,227 yards in Pats' Super Bowl season in 1985... New England obtained him with seventh-round draft pick in 1983, making selection despite fact he already had signed contract with Washington Federals in USFL. Ran for 823 yards, caught 40 passes for Generals in 1983... Jumped to Pats in 1985... All-Southwest Conference performer at SMU and second-leading rusher behind Eric Dickerson in Mustang history... Once had 96-yard pass reception against North Texas State... On losing side only 11 times in high school and college career... Younger brother Chris is outfielder for Philadelphia Phillies... Born Jan. 2, 1961, in Jacksonville, Tex.

COACH RAYMOND BERRY: Hall of Fame receiver is considered epitome of a players' coach... Only coach in Pats' history to guide team to successive playoff appearances. Took 1985 team to Super Bowl. Team returned to playoffs next season, but was eliminated in semifinal game by eventual AFC champion Denver... Had been out of football when he was named to replace Ron Meyer after eighth game of 1984

season and directed team to 4-4 record . . . Has 37-23 record, including playoffs, as head coach . . . Starred at Colts' receiver (1955-67) and helped team to two NFL championships. At best in famed 1958 sudden-death title game against New York Giants when he had 12 receptions for 178 yards, both NFL championship-game records . . . Inducted into Hall of Fame in 1973, first year he was eligible . . . Born Feb. 27, 1933, in Corpus Christi, Tex. . . . Son Mark is a receiver at Vanderbilt.

LONGEST PLAY

Dec. 18, 1977. It was the biggest day in more than a decade for the Patriots. If they could defeat the Baltimore Colts, defending AFC-East champions, the Pats would make the conference playoffs as division champions themselves under the complicated NFL tie-breaking formula.

New England seemed on its way to the title after rookie cornerback Raymond Clayborn returned the second-half kickoff 101 yards for a touchdown that gave the Pats a 21-3 lead. But three TD passes by Bert Jones in the second half and a three-yard run by Don McCauley with 3:16 left brought the Colts back for a 30-24 victory.

Clayborn also had a 100-yard kickoff return against the New York Jets in Shea Stadium on Oct. 2, 1977. The Pats lost that game, too, 30-27.

INDIVIDUAL PATRIOT RECORDS

Rushing

Most Yards Game:	212	Tony Collins, N.Y. Jets, 1983
Season:	1,458	Jim Nance, 1966
Career:	5,453	Sam Cunningham, 1973-79, 1981-82

Passing

Most TD Passes Game:	5	Babe Parilli, vs Buffalo, 1964
	5	Babe Parilli, vs Miami, 1967
	5	Steve Grogan, vs N.Y. Jets, 1979
Season:	31	Babe Parilli, 1964
Career:	165	Steve Grogan, 1975-87

Receiving

Most TD Passes Game:	3	Billy Lott, vs Buffalo, 1961
	3	Gino Cappelletti, vs Buffalo, 1964
	3	Jim Whalen, vs Miami, 1967
	3	Harold Jackson, vs N.Y. Jets, 1979
	3	Derrick Ramsey, vs Indianapolis, 1984
	3	Stanley Morgan, vs Seattle, 1986
Season:	12	Stanley Morgan, 1979
Career:	60	Stanley Morgan, 1977-87

Scoring

Most Points Game:	28	Gino Cappelletti, vs Houston, 1965
Season:	155	Gino Cappelletti, 1964
Career:	1,130	Gino Cappelletti, 1960-70
Most TDs Game:	3	Billy Lott, vs Buffalo, 1961
	3	Billy Lott, vs Oakland, 1961
	3	Larry Garron, vs Oakland, 1964
	3	Gino Cappelletti, vs Buffalo, 1964
	3	Larry Garron, vs San Diego, 1966
	3	Jim Whalen, vs Miami, 1967
	3	Sam Cunningham, vs Buffalo, 1974
	3	Mack Herron, vs Buffalo, 1974
	3	Sam Cunningham, vs Buffalo, 1975
	3	Harold Jackson, vs N.Y. Jets, 1979
	3	Tony Collins, vs N.Y. Jets, 1983
	3	Mosi Tatupu, vs L.A. Rams, 1983
	3	Derrick Ramsey, vs Indianapolis, 1984
	3	Stanley Morgan, vs Seattle, 1986
Season:	13	Steve Grogan, 1976
	13	Stanley Morgan, 1979
Career:	61	Stanley Morgan, 1977-87

NEW YORK JETS

TEAM DIRECTORY: Chairman: Leon Hess; Pres.: Jim Kensil; Dir. Player Personnel: Mike Hickey; Dir. Pro Personnel: Jim Royer; Dir. Pub. Rel.: Frank Ramos; Head Coach: Joe Walton. Home field: Giants Stadium (76,891). Colors: Kelly green and white.

SCOUTING REPORT

OFFENSE: Coach Joe Walton calls it a "refurbishing," rather than a rebuilding. Whatever it is, New York (6-9 in the AFC-East cellar in '87) will have a new look in its offensive line in 1988.

The draft could be a major factor. The Jets' first pick, 6-5,

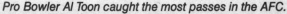

Pro Bowler Al Toon caught the most passes in the AFC.

285-pound Dave Cadigan of USC, is an awesome blocker who figures to start at left tackle, enabling the Jets to move Jim Sweeney to center. Another change will be at left guard, where third-year Mike Haight is expected to take over in place of utility man Ted Banker. The right side is set with Reggie McElroy at tackle and Dan Alexander at guard.

Cadigan will be welcomed by the backs, who averaged only 3.6 yards per carry, and the quarterbacks, who were sacked 50 times.

Otherwise, the Jets don't lack for talent with quarterback Ken O'Brien, running backs Freeman McNeil, Johnny Hector and Roger Vick, wide receivers Al Toon and Wesley Walker and tight end Mickey Shuler. Walker missed seven games with a shoulder injury and is 32 now. When he's out, the Jets have nobody close with his ability to stretch a defense and take the heat off Toon, who caught 68 passes last season.

DEFENSE: The Jets are in trouble here. Gone is tackle Joe Klecko, who refused to accept his medical discharge and now is a Colt. The Jets traded defensive end Barry Bennett to the Raiders. They are running short of defensive linemen. Hoping to fill in the secondary, the team made defensive backs their No. 2, No. 3 and No. 4 draft picks: Bethune-Cookman's Terry Williams, Missouri's Erik McMillan and Washington State's James Hasty.

Where New York is strongest is at linebacker with Alex Gordon, Troy Benson, Bob Crable and Kevin McArthur. Crable was probably New York's best defensive player. Whatever it was Mark Gastineau once had, he seems to have lost. The former All-Pro had only 4½ sacks. Marty Lyons on the other side has slipped badly, too. New York has no replacements ready.

KICKING GAME: With Dave Jennings retired, the Jets' punting job for now goes to Tom O'Connor, who averaged only 33.4 yards for the replacement Jets. Pat Leahy seems to improve with age. Leahy made 18 of his 22 field-goal tries last season and was 16-17 inside 40 yards. JoJo Townsell was a dangerous punt-return threat, averaging 11.9 on 32 runbacks. Bobby Humphery, however, disappointed with his 19.8 kickoff-return mark. The Jets covered kicks and punts better than most teams in the NFL.

THE ROOKIES: Arrival of Cadigan serves team's most pressing need—blocking. "A little bit of a throwback," says Mike Hickey, Jets' player personnel director. "He loves to practice hard, he likes to block for the run and the pass." The Jets are also high on cornerback Williams, who is known to be demonic on

JETS VETERAN ROSTER

HEAD COACH—Joe Walton. Assistant Coaches—Zeke Bratkowski, Ray Callahan, Bud Carson, Wally Chambers, Mike Faulkiner, Bobby Hammond, Rich Kotite, Larry Pasquale, Dan Radakovich, Jim Vechiarella.

No.	Name	Pos.	Ht.	Wt.	NFL Exp.	College
60	Alexander, Dan	G-T	6-4	274	12	Louisiana State
97	Baldwin, Don	DE	6-3	263	2	Purdue
95	Baldwin, Tom	DT	6-4	270	4	Tulsa
63	Banker, Ted	G-C	6-2	275	5	Southeast Missouri
31	Barber, Marion	RB	6-3	228	7	Minnesota
54	Benson, Troy	LB	6-2	235	3	Pittsburgh
64	Bingham, Guy	C-G	6-3	260	9	Montana
23	Bligen, Dennis	RB	5-11	215	4	St. John's
59	Clifton, Kyle	LB	6-4	236	5	Texas Christian
50	Crable, Bob	LB	6-3	230	7	Notre Dame
22	Dykes, Sean	CB	5-10	170	2	Bowling Green
52	Elam, Onzy	LB	6-2	225	2	Tennessee State
30	Faaola, Nuu	RB	5-11	210	3	Hawaii
8	Flick, Tom	QB	6-2	190	5	Washington
98	Foster, Jerome	DE-DT	6-2	275	4	Ohio State
99	Gastineau, Mark	DE	6-5	255	10	East Central Oklahoma
35	Glenn, Kerry	CB	5-9	175	3	Minnesota
55	Gordon, Alex	LB	6-5	245	2	Cincinnati
81	Griggs, Billy	TE	6-3	230	4	Virginia
79	Haight, Mike	G-T	6-4	270	3	Iowa
39	Hamilton, Harry	S	6-0	195	5	Penn State
84	Harper, Michael	WR	5-10	180	3	Southern California
51	Haslett, Jim	LB	6-3	236	9	Indiana, Pa.
34	Hector, Johnny	RB	5-11	200	6	Texas A&M
47	Holmes, Jerry	CB	6-2	175	7	West Virginia
28	Howard, Carl	CB-S	6-2	190	5	Rutgers
48	Humphery, Bobby	CB-KR	5-10	180	5	New Mexico State
89	Klever, Rocky	TE	6-3	230	6	Montana
5	Leahy, Pat	K	6-0	193	15	St. Louis
21	Lewis, Sid	CB	5-11	180	2	Penn State
26	Lyles, Lester	S	6-3	218	4	Virginia
93	Lyons, Marty	DE-DT	6-5	269	10	Alabama
86	Martin, Tracy	WR-KR	6-3	205	2	North Dakota
57	McArthur, Kevin	LB	6-2	245	3	Lamar
68	McElroy, Reggie	T	6-6	275	6	West Texas State
24	McNeil, Freeman	RB	5-11	214	8	UCLA
56	Mehl, Lance	LB	6-3	233	9	Penn State
94	Mersereau, Scott	DE	6-3	278	2	Southern Connecticut
36	Miano, Rich	S	6-0	200	4	Hawaii
58	Monger, Matt	LB	6-1	238	4	Oklahoma State
77	Nichols, Gerald	DT	6-2	261	2	Florida State
7	O'Brien, Ken	QB	6-4	208	6	California-Davis
25	Radachowsky, George	S	5-11	190	4	Boston College
92	Rose, Ken	LB	6-1	215	2	Nevada-Las Vegas
10	Ryan, Pat	QB	6-3	210	11	Tennessee
82	Shuler, Mickey	TE	6-3	231	11	Penn State
87	Sohn, Kurt	WR-KR	5-11	180	7	Fordham
53	Sweeney, Jim	T-G	6-4	260	5	Pittsburgh
88	Toon, Al	WR	6-4	205	4	Wisconsin
83	Townsell, JoJo	WR-KR	5-9	180	4	UCLA
43	Vick, Roger	RB	6-3	230	2	Texas A&M
85	Walker, Wesley	WR	6-0	182	12	California
38	Zordich, Mike	S	5-11	207	2	Penn State

TOP DRAFT CHOICES

Rd.	Name	Sel. No.	Pos.	Ht.	Wt.	College
1	Dave Cadigan	8	T	6-3	276	Southern California
2	Terry Williams	37	CB	5-10	192	Bethune-Cookman
3	Erik McMillan	63	DB	6-2	199	Missouri
3	James Hasty	74	S	5-11	200	Washington State
5	Mike Withycombe	119	T	6-5	308	Fresno State

special teams. He'll get a shot to play right away in an undistinguished secondary.

OUTLOOK: Before the draft, Walton said, "Our new direction is to go for some more young players and to think more about size." He's taken a big step in that direction and hopes it'll make the difference in pass protection, pass rush and in the secondary.

JET PROFILES

KEN O'BRIEN 27 6-4 208   Quarterback

His rating as passer dropped to a respectable 82.8 last season compared to his league-leading 96.4 in 1985 . . . Coach Joe Walton thinks team's fortunes have affected his play. "There is no doubt in my mind that when the offense is working on all cylinders that he can be one of the best," says Walton . . . One of Jets' objectives is to improve pass protection for Obie. He was sacked 50 times last season in 12 games . . . Completed 59.5 percent last year with 13 TDs and just eight interceptions . . . Was college roommate of Houston safety Bo Eason at Cal State-Davis . . . Fifth of six quarterbacks taken in first round of 1983 draft after John Elway, Todd Blackledge, Jim Kelly, Tony Eason, and before Dan Marino . . . Father is orthopedic surgeon . . . Born Nov. 27, 1960, in Long Island, N.Y., but family moved to Sacramento when he was three.

AL TOON 25 6-4 205   Wide Receiver

The AFC's leading receiver and second overall in the league with 68 catches for 976 yards and five TDs last season and earned starting Pro Bowl nod at wide receiver with Seattle's Steve Largent . . . Hasn't gone without a catch in a regular-season game since early in his rookie season . . . When Jets have Wesley Walker in the lineup as deep threat Toon just eats up underneath defenses with his quickness, range and soft hands . . . Had 85 catches in 1986 to set club record . . . First Jet since Joe Namath (1968-69) to be voted team's MVP two seasons in succession . . . Has 199 career catches in just three seasons . . . First-rounder out of Wisconsin in 1985 . . . Born April 30, 1963, in Newport News, Va.

JOHNNY HECTOR 27 5-11 200   Running Back

Tied with Rams' Charles White for NFL lead in rushing touchdowns with 11. "He has developed into an excellent short-yardage and goal-line runner. He can smell the end zone," says Joe Walton...Combined with Freeman McNeil to give Jets 965 yards from halfback position. Hector had 435 and caught 32 passes for 249 yards...In 1986 came through with 117 and 143-yard rushing performances filling in for injured McNeil...Ran for 2,587 yards and 20 TDs at Texas A&M... Set Aggie long-jump record with 26-4 leap and was second to Carl Lewis in long jump during 1982 Southwest Conference meet...Born Nov. 26, 1960, in Lafayette, La.

BOB CRABLE 29 6-3 230   Outside Linebacker

His pro career finally got rolling in 1986 when he completed a comeback from a major knee injury suffered in 1984...Started all 16 games in 1986 at either outside linebacker position or at left inside. Now is fixture on right outside...Last season led Jets with 95 tackles, including 66 solo hits. Had two sacks and was credited with 15 quarterback pressures and seven passes broken up...Biggest play came in season opener at Buffalo, when he deflected a Jim Kelly pass, then made interception to set up what proved to be the winning touchdown in a 31-28 game...Has degree in marketing and runs own embroidery company...First-round draft choice out of Notre Dame in 1982...Born Aug. 22, 1959, in Cincinnati.

FREEMAN McNEIL 29 5-11 214   Running Back

What kind of numbers would the former UCLA star put up if he were healthy for an entire season?...The only time that has happened was in strike-shortened 1982 season... Led Jets in rushing last year for club-record seventh season in a row with 530 yards despite missing three games with hamstring injury and sharing some action with Johnny Hector... Best season was 1985 when he ran for 1,331 yards and also caught 38 passes...Collects old cars and calls 1938 Chevy Coupe his favorite...Ran for 3,195 yards at UCLA...Third pick overall in 1981 draft...Born April 22, 1959, in Jackson, Miss.

HARRY HAMILTON 25 6-0 195   **Right Safety**

Smart, tough safety who is known as hitter in Jets' secondary... Tied for second on team with 83 tackles... Dedicated, hard-working player, a key man in the defense... Played so-called "Hero" position in Penn State defense, meaning a cross between safety and linebacker... One of only seven Jets to start all 12 non-strike games last year... Goes into season with second-longest starting streak (22 games) among Jets' defenders, not including strike games... Tied for team lead with three interceptions in '87... Only a seventh-rounder out of Penn State in 1984... Has begun studies for degree at Cardoza Law School in New York... Father Stan was a writer for "Sesame Street"... Born Nov. 29, 1962, in Jamaica, N.Y.

JIM SWEENEY 26 6-4 260   **Offensive Tackle**

One of group of young offensive linemen Jets feel is just beginning to establish themselves... Made switch from left guard two seasons ago to left tackle. Can and has played center as well... Graded out well in first season after switch to tackle (in 1986) despite shoulder problem which hampered him and has since been alleviated through surgery... Born Aug. 8, 1962, in Pittsburgh and idolized Steeler center great Mike Webster... A second-round pick out of Pittsburgh in 1984... Serves as Big Brother for 23-year-old mentally handicapped cousin.

WESLEY WALKER 33 6-0 182   **Wide Receiver**

Started only three games in '87 because of shoulder injury and ended up with only nine catches for 190 yards and one TD... Averaged 21.1 per catch, which are Walker-type figures... Team sorely missed his deep-threat speed... Has averaged 20 yards or more per catch in seven of his 11 seasons as pro... Had Jets' record 96-yard TD reception against Buffalo in 1985... Legally blind in left eye because of cataract he's had since birth... Was 1977 second-round pick out of California, where he set NCAA record for average gain per pass reception in career (25.7)... Born May 26, 1955, in San Bernardino, Cal.... Father is a Vietnam vet.

ALEX GORDON 23 6-5 245   Outside Linebacker

His size exemplifies the new look Joe Walton is trying to bring to Jets in latest makeover... Expected to be late first-round pick out of the University of Cincinnati in 1987, Jets relieved to find him when they picked in second round ... They plugged him right into linebacker foursome on left side and he started all 12 regular games, finishing sixth on team with 61 tackles, but with a team-high five sacks... Defensive MVP in Blue-Gray game... Had 12 tackles and two sacks against Penn State his senior year... Born Sept. 14, 1964, in Jacksonville, Fla.

ROGER VICK 24 6-3 230   Fullback

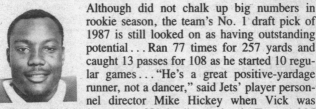

Although did not chalk up big numbers in rookie season, the team's No. 1 draft pick of 1987 is still looked on as having outstanding potential... Ran 77 times for 257 yards and caught 13 passes for 108 as he started 10 regular games... "He's a great positive-yardage runner, not a dancer," said Jets' player personnel director Mike Hickey when Vick was drafted... Finished career as fifth-leading rusher in Texas A&M history with 2,471 yards and 22 TDs... Born Aug. 11, 1964, in Conroe, Tex.... Went to high school in Tomball, Tex.

COACH JOE WALTON: Not afraid to make bold, controversial moves and he's done so again with axing of

some popular Jet veterans. He's left himself open to media criticism and perhaps some from within organization... With career record of 41-38, he has best mark of any Jet coach, but saw team drop to disappointing 6-9 in 1987 after two consecutive playoff years ... Took over for Walt Michaels as head coach in 1983... Had joined the team in 1981 from Washington Redskins, where he was assistant coach from 1974 and served as offensive coordinator from 1978... With Skins earned acclaim for his work with Joe Theismann... As a player (tight end) he spent four seasons with Washington and three more with the Giants after an All-American career at Pittsburgh... He was a second-round draft choice in 1957... Father Frank also played at Pitt and in the first college All-Star Game in 1934. Dad went on to play for the Redskins... Born Dec. 15, 1935, in Beaver Falls, Pa.... Joe's son, Joseph Jr., known as Tiger, is quarterback at East Islip (N.Y.) High School.

LONGEST PLAY

The Jets were known as the Titans then. Their owner was Harry Wismer and their home stadium was the Polo Grounds. It was the fall of 1960.

That first New York team, coached by Sammy Baugh, included a speedy little halfback named Leon Burton, a 172-pounder who played at Arizona State.

The Titans harbored visions of challenging for the first AFL title when Eddie Erdelatz' Oakland Raiders rolled into town.

When Burton returned a kickoff 101 yards, Titans hopes were high. But the Raiders won, 28-27, and the Titans soon fell from serious contention.

The second longest play in Jets' history is also the longest punt in pro football history, 98 yards by rookie Steve O'Neal in a 21-19 loss at Denver, Sept. 21, 1969.

INDIVIDUAL JET RECORDS

Rushing

Most Yards Game:		192	Freeman McNeil, vs Buffalo, 1985
	Season:	1,331	Freeman McNeil, 1985
	Career:	5,850	Freeman McNeil, 1981-87

Passing

Most TD Passes Game:		6	Joe Namath, vs Baltimore, 1972
	Season:	26	Al Dorow, 1960
		26	Joe Namath, 1967
	Career:	170	Joe Namath, 1965-76

Receiving

Most TD Passes Game:		4	Wesley Walker, vs Miami, 1986
	Season:	14	Art Powell, 1960
		14	Don Maynard, 1965
	Career:	88	Don Maynard, 1960-72

Scoring

Most Points Game:		19	Jim Turner, vs Buffalo, 1968
		19	Pat Leahy, vs Cincinnati, 1984
	Season:	145	Jim Turner, 1968
	Career:	1,078	Pat Leahy, 1974-87
Most TDs Game:		4	Wesley Walker, vs Miami, 1986
	Season:	14	Art Powell, 1960
		14	Don Maynard, 1965
		14	Emerson Boozer, 1972
	Career:	88	Don Maynard, 1960-72

PITTSBURGH STEELERS

TEAM DIRECTORY: Chairman: Art Rooney; Pres.: Daniel Rooney; VP: John McGinley; VP: Art Rooney Jr.; Dir. Player Personnel: Dick Haley; Bus. Mgr.: Joe Gordon; Dir. Publicity: Dan Edwards; Head Coach: Chuck Noll. Home field: Three Rivers Stadium (59,000). Colors: Black and gold.

SCOUTING REPORT

OFFENSE: The Steeler philosophy will not change. Pittsburgh still will rely on establishing its running game. However, the passing game has to improve if Chuck Noll's team (8-7 in '87) is to mount any challenge in the AFC Central. The Steelers were last in the AFC in passing and had only 13 touchdown completions. They completed just 50.3 percent of their passes and the interception total was 25.

Most of that was compiled by Mark Malone, who was traded to San Diego. The likely QB in '88 is Todd Blackledge, whom the Steelers will try to retread. The former Penn State star and

LB Bryan Hinkle came up with three interceptions.

No. 1 draft pick in '83 was obtained in a trade from Kansas City, where he was almost as ineffective as Malone.

The Steelers need receivers, too, even if Louis Lipps comes back to his 1985 form. A comeback by Lipps is important because John Stallworth, who led the team with 41 receptions last season, retired. The Steelers also have no tight end to speak of.

There's no explosiveness in the running game either, but Earnest Jackson, Frank Pollard and Walter Abercrombie give Pittsburgh three productive plodders who can pound for yardage behind a trapping line.

DEFENSE: Employing a physical, relentless style, the Steelers made dramatic improvement last season, especially in the secondary, where three draft picks transformed that area from a weakness to a strength. Pittsburgh's defenders scored a league-high seven touchdowns. The Steelers gave up more passing yards than any AFC team, but intercepted 27. Pittsburgh traded yardage for big plays and had 44 takeaways.

The picture would get even better if the sack total of 26 were to increase dramatically. Just 10 of the sacks were by defensive linemen. The Steelers hope No. 1 pick DE Aaron Jones of Eastern Kentucky will be a pass-rushing force. Bryan Hinkle and Mike Merriweather stand out in the linebacker foursome. The Steelers think an improved Gregg Carr can move into the lineup in his fourth season. Rookie secondary stars were Delton Hall, Thomas Everett and Rod Woodson. They join veteran Dwayne Woodruff, who made a comeback from knee surgery.

KICKING GAME: Gary Anderson had a good year, hitting 22 of 27 field-goal attempts and was 10 of 14 from 40 and out, including 50 and 52-yard efforts. Punter Harry Newsome had his best season with a 41.8 gross average, but his net of 31.5 was second-lowest in the AFC. Dwight Stone on kickoffs (20.3) and Woodson on kickoffs (22.3) and punts (8.4) give the Steelers two dangerous return threats. Pittsburgh covered kickoffs well (16.7 yield) but were only so-so in punt coverage (8.6).

THE ROOKIES: The fans at a Pirates' baseball game booed announcement of the Steelers' selection of Jones in the first round when their need was speed at RB and WR. Then, the Steelers went for squat offensive linemen they seem to favor—guard Dermontti Dawson of Kentucky and center Chuck Lanza of Notre Dame. Versatile Gordie Lockbaum of Holy Cross, picked in the ninth round as RB, could find a spot.

STEELERS VETERAN ROSTER

HEAD COACH—Chuck Noll. Assistant Coaches—Ron Blackledge, Tom Dungy, Dennis Fitzgerald, Joe Greene, Dick Hoak, Jed Hughes, Hal Hunter, Jon Kolb, Tom Moore, Dwain Painter.

No.	Name	Pos.	Ht.	Wt.	NFL Exp.	College
34	Abercrombie, Walter	RB	6-0	210	7	Baylor
81	Alston, Lyneal	WR	6-1	205	2	Southern Mississippi
1	Anderson, Gary	K	5-11	170	7	Syracuse
72	Aydelette, Buddy	T-C	6-4	262	3	Alabama
66	Behning, Mark	T	6-6	277	2	Nebraska
—	Blackledge, Todd	QB	6-3	225	6	Penn State
60	Blankenship, Brian	G-C	6-1	281	2	Nebraska
15	Bono, Steve	QB	6-4	215	4	UCLA
65	Boyle, Jim	T	6-5	270	2	Tulane
6	Brister, Bubby	QB	6-3	195	3	Northeast Louisiana
10	Bruno, John	P	6-2	190	2	Penn State
91	Carr, Gregg	LB	6-2	224	4	Auburn
44	Carter, Rodney	RB	6-0	212	2	Purdue
88	Clinkscales, Joey	WR	6-0	204	2	Tennessee
56	Cole, Robin	LB	6-2	225	12	New Mexico
67	Dunn, Gary	NT	6-3	278	12	Miami
24	Erenberg, Rich	RB	5-10	205	4	Colgate
27	Everett, Thomas	S	5-9	179	2	Baylor
68	Freeman, Lorenzo	NT-DT	6-5	270	2	Pittsburgh
92	Gary, Keith	DE	6-3	260	6	Oklahoma
86	Gothard, Preston	TE	6-4	242	4	Alabama
29	Gowdy, Cornell	S-CB	6-1	197	3	Morgan State
22	Griffin, Larry	S-CB	6-0	199	3	North Carolina
35	Hall, Delton	CB	6-1	205	2	Clemson
96	Henton, Anthony	LB	6-1	234	2	Troy State
53	Hinkle, Bryan	LB	6-2	215	7	Oregon
33	Hoge, Merril	RB	6-2	212	2	Idaho State
62	Ilkin, Tunch	T	6-3	265	9	Indiana State
43	Jackson, Earnest	RB	5-9	218	6	Texas A&M
78	Johnson, Tim	DE-DT	6-3	260	2	Penn State
84	Lee, Danzell	TE	6-2	229	2	Lamar
83	Lipps, Louis	WR	5-11	190	5	Southern Mississippi
50	Little, David	LB	6-1	230	8	Florida
89	Lockett, Charles	WR	6-0	179	2	Long Beach State
74	Long, Terry	G	5-11	275	5	East Carolina
—	Lucas, Jeff	T	6-7	288	2	West Virginia
57	Merriweather, Mike	LB	6-2	221	7	Pacific
—	Minter, Michael	DT	6-3	275	2	North Texas State
64	Nelson, Edmund	DE-DT	6-3	266	7	Auburn
18	Newsome, Harry	P	6-0	189	4	Wake Forest
54	Nickerson, Hardy	LB	6-2	224	2	California
30	Pollard, Frank	RB	5-10	230	9	Baylor
76	Quick, Jerry	T-G	6-5	273	2	Wichita State
79	Rienstra, John	G	6-5	269	3	Temple
47	Riley, Cameron	S	6-1	195	2	Missouri
28	Sanchez, Lupe	S-KR	5-10	195	3	UCLA
20	Stone, Dwight	RB-KR	6-0	188	2	Middle Tenn. State
90	Stowe, Tyronne	LB	6-1	232	2	Rutgers
87	Thompson, Weegie	WR	6-6	210	5	Florida State
52	Webster, Mike	C	6-2	254	15	Wisconsin
98	Williams, Gerald	DE-DT	6-3	270	3	Auburn
93	Wills, Keith	DE	6-1	260	7	Northeastern
73	Wolfley, Craig	G	6-1	272	9	Syracuse
49	Woodruff, Dwayne	CB	6-0	198	9	Louisville
26	Woodson, Rod	CB-S-KR	6-0	202	2	Purdue
80	Young, Theo	TE	6-2	237	2	Arkansas

TOP DRAFT CHOICES

Rd.	Name	Sel. No.	Pos.	Ht.	Wt.	College
1	Aaron Jones	18	DE	6-4	255	Eastern Kentucky
2	Dermontti Dawson	44	G	6-2	265	Kentucky
3	Chuck Lanza	70	C	6-2	270	Notre Dame
5	Darin Jordan	121	LB	6-2	240	Northeastern
5	Jerry Reese	128	NT	6-2	270	Kentucky

OUTLOOK: The Steelers' gambling defensive style could backfire, but they don't take many chances on offense. They need more efficient passing to be a playoff threat and Blackledge may not be the answer.

STEELER PROFILES

TODD BLACKLEDGE 27 6-3 225   Quarterback

In Three Rivers quarterback hotseat, following offseason trade which brought him from Kansas City...After quarterbacking 1982 Penn State team to national championship, he was the second of six quarterbacks taken in the 1983 NFL draft (seventh overall). He's had the least success of the half dozen...Threw only 31 times with 15 completions for 154 yards and one TD last season...Career completion percentage is under 50 percent and TD-INT ratio is 26-32, yet those are better numbers than Mark Malone put up for Pittsburgh last season...Steelers feel he can be a factor in their resurgence...Father Ron is Steelers' offensive line coach...Born Feb. 25, 1961, in Canton, Ohio.

MIKE WEBSTER 36 6-2 254   Center

Will set a Steeler record for longevity assuming he goes ahead with plans to play a 15th season this year. Was considering retirement but is coming back for at least one more shot...Established team record for games played. Now has 204 regular-season games, passing Mel Blount's 200...Played in Pro Bowl as first alternate, replacing injured Dwight Stephenson. It was his ninth appearance...A fifth-round choice out of Wisconsin in 1974...Hosts annual charity golf tournament benefitting Spinal Bifida...Born March 18, 1952, in Tomahawk, Wis.

TERRY LONG 29 5-11 275   Guard

Starter at right guard last three seasons after opening seven games at left guard in rookie season...Squat, powerful blocker the Steelers like in their trapping offense...Dedicated weight-lifter. Great quickness and agility despite bulk...One of leaders in offensive line that allowed only 27 sacks in '87 ...East Carolina product chosen in fourth round of 1984 draft ... Touted as nation's strongest college football player after winning super heavyweight division of North Carolina powerlifting championship ... Joined army before going to college ... Made more than 60 parachute jumps with 82nd Airborne Division ... Born July 21, 1959, in Columbia, S.C.

LOUIS LIPPS 26 5-11 190   Wide Receiver

Suffered through second successive disappointing season because of injuries ... Caught only 11 passes for 164 yards and 14.9 average, and no TDs last year. Returned seven punts for 6.6-yard average ... In 1986 he caught 59 for 1,134 and returned 36 punts for 12.1-yard average and two TDs ... With John Stallworth retired, his return to health is vital to Steelers ... First-round draft pick in 1984 out of Southern Mississippi ... Born Aug. 9, 1962, in New Orleans.

EARNEST JACKSON 28 5-9 218   Running Back

Was leading AFC in rushing before taking a helmet in back against Houston and missing some playing time ... With 686 yards rushing on 180 carries, he lost chance to be first player in NFL history to rush for 1,000 for three different teams; he totaled 1,179 for San Diego in 1984, 1,028 for Philadelphia in '85 ... Steelers' rushing leader had four 100-yard games in '87 ... Chargers drafted him in eighth round out of Texas A&M in 1983 ... Signed with Steelers as free agent in 1986 after being purged from Eagles by Buddy Ryan ... Born Dec. 18, 1959, in Needville, Tex. ... Has degree in building construction.

BRYAN HINKLE 29 6-2 215   Outside Linebacker

Fifth on team with 56 tackles in '87 after being selected Steelers' MVP in 1986 when he was leading tackler and big-play linebacker ... A sixth-round draft pick in 1981, but has been starter since 1984 opposite Mike Merriweather. Probably is overshadowed by his counterpart on other side ... Now has 10 career interceptions, including three last season ... Began career as quarterback at Oregon and played some strong safety ... Came on as senior after injuries hampered him early. That's probably why he was only 156th draft pick ... Born June 4, 1959, in Long Beach, Cal.

MIKE MERRIWEATHER 27 6-2 221 Outside Linebacker

Three-time Pro Bowler who was voted MVP by his teammates, making him only fourth linebacker in Steeler history to earn that honor ... Others were Andy Russell, Jack Lambert and Bryan Hinkle ... Was third-leading tackler with 65 (56 solo), sack leader with 5½ and team leader in fumble recoveries with three. Also intercepted two passes, forced three fumbles and broke up 10 passes ... Did not make Pro Bowl, however, ending 17-year streak when there was at least one Steeler LB chosen ... Was third-round draft pick in 1982 out of Pacific ... Born Nov. 26, 1960, in St. Albans, N.Y.

DWAYNE WOODRUFF 31 6-0 198   Cornerback

Made remarkable comeback from serious '86 knee injury and made five interceptions to lead team for third time in his career. It was his fourth campaign with five thefts and now is seventh in team history with 26 for career ... Senior leader of talented group of secondary players in Pittsburgh ... Became full-time starter in 1981 when Ron Johnson was moved from corner to safety ... Was sixth-round draft choice out of Louisville in 1979 ... One of players he beat out was Tony Dungy, now his position coach ... Has been working on law degree at Duquesne in offseason ... Born Feb. 18, 1957, in Bowling Green, Ky.

ROD WOODSON 23 6-0 202   Free Safety

Checked in as late-signee with Steelers and made big impact as nickle back who backed up at corner and safety ... Could end up starting at corner eventually, or who knows? Could play wide receiver or even running back. He's that talented ... Returned interception 45 yards for touchdown. Also returned 16 punts for 8.4-yard average and 13 kickoffs for 22.3 ... All-American at Purdue was 10th pick in '87 draft ... Established 13 Boilermaker records for tackles, interceptions, interception returns, kickoff returns and kickoff-return yardage ... Was outstanding hurdler ... Born March 10, 1965, in Fort Wayne, Ind.

DELTON HALL 23 6-1 205   Cornerback

Drew costly unsportsmanlike penalties and disqualification when he blew his top at calls in key late-season game against Cleveland... Second-round pick from Clemson intercepted three passes and returned a pass and a fumble for a touchdown... Was selected Steeler Rookie of Year by Pittsburgh writers... Started all 12 games, more than any other Steeler rookie. His two defensive scores were most by a defensive rookie in NFL... Ranked seventh on team with 49 tackles, first in passes defensed with 16 and also forced a fumble and recovered two... Born Jan. 16, 1965, in Greensboro, N.C.

COACH CHUCK NOLL: Became the fifth-winningest coach in NFL history with 171st victory on opening day over San Francisco... Overall record through 19 seasons is 178-121-1 (.595) and he's only four-time Super Bowl winner in history... Still tough and feisty as his late-season encounter with Houston's Jerry Glanville over alleged dirty play demonstrated... Came to Steelers in 1969 from Don Shula's Baltimore staff... Manages to stay modern and adapt despite all his years as head coach and success he's had... Born Jan. 5, 1932, in Cleveland... Played guard and linebacker at Dayton and for seven seasons with Browns.

LONGEST PLAY

There have been seasons during Chuck Noll's tenure as head coach the Steelers didn't give up 52 points in a month, let alone one game. However, 1969 was not one of them. Noll's first Steeler team went 1-13 and that included a 52-14 loss to the Vikings in Bloomington, Minn., Nov. 23.

Biggest play for the Steelers that day was a 101-yard kickoff return by Don McCall, a running back from USC who had been acquired from the Saints.

Longest pass play in Steeler history went from one quarterback to another, ironically. It was a 91-yard connection from

Terry Bradshaw to No. 3 quarterback Mark Malone on Nov. 8, 1981, in Seattle. It went for a touchdown, but the Steelers lost, 24-21.

INDIVIDUAL STEELER RECORDS

Rushing

Most Yards Game:	218	John Fuqua, vs Philadelphia, 1970
Season:	1,246	Franco Harris, 1975
Career:	11,950	Franco Harris, 1972-83

Passing

Most TD Passes Game:	5	Terry Bradshaw, vs Atlanta, 1981
	5	Mark Malone, vs Indianapolis, 1985
Season:	28	Terry Bradshaw, 1978
Career:	210	Terry Bradshaw, 1970-82

Receiving

Most TD Passes Game:	4	Roy Jefferson, vs Atlanta, 1968
Season:	12	Buddy Dial, 1961
	12	Louis Lipps, 1985
Career:	63	John Stallworth, 1974-87

Scoring

Most Points Game:	24	Ray Mathews, vs Cleveland, 1954
	24	Roy Jefferson, vs Atlanta, 1968
Season:	139	Gary Anderson, 1985
Career:	731	Roy Gerela, 1971-78
Most TDs Game:	4	Ray Mathews, vs Cleveland, 1954
	4	Roy Jefferson, vs Atlanta, 1968
Season:	14	Franco Harris, 1976
Career:	100	Franco Harris, 1972-83

SAN DIEGO CHARGERS

TEAM DIRECTORY: Owner/Chairman of Board: Alex G. Spanos; Dir. of Administration: Jack Teele; Dir. Football Operations: Steve Ortmayer; Dir. Pub. Rel.: Rick Smith; Head Coach: Al Saunders. Home field: San Diego Jack Murphy Stadium (60,100). Colors: Blue, white and gold.

SCOUTING REPORT

OFFENSE: Once a state-of-the-art offensive machine, the Chargers now are pedestrian. They have no running game to speak of. With the retirement of Dan Fouts, the quarterbacking

Gary Anderson assembled 1,596 all-purpose yards.

becomes a mystery. Most likely the job will be turned over to former Steeler Mark Malone or untested Mark Vlasic.

Al Saunders' team averaged only 3.3 yards a crack running the ball and fell short of the 100-yard mark in eight of its 12 regular games. The high game was only 130 and the longest run from scrimmage just 25 yards despite the presence of swift Gary Anderson in the backfield.

Whoever ends up as the quarterback won't have quite the same caliber receivers Fouts used to throw to. Wes Chandler (now a 49er) caught only 39 balls last season. Little Lionel James caught 41 coming out of the backfield. Leading receiver was tight end Kellen Winslow with 53 catches, but his average per catch was only 9.8. So the Chargers hope to get help from first-round draft pick Anthony Miller, a wide receiver from Tennessee.

San Diego is seeking a counterpart to left tackle Jim Lachey, hoping that another quality offensive lineman will unlock some semblance of a running game.

Malone completed just 46.4 percent and threw 19 interceptions at Pittsburgh last season. He needed a change of scenery badly. Going to San Diego may help, but don't bet on it.

DEFENSE: The Chargers made progress, moving up from 23rd to 15th in the NFL defensive standings between '86 and '87. Still, San Diego has a way to go. The club needs two top cornerbacks, a linebacker and a defensive lineman to build a quality defense. If Leslie O'Neal, the brilliant rookie pass rusher of '86, is able to return from major knee surgery, it would be a big help. He had 12½ sacks in 13 games as a rookie before he was injured.

Defensive standouts are end Lee Williams, outside linebackers Billy Ray Smith and Chip Banks and free safety Vencie Glenn.

KICKING GAME: Vince Abbott was just adequate as the Chargers' kicker, hitting 13 of 22 on field goals. He was only 2 of 6, however, in the 40s and missed all three tries from beyond 50 yards. Punter Ralf Mojsiejenko made the Pro Bowl with a 42.9 net average even though opposing return men averaged in double figures against him. James led the AFC with a 12.5 punt-return average. Rookie Jamie Holland had a 21.6 kickoff average. San Diego coverage teams were nothing to write home about, though.

THE ROOKIES: "We were looking to add speed and explosion to our team," Saunders said after selecting wide receivers Miller and Iowa's Quinn Early in first two rounds. They will free An-

CHARGERS VETERAN ROSTER

HEAD COACH—Al Saunders. Assistant Coaches—Gunther Cunningham, Mike Haluchak, Bobby Jackson, Charlie Joyner, Dave Levy, Ron Lynn, Jerry Rhome, Wayne Sevier, Jerry Wampfler.

No.	Name	Pos.	Ht.	Wt.	NFL Exp.	College
10	Abbott, Vince	K	5-11	206	2	Cal State-Fullerton
42	Adams, Curtis	RB	5-11	194	3	Central Michigan
40	Anderson, Gary	RB	6-0	181	4	Arkansas
96	Baldwin, Keith	DE	6-4	270	6	Texas A&M
56	Banks, Chip	LB	6-4	233	7	Southern California
44	Bayless, Martin	S	6-2	200	5	Bowling Green
57	Benson, Thomas	LB	6-2	235	5	Oklahoma
82	Berstine, Rod	TE	6-3	235	2	Texas A&M
58	Brandon, David	LB	6-4	225	2	Memphis State
—	Brookins, Mitchell	WR	5-11	192	3	Illinois
55	Busick, Steve	LB	6-4	227	8	Southern California
22	Byrd, Gill	CB-S	5-11	196	6	San Jose State
71	Charles, Mike	NT	6-4	287	6	Syracuse
77	Claphan, Sam	G-T	6-6	288	8	Oklahoma
37	Dale, Jeff	S	6-3	213	3	Louisiana State
61	Dallafior, Ken	G	6-4	278	4	Minnesota
36	Davis, Mike	S	6-3	205	10	Colorado
78	Ehin, Chuck	NT	6-4	266	6	Brigham Young
70	FitzPatrick, James	G-T	6-7	286	3	Southern California
25	Glenn, Vencie	S	6-0	187	3	Indiana State
92	Hardison, Dee	DE	6-4	291	11	North Carolina
86	Holland, Jamie	WR	6-1	186	2	Ohio State
88	Holohan Pete	TE	6-4	235	6	Norte Dame
27	Hunter, Daniel	CB	5-11	178	4	Henderson State
52	Jackson, Jeffery	LB	6-1	230	4	Auburn
26	James, Lionel	WR	5-6½	170	5	Auburn
—	Johnson, Demetrious	S	6-0	196	6	Missouri
10	Kelly, Mike	QB	6-3	195	2	Georgia Tech
94	Kirk, Randy	LB	6-2	235	2	San Diego State
68	Kowalski, Gary	G-T	6-6	273	5	Boston College
74	Lachey, Jim	T	6-6	289	4	Ohio State
62	Macek, Don	C	6-2	270	13	Boston College
—	Malone, Mark	QB	6-4	222	9	Arizona State
60	McKnight, Dennis	C-G	6-3	270	7	Drake
69	Miller, Les	DE	6-7	285	2	Fort Hays State
—	Moffett, Tim	WR	6-2	190	4	Mississippi
2	Mojsiejenko, Ralf	P	6-2	212	4	Michigan State
91	O'Neal, Leslie	DE	6-4	255	2	Oklahoma State
34	Patterson, Elvis	CB	5-11	198	5	Kansas
93	Pettitt, Duane	DE	6-4	265	2	San Diego State
75	Phillips, Joe	DE	6-5	275	3	Southern Methodist
50	Plummer, Gary	LB	6-2	240	3	California
53	Price, Stacey	LB	6-2	194	2	Arkansas State
—	Quillan, Fred	C	6-5	266	11	Oregon
20	Redden, Barry	RB	5-10	219	7	Richmond
66	Rosado, Dan	G-T	6-3	280	2	Northern Illinois
79	Rouse, Curtis	G-T	6-3	340	7	Tenn.-Chattanooga
85	Sievers, Eric	TE	6-4	230	8	Maryland
54	Smith, Billy Ray	LB	6-3	236	6	Arkansas
43	Spencer, Tim	RB	6-1	227	4	Ohio State
—	Stadnik, John	C-G	6-4	265	2	Western Illinois
59	Taylor, John	LB	6-4	235	4	Hawaii
76	Thompson, Broderick	G-T	6-4	290	3	Kansas
98	Unrein, Terry	NT-DE	6-5	280	3	Colorado State
13	Vlasic, Mark	QB	6-3	206	2	Iowa
23	Walters, Danny	CB	6-1	200	5	Arkansas
81	Ware, Timmie	WR	5-10	170	3	Southern California
84	Williams, Al	WR	5-10	180	2	Nevada-Reno
99	Williams, Lee	DE	6-5½	263	5	Bethune-Cookman
72	Wilson, Karl	DE	6-4	268	2	Louisiana State
80	Winslow, Kellen	TE	6-5½	251	10	Missouri
33	Zachary, Ken	RB	6-0	222	2	Oklahoma State

TOP DRAFT CHOICES

Rd.	Name	Sel. No.	Pos.	Ht.	Wt.	College
1	Miller, Anthony	15	WR	5-11	187	Tennessee
3	Early, Quinn	60	WR	5-11	185	Iowa
4	Campbell, Joe	91	DE	6-3	236	New Mexico State
4	Searels, Stacy	93	T	6-4	270	Auburn
4	Richards, Dave	98	T	6-4	300	UCLA

derson and James for more RB duty. Watch for later picks, Stacy Searels of Auburn and Dave Richards of UCLA, to challenge for OL jobs.

OUTLOOK: Last year's 8-1 start (8-7 overall) fooled some people. This is not a solid team and now there is a quarterback problem. The defense would look even better if the Chargers could develop some kind of a ball-control game. San Diego doesn't scare many teams with its passing game anymore.

CHARGER PROFILES

MARK MALONE 29 6-4 222   **Quarterback**

An April 12 trade took him away from Three Rivers Stadium boo-birds to Mission Valley, where he tries to replace a San Diego legend, Dan Fouts... Actually, it's a homecoming for former Arizona State star born Nov. 22, 1958, in San Diego suburb of El Cajon... Was last-rated quarterback (46.7) among NFL regulars in 1987. Completed only 46.4 percent for just 1,896 yards, six TDs with 19 interceptions... Had career highs in attempts, completions and yards in 1986 and was off to good start in 1985 before a dislocated toe cut season short... Led Steelers to AFC championship game in 1984... Had 90-yard pass reception from Terry Bradshaw against Seattle in '81 that is longest in team history... Last player taken in first round of 1980.

LIONEL JAMES 26 5-6 170   **Wide Receiver**

"If I were 6-2 I'd be playing basketball," says Lionel, who can dunk a basketball. Instead, he's among NFL's most versatile and exciting performers... Led AFC in punt returns until final game and finished with 12.5 average, including 81-yard TD bolt for touchdown. Caught 41 passes for 593 yards and three TDs. Also rushed 27 times for 102 yards... Has played at running back... Set two NFL records in 1985—2,535 all-purpose yards and his receiving yards (1,027) were an all-time high for a running back... Often blocked for Bo Jackson in senior season at Auburn... Born May 25, 1962, in Albany, Ga. ... Fifth-rounder in '84.

KELLEN WINSLOW 30 6-5 251   Tight End

Crowned courageous comeback from major knee injury by earning first Pro Bowl appearance since the '83 season and fifth of career ... Led Chargers and trailed only Giants' Mark Bavaro (55) among NFL tight ends with 53 receptions ... Voted by teammates as outstanding offensive player in '87 ... Finished ninth season with 541 career catches and ranks fifth among active receivers and 14th all-time ... Born Nov. 5, 1957, in St. Louis, Mo., but grew up across Mississippi River in East St. Louis, Ill ... First-round pick out of Missouri in 1979.

LEE WILLIAMS 25 6-5 263   Defensive End

Racked up team-leading eight sacks after his 15 in 1986 was second-best in AFC and fourth in league. Now has 32 sacks in 3½ full NFL seasons after coming over from USFL Los Angeles Express in middle of 1984 ... An attacking lineman who is getting better against run ... Born Oct. 15, 1962, in Fort Lauderdale, Fla., and went to Stranahan High, same school as former Bronco Rubin Carter ... Four-year starter at Bethune-Cookman.

CHIP BANKS 28 6-4 233   Outside Linebacker

Came over from Cleveland in draft-day trade in 1987 and was second on team in tackles with 71. Also had three sacks, an interception, two recovered fumbles ... Was Pro Bowl selection four of previous five seasons ... During career in Cleveland, started all 73 games he played ... Was third player chosen in 1982 draft and was named NFL Defensive Rookie of the Year by *Pro Football Weekly*, UPI and AP ... All Pac-10 player at USC ... Born William Banks Sept. 18, 1959, in Fort Lawton, Okla.

GARY ANDERSON 27 6-0 181   Running Back

Exciting, versatile performer totaled 1,296 all-purpose yards in 1987 (260 rushing, 503 receiving and 433 on kickoffs)...That followed a Pro Bowl season when he ran for 442, caught 80 passes for 871 more, returned punts for 9.1 average and 227 yards and kickoffs for 20.1 average and 482, giving him 2,022 all-purpose yards...Joined team from USFL in 1985 when given release by Tampa Bay Bandits. Highlight was 98-yard kickoff return for score...Led Arkansas to four bowl appearances under Lou Holtz...Born April 18, 1961, in Columbia, Mo.

BILLY RAY SMITH 27 6-3 236   Outside Linebacker

Classic NFL linebacker voted team's MVP after leading in tackles third year in a row with 88...Also led Chargers with five interceptions and was second alternate to the Pro Bowl...Career took upswing when Chargers moved him to outside position in '86 after three seasons on inside. Had 11 sacks that year, second among NFL linebackers behind Giants' Lawrence Taylor...Was defensive end at Arkansas under Lou Holtz...First of three first-rounders taken by Chargers in 1983...Born Billy Ray Smith Jr. Aug. 10, 1961, in Fayetteville, Ark. Billy Ray Sr. played 14 seasons in NFL with Baltimore.

VENCIE GLENN 23 6-0 187   Free Safety

Set an NFL record with 103-yard interception return for touchdown Nov. 29 against Denver, but Chargers lost...Did set up Vince Abbott's 33-yard game-winning field goal in overtime against Cleveland by intercepting a Bernie Kosar pass, one of four interceptions on season...Also blocked a punt and finished third on team with 66 tackles...Voted team's Outstanding Defensive Player...Patriots selected him out of Indiana State in second round of 1986 draft and was traded to Chargers after four games......Father George coached at Grambling under Eddie Robinson, 1954-70.

RALF MOJSIEJENKO 25 6-2 212   Punter

The AFC's Pro Bowl punter after leading conference with career-high 42.9 gross average and finishing third in league with net average of 33.5 . . . Left-footed punter who also kicks off for Chargers. Also holds on field-goal and extra-point attempts . . . Born Jan. 28, 1963, in Salzgitter Lebenstadt, West Germany, moved to Bridgeman, Mich., when he was nine months old . . . Exceptional kicker and punter at Michigan State, where he set career record with 43.8-yard average on punts . . . Also pitched on baseball team.

COACH AL SAUNDERS: Nobody thought it possible, but he's succeeded in changing the look of the Chargers from the Air Coryell offensive machine to a burgeoning defensive power . . . Team got off to 8-1 start with help of 3-0 record in strike games, then ended with six-game losing streak . . . Replaced Don Coryell Oct. 19, 1986, and was youngest head coach in NFL at the time, 39 . . . Dedicated to building consistent defense as evidenced by acquisition of Chip Banks . . . Was receivers' coach for San Diego 1983-85 and was named assistant head coach prior to '86 season . . . Coached 13 years in colleges, beginning as graduate assistant at USC in 1970 . . . Born Feb. 1, 1947, in London, making him only third foreign-born head coach in NFL history . . . Was defensive back at San Jose State . . . Holds masters in education from Stanford and is working on doctorate from Southern Cal. . . . Was prep All-America swimmer at San Francisco's St. Ignatius High.

LONGEST PLAY

On Denver's first offensive series against the Chargers Nov. 29, 1987, quarterback John Elway confidently moved his team to the Chargers' six-yard line in 12 plays. It was an impressive start for Denver in the game some thought would decide the title in the AFC West. Then Charger safety Vencie Glenn of the Chargers stepped in front of an Elway throw into the end zone and raced untouched 103 yards to put San Diego ahead, 7-0.

But Elway threw three touchdowns in a 31-17 Bronco victory as Denver closed to within a half-game of the first-place Chargers in the division and eventually went on to the title and the Super Bowl.

Former Charger back Keith Lincoln was involved in two of the longest plays in the team's history. His 103-yard kickoff return vs. the New York Titans on Sept. 16, 1962, is a club record, as is the 91-yard pass from Jack Kemp at Denver on Nov. 12, 1961.

INDIVIDUAL CHARGER RECORDS

Rushing

Most Yards Game:	206	Keith Lincoln, vs Boston, 1964
Season:	1,179	Earnest Jackson, 1984
Career:	4,963	Paul Lowe, 1960-67

Passing

Most TD Passes Game:	6	Dan Fouts, vs Oakland, 1981
Season:	33	Dan Fouts, 1981
Career:	254	Dan Fouts, 1973-87

Receiving

Most TD Passes Game:	5	Kellen Winslow, vs Oakland, 1981
Season:	14	Lance Alworth, 1965
Career:	81	Lance Alworth, 1962-70

Scoring

Most Points Game:	30	Kellen Winslow, vs Oakland, 1981
Season:	118	Rolf Benirschke, 1980
Career:	766	Rolf Benirschke, 1977-86
Most TDs Game:	5	Kellen Winslow, vs Oakland, 1981
Season:	19	Chuck Muncie, 1981
Career:	83	Lance Alworth, 1962-70

SEATTLE SEAHAWKS

TEAM DIRECTORY: Pres./GM: Mike McCormack; VP/Asst. GM: Chuck Allen; Dir. Player Personnel: Mike Allman; VP/Dir. Pub. Rel.: Gary Wright; Head Coach: Chuck Knox. Home field: Kingdome (64,757). Colors: Blue, green and silver.

SCOUTING REPORT

OFFENSE: Curt Warner ran for 985 yards, second in the AFC; Steve Largent caught 58 passes and quarterback Dave Krieg chalked up a more-than-respectable 87.6 rating. Still, the Sea-

Off the field and on, Brian Bosworth made his presence felt.

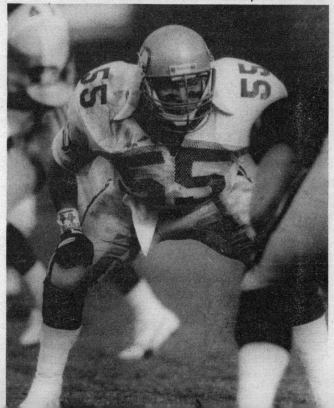

hawks were outgained both on the ground and in the air by their opponents and were only 17th in the NFL in total offense. Seattle did lead the league in third-down efficiency, 48.7, a vital statistic for a team that relies on ball control.

Kelly Stouffer, the Cardinals' No. 1 pick who was a contract holdout in '87, arrives as quarterback of the future.

Except at fullback, where third-year man John L. Williams could turn into even more of a force than he was in '87, it's difficult to see where the Seahawks will improve in 1988. The offensive line is ordinary and the Seahawks are so thin at the skill positions it wouldn't be surprising to see them dip from the ranks of contenders in the AFC West, except there is no up-and-coming team to replace them as the main challengers to Denver.

DEFENSE: Whether it was jealousy over the $11-million contract rookie linebacker Brian Bosworth signed or the NFL players' strike, the Seattle defense didn't play with its usual enthusiasm in '87. The Seahawks allowed 343 yards a game and weren't as opportunistic as usual during a 9-6 campaign.

Despite the brilliant season inside linebacker Fredd Young had and the addition of Bosworth, Seattle opponents averaged 4.7 yards per carry. Young made the Pro Bowl again. "I'd rather skin a bobcat's butt in a phone booth than be tackled by Fredd," says teammate Bryan Millard.

Bosworth should become a force in '88 and young secondary players such as Eugene Robinson and Patrick Hunter should improve. Also, outside linebacker Tony Woods may be ready to move into the lineup. However, nose tackle Joe Nash did not play up to his past standards and the Seahawks no longer have their defensive leader, strong safety Kenny Easley. He was slated to go to the Cardinals in the Stouffer deal, but a kidney ailment appears to have ended his career.

KICKING GAME: Kicker Norm Johnson hit 15 of 20 field-goal tries but was only 4-7 in the 30-39-yard range. Rookie punter Ruben Rodriguez had his shaky moments as he averaged 40.0. Bobby Joe Edmonds was the Pro Bowl return man for the AFC, after averaging 12.6 on punts and 20.9 on kickoffs. The Seahawks did not cover punts and kicks as well as they have in recent years.

THE ROOKIES: Seattle's No. 1 pick last year went for Bosworth and this time the concentration was on offense in the Seahawks' first three selections. Wide receivers Brian Blades of Miami and Tommy Kane of Syracuse and RB Kevin Harmon of

SEAHAWKS VETERAN ROSTER

HEAD COACH—Chuck Knox. Assistant Coaches—Tom Catlin, George Dyer, Chick Harris, Ralph Hawkins, Ken Meyer, Steve Moore, Russ Purnell, Kent Stephenson, Rusty Tillman, Joe Vitt.

No.	Name	Pos.	Ht.	Wt.	NFL Exp.	College
65	Bailey, Edwin	G	6-4	276	8	South Carolina State
62	Barbay, Roland	NT	6-4	260	2	Louisiana State
76	Borchardt, Jon	T	6-5	272	10	Montana State
55	Bosworth, Brian	LB	6-2	248	2	Oklahoma
77	Bryant, Jeff	DE	6-5	272	7	Clemson
97	Burnham, Tim	T	6-5	280	2	Washington
34	Burse, Tony	RB	6-0	220	2	Middle Tenn. State
59	Bush, Blair	C	6-3	272	11	Washington
53	Butler, Keith	LB	6-4	239	11	Memphis State
83	Butler, Ray	WR	6-3	206	9	Southern California
84	Clark, Louis	WR	6-0	206	2	Mississippi State
30	Edmonds, Bobby Joe	RB	5-11	186	3	Arkansas
54	Feasel, Grant	C	6-7	280	4	Abilene Christian
88	Franklin, Byron	WR	6-1	183	7	Auburn
56	Gaines, Greg	LB	6-3	222	7	Tennessee
7	Gilbert, Gale	QB	6-3	206	3	California
79	Green, Jacob	DE	6-3	252	9	Texas A&M
47	Hardy, Andre	RB	6-1	233	3	St. Mary's (Calif.)
78	Heller, Ron	T	6-6	280	5	Penn State
25	Hollis, David	CB	5-11	175	2	Nevada-Las Vegas
29	Holloway, Johnny	CB	5-11	182	3	Kansas
23	Hunter, Patrick	CB	5-11	185	3	Nevada-Reno
24	Jenkins, Melvin	CB	5-10	170	2	Cincinnati
52	Johnson, M.L.	LB	6-3	225	2	Hawaii
9	Johnson, Norm	K	6-2	198	7	UCLA
26	Justin, Kerry	CB	5-11	185	9	Oregon State
15	Kemp, Jeff	QB	6-0	201	8	Dartmouth
17	Krieg, Dave	QB	6-1	196	9	Milton
37	Lane, Eric	RB	6-0	201	8	Brigham Young
80	Largent, Steve	WR	5-11	191	13	Tulsa
13	Mathison, Bruce	QB	6-3	205	5	Nebraska
70	Mattes, Ron	T	6-6	306	3	Virginia
51	Merriman, Sam	LB	6-3	232	6	Idaho
71	Millard, Bryan	G	6-5	284	5	Texas
61	Mitz, Alonzo	DE	6-3	273	3	Florida
35	Moore, Mark	S	6-0	194	2	Oklahoma State
43	Morris, Randall	RB	6-0	200	5	Tennessee
21	Moyer, Paul	S	6-1	201	6	Arizona State
72	Nash, Joe	NT	6-2	257	7	Boston College
73	Powell, Alvin	G	6-5	296	2	Winston-Salem State
41	Robinson, Eugene	S	6-0	186	4	Colgate
5	Rodriguez, Ruben	P	6-2	220	2	Arizona
27	Romes, Charles	CB	6-1	190	12	North Carolina Central
58	Scholtz, Bruce	LB	6-6	242	7	Texas
74	Singer, Curt	T	6-5	279	2	Tennessee
82	Skansi, Paul	WR	5-11	183	6	Washington
87	Strozier, Wilbur	TE	6-4	255	2	Georgia
20	Taylor, Terry	CB	5-10	191	4	Southern Illinois
85	Teal, Jimmy	WR	5-11	175	4	Texas A&M
86	Tice, Mike	TE	6-7	247	8	Maryland
90	Tipton, Rico	LB	6-2	240	2	Washington State
81	Turner, Daryl	WR	6-3	194	5	Michigan State
28	Warner, Curt	RB	5-11	205	5	Penn State
32	Williams, John L.	RB	5-11	226	3	Florida
91	Williams, Lester	NT	6-3	290	6	Miami
75	Wilson, Mike	T	6-5	280	11	Georgia
57	Woods, Tony	LB	6-4	244	2	Pittsburgh
92	Wyman, David	LB	6-2	229	2	Stanford
50	Young, Fredd	LB	6-1	233	5	New Mexico State

TOP DRAFT CHOICES

Rd.	Name	Sel. No.	Pos.	Ht.	Wt.	College
2	Brian Blades	49	WR	5-11	182	Miami
3	Tommy Kane	75	WR	5-11	178	Syracuse
4	Kevin Harmon	101	RB	6-0	200	Iowa
6	Roy Hart	158	NT	6-0	272	South Carolina
7	Ray Jackson	185	DB	5-11	190	Ohio State

Iowa, who could become a third-down receiving specialist, have a chance of making it.

OUTLOOK: As long as Chuck Knox is on the job Seattle (9-6 last year) will put a solid team on the field. The Seahawks seemed to have hit a plateau, however. A team that some considered Super Bowl timber a year ago doesn't look like a legitimate contender now.

SEAHAWK PROFILES

DAVE KRIEG 29 6-1 196   **Quarterback**

Quietly enjoyed good season for Seahawks, setting club records for pass completion percentage (60.5) and percentage of touchdown passes (7.8) along with raising career record for TD passes (130)...Has thrown for more touchdowns in last five seasons (121) than any other NFL quarterback except Dan Marino... Ranked third in AFC in quarterback rating with 87.6 mark, trailing only Cleveland's Bernie Kosar and Miami's Marino. TD passes thrown (23) second only to Marino's...Entered the 1987 season as NFL's fourth-ranked quarterback of all-time based on minimum of 1,500 career attempts...His 84.5 rating ranked behind Dan Marino (95.2), Joe Montana (91.2) and Otto Graham (86.6)...Signed as free agent out of Milton College in 1980...Born Oct. 20, 1958, in Ioia, Wis.

STEVE LARGENT 33 5-11 191   **Wide Receiver**

Made Pro Bowl for seventh time last season and became NFL's all-time leading receiver with 752 catches, passing Charlie Joiner's mark of 750...Caught 58 passes for 912 yards to finish second in AFC in each category and caught eight for TDs...Now has ten 50-catch seasons, breaking his own NFL record and has moved into second in all-time career receiving yards with 12,041, trailing only Joiner (12,146)... With 95 TD catches is closing in on Don Hutson's league mark of 99...Hinting that this season could be his last...Originally drafted out of Tulsa in fourth round of 1976 draft by Houston, was traded to expansion Seahawks... Born Sept. 28, 1954, in Tulsa, Okla.

CURT WARNER 27 5-11 205   Running Back

Seahawks believe they would have gone beyond wild-card round of playoffs if they hadn't lost AFC's second-leading rusher with ankle injury in final regular-season game at Kansas City... He finished with 985 yards and probably would have passed 1,000 for the fourth time in his career... Total of 1,152 yards from scrimmage (including 167 receiving) was third in the conference. Had 10 TDs... Voted to Pro Bowl for third time... Led AFC in rushing in 1983 with 1,481 yards, then missed nearly all of 1984 season with knee injury in opener, but came back to start all 16 games each of next two seasons... Third player selected in 1983 draft, out of Penn State ... Born March, 18, 1961, in Wyoming, W. Va.

JOHN L. WILLIAMS 23 5-11 226   Fullback

Second on team in rushing with 500 yards and receiving with 38 catches for 420 yards in second NFL season... Ran for 538 yards as rookie when he started all 16 games... Fumbled only once during entire rookie season when he handled ball 162 times... Was first-round pick out of Florida in 1986... Broke away for 86-yard TD run against West Texas State as freshman... Ideal fullback for Chuck Knox offense because of lead blocking ability and receiving talents... Born Nov. 23, 1964, in Palatka, Fla.

JACOB GREEN 31 6-3 252   Defensive End

Registered 9½ sacks in 12 games to lead Seahawks as he earned second straight Pro Bowl selection... That increased team record he holds to 86... Also tied team record with 11 fumble recoveries during career... Has hit double figures in sacks in five of his eight seasons since he was drafted in 1980 first round out of Texas A&M... Was AP All-American and was voted Defensive MVP of East-West Shrine game... Born Jan. 21, 1957, in Pasadena, Tex.... Operates landscaping business in Houston in offseason.

FREDD YOUNG 26 6-1 233   Inside Linebacker

Grown from special-teams whiz to Pro Bowl inside linebacker... Made Pro Bowl for two years as special-teams man, but last two years he made it on his merit as linebacker... Gave notice of his special-teams potential in very first pro game when he blocked punt, forced fumble and had four tackles inside 20 on kickoff coverage... Seahawks' leader in tackles the last two seasons... Registered 101 tackles in 1987 and had nine sacks, second on team. Also forced five fumbles and recovered four... Born Nov. 14, 1961, in Dallas... A third-rounder out of New Mexico State in 1984... Great speed... Majored in criminal justice.

BRIAN BOSWORTH 23 6-2 248   Inside Linebacker

Controversy dogged The Boz all of 1987 but he finished as Seahawks' second-leading tackler with 81 and had four sacks... Much was made of him getting bowled over by Bo Jackson in loss to Raiders but Boz, earrings, punk hairdo and all, figures to be standout defender for many seasons... Selected with first pick on first round of the 1987 supplemental draft... In supplemental because he was fourth-year junior who graduated from Oklahoma after regular draft in April... Won Dick Butkus Award as nation's outstanding linebacker in 1985 and 1986... First team Academic All-American and graduated with 3.3 average in business... Born March 9, 1965, in Irving, Tex.

BOBBY JOE EDMUNDS 23 5-11 186   Kick Returner

Led the AFC with 12.6-yard punt-return average in 1987, finishing .01 ahead of San Diego's Lionel James... Also was fifth in kickoff-return average at 20.9... In rookie season, 1986, he led NFL in punt-return average and was selected to AFC Pro Bowl squad as return man. Averaged 22.5 on kickoff returns as well... Second-leading punt returner in Arkansas history... Fifth-round pick... Born Sept. 26, 1964, in Nashville, Tenn.... Drafted by St. Louis baseball Cardinals on 12th round out of high school in St. Louis... Father Bobby Joe Sr. played with Indiana Pacers of American Basketball Association.

EUGENE ROBINSON 25 6-0 186   Safety

Another free-agent find who is paying off... Signed after 1985 draft, he played in all 16 games as extra defensive back... Became starter for entire 1986 season and ranked second on team in tackles... Second on team with three interceptions in '87... Played at Colgate... Graduated with degree in computer science... Spends offseason in Kirkland, Wash., working for computer research and development company... Born May 28, 1963, in Hartford, Conn.

COACH CHUCK KNOX: Never been to the Super Bowl but

that's about only argument against ranking him among greatest coaches in NFL history. Only coach to take three different franchises to playoffs... Has won six divisional titles, five with Los Angeles Rams (1973-77), one with Buffalo Bills (1980)... In five seasons in Seattle his teams have compiled 48-31 record in regular season, good for sixth in league during that time... Finished last season ranked seventh in NFL history with winning percentage of .628 (139-81-1) among coaches with at least 10 seasons... Has gone to playoffs 10 times in 15 seasons as head coach... Known as a players' coach, but don't think that doesn't mean he's tough. A glare from Chuck's steely blues is worth 10 verbal tirades by another coach... Success stems from steely determination, preparation, knowing the percentages and an occasional trick or two... Holds degree in history from Juniata College, where he played tackle... Born April 27, 1932, in Sewickley, Pa.... Son Chuck was running back at Arizona.

LONGEST PLAY

The Seahawks, fresh from key victories over the Raiders and Broncos, had fallen behind the Cardinals, 7-0, at Busch Memorial Stadium on Nov. 13, 1983.

Then journeyman running back Zachary Dixon fielded Neil

O'Donoghue's short kickoff and brought it back 94 yards for a touchdown. No player in the history of the Seahawks had ever returned a kickoff for a touchdown.

The Cardinals, with Neil Lomax throwing four TD passes, wound up winning, 33-28. But the Seahawks went on to the playoffs for the first time and made it to the AFC finals before bowing to the eventual Super Bowl champion Raiders.

INDIVIDUAL SEAHAWK RECORDS

Rushing

Most Yards Game:	207	Curt Warner, vs Kansas City, 1983
Season:	1,481	Curt Warner, 1986
Career:	5,049	Curt Warner, 1983-87

Passing

Most TD Passes Game:	5	Dave Krieg, vs Detroit, 1984
	5	Dave Krieg, vs San Diego, 1985
Season:	32	Dave Krieg, 1984
Career:	130	Dave Krieg, 1980-87

Receiving

Most TD Passes Game:	4	Daryl Turner, vs San Diego, 1985
Season:	13	Daryl Turner, 1985
Career:	95	Steve Largent, 1976-87

Scoring

Most Points Game:	24	Daryl Turner, vs San Diego, 1985
Season:	110	Norm Johnson, 1984
Career:	677	Steve Largent, 1976-87
Most TDs Game:	4	Daryl Turner, vs San Diego, 1985
Season:	15	David Sims, 1978
	15	Sherman Smith, 1979
Career:	96	Steve Largent, 1976-87

Dave Krieg keeps adding to Seahawk records.

INSIDE THE NFC

By MARTY HURNEY

PREDICTED ORDER OF FINISH

EAST	CENTRAL	WEST
N. Y. Giants	Chicago	San Francisco
Washington	Minnesota	New Orleans
Philadelphia	Detroit	Los Angeles
Dallas	Tampa Bay	Atlanta
Phoenix	Green Bay	

NFC Champion: San Francisco

What's new as the NFC enters '88 in quest of its fifth straight NFL championship?

A city (St. Louis) has vanished. A legend (Walter Payton) is gone. And Green Bay has a new coach (Lindy Infante).

Phoenix is the new home of the Cardinals, marking the first franchise shift since the Baltimore Colts stole off to Indianapolis in the middle of the night in 1984.

The 49ers, king of the West in '87 but ousted by Minnesota in the divisional playoffs, come into the new season loaded for a repeat. Blessed with two starting quarterbacks in Joe Montana and Steve Young, a receiver in Jerry Rice who is headed for the Hall of Fame, and a powerful defense, the 49ers have to be favorites for their third straight divisional title.

New Orleans, heady over the finest season in its 21-year history, doesn't figure to unseat the 49ers, but Reuben Mayes,

---

Marty Hurney was covering pro football for the Washington Times *when he took on the NFC assignment for the Handbook. Alas, he's wearing a new uniform for the 1988 season as public relations director of the Super Bowl champion Redskins.*

Bobby Hebert & Co. could be on a roll. Their worst years are behind them.

The Rams could be a factor if quarterback Jim Everett continues to develop under Ernie Zampese and the offensive line isn't too old to keep opening holes for NFL rushing champ Charles White.

Atlanta, with up-and-coming Chris Miller geared for the No. 1 quarterback role and Pro Bowl running back Gerald Riggs, isn't ready to climb out of the cellar.

The NFC East shapes up as a two-team battle between Washington's Super Bowl defender and the Giants, with the 1986 champion getting the edge at least on the strength of schedule. If the Giants can survive through their first five games—Washington, San Francisco, Dallas, Los Angeles Rams and Washington—they could go the distance to the division crown. Of course, this doesn't preclude an encore for Doug Williams and a Redskin team reinforced by the arrival of ex-Bear linebacker Wilber Marshall.

The Eagles should keep improving as quarterback Randy Cunningham keeps maturing, but the Herschel Walker-led Cowboys and the *Phoenix* Cardinals (it'll take a while to get used to) will bring up the rear.

In the NFC Central, Chicago and Minnesota will be head-to-head again, but this time the Bears will have to do it without the retired Payton and with the omnipresent uncertainty of quarterback Jim McMahon. The Vikings still have to decide whether Tommy Kramer or Wade Wilson is the quarterback.

After the Bears and Vikings, the Central falls off quickly. No matter the progress of Chuck Long at quarterback, Detroit needs healthy running backs and help in other sectors before it can become a serious contender.

Tampa Bay's Vinny Testaverde will assert himself in his sophomore season, but he alone can't turn around a Buccaneer team that, like Detroit, was 4-11 last year.

Infante inherits quarterback uncertainties, among other problems, at Green Bay in his rookie season as a head coach. He'll need all of his impressive credentials as a former offensive coordinator of the Cleveland Browns.

Playoffs? Make it Washington and Minnesota as the wild-card teams to go with the Giants, Chicago and San Francisco.

Who'll be in Miami's Joe Robbie Stadium on Super Sunday? Bill Walsh's 49ers.

ATLANTA FALCONS

TEAM DIRECTORY: Chairman: Rankin Smith Sr.; Pres.; Rankin Smith Jr.; VP: Taylor Smith; Dir. Pub. Rel.: Charlie Taylor; Head Coach: Marion Campbell. Home field: Atlanta Stadium (59,643). Colors: Red, black, silver and white.

SCOUTING REPORT

OFFENSE: It took most of last season to sign him, but the Falcons believe they finally have found a quarterback around which to build their future. Chris Miller, the team's top draft pick in 1987, played the final 2½ games and showed the ability to throw deep as well as complete the touch pass.

The Falcons know what they can do with running back Gerald Riggs, the only running back in the league to play in the last three Pro Bowls. He's being counted on again as the leader in the offensive backfield. If the line, led by Bill Fralic and Mike Kenn, can stay healthy, the Falcons should improve on their last-place offensive ranking of last season.

Atlanta finished 28th in rushing and 22nd in passing, which needs better depth at receiver behind Floyd Dixon. Stacey Bailey filled the No. 2 spot last season, but Dixon was the only consistent receiver on the team.

DEFENSE: The team's greatest need is defense and coach Marion Campbell, with the overall first pick in the draft, accordingly went for Auburn linebacker Aundray Bruce. The rookie and Tim Green, 1986 first-rounder, should strengthen a linebacking corps that plays behind a potentially good defensive line.

Green won a starting job one game after the strike, but missed the last six games because of a knee injury.

In all, the Falcons started nine different linebackers because of injuries. It got so bad that they went from a 3-4 set to a 4-3. But if most can stay healthy in '88, the team's rushing defense should upgrade its last-place ranking. Joe Costello and second-year hopefuls Jessie Tuggle and Michael Reid are expected to press for more playing time.

The Falcons' defensive front is capable of helping make the team's linebackers look good. Nose tackle Tony Casillas and ends Rick Bryan and Mike Gann all are of Pro-Bowl caliber. But like most of the team's defensive players, the line was riddled with injuries.

Cornerback Bobby Butler was the only defensive player to start all 12 non-strike games at the same position and led the team

Pro Bowler Gerald Riggs was fourth in NFC rushing.

in interceptions for the fourth straight season. Other than Butler, Atlanta's backs had less than four seasons' experience and were at a disadvantage because of a limited pass rush. Free safety Brett Clark fractured his leg on the fifth play of the season opener and the team went through three starters at free safety before discovering rookie Tim Gordon.

KICKING GAME: The Falcons had the NFL's leading kick-returner in Sylvester Stamps and the leading punter in Rick Donnelly. But they'll be hurt by the loss of veteran placekicker Mick Luckhorst, who retired. He had a career field-goal percentage of 70.1 and was on a streak of 134 consecutive extra points. The only downside on special teams was that opponents scored twice on returns. The Falcons will be looking for a punt-returner to replace Billy (White Shoes) Johnson. But in all, special teams are the Falcons' most stable unit.

THE ROOKIES: The Falcons got a running start in resurrecting the NFL's worst-rated defense by selecting Bruce—regarded as the nation's premier outside linebacker—and USC linebacker Marcus Cotton in the first two rounds. Bruce had 15 sacks last season, Cotton 12. The Falcons had a league-worst 17. Third-rounder Alex Higdon, a 6-5, 252-pound tight end from Ohio State, has the size and potential.

OUTLOOK: Health permitting, the Falcons should improve on last season's 3-12 mark. But as Campbell readily admits, it will take more than a year to turn Atlanta into a playoff contender.

FALCON PROFILES

GERALD RIGGS 27 6-1 232   **Running Back**

Only NFL running back to make the Pro Bowl the last three years . . . . . . Second only to Eric Dickerson in yards gained over last four seasons . . . Hard-nosed, overpowering runner. "Gerald is so tough, and when we can stay close, he's exceptionally hard on defenses in the fourth quarters," says coach Marion Campbell. . . . . Finished fourth among NFC rushers, carrying 203 times for 875 yards. . . . First-round draft choice out of Arizona State in 1982. . . . Has carried the running load for Atlanta since knee injury sidelined William Andrews in 1984. . . . Avid tennis player. . . . Looks forward to a career in television after football. . . . Born Nov. 6, 1960, in Tullos, Cal.

CHRIS MILLER 23 6-2 195   **Quarterback**

The starter . . . A No. 1 pick out of Oregon, Miller started twice as a rookie and threw the team's three longest passes of the season. . . . Took first NFL snap after replacing Scott Campbell in second half against Rams in Falcons' 13th game . . . Completed 10 of 20 passes for 170 yards . . . First start came against 49ers and league's No. 1-ranked defense . . . Only fourth rookie in team history to start at quarterback. Three have done it during Marion Campbell's term as head coach . . . Started slowly after holding out in a contract dispute until Oct. 30 . . . Looking forward to first NFL training camp. . . . Rewrote the record books at Oregon, where he passed

FALCONS VETERAN ROSTER

HEAD COACH—Marion Campbell. Assistant Coaches—Tom Brasher, Fred Bruney, Scott Campbell, Chuck Clausen, Steve Crosby, Rod Dowhower, Foge Fazio, Jim Hanifan, Claude Humphrey, Tim Jorgensen, Jimmy Raye.

No.	Name	Pos.	Ht.	Wt.	NFL Exp.	College
47	Badanjek, Rick	RB	5-8	217	2	Maryland
82	Bailey, Stacey	WR	6-0	157	7	San Jose State
93	Bohm, Ron	DE	6-3	253	2	Illinois
98	Brown, Greg	DE	6-5	265	8	Kansas State
77	Bryan, Rick	DE	6-4	265	5	Oklahoma
23	Butler, Bobby	CB	5-11	175	8	Florida State
10	Campbell, Scott	QB	6-0	195	5	Purdue
25	Case, Scott	CB	6-0	178	5	Oklahoma
75	Casillas, Tony	NT	6-3	280	3	Oklahoma
28	Clark, Bret	S	6-3	198	2	Nebraska
56	Costello, Joe	LB	6-3	244	3	Cent. Conn. State
88	Cox, Arthur	TE	6-2	262	6	Texas Southern
30	Croudip, David	CB	5-8	183	5	San Diego State
86	Dixon, Floyd	WR	5-9	170	3	Stephen F. Austin
3	Donnelly, Rick	P	6-0	190	4	Wyoming
64	Dukes, Jamie	G	6-1	278	3	Florida State
24	Emery, Larry	RB	5-9	195	2	Wisconsin
39	Everett, Major	RB	5-10	218	5	Mississippi College
48	Flowers, Kenny	RB	6-0	210	2	Clemson
79	Fralic, Bill	T-G	6-5	280	4	Pittsburgh
76	Gann, Mike	DE	6-5	275	4	Notre Dame
41	Gordon, Tim	S	6-0	188	2	Tulsa
99	Green, Tim	LB	6-2	245	3	Syracuse
96	Hall, James	LB	6-1	252	2	NW Louisiana
21	Huff, Charles	CB	5-11	195	2	Presbyterian
68	Jackson, Lawrence	G	6-1	275	2	Presbyterian
84	Jones, Joey	WR	5-8	165	2	Alabama
78	Kenn, Mike	T	6-7	277	11	Michigan
63	Klewel, Jeff	G	6-3	277	3	Arizona
14	Kramer, Erik	QB	6-0	192	2	North Carolina State
52	Kraynak, Rich	LB	6-1	230	6	Pittsburgh
—	Lavette, Robert	RB	5-11	190	3	Georgia Tech
83	Matthews, Aubrey	WR	5-7	165	3	Delta State
87	Middleton, Ron	TE	6-2	252	3	Auburn
62	Miller, Brett	T	6-7	300	6	Iowa
12	Miller, Chris	QB	6-2	195	2	Oregon
73	Mitchell, Leonard	T	6-7	295	8	Houston
34	Moore, Robert	S	5-11	190	3	NW Louisiana
35	Moss, Gary	S	5-10	192	2	Georgia
67	Mraz, Mark	DE	6-4	255	2	Utah State
72	Provence, Andrew	DE	6-3	267	6	South Carolina
59	Rade, John	LB	6-1	240	6	Boise State
55	Radloff, Wayne	C	6-5	277	4	Georgia
95	Reid, Michael	LB	6-2	226	2	Wisconsin
42	Riggs, Gerald	RB	6-1	232	7	Arizona State
61	Scully, John	G	6-6	270	8	Notre Dame
44	Settle, John	RB	5-9	207	2	Appalachian
37	Shelley, Elbert	S	5-11	180	2	Arkansas State
29	Stamps, Sylvester	RB	5-7	171	4	Jackson State
45	Whisenhunt, Ken	TE	6-3	240	4	Georgia Tech
54	Williams, Joel	LB	6-1	227	10	Wisconsin-LaCrosse

TOP DRAFT CHOICES

Rd.	Name	Sel. No.	Pos.	Ht.	Wt.	College
1	Bruce, Aundray	1	LB	6-5	236	Auburn
2	Cotton, Marcus	28	LB	6-3	214	Southern California
3	Higdon, Alex	56	TE	6-5	252	Ohio State
5	Dimry, Charles	110	CB	6-0	165	Nevada-Las Vegas
6	Thomas, George	138	WR	5-9	169	Nevada-Las Vegas

for 6,681 yards and became first Pac-10 quarterback since Jim Plunkett to earn All-League honors in back-to-back seasons . . . A shortstop in baseball, he was drafted by Blue Jays June 6, 1983 and later drafted by the Mariners Jan. 9, 1985 . . . He had a year in the minors, but opted for football . . . Born Aug. 9, 1965, in Pomona, Cal.

BILL FRALIC 25 6-5 280   Guard

His dad, Bill Sr., was a Marine and is a steel worker, 6-3, 250, so Bill Jr. wasn't going to be a tennis player . . . Neither were brothers Joe, who played at John Marshall, and Mike, who played at South Carolina . . . How tough was dad? He had a sign in the front yard that read: "Forget the dog, beware the owner!" . . . Bill has played in last two Pro Bowls . . . Selected AP All-Pro in 1987 . . . Will earn $300,000 base salary in last year of contract . . . Taken as second player in 1985 draft out of Pittsburgh and was selected as NFL Rookie of the Year by *Sports Illustrated* . . . Born Oct. 31, 1962, in Pittsburgh . . . Outspoken on drug issues . . . Avid weightlifter.

TONY CASILLAS 24 6-3 280   Nose Tackle

Tony the Terminator . . . He stops opposing running backs and makes the Falcon defense go . . . Averaged nine tackles a game . . . Missed last four games with hairline fracture in right ankle . . . Will earn $250,000 in base salary this season. . . . Combined with Rick Bryan and Mike Gann, Casillas gives Falcons one of most promising defensive fronts in league. . . . Makes linebackers look good because he plugs up the middle. Played in front of Brian Bosworth at Oklahoma . . . Was No. 2 overall pick in 1986 draft . . . Of Mexican-American descent . . . Born Oct. 26, 1963, in Tulsa, Okla. . . . Owns a black chow dog named "Bobo."

RICK BRYAN 26 6-4 265   Defensive End

Sooner or later, this former Oklahoma star was due to miss a game because of injury. After starting all 48 games his first three seasons, a groin pull Nov. 22 took him out of the lineup for three games . . . Still finished fourth on the team in tackles with 85 . . . Coaches say it's just a matter of time before he makes it to his first Pro Bowl . . . Will concentrate on helping

Falcons improve pass rush this season. Has 20.5 sacks in four years... Earned $325,000 in last year of contract last season... Falcons can't afford a lengthy contract dispute... Born March 20, 1962, in Coweta Okla., he wears the "Good Ole Boy" label with pride.

FLOYD DIXON 24 5-9 170   Wide Receiver

Runs in open track meets in Texas in the spring; runs past defensive backs in the fall. ...Caught 36 passes for 600 yards and five touchdowns... Gary Clark-type of receiver. Runs accurate patterns and has good hands ...Billy "White Shoes" Johnson was his teenage hero... Voted NFC Rookie of the Year in 1986 when he caught 42 passes for 617 yards

...Sixth-round choice out of Stephen F. Austin... Has 4.4 speed in the 40-yard dash, a standing vertical leap of 33½ inches and he bench-presses more than 300 pounds... Majored in business... Born April 9, 1964, in Houston.

TIM GREEN 24 6-2 245   Linebacker

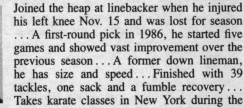

Joined the heap at linebacker when he injured his left knee Nov. 15 and was lost for season ...A first-round pick in 1986, he started five games and showed vast improvement over the previous season... A former down lineman, he has size and speed... Finished with 39 tackles, one sack and a fumble recovery... Takes karate classes in New York during the offseason... An All-American at Syracuse, he had 28½ sacks during final two seasons. Finished with 43... Graduated with a 3.83 grade-point average and was valedictorian of senior class ...Enjoys the outdoors: hunting, windsurfing and skiing. Born Dec. 16, 1963, in Liverpool, N.Y.

BOBBY BUTLER 29 5-11 175   Cornerback

Falcons' only defensive player to start all 12 games at the same spot... Had four interceptions, 31 tackles and one fumble recovery... Only starter in secondary with over four years' experience... Has 23 career interceptions in eight seasons... Missed last half of 1986 with broken leg... Was voted Comeback Player of the Year in '87... First-round draft choice in 1981... Manager-trainee at Domino's pizza last two offseasons

... Member of Florida State track team ... Earned $264,000 in final year of contract last season ... Born May 28, 1959, in Boynton Beach, Fla.

SYLVESTER STAMPS 27 5-7 171   Returner

Led the NFL in kick returns with a 27.5-yard average. Voted as Pro Bowl alternate ... Has 4.3 speed ... Used in a pinch as third-down receiver ... Caught four passes for 40 yards ... Four-year vet's career kickoff return average is second among active players ... Signed with Falcons twice: May 2, 1984, and Dec. 10, 1985. Was working as a fireman in Vicksburg, Miss., when Falcons called the second time ... Played at Jackson State ... Nicknames abound: Zip Code, Special Delivery, Sly and Mighty Mouse ... Born Feb. 24, 1961, in Vicksburg, Miss.

MICK LUCKHURST 30 6-2 183   Kicker

Owns 10 club records and a career field-goal percentage of 70.1 percent ... Has made 134 consecutive extra points ... Only kicker in NFL history ever to make two field goals of 50 or more yards in one game ... Member of eight-man players' union executive board ... Only attempted 13 field goals last season, making nine. "We need to get Mick more attempts," said special teams coach Foge Fazio ... Signed as free agent May 5, 1981 ... Born March 31, 1958, in Redbourn, England, he grew up playing soccer and rugby ... Writes a column for an English publication called "First Down."

COACH MARION CAMPBELL: Registered 3-12 record his first season as head coach. It was the worst record in the league ... Was given vocal support by owner Rankin Smith, who blamed the Falcons' problems more on personnel than on coaching ... Considered one of the best defensive coaches in the league ... Has 27 years of professional coaching experience ... Served as the Falcons' defensive coordinator for a season before replacing Dan Henning ... Started his coaching career in 1962 as line coach of the Boston Patriots. Served as defensive line coach for the Vikings 1964-66 and worked with the "Fearsome Foursome" at Los Angeles from 1967-68 . . . Was defensive coordinator for Atlanta the next six seasons before becoming head coach 1974-76 . . . Went to the Super Bowl in 1980 as defensive coordinator of Eagles . . . Became Eagles' head coach in 1983, was fired in '85 and rehired by Atlanta in '86 . . . Born May 25, 1929, in Chester, S.C. . . . Was All-SEC defensive lineman at Georgia and played for the 49ers in 1954 and 1955 and Eagles from 1956-61 . . . A two-time Pro Bowl selection.

LONGEST PLAY

The Falcons had already clinched a wild-card berth heading into their game with the Cardinals on Dec. 17, 1978. They trailed, 14-7, midway in the second quarter when St. Louis' Steve Little punted to the Falcons' goal line.

Dennis Pearson, a rookie wide receiver and kick-returner who had played at Washington State and San Diego State, caught the kick on the goal line, eluded a covey of Cardinals and went the distance for a 100-yarder. It tied the game, but the Cardinals won, 42-21.

INDIVIDUAL FALCON RECORDS

Rushing

Most Yards Game:	202	Gerald Riggs, vs New Orleans, 1984
Season:	1,719	Gerald Riggs, 1985
Career:	6,143	Gerald Riggs, 1982-87

Passing

Most TD Passes Game:	4	Randy Johnson, vs Chicago, 1969
	4	Steve Bartkowski, vs New Orleans, 1980
	4	Steve Bartkowski, vs St. Louis, 1981
Season:	31	Steve Bartkowski, 1980
Career:	149	Steve Bartkowski, 1975-85

Receiving

Most TD Passes Game:	3	Lynn Cain, vs Oakland, 1979
	3	Alfred Jenkins, vs New Orleans, 1981
	3	William Andrews, vs Denver, 1982
	3	William Andrews, vs Green Bay, 1983
	3	Lynn Cain, vs L.A. Rams, 1984
	3	Gerald Riggs, vs. L.A. Rams, 1985
Season:	13	Alfred Jenkins, 1981
Career:	40	Alfred Jenkins, 1975-83

Scoring

Most Points Game:	18	Lynn Cain, vs Oakland, 1979
	18	Alfred Jenkins, vs New Orleans, 1981
	18	William Andrews, vs Denver, 1982
	18	William Andrews, vs Green Bay, 1983
	18	Lynn Cain, vs L.A. Rams, 1984
	18	Gerald Riggs, vs L.A. Rams, 1985
Season:	114	Mick Luckhurst, 1981
Career:	558	Mick Luckhurst 1981-87
Most TDs Game:	3	Shared by Lynn Cain, Alfred Jenkins, William Andrews and Gerald Riggs
Season:	13	Alfred Jenkins, 1981
	13	Gerald Riggs, 1984
Career:	47	Gerald Riggs 1982-87

CHICAGO BEARS

TEAM DIRECTORY: Chairman: Edward B. McCaskey; Pres.: Michael B. McCaskey; VP Player Personnel: Bill Tobin; Dir. Administraton: Bill McGrane; Dir. Finance: Ted Phillips; Pub. Rel. Dir.: Ken Valdiserri; Head Coach: Mike Ditka. Home field: Soldier Field (66,030). Colors: Orange, navy blue and white.

SCOUTING REPORT

OFFENSE: One of the biggest changes in the Bears' offense will involve receivers and quarterback coach Greg Landry. The former NFL and USFL quarterback will take an active role in the play-calling.

"I have no desire to call plays," coach Mike Ditka said. "I've done it my way and I'm willing to back off. We haven't won the big games."

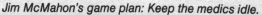

Jim McMahon's game plan: Keep the medics idle.

The Bears have won four consecutive division titles, but they need a healthy Jim McMahon. He has missed much of the past two seasons because of injuries and he proved human last January in the first-round playoff loss to Washington after coming back from a six-week layoff.

He had arthroscopic surgery on his right shoulder during the offseason and history says the Bears better have a dependable backup. Jim Harbaugh, the team's top pick in '87, will challenge Mike Tomczak for that role.

Walter Payton is gone and that has to leave a huge gap in the running game. Even with No. 1 pick Brad Muster of Stanford and Neal Anderson, who led the team in rushing and receiving last season, the Bears will miss Sweetness' immense contributions.

The offensive line, anchored by center Jay Hilgenberg and tackle Jimbo Covert, remains among the best in the league and the receiving corps is headed by bobsledder Willie Gault and the outspoken Dennis McKinnon.

DEFENSE: The defense wasn't the dominant force it had been in previous seasons. One big difference was reflected in turnovers; Chicago's 24 ranked last in the league. Still, the defense ranked second, first against the rush and seventh against the pass. But the Bears suffered a big loss in the defection of All-Pro linebacker Wilber Marshall to Washington. And Otis Wilson, the team's other outside linebacker, was still debating with Ditka and could be headed elsewhere.

Add the retirement of free safety Gary Fencik, aging years to tackles Dan Hampton and Steve McMichael, and perhaps 50 pounds to William Perry and there are questions about Chicago's highly regarded defense.

The linebackers arguably have been the best group in the league since 1985. Mike Singletary remains a solid force in the middle, but the perimeters are uncertain. The team needs a consistent pass rush. Dave Duerson will stay at strong safety and battle Todd Bell for the starting post. Cornerback Vestee Jackson heads a group of cross-your-fingers corners.

Three 1987 draft picks—end Sean Smith, linebacker Will Johnson and tackle Dick Chapura—will have greater opportunity.

KICKING GAME: Kevin Butler ranked ninth in the league in scoring among kickers with 85 points, but Ditka goes through punters like the Cubs go through managers. The Bears had three in '87—Bryan Wagner, Kevin Brown and Tommy Barnhardt.

BEARS VETERAN ROSTER

HEAD COACH—Mike Ditka. Assistant Coaches—Jim Dooley, Ed Hughes, Steve Kazor, Greg Landry, Jim LaRue, John Levra, Dave McGinnis, Johnny Roland, Dick Stanfel, Vince Tobin.

No.	Name	Pos.	Ht.	Wt.	NFL Exp.	College
54	Adickes, John	C	6-3	264	2	Baylor
47	Allen, Egypt	CB-S	6-0	203	2	Texas Christian
70	Althoff, Jim	DT	6-3	278	2	Winona State
35	Anderson, Neal	RB	5-11	210	3	Florida
81	Barnes, Lew	WR	5-8	163	2	Oregon
17	Barnhardt, Tommy	P	6-3	205	2	North Carolina
79	Becker, Kurt	G	6-5	270	7	Michigan
68	Blair, Paul	T	6-4	295	3	Oklahoma State
62	Bortz, Mark	G	6-6	269	6	Iowa
86	Boso, Cap	TE	6-3	224	2	Illinois
6	Butler, Kevin	K	6-1	195	4	Georgia
94	Capura, Dick	DT	6-3	280	2	Missouri
74	Covert, Jim	T	6-4	271	6	Pittsburgh
95	Dent, Richard	DE	6-5	260	6	Tennessee State
36	Douglass, Maurice	CB-S	5-11	200	3	Kentucky
22	Duerson, Dave	S	6-1	203	6	Norte Dame
83	Gault, Willie	WR	6-1	183	6	Tennessee
23	Gayle, Shaun	CB	5-11	193	5	Ohio State
29	Gentry, Dennis	WR	5-8	181	7	Baylor
99	Hampton, Dan	DE	6-5	270	10	Arkansas
4	Harbaugh, Jim	QB	6-3	202	2	Michigan
90	Jarris, Al	LB	6-5	253	9	Arizona State
63	Hilgenberg, Jay	C	6-3	265	8	Iowa
24	Jackson, Vestee	CB	6-0	186	3	Washington
31	Jeffries, Eric	CB-S	5-10	161	2	Texas
93	Johnson, Will	LB	6-4	245	2	Northeast Louisiana
88	Kozlowski, Glen	WR	6-1	193	2	Brigham Young
43	Lynch, Lorenzo	CB-S	5-9	197	2	Cal State-Sacramento
—	McKeever, Vito	CB	6-0	180	2	Florida
85	McKinnon, Dennis	WR	6-1	185	5	Florida State
9	McMahon, Jim	QB	6-1	190	7	Brigham Young
76	McMichael, Steve	DT	6-2	260	9	Texas
87	Moorehead, Emery	TE	6-2	220	12	Colorado
84	Morris, Ron	WR	6-1	187	2	Southern Methodist
51	Morrissey, Jim	LB	6-3	215	4	Michigan State
46	Mosley, Anthony	RB	5-9	204	1	Fresno State
91	Novell, Jay	LB	6-2	232	2	Iowa
89	Ortego, Keith	WR	6-0	180	4	McNeese State
72	Perry, William	DT	6-2	325	4	Clemson
48	Phillips, Reggie	CB	5-10	170	4	Southern Methodist
27	Richardson, Mike	CB	6-0	188	6	Arizona State
59	Rivera, Ron	LB	6-3	239	5	California
53	Rodenhauser, Mark	C	6-5	260	2	Illinois State
52	Rubens, Larry	C	6-2	262	4	Montana State
20	Sanders, Thomas	RB	5-11	203	4	Texas A&M
50	Singletary, Mike	LB	6-0	228	8	Baylor
97	Smith, Sean	DE	6-4	275	2	Grambling
26	Suhey, Matt	RB	5-11	216	9	Penn State
57	Thayer, Tom	G	6-4	261	4	Notre Dame
33	Thomas, Calvin	RB	5-11	245	7	Illinois
18	Tomczak, Mike	QB	6-1	195	4	Ohio State
78	Van Horne, Keith	T	6-6	280	8	Southern California
15	Wagner, Bryan	P	6-2	195	2	Cal State-Northridge
55	Wilson, Otis	LB	6-2	232	9	Louisville
73	Wojciechowski, John	G	6-4	262	2	Michigan State

TOP DRAFT CHOICES

Rd.	Name	Sel. No.	Pos.	Ht.	Wt.	College
1	Muster, Brad	23	RB	6-3	220	Stanford
1	Davis, Wendell	27	WR	5-11	190	LSU
2	Jones, Dante	51	LB	6-1	225	Oklahoma
3	Jarvis, Ralph	78	DE	6-5	261	Temple
4	Thornton, Jim	105	TE	6-2	242	Cal St.-Fullerton

THE ROOKIES: The Bears went for offensive spark with their two first-round picks. Muster, a 6-3, 220-pounder, is a solid combination of runner, receiver and blocker, and Wendell Davis, a wide receiver from LSU, has great quickness. No. 2 pick Dante Jones from Oklahoma is a rugged, Bears-type inside linebacker. Defensive end Ralph Jarvis, a third-rounder from Temple, could be a sleeper in the same manner Richard Dent was in the 1983 draft.

OUTLOOK: Still a very good football team, but not a dominant one. If McMahon stays healthy and the defense finds someone to replace Marshall, they will challenge again. If not, they might not beat out the Vikings in the Central Division.

BEAR PROFILES

JIM McMAHON 29 6-1 190   Quarterback

The flamboyant Bear proved mortal when, after missing six games, he threw three second-half interceptions in last season's opening-round playoff loss to the championship-bound Redskins...It was the first time the Bears dropped a playoff game with McMahon as a starter...Reinjured in the game, McMahon did little to enhance his record in a season in which he ranked seventh in the league among passers (125 of 210 for a 59.5 percentage)...He threw eight interceptions in the regular season...Perhaps the magic—like Walter Payton—is gone for the rebel quarterback who led the Bears to victory in Super Bowl XX...The injury-dogged McMahon, whose autobiography, *McMahon*, was a best-seller after the Super Bowl season, embarks on his seventh season.... He was a first-round draft choice out of Brigham Young in 1982 ...Born Aug. 21, 1959, in Jersey City, N.J.

WILLIE GAULT 27 6-1 183   Wide Receiver

The U.S. Olympic bobsled team didn't use him at Calgary, but the Bears certainly did... Willie led Chicago in receiving yards (705), yards per catch (20.1) and touchdowns (7)... Once one of the world's leading hurdlers, he adapted his trackman's speed and agility to football as a wide receiver at Tennessee... Was a first-round selection in the 1983 draft and has led the Bears in yards receiving and TD catches four times . . . Earned a base salary of $347,000 in final year of contract and was the team's sixth-highest-paid player on offense . . . Born Sept. 5, 1960, in Griffin, Ga.

NEAL ANDERSON 24 5-11 210   Running Back

Started to fill the shoes of Walter Payton even before Sweetness retired . . . Led the Bears in rushing (586 yards on 129 carries) and receiving (467 yards, 47 catches) in his first full season as a starter . . . Became first player other than Payton to lead team in rushing since Ken Grandberry in 1974 . . . His absence because of a sprained knee hurt the Bears in their playoff loss to the Redskins . . . With Payton retired, he'll move from fullback to tailback this season and his production surely will increase . . . A first-round selection out of the University of Florida in 1986, he was the school's all-time leading rusher . . . Born Aug. 4, 1964, in Graceville, Fla.

MIKE SINGLETARY 29 6-0 228   Linebacker

Team's defensive leader, Singletary indirectly was the reason the team let Wilber Marshall go to the Redskins . . . He recently negotiated a new contract worth $750,000 this season and the team promised not to pay more to any other linebacker . . . So Marshall headed for Washington after receiving a five-year, $6-million offer from Redskins . . . Has certainly played like a Six-Million-Dollar Man for the Bears in his last five Pro-Bowl seasons . . . Selected first-team All-Pro by Associated Press, Pro Football Writers, *Pro Football Weekly* and *The Sporting News* . . . A second-round draft choice out of Baylor, he was Southwest Conference Player of the Year in 1979 and 1980. Born Oct. 9, 1958, in Houston.

DAVE DUERSON 27 6-1 203   Safety

Led the team in tackles (116) and interceptions (three) despite moving from strong safety to free safety . . . Just missed making Pro Bowl for third time. Voted an alternate . . . Has proven to be another gem in a cluster of valuable overlooked draft choices that Bears have selected . . . A third-rounder out of Notre Dame in 1983, Duerson has bailed the Bears out twice in last three seasons . . . He replaced Todd Bell at strong safety in '85 when Bell sat out because of a contract dispute and he switched to free safety last season when the Bears needed someone to start over aging Gary Fencik. Worth every penny of the $375,000 he will earn this season . . . Born Nov. 28, 1960, in Muncie, Ind.

KEVIN BUTLER 26 6-1 195   Kicker

Jim McMahon's favorite teammate . . . You know he's different . . . Actually, Butler seems normal for a kicker, but he's far from average. Finished the season with a streak of 18 field goals inside the 40 . . . Didn't miss one from that range all season (16-for-16) and had two from 52 yards out, matching his career long . . . His 85 points ranked him ninth in league among kickers and moved him from 11th to eighth on team's all-time scoring list . . . Has made 349 points in only three seasons . . . Despite his credentials, Butler was one of lowest-paid kickers in the league last season with a $110,000 base. His contract expired Feb. 1, but with the Bears' track record in salaries, this is one time Butler may come away short of his mark . . . Born July 24, 1962, in Savannah, Ga.

DAN HAMPTON 31 6-5 270   Defensive Tackle

Anytime you have a guy nicknamed Danimal, it's wise to play him near all the action . . . The Bears caught onto that late in the season and moved him back from end to tackle . . . The defense seemed to respond and began approaching the level that had made it so famous in past seasons . . . The second-highest-paid player on the defense behind Mike Singletary, Hampton is scheduled to earn $725,000 this season . . . Has made the Pro Bowl as both a tackle and end but should remain at tackle since he made such a difference . . . A first-round choice (fourth overall) out of Arkansas in 1979, he made 32 tackles behind the line of scrimmage for Razorbacks . . . Has made Pro Bowl in 1980, '82, '84 and '85 . . . Grew up on 42-acre farm near Cabot, Ark. Plays bass guitar, classical guitar, drums, saxophone, piano and organ . . . Born Jan. 19, 1957, in Oklahoma City, Okla.

STEVE McMICHAEL 30 6-2 260   Defensive Tackle

Imagine, he never made it as a Patriot . . . Got cut by Ron Erhardt in 1980 as a third-round selection in the draft and wound up as a free-agent signee with the Bears in '81 . . . He finished in a fury last season with 5½ sacks in the last four games for seven on the season and All-Pro honors from Associated Press, *Pro Football Weekly*, the Pro Football Writers and *The Sporting News* . . . Hasn't missed a game in four seasons and now owns the Bears' longest consecutive-game starting streak with 68 . . . Just missed his second consecutive trip to the Pro Bowl; was an alternate . . . Earned $275,000 last year . . . Played at Texas, where he was a finalist for the Outland Trophy and Lonbardi Award . . . Hunts rattlesnakes—and quarterbacks . . . Born Oct. 17, 1957, in Houston.

JAY HILGENBERG 29 6-3 265   Center

This guy was meant to play in Chicago . . . Has started 67 consecutive games despite elbow and shoulder injuries last season . . . Played several games with a harness and needed off-season surgery . . . Heart of a highly regarded line . . . Made third consecutive trip to Pro Bowl as starter . . . Selected first-team All-Pro by *Sporting News* . . . Extremely strong against nose guards but is agile enough to pull . . . Father Jerry was All-American center at Iowa in 1950s . . . Brother Joel plays for the Saints . . . Avid outdoorsman . . . Signed with Bears May 8, 1981 as free agent . . . Born March 21, 1959, in Iowa City, Iowa.

RICHARD DENT 27 6-5 260   Defensive End

His 4½ sacks against the Rams in the regular-season finale were most by any player in 1987 . . . Finished second in the NFL with 13½, behind Eagles' Reggie White (21) . . . Has 29½ sacks over the last four seasons, leading Bears each year in that category . . . Classic example of Bears' drafting abilities: Bill Tobin took him in Round 8 of 1983 draft . . . Immediately underwent dental work, which presumably helped him to eat more, so went from playing weight of 235 at Tennessee State to 265 with Bears...Hobbies include racquetball, tennis, swimming and horseback riding...Born Dec. 13, 1960, in Atlanta.

COACH MIKE DITKA: Outspoken leader who has no qualms about firing up the opposition...Before Bears' playoff against Washington he created a storm when he said Redskins' Dexter Manley had an IQ of a grapefruit...Did it make a difference? Well, Redskins won...No love lost between him and Eagles' coach Buddy Ryan, former Bears' defensive coordinator ...Career record is 65-30 in six seasons... Team has made the playoffs every year since 1984...He's been in NFL as player and coach for 26 years...Played 12 years at tight end for the Bears (1961-66), Eagles (1967-68) and Cowboys (1970-72)...Cowboys' offensive coach 1973-81 before becoming Bears' head man in '82...Was Coach of the Year in 1986 when Chicago won Super Bowl XX...Unpredictable. Week before the team played in Minnesota's Metrodome last year, he wore roller skates at the Bears' office, mocking the Vikings' indoor facility he called a roller rink...Was an All-American at Pitt (tight end, linebacker)...Born Oct. 13, 1939, in Carnegie, Pa.

LONGEST PLAY

He'd made the Pro Bowl as a rookie in 1966. Now he was opening his second season for the Bears, on Sept. 17, 1967, against the Steelers at Forbes Field.

With 5:40 gone in the first period, the Steelers kicked a field goal to lead, 3-0. Gale Sayers lined up deep for the ensuing kick. He took the ball three yards into the end zone, drove up the center of the field, then cut for the left sideline. With one man to beat near midfield, he veered right and ran untouched for a 103-yard touchdown, the longest in team history.

That was the only highlight of the day for the Bears. The Steelers went on to win, 41-13, and Sayers was held to two yards rushing.

INDIVIDUAL BEAR RECORDS

Rushing

Most Yards Game:	275	Walter Payton, vs Minnesota, 1977
Season:	1,852	Walter Payton, 1977
Career:	16,726	Walter Payton, 1975-87

Passing

Most TD Passes Game:	7	Sid Luckman, vs N.Y. Giants, 1943
Season:	28	Sid Luckman, 1943
Career:	137	Sid Luckman, 1939-50

Receiving

Most TD Passes Game:	4	Harlon Hill, vs San Francisco, 1954
	4	Mike Ditka, vs Los Angeles, 1963
Season:	13	Dick Gordon, 1970
	13	Ken Kavanaugh, 1947
Career:	50	Ken Kavanaugh, 1940-41, 1945-50

Scoring

Most Points Game:	36	Gale Sayers, vs San Francisco, 1965
Season:	144	Kevin Butler, 1985
Career:	750	Walter Payton, 1975-87
Most TDs Game:	6	Gale Sayers, vs San Francisco, 1965
Season:	22	Gale Sayers, 1965
Career:	125	Walter Payton, 1975-87

DALLAS COWBOYS

TEAM DIRECTORY: General Partner: H.R. Bright; Pres./GM: Tex Schramm; VP-Player Development: Gil Brandt; VP-Administration: Joe Bailey; VP-Treasurer: Don Wilson; VP-Pro Personnel: Bob Ackles; Pub. Rel. Dir.: Doug Todd; Head Coach: Tom Landry. Home field: Texas Stadium (63,855). Colors: Royal blue, metallic blue and white.

SCOUTING REPORT

OFFENSE: With Danny White's career nearing its end, coach Tom Landry is counting on Steve Pelluer to solve things at quarterback. White, now 36 and with wrist problems, had a 59.4 percentage completion average (215 for 362), while the 26-year-old Pelluer posted a 54.5 percentage (55 for 101). Pelluer will get his chance for full-time duty.

The Cowboys, ninth in NFC rushing, are expecting a 1,000-yard campaign from Herschel Walker, whose 891 yards (4.3 average) are only a hint of things to come. Tony Dorsett (456, 3.5) is now a Bronco and Walker, third-leading rusher in the NFC, still will need a supporting cast.

The Cowboys expect wide receiver Michael Irvin, No. 1 pick out of Miami, will put back some zip in the passing game. With Mike Sherrard uncertain after missing a year with a broken leg, wide receiver is in the hands of Kelvin Edwards and Kelvin Martin. Tight end Doug Cosbie fell off some last season, so Thornton Chandler may see a bigger role.

The offensive-line situation isn't too bright when the guy you labeled as your best lineman at the start of the 1987, Nate Newton, reports to a 1988 minicamp some 50 pounds overweight. The Cowboys also considering moving Daryle Smith from tackle to center.

DEFENSE: The main priority is to rediscover a consistent pass rush. Danny Noonan had replaced veteran Randy White as a full-time player by the end of last season, John Dutton is gone, Ed (Too Tall) Jones is 37 and Jim Jeffcoat has yet to play up to expectations.

Because the Cowboys are expected to play the 3-4 frequently this season—perhaps with White as a standup linebacker—they need a big-play person to join Jeff Roher, Ron Burton, Jess Penn, Eugene Lockhart and Mike Hegman. They'll also need healthy linebackers; Lockhart, Penn and Hegman all suffered broken legs last season.

Herschel Walker led Cowboys in rushing, pass-receiving.

In the secondary, the corners seem secure with Everson Walls and Ron Francis, but there's a question at safety since Michael Downs didn't have one of his best seasons and Bill Bates isn't one of the fastest strong safeties in the league.

KICKING GAME: Not many questions here. Roger Ruzek arguably could have made the Pro Bowl last season, more than adequately replacing Rafael Septien. He set a team record by kicking five field goals against the Rams and tied a league record with four field goals in the fourth quarter against the Giants.

THE ROOKIES: The selection of Irvin, who reminds scouts of Jerry Rice, brought the Cowboys "back to the land of the living," according to Tex Schramm. No. 2 pick Ken Norton Jr. of UCLA will vie for an outside linebacker spot. The Cowboys went for huge offensive linemen in rounds three and four in G Mark Hutson, a 6-3, 292-pounder from Oklahoma, and T David Widell, a 6-6, 280-pounder from Boston College who'll likely be tried at center.

COWBOYS VETERAN ROSTER

HEAD COACH—Tom Landry. Assistant Coaches—Ben Agajanian, Neill Armstrong, Jim Erkenbeck, Paul Hackett, Al Lavan, Alan Lowry, Dick Nolan, Mike Solari, Ernie Stautner, Jerry Tubbs, Bob Ward.

No.	Name	Pos.	Ht.	Wt.	NFL Exp.	College
36	Albritton, Vince	S	6-2	217	5	Washington
2	Alexander, Ray	WR	6-4	196	2	Florida A&M
87	Banks, Gordon	WR	5-10	170	6	Stanford
80	Barksdale, Rod	WR	6-1	193	3	Arizona
40	Bates, Bill	S	6-1	199	6	Tennessee
99	Brooks, Kevin	DE	6-6	278	4	Michigan
15	Burbage, Cornell	WR	5-10	181	2	Kentucky
57	Burton, Ron	LB	6-1	250	2	North Carolina
85	Chandler, Thornton	TE	6-5	242	3	Alabama
70	Clsowski, Steve	T	6-5	275	2	Santa Clara
42	Clack, Darryl	RB	5-10	220	3	Arizona State
84	Cosbie, Doug	TE	6-6	241	10	Santa Clara
55	DeOssie, Steve	LB	6-2	249	5	Boston College
26	Downs, Michael	S	6-3	212	8	Rice
81	Edwards, Kelvin	WR	6-2	205	3	Liberty
85	Folsom, Steve	TE	6-5	236	3	Utah
46	Fowler, Todd	RB	6-3	222	4	Stephen F. Austin
38	Francis, Ron	CB	5-9	201	2	Baylor
66	Gogan, Kevin	T	6-7	310	2	Washington
27	Haynes, Tommy	S	6-0	190	2	Southern California
58	Hegman, Mike	LB	6-1	226	13	Tennessee State
45	Hendrix, Manny	CB-S	5-10	181	3	Utah
52	Hurd, Jeff	LB	6-2	245	2	Kansas State
53	Jax, Garth	LB	6-2	222	3	Florida State
77	Jeffcoat, Jim	DE	6-5	263	6	Arizona State
72	Jones, Ed	DE	6-9	275	14	Tennessee State
68	Ker, Crawford	G	6-3	283	4	Florida
67	Lilja, George	C	6-4	282	7	Michigan
56	Lockhart, Eugene	LB	6-2	230	5	Houston
14	McDonald, Paul	QB	6-2	182	9	Southern California
83	Martin, Kelvin	WR	5-9	163	2	Boston College
30	Newsome, Timmy	RB	6-1	235	9	Winston-Salem State
67	Newton, Nate	G	6-3	305	3	Florida A&M
73	Noonan, Danny	DT	6-3	282	2	Nebraska
16	Pelluer, Steve	QB	6-4	208	5	Washington
59	Penn, Jesse	LB	6-3	224	4	Virginia Tech
64	Rafferty, Tom	C	6-3	263	13	Penn State
82	Renfro, Mike	WR	6-0	184	11	Texas Christian
50	Rohrer, Jeff	LB	6-2	227	7	Yale
9	Ruzek, Roger	K	6-1	185	2	Weber State
4	Saxon, Mike	P	6-3	193	4	San Diego State
22	Scott, Victor	CB-S	6-0	203	5	Colorado
86	Sherrard, Mike	WR	6-2	187	2	UCLA
60	Smerek, Don	DT	6-7	266	7	Nevada-Reno
79	Smith, Daryle	T	6-5	278	2	Tennessee
19	Sweeney, Kevin	QB	6-0	193	2	Fresno State
63	Titensor, Glen	G	6-4	275	7	Brigham Young
71	Tuinei, Mark	C	6-5	282	6	Hawaii
95	Walen, Mark	DT	6-5	262	2	UCLA
34	Walker, Herschel	RB	6-1	223	3	Georgia
24	Walls, Everson	CB	6-1	193	8	Grambling
94	Watts, Randy	DE	6-6	305	2	Catawba
65	White, Bob	T	6-5	267	2	Rhode Island
11	White, Danny	QB	6-3	198	13	Arizona State
37	White, Gerald	RB	5-11	223	2	Michigan
54	White, Randy	DT	6-4	263	14	Maryland
23	Williams, Robert	CB-S	5-10	195	2	Baylor
76	Zimmerman, Jeff	T	6-3	316	2	Florida

TOP DRAFT CHOICES

Rd.	Name	Sel. No.	Pos.	Ht.	Wt.	College
1	Irvin, Michael	11	WR	6-2	202	Miami
2	Norton, Ken Jr.	41	LB	6-2	224	UCLA
3	Hutson, Mark	67	G	6-3	292	Oklahoma
4	Widell, David	94	OT	6-6	280	Boston College
6	Secules, Scott	151	QB	6-3	218	Virginia

OUTLOOK: The Cowboys, coming off a 7-8 season that followed a 7-9 in '86, haven't made the playoffs in two years and it will be another struggle this time unless Walker and Pelluer can lead the way to a turnaround. But nobody ever counts out a team coached by Landry.

COWBOY PROFILES

HERSCHEL WALKER 26 6-1 223   **Running Back**

Winner by TKO over Tony Dorsett. He won full-time duty in the backfield . . . Gained 891 yards on 209 carries and caught 60 passes for 715 yards, leading team in both categories . . . Only NFL player to gain more than 700 yards rushing and receiving in each of past two seasons . . . Started asking for ball more about midseason. Once he got it, he carried it all the way to the Pro Bowl . . . Has shattered records wherever he has played, from Johnson County High School in Wilkerson, Ga., to the University of Georgia where he won the Heisman Trophy in 1982, to the New Jersey Generals of the United States Football League . . . Dallas selected him in fifth round of 1985 draft and waited until USFL folded . . . Signed him Aug. 13, 1986 . . . Will earn $500,000 base salary this season . . . Born March 3, 1962, in Wrightsville, Ga.

STEVE PELLUER 26 6-4 208   **Quarterback**

Projected by coach Tom Landry to emerge as the starter over Danny White. "Obviously, this is where we are leaning," Landry said. "I would think that from his last two games, Pelluer probably will be in pretty good position coming out of training camp" . . . Completed 25 of 52 passes for 305 yards in last two games . . . Replaced 36-year-old White, who has been hampered the past two seasons by a broken wrist . . . Didn't have a good training camp last year . . . Mobile. Playmaker . . . Has completed 275 of 487 passes for 3,416 yards in three-year career . . . Named Pac-10 Player of the Year in 1983 after setting six University of Washington records . . . The Huskies' second all-time leading passer . . . Born July 29, 1962, in Yakima, Washington . . . Will earn $302,000 in last year of contract.

NATE NEWTON 27 6-3 305   Guard

Loves french fries. Can't stay away from them. That's one reason he reported to minicamp at 354 pounds, to the dismay of Cowboy coaches . . . If he can handle his weight problem, he could be a force on the line, offensive line coach Jim Erkenbeck says . . . Considered Dallas' top lineman before he ballooned from 310 to 330 during the strike . . . Strong and unusually quick for one so big . . . Cut by the Redskins as a rookie free agent in 1983 . . . Played two seasons with the Tampa Bay Bandits . . . Loves to laugh and smile . . . Four-year letterman at Florida A&M . . . Younger brother Tim is nose tackle with Vikings . . . Born Dec. 20, 1960, in Orlando, Fla.

KELVIN EDWARDS 24 6-4 205   Wide Receiver

Joined Cowboys during '87 strike and impressed in three replacement games . . . Caught 14 passes for 272 yards . . . Started in six games after strike . . . Finished with 34 receptions for 521 yards, three TDs . . . Added much-needed speed to Cowboy receiver corps, complementing possession receiver Mike Renfro . . . Will be counted on, especially if Mike Sherrard doesn't make it back off the injury list . . . Selected by New Orleans in fourth round of 1986 draft and was released in summer of '87 . . . Set numerous records at Virginia's Liberty Baptist College, where he also was outstanding as a runner in track . . . Born July 19, 1964, in Birmingham, Ala. . . . Signed with Dallas as a free agent before the strike.

DANNY NOONAN 23 6-4 282   Defensive Tackle

He pushed 36-year-old John Dutton off the roster by midseason and by the end he was splitting time with Randy White . . . The Cowboys' No. 1 pick in 1987 out of Nebraska, he quickly emerged as a solid backup to tackle Kevin Brooks and White. That made Dutton expendable . . . Started over White late in season . . . Expected to start at right tackle this season, moving White either to an end or pass-rushing linebacker...Can bench-press over 500 pounds...Excellent work habits..."He's got the size, speed and quickness you look for in a defensive lineman," Tom Landry said...Consensus All-American and Big-Eight pick as a senior. Anchored Nebraska defense that ranked second in nation...Born July 14, 1965, in Lincoln, Neb.

RON BURTON 24 6-1 250 — Linebacker

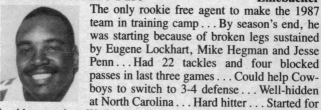

The only rookie free agent to make the 1987 team in training camp...By season's end, he was starting because of broken legs sustained by Eugene Lockhart, Mike Hegman and Jesse Penn...Had 22 tackles and four blocked passes in last three games...Could help Cowboys to switch to 3-4 defense...Well-hidden at North Carolina...Hard hitter...Started for Lockhart against Washington and on outside against Cardinals. Probably will be moved permanently to outside this season... Born May 2, 1964, in Richmond, Va.

EVERSON WALLS 28 6-1 193 — Cornerback

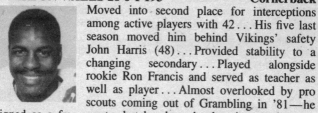

Moved into second place for interceptions among active players with 42...His five last season moved him behind Vikings' safety John Harris (48)...Provided stability to a changing secondary...Played alongside rookie Ron Francis and served as teacher as well as player...Almost overlooked by pro scouts coming out of Grambling in '81—he signed as a free agent—but has been hard to ignore since... Played in four Pro Bowls first six seasons...A gambler, scrapper...Key to the secondary...Led the nation in interceptions his senior season at Grambling with 11...Nicknamed "Chubby"...Active in Big Brothers, American Heart Association and Foster Parents program...Born Dec. 28, 1959, in Dallas.

RON FRANCIS 24 5-9 201 — Cornerback

He played like a rookie is expected to play. He looked good at times, and he looked bad at times. Lowpoint: an interference penalty in the waning seconds against the Eagles that allowed coach Buddy Ryan to go for a "slap-in-the-face" touchdown...Highpoint: An 18-yard interception return for a touchdown against the Patriots...Given starting job when Ron Fellows was traded...Landry was pleased with rookie's performance...Cowboys drafted him in second round because of his "quickness and competitiveness"...Led Southwest Conference in interceptions his final two seasons at Baylor ...Recruited out of high school as running back, then switched to corner after being red-shirted...Brother James starts at Baylor as linebacker...Born April 7, 1964, in Galveston, Tex.

ROGER RUZEK 27 6-1 185　　　　　　　　**Placekicker**

In first year in the NFL he set club record for field-goal accuracy, making 22 of 25 attempts (.880)...Set team mark against the Rams with five of five in 29-21 victory...Led Cowboys in scoring with 92 points, fourth in the NFL among kickers..."Ruzek was a real bright spot for us," said Tom Landry. "He has a chance to be a top kicker for many years." ...Curiously, he was cut by Cowboys in training camp, then given another chance when it was discovered that an ankle injury had caused him to alter kicking style...A former teammate of Herschel Walker's on the New Jersey Generals in the USFL, where he played for two seasons after attending Weber State... Born Dec. 17, 1960, in San Francisco.

JEFF ROHRER 29 6-2 227　　　　　　　　**Linebacker**

Marks his third year as a starting right outside linebacker...Finished fourth on team in tackles with 74 and tied Kevin Brooks for fourth in sacks with four...Selected in second round of 1982 draft...Was highest NFL draft choice out of Yale since 1969, when Cowboys chose Calvin Hill in first round... Spent first three years making progress on special teams...Wore an earring for a month in 1986 to win a bet...Was a National Football Foundation Hall of Fame Scholar-Athlete in high school at Manhattan Beach, Cal., where he was born Dec. 25, 1958.

The pressure is on QB Steve Pelluer.

COACH TOM LANDRY: Learned last season that even the greatest coaches have their critics . . . With Cowboys struggling late in season, Dallas president Tex Schramm questioned publicly the job that Landry was doing . . . This is expected to be his last year . . . Oldest head coach at 64 . . . Coming off his first two consecutive losing seasons since 1963-64 . . . Under his direction, the Cowboys have won 12 division championships, five NFC titles and two Super Bowls (VI and XII) . . . After team finished 7-8 last year, Landry sent a letter to players that read: "You passed the test that Harry Truman quoted: 'The way you endure is more important than the crisis itself.'" Has endured 28 seasons with the Cowboys . . . Was a defensive back for the New York Yankees of the All-American Conference in 1949 after starring as a fullback and defensive back at Texas . . . Joined Giants in 1950 and was an All-Pro defensive back in 1954 . . . Became defensive coach for the team the following season . . . Born Sept. 11, 1924, in Mission, Tex.

LONGEST PLAY

It happened in the 1982 season—a year marked by the players' strike that caused a two-month interruption of play.

In a rescheduled finale of the regular season against Minnesota on Jan. 3, 1983, Tony Dorsett ran 99 yards for a touchdown, the longest run from scrimmage in NFL history.

Minnesota won, 31-27, but Dorsett won the league rushing crown and Dallas subsequently made it to the NFC championship game. There the Cowboys lost, 31-17, to Washington, which went on to win Super Bowl XVII, 27-17, over Miami.

INDIVIDUAL COWBOY RECORDS
Rushing

Most Yards Game:	206	Tony Dorsett, vs Philadelphia, 1978
Season:	1,646	Tony Dorsett, 1981
Career:	12,036	Tony Dorsett, 1977-87

Passing

Most TD Passes Game:	5	Eddie LeBaron, vs Pittsburgh, 1962
	5	Don Meredith, vs N.Y. Giants, 1966
	5	Don Meredith, vs Philadelphia, 1966
	5	Don Meredith, vs Philadelphia, 1968
	5	Craig Morton, vs Philadelphia, 1969
	5	Craig Morton, vs Houston, 1970
	5	Danny White, vs N.Y. Giants, 1983
Season:	29	Danny White, 1983
Career:	154	Danny White, 1976-87

Receiving

Most TD Passes Game:	4	Bob Hayes, vs Houston, 1970
Season:	14	Frank Clarke, 1962
Career:	71	Bob Hayes, 1965-74

Scoring

Most Points Game:	24	Dan Reeves, vs Atlanta, 1967
	24	Bob Hayes, vs Houston, 1970
	24	Calvin Hill, vs Buffalo, 1971
	24	Duane Thomas, vs St. Louis, 1971
Season:	123	Rafael Septien, 1983
Career:	874	Rafael Septien, 1978-86
Most TDs Game:	4	Dan Reeves, vs Atlanta, 1967
	4	Bob Hayes, vs Houston, 1970
	4	Calvin Hill, vs Buffalo, 1971
	4	Duane Thomas, vs St. Louis, 1971
Season:	16	Dan Reeves, 1966
Career:	86	Tony Dorsett, 1977-87

DETROIT LIONS

TEAM DIRECTORY: Pres.: William Clay Ford; Exec. VP/GM: Russ Thomas; Dir. Football Operations/Head Coach: Darryl Rogers; Dir. Pub. Rel.: Bill Keenist. Home field: Pontiac Silverdome (80,638). Colors: Honolulu blue and silver.

SCOUTING REPORT

OFFENSE: Chuck Long needs more receiving help and he didn't have a consistent offensive line or healthy running backs to work with, but he stamped himself as the team's answer at quarterback. He had a 55.8 completion percentage (232 for 416).

James Jones (342 yards on 96 carries and 262 yards receiving) didn't score a touchdown and was the team's leading rusher as Garry James (270 yards on 82 carries) missed seven games with injuries. That's one of the many reasons Darryl Rogers' team was 4-11 and tied for last place with Tampa Bay in the Central Division.

Harvey Salem and Lomas Brown were solid on the offensive line and Kevin Glover could fill a need if he starts at center.

Wide receiver Pete Mandley, voted the team's MVP, was fifth in the NFC in pass receiving (58 catches for 720 yards), but a priority is finding another wide receiver as well as a productive tight end.

DEFENSE: Except for outside linebacker, there are many gaps. The defensive backfield is probably the greatest need, where top pick Bennie Blades of Miami is a natural at free safety but could play and excel anywhere. Devon Mitchell will help out if he can return from a knee injury that sidelined him the entire 1987 season. Free safety Raphel Cherry came on at the end of the season and this could be the year he shows the talents the Redskins thought he had when they started him as a rookie in 1985.

Linebacker could be one of the strongest positions on the team if another Dennis Gibson can come along to play inside. Gibson was an eighth-round draft choice in '87 and again should start inside. The Lions are tough at outside linebacker with Jimmy Williams and Michael Cofer.

Up front, they'll be counting on their top two picks in 1987—nose tackle Jerry Ball and end Reggie Rogers—to keep improving.

KICKING GAME: If the other units were as dependable as the kicking game, the Lions might be pressing the top teams in the

Chuck looks forward to Long future as a Lion.

NFC Central. Jim Arnold broke Reggie Roby's NFL record for net average with 39.6 yards a punt while making the Pro Bowl. Kicker Eddie Murray didn't have his best season, but he finished strong by making 11 of his last 14 field goals.

THE ROOKIES: Blades is an outstanding coverage man and led the nation in interceptions his junior year. Middle linebacker Chris Spielman of Ohio State, a No. 2 pick, is a little short at 6-0 but has great lateral quickness and may be a starter. Another second-rounder, Pat Carter of Florida State, is a bruising blocker at tight end. No. 3 choice Ray Roundtree of Penn State has potential at wide receiver.

OUTLOOK: If the Long-led offense can stay healthy and if the young hopefuls mature on defense and if—well, a lot of ifs—the

LIONS VETERAN ROSTER

HEAD COACH—Darryl Rogers. Assistant Coaches—Bob Baker, Carl Battershell, Lew Carpenter, Don Doll, Wayne Fontes, Bill Muir, Mike Murphy, Rex Norris, Vic Rapp, Willie Shaw.

No.	Name	Pos.	Ht.	Wt.	NFL Exp.	College
6	Arnold, Jim	P	6-3	211	6	Vanderbilt
68	Baack, Steve	G	6-4	265	5	Oregon
93	Ball, Jerry	NT	6-1	283	2	Southern Methodist
61	Barrows, Scott	G-C	6-2	278	3	West Virginia
—	Benson, Charles	DE	6-1	267	4	Baylor
25	Bernard, Karl	RB	5-11	205	2	Southwest Louisiana
80	Bland, Carl	WR	5-11	182	5	Virginia Union
75	Brown, Lomas	T	6-4	282	4	Florida
96	Butcher, Paul	LB	6-0	219	3	Wayne State
—	Carr, Carl	LB	6-3	230	2	North Carolina
89	Chadwick, Jeff	WR	6-3	190	6	Grand Valley State
45	Cherry, Raphel	S	6-0	194	3	Hawaii
55	Cofer, Michael	LB	6-5	245	6	Tennessee
—	Davis, Jerome	NT	6-1	260	2	Ball State
70	Dorney, Keith	G-T	6-5	285	10	Penn State
42	Ellerson, Gary	RB-KR	5-11	220	4	Wisconsin
77	Ferguson, Keith	DE	6-5	260	8	Ohio State
40	Galloway, Duane	CB-S	5-8	181	3	Arizona State
98	Gibson, Dennis	LB	6-2	240	2	Iowa State
53	Glover, Kevin	C-G	6-2	267	4	Maryland
62	Green, Curtis	DE-NT	6-3	265	8	Alabama State
34	Griffin, James	S	6-2	197	6	Middle Tenn. State
17	Hipple, Eric	QB	6-2	198	8	Utah State
32	James, Garry	RB	5-10	214	3	Louisiana State
95	Jamison, George	LB	6-1	226	2	Cincinnati
—	Johnson, Earl	CB	6-0	190	2	South Carolina
30	Jones, James	RB	6-2	229	6	Florida
87	Kab, Vyto	TE	6-5	240	6	Penn State
83	Lee, Gary	WR-KR	6-1	202	2	Georgia Tech
81	Lewis, Mark	TE	6-2	250	3	Texas A&M
50	Lockett, Danny	LB	6-2	228	2	Arizona
16	Long, Chuck	QB	6-4	211	3	Iowa
82	Mandley, Pete	WR-KR	5-10	191	5	Northern Arizona
57	Maxwell, Vernon	LB	6-2	235	6	Arizona State
—	McDuffie, George	DE	6-6	270	2	Findlay
29	McNorton, Bruce	CB	5-11	175	7	Georgetown (Ky.)
74	Milinichik, Joe	G-T	6-5	275	2	North Carolina State
31	Mitchell, Devon	S	6-1	194	2	Iowa
52	Mott, Steve	C	6-3	270	6	Alabama
3	Murray, Ed	K	5-10	175	9	Tulane
86	Nichols, Mark	WR	6-2	208	7	San Jose State
49	Paige, Tony	RB	5-10	230	5	Virginia Tech
51	Robinson, Shelton	LB	6-2	236	7	North Carolina
60	Rogers, Reggie	DE	6-6	272	2	Washington
84	Rubick, Rob	TE	6-3	234	7	Grand Valley State
97	Saleaumua, Dan	NT	6-0	285	2	Arizona State
73	Salem, Harvey	G	6-6	285	6	California
64	Sanders, Eric	T-G	6-7	280	8	Nevada-Reno
28	Sheffield, Chris	CB	6-1	200	3	Albany State
41	Smith, Ricky	WR-CB	6-0	188	5	Alabama State
—	Thompson, Robert	LB	6-3	225	4	Michigan
27	Watkins, Bobby	CB	5-10	184	7	SW Texas State
—	Wester, Cleve	RB	5-8	188	2	Concordia (Neb.)
—	Wheeler, Mark	TE	6-2	232	2	Kentucky
76	Williams, Eric	NT	6-4	280	5	Washington State
59	Williams, Jimmy	LB	6-3	230	7	Nebraska
38	Williams, Scott	RB	6-2	234	3	Georgia
21	Woolfolk, Butch	RB	6-1	212	7	Michigan

TOP DRAFT CHOICES

Rd.	Name	Sel. No.	Pos.	Ht.	Wt.	College
1	Blades, Bennie	3	S	6-1	213	Miami
2	Spielman, Chris	29	LB	6-0	234	Ohio State
2	Carter, Pat	32	TE	6-4	260	Florida State
3	Roundtree, Ray	58	WR	6-0	180	Penn State
4	White, William	85	DB	5-10	189	Ohio State
5	Andolsek, Eric	111	G	6-2	281	LSU

Lions might have a shot at third as the Bears and Vikings fight it out for No. 1 in the division.

LION PROFILES

CHUCK LONG 25 6-4 211   Quarterback

Took every offensive snap during the 12 non-strike games . . . Led team in minutes played . . . Threw 416 passes, second-highest single-season number in team history. Completed 232, third-highest . . . Of 20 interceptions, three were Hail Mary passes and four others were tipped . . . Sacked only 17 times in 12 games . . . Threw for 362 yards in 34-33 loss to Green Bay. Hall of Famer Bobby Layne was only Lions' quarterback to throw for more yards in a single game—374 against Chicago in 1950 and 364 against Pittsburgh in 1953 . . . The former Iowa star gained valuable experience last year and should improve . . . Eric Hipple, who missed the entire season after breaking his right thumb in training camp, will be the backup . . . Judging from last season, Lions made right choice when they tagged Long as their first, first-round quarterback since 1968 . . . He was the Heisman Trophy runnerup to Auburn's Bo Jackson in 1985 . . . Born Feb. 18, 1963, in Norman, Okla.

JAMES JONES 27 6-2 229   Running Back

Perhaps being a player rep during a strike season was a factor in his below-par performance, but his 342 yards on 96 carries was enough to lead the Lions . . . He's considered by his coaches as one of the most underrated full-backs in the league . . . Caught 34 passes for 262 yards . . . Missed one game and most of two others because of neck injury . . . Missed running mate Garry James, who was sidelined for seven games because of rib and shoulder injuries . . . First-round draft choice out of Florida in 1983, the 13th player selected overall . . . One of the most physical runners in the league . . . "He's the toughest to tackle," claims Dallas defensive back Michael Downs . . . Born March 21, 1961, in Pompano Beach, Fla.

PETE MANDLEY 27 5-19 191   Wide Receiver

Team's Most Valuable Player on offense... Pro Bowl alternate... His seven touchdown receptions were most in a season by a Detroit receiver since 1968... His 58 catches were the sixth-highest in team history... Scheduled to earn $242,000 base salary in last year of contract... Ranks fourth in team history in both career punt returns (106) and career punt return yardage (1,703)... "He has good hands, good speed, and the ability to make the first guy miss," said special teams coach Carl Battershell... Would have returned a punt for a touchdown for third consecutive season if 73-yarder versus Minnesota had not been nullified because of penalty... Attended same high school as Dallas quarterback Danny White (Westwood High in Mesa, Ariz.)... Second-round draft choice out of Northern Arizona in 1984... Born July 29, 1961, in Mesa, Ariz.

LOMAS BROWN 25 6-4 282   Tackle

Might have made Pro Bowl if he was on a winning team... Leader of offensive line that allowed only 17 sacks in 12 games... In his third season he missed one game and most of two others because of knee injury... Started every game his first two seasons... Played well against some of the best defensive ends in the league, including Washington's Dexter Manley... "The expectations we had when we drafted Lomas have been fulfilled and then some," said offensive line coach Bill Muir.... First-round 1985 draft choice out of Florida, where he was a two-time All-American... Cousin of 49ers' Guy McIntyre ... Born March 30, 1963, in Miami, Fla.

DENNIS GIBSON 24 6-2 240   Linebacker

Could be considered the best choice of the 1987 draft. An eighth-rounder out of Iowa State, he moved inside and became first rookie to lead Lions in tackles (90) in recorded team history... Started every game... Although he played outside for Iowa State, Lions projected him as an inside backer. "He's a big, smart player," said director of player personnel Joe Bushofsky... Voted Iowa State's Most Valuable Player as a senior... Played in Blue-Gray and Senior Bowl games... Engineering major... Has a 35-inch vertical jump... Born Feb. 2, 1964, in Ankeny, Iowa.

GARRY JAMES 24 5-10 214   Running Back

Moved to Detroit in offseason for first time since he joined team in 1986 . . . Coaches hope offseason weight program will help decrease injuries that have hampered him past two seasons . . . Very dangerous when healthy . . . Led team with four rushing touchdowns despite missing seven games because of rib and shoulder injuries . . . Carried 82 times for 270 yards . . . Outside threat and good receiver . . . Fourth-most productive career rusher at LSU . . . A second-round draft pick in 1986 . . . Finished second behind Reuben Mayes in rushing yardage among rookie running backs in '86 . . . Will earn $215,000 this season . . . Born Sept. 4, 1963, in Gretna, La.

JIMMY WILLIAMS 27 6-3 230   Linebacker

Most Valuable Player on the Lions' defense . . . Finished second on team with 69 tackles . . . Signed a three-year contract after settling on a one-year agreement before 1986 and performed like a happy player. Will earn $325,000 in base salary this season . . . Coaches said he should have made the Pro Bowl. They compare him to the Giants' Carl Banks . . . Exceptional against run; improved against the pass . . . Leader of linebacker corps that could emerge this season as one of league's best . . . Brother Toby starts for the Patriots . . . Both made Nebraska team as walk-ons . . . They're two of eight children . . . Born Nov, 15, 1960, in Washington, D.C. . . . A graduate of Washington's Woodrow Wilson High, he didn't receive a single scholarship offer from a major university.

RAPHEL CHERRY 26 6-0 194   Safety

Signed during strike, he started last 10 nonstrike games and finished as team's sixth-leading tackler . . . Can apply bone-crushing hits . . . Drafted in fifth round out of Hawaii by the Redskins in 1985 and was starting by end of rookie season . . . Fell off in performance the following summer and was released . . . Signed with 49ers in December 1986, but never got to play . . . Born Dec. 19, 1961, in Little Rock, Ark. . . . Is a cousin of Kansas City's Deron Cherry . . . Was a first-round pick (No. 6) of the Houston Gamblers in the 1985 USFL draft.

MICHAEL COFER 28 6-5 245   Linebacker

Turn-'em-loose type of player. Led team in sacks with 8½...Excellent speed. Best athlete on defense...Switched from defensive end after 1984 season and has combined with Jimmy Williams to give Lions two solid outside linebackers..."We expected him to improve, but I think his progress even has surprised us a bit," said defensive coordinator Wayne Fontes. "He can become a dominant linebacker in this league."...Working toward getting his real-estate license...Was an aspiring actor in college...Four-year letterman at Tennessee...Third-round draft choice in 1983...Will earn $260,000 in final year of contract...Born April 7, 1960, in Knoxville, Tenn.

JIM ARNOLD 27 6-3 211   Punter

Team's only Pro Bowl representative...Set NFL record for net average per punt (39.6 yards)...His performance helped Lions' punt team improve significantly over 1986, when opponents returned two punts for touchdowns and blocked another for a score...A fifth-round selection by Kansas City in 1983, he led the league in punting in '84...Signed with Lions as a free agent late in 1986...Led the nation in punting his senior year at Vanderbilt...Born Jan 31, 1961, in Dalton, Ga.

COACH DARRYL ROGERS: Survived his third season amid

speculation that he would be fired...Finished 4-11 to bring three-year total to 16-31...Had to overcome several obstacles including the 24-day players strike and the lingering uncertainty of his job status. "There were a number of distractions that hurt our continuity and consequently our ability to succeed," he said. "I think the players' strike hurt us as much, if not more, than any other football team."...Team won two of last three games after owner William Clay Ford assured players their coach would not be fired...Detroit's 16th head coach...Named Big Ten Coach of the Year in 1977 after leading probation-saddled Michigan State to 7-3-1 record...Served 20 years as a coach at Hayward (1965), Fresno State (1966-73), San Jose State (1973-76), Michigan State (1976-80) and Arizona State

(1980-85). Compiled 129-84-7 record over that span...Born May 28, 1935, in Los Angeles...Was a leading passer at Fresno State...Served in the Marine Corps.

LONGEST PLAY

The Lions were out of it in their Oct. 16, 1966, game against the Colts. They trailed, 38-7, with 10:04 remaining in the game. After a Baltimore kickoff they were on their own one. On first down, quarterback Karl Sweetan, who had replaced Milt Plum, hit Pat Studstill at the Lions' 45 and he romped for the score.

You can't make 'em any longer than that. The 99-yard pass play is an NFL record, achieved six times in NFL history.

The Colts wound up winning, 45-14. Sweetan only completed three other passes in 11 attempts, but he made the record book.

INDIVIDUAL LION RECORDS

Rushing

Most Yards Game:	198	Bob Hoernschemeyer, vs N.Y. Yanks, 1950
Season:	1,437	Billy Sims, 1981
Career:	5,106	Billy Sims, 1980-84

Passing

Most TD Passes Game:	5	Gary Danielson, vs Minnesota, 1978
Season	26	Bobby Layne, 1951
Career:	118	Bobby Layne, 1950-58

Receiving

Most TD Passes Game:	4	Cloyce Box, vs Baltimore, 1950
Season:	15	Cloyce Box, 1952
Career:	35	Terry Barr, 1957-65

Scoring

Most Points Game:	24	Cloyce Box, vs Baltimore, 1950
Season:	128	Doak Walker, 1950
Career:	765	Eddie Murray, 1980-87
Most TDs Game:	4	Cloyce Box, vs Baltimore, 1950
Season:	16	Billy Sims, 1980
Career:	47	Billy Sims, 1980-84

GREEN BAY PACKERS

TEAM DIRECTORY: Chairman: Dominic Olejiniczak; Pres.: Robert Parins; Sec.: Peter Platten III; Exec. VP-Adm.: Bob Harlan; VP-Football Operations: Tom Braatz; Dir. Pub. Rel.: Lee Remmel; Head Coach: Lindy Infante. Home fields: Lambeau Field (56,926) and County Stadium, Milwaukee (55,976). Colors: Green and gold.

SCOUTING REPORT

OFFENSE: New coach Lindy Infante, ex-Browns' offensive co-ordinator, doesn't have a Bernie Kosar in Green Bay. He inherits a team that was 5-9-1, third in the NFC Central, and finished 25th in the NFL in scoring with 255 points.

At quarterback he'll have to choose from veteran Randy Wright and Don Majkowski, a 10th-rounder in '87. Wright completed 132 of 247 (53.4), Majkowski 55 of 127 (43.3). Another outside contender is Robbie Bosco, who missed his first two seasons due to arm trouble.

Running back should be a plus with Ken Davis, the team's leading rusher (413 yards on 109 attempts) and Brent Fullwood, who rushed for 274 yards on 84 carries as a rookie. They alternated at tailback last year, but Infante plans to use Fullwood at fullback.

No. 1 pick Sterling Sharpe of South Carolina beefs up the smallish, but speedy receiver corps of Walter Stanley and Phil Epps. The Packers, though, could use additional help at tight end, where five-year pro Ed West had his best season.

The offensive line is solid with returning starters Ken Ruettgers, Keith Uecker, Rich Moran, Ron Hallstrom and Mark Cannon.

DEFENSE: Only four teams in the NFC gave up fewer points than the Packers. They ranked 18th in the league against the rush, but finished fourth in the NFC in takeaways.

Returning starters on the defensive line are Alphonso Carreker, Robert Brown and Jerry Boyarsky. Ex-Bengal Ross Browner contributed at end and tackle last season.

The linebackers are led by Tim Harris, a linebacker-defensive end who emerged as a team leader; Brian Noble, John Anderson and Johnny Holland, voted the Pack's Rookie of the Year.

Veteran Dave Brown showed he still had it at 35 as a cornerback and strong safety Mark Murphy returned to his old form after a leg fracture.

Ken Davis topped Pack in rushing, but it's not enough.

KICKING GAME: Punter Don Bracken finished ninth in the league with a 40.9-yard average and Max Zendejas kicked 16 field goals in 19 attempts.

THE ROOKIES: Sharpe caught 130 passes for 1,968 yards his last two collegiate seasons as a Gamecock and is also a solid return man. The Pack added muscle on the defensive line with No. 2 pick Shawn Patterson of Arizona State and No. 4 pick Rollin Putzier of Oregon, both tackles. Third-rounder Keith Woodside of Texas A&M is an elusive runner and impressive pass-catcher coming out of the backfield.

PACKERS VETERAN ROSTER

HEAD COACH—Lindy Infante. Assistant Coaches—Hank Bullough, Greg Blache, Charlie Davis, Buddy Geis, Dick Jauron, Virgil Knight, Dick Moseley, Willie Peete, Howard Tippett.

No.	Name	Pos.	Ht.	Wt.	NFL Exp.	College
59	Anderson, John	LB	6-3	228	11	Michigan
61	Boyarsky, Jerry	NT	6-3	290	8	Pittsburgh
17	Bracken, Don	P	6-0	211	4	Michigan
32	Brown, David	CB	6-1	197	14	Michigan
93	Brown, Robert	DE	6-2	267	7	Virginia Tech
79	Browner, Ross	DE	6-3	265	11	Notre Dame
58	Cannon, Mark	C	6-3	258	5	Texas-Arlington
76	Carreker, Alphonso	DE	6-6	271	5	Florida State
30	Carruth, Paul Ott	RB	6-1	220	3	Alabama
69	Cherry, Bill	C-G	6-4	277	3	Middle Tenn. State
33	Clark, Jessie	RB	6-0	228	6	Arkansas
64	Collier, Steve	T	6-7	342	2	Bethune-Cookman
20	Cook, Kelly	RB	5-10	225	2	Oklahoma State
36	Davis, Kenneth	RB	5-10	209	3	Texas Christian
56	Dent, Burnett	LB	6-1	236	3	Tulane
99	Dorsey, John	LB	6-2	243	5	Connecticut
85	Epps, Phillip	WR	5-9½	165	7	Texas Christian
21	Fullwood, Brent	RB	5-11	209	2	Auburn
23	Green, George	CB-S	6-0	194	4	Western Carolina
89	Hackett, Joey	TE	6-5	267	3	Elon College
65	Hallstrom, Ron	G	6-6	290	7	Iowa
97	Harris, Tim	LB	6-6	245	3	Memphis State
50	Holland, Johnny	LB	6-2	221	2	Texas A&M
38	Jefferson, Norman	CB-S	5-10	183	2	Louisiana State
39	Johnson, Kenneth	CB	6-0	185	2	Mississippi State
22	Lee, Mark	CB-S	5-11	189	9	Washington
7	Majkowski, Don	QB	6-2	197	2	Virginia
44	Mandeville, Chris	S	6-1	213	2	California-Davis
98	Moore, Brent	LB	6-5	242	2	Southern California
57	Moran, Rich	C-G	6-2	275	4	San Diego State
47	Morris, Jim Bob	CB-S	6-3	211	2	Kansas State
81	Morris, Lee	WR	5-10	180	2	Oklahoma
37	Murphy, Mark	S	6-2	201	7	West Liberty
80	Neal, Frankie	WR	6-1	202	2	Fort Hays State
72	Neville, Tom	T-G	6-5	306	3	Fresno State
91	Noble, Brian	LB	6-4	250	4	Arizona State
82	Paskett, Keith	WR	5-11	180	2	Western Kentucky
77	Robison, Tommy	G	6-4	290	2	Texas A&M
75	Ruettgers, Ken	T	6-5	285	4	Southern California
83	Scott, Patrick	WR	5-10	170	2	Grambling
87	Stanley, Walter	WR-KR	5-9	179	4	Mesa College (Colo.)
54	Stephen, Scott	LB	6-2	232	2	Arizona State
29	Stills, Ken	CB-S	5-10	186	4	Wisconsin
48	Summers, Don	TE	6-4	235	3	Boise State
92	Thomas, Ben	DE-NT	6-4	275	3	Auburn
70	Uecker, Keith	G-T	6-5	284	6	Auburn
73	Veingrad, Alan	T-G	6-5	277	3	East Texas State
28	Watts, Elbert	CB	6-1	205	2	Southern California
52	Weddington, Mike	LB	6-4	245	3	Oklahoma
51	Weisnuhn, Clayton	LB	6-1	218	5	Angelo State
86	West, Ed	TE	6-1	243	5	Auburn
35	Willhite, Kevin	RB	5-11	208	2	Oregon
—	Winter, Blaise	NT	6-3	274	4	Syracuse
16	Wright, Randy	QB	6-2	203	5	Wisconsin
8	Zendejas, Max	K	5-11	184	3	Arizona

TOP DRAFT CHOICES

Rd.	Name	Sel. No.	Pos.	Ht.	Wt.	College
1	Sharpe, Sterling	7	WR	5-11	196	South Carolina
2	Patterson, Shawn	34	DT	6-5	263	Arizona State
3	Woodside, Keith	61	RB	5-11	204	Texas A&M
4	Putzier, Rollin	88	DT	6-4	283	Oregon
4	Cecil, Chuck	89	DB	6-0	184	Arizona
5	Reed, Darrell	116	LB	6-1	220	Oklahoma

OUTLOOK: Infante acknowledges in his first year as a head coach that the key concern revolves around quarterback. There'll be no easy solution. "I think that, hopefully, we're not as far away as some people think we are," he said. But it won't happen overnight.

PACKER PROFILES

TIM HARRIS 23 6-6 245   Linebacker

Closest player to a dominant linebacker the Pack has had since Ted Hendricks left in 1974 ...Led team in sacks (7) for second straight year... Talkative, exuberant, sometimes more vocal on the field than coaches would like... Entering third season, the towering Memphis State product should press for All-Pro honors ...Named team's Rookie of the Year in '86 ...Enters final year of four-year contract and is scheduled to earn a base of $130,000... Born Sept. 10, 1964, in Birmingham, Ala.... Was a fourth-round Packer pick in 1986 draft.

KENNETH DAVIS 26 5-10 209   Running Back

This Lone Star turned into a shining star last season... A second-round choice out of Texas Christian in 1986, Davis led team in rushing (413 yards) for the second year in a row but played much better than he did as a rookie... Admitted he was confused at times in passing game his first season but adopted well as a sophomore... Good quickness and open-field speed... Lists professional pool champions Willie Mosconi and Minnesota Fats as his sports heroes and hopes to follow their leads after his football career is over... Born April 16, 1962, in Temple, Tex.

PHILLIP EPPS 29 5-9½ 165   Wide Receiver

Hurdled John Jefferson and Eddie Lee Ivory to become 10th-ranked receiver in team history ...Made 40 catches for 516 yards despite missing three games because of the strike and 2½ more because of an abdominal muscle pull... Hampered with injuries last two years. Broken ankle forced him to sit out last four games in '86 ... Still, after six seasons, one of fastest receivers in the league . . . Off the field, very quiet, spends a lot of time with his family . . . Spends offseason working as sales representative for an automobile dealer . . . Became free agent at the end of last season. Made base salary of $295,000 in '87 . . . Born Nov. 11, 1958, in Fort Worth, Tex.

RANDY WRIGHT 27 6-2 203   Quarterback

Not certain what '88 will hold for this four-year veteran . . . First-year coach Lindy Infante has acknowledged that quarterback is a problem area . . . He is looking for better play than team received from either Wright or Don Majkowski last season . . . Rating of 61.6 was last among NFC starters . . . Completed 132 of 247 for 1,507 yards. Threw for six touchdowns and 11 interceptions . . . First-string personality. Reportedly plays piano for his dog at night to lull him to sleep . . . Sixth-round draft choice out of Wisconsin in 1984, where he led Badgers to assorted offensive marks . . . He was MVP in the Blue-Gray game . . . Born Jan. 12, 1961, in Austin, Tex.

RON HALLSTROM 29 6-6 290   Guard

Improvement off last season could earn him a trip to Hawaii this January . . . Coming off most consistent season in six-year career. Only allowed one-half of a quarterback sack in 12 games . . . A first-round choice out of Iowa in 1982, he broke his nose as a rookie and took a while to adjust to the pros . . . In '86, he was voted offensive captain and later admitted that he might have worried too much about the team and not enough about his own performance . . . Became All-Big Ten as an offensive lineman at Iowa after spending his freshman year as a defensive tackle at Iowa Central Junior College . . . Born June 11, 1959, in Holden, Mass., but grew up in Moline, Ill., where he still makes his home.

BRENT FULLWOOD 24 5-11 209   Running Back

Can provide all the electricity any backfield needs but he suffered a pulled hamstring in the second game of his rookie season and from there on he and coach Forrest Gregg seemed to cross wires . . . Wasn't in as good playing shape as Gregg would have liked . . . Carried only 84 times for 274 yards, not quite what the Pack expected when they drafted him in the first round (No. 4) out of Auburn . . . Shared time at tailback with Kenneth Davis but could move to fullback this season . . . Will be featured on return teams . . . Finished fifth in NFC in kickoff returns and can do much better . . . Should emerge this season as an explosive power runner and hopes to remind Packer fans of his most admired athlete, Tony Dorsett . . . Born Oct. 10, 1963, in Kissimmee, Fla.

BRIAN NOBLE 25 6-4 250　　　　　　　　Linebacker

Moved into a new level of performance last season, upgrading mental part of his game . . . Stepped into leadership role on defense while leading team in tackles for second straight year . . . Has Pro Bowl potential . . . Was voted team's Rookie of the Year in '85 . . . A fifth-rounder out of Arizona State . . . Won junior college All-American honors at Fullerton (Cal.) JC . . . Born Sept. 6, 1962, in Anaheim, Cal. . . . He played defensive end and also punted in high school . . . Works as sales manager in his father's plating business in offseason.

MARK MURPHY 30 6-2 201　　　　　　　Strong Safety

Green Bay's Comeback Player of the Year . . . Turned in successful season after sitting out '86 because of a stress fracture in his left foot . . . Regained starting job and added stability to safety spot . . . Hard hitter . . . Intelligent . . . Doesn't make the killing mental mistake . . . The investment was minimal for the Packers, who signed him in 1980 as a free agent out of West Liberty State in Pennsylvania . . . Born April 22, 1958, in Canton, Ohio, once home of the famous Canton Bulldogs and now site of the Pro Football Hall of Fame.

KEN RUETTGERS 26 6-5 285　　　　　　　　Tackle

He could write a book—and does. It includes scouting reports on every defensive end he has faced or seen on film . . . He notes their strengths, favorite moves and anything else he can come up with . . . It works becsuse he has become one of the NFL's premier offensive tackles . . . The three-year veteran out of USC is only the second lineman in team history to be voted MVP of the offense. The other was Ken Bowman in 1971 . . . Selected in first round (No. 7) of 1985 draft after co-captaining the Trojans as a senior and playing in Japan Bowl . . .

Born Aug. 20, 1962, in Bakersfield, Cal., where, in addition to football, he played basketball, threw the shot and discus and was a member of the golf team . . . Will earn $280,000 base salary in final year of contract.

DAVID BROWN 35 6-1 197   Cornerback

Signed as a free agent after 11 years as a mainstay in Seattle, he proved himself anew as a leader in the secondary . . . His knowledge and experience made up for any lost speed . . . Shared lead in interceptions with three . . . He's the active career leader in the NFL with 53 interceptions . . . When he left Seattle he ranked second on the Seahawks in games played (159) and games started (159), trailing Steve Largent in each category . . . Was a first-round Steeler pick out of the University of Michigan in 1975 and joined the Seahawks in the expansion draft in '76 . . . Named to Michigan's all-time team for second 50 years of Wolverine football in 1983 . . . Born Jan. 16, 1953, in Akron, Ohio.

LINDY INFANTE: Offensive coordinator for the Browns the

past two seasons, Infante was named to succeed Forrest Gregg last February after Gregg accepted the head coaching job at SMU . . . Under Infante's direction, Browns' offense was ranked ninth in the league last season, averaging 26 points per game during the regular season and 35.5 points in the AFC playoffs . . . Helped develop quarterback Bernie Kosar into one of the league's premier passers . . . Expected to groom a quarterback for the future . . . Served two years as head coach of the Jacksonville Bulls of the USFL before joining the Browns in 1986 . . . Served as quarterback/receivers coach for the Bengals two years before that . . . Began coaching career in 1965 at Miami Senior High School, then moved to the University of Florida in 1966 as freshman team coach . . . Coached Gator offensive backs from 1967-71 . . . Served as Memphis State offensive coordinator 1972-73, quarterback coach of Charlotte Hornets (World Football League) in 1975 and offensive coordinator at Tulane in 1976 . . . Joined New York Giants' offensive staff in 1977 . . . An All-Southeastern Conference defensive back at the Florida, he was drafted in 12th round by Browns in 1963 but opted to play for Hamilton in the Canadian Football League . . . Born May 27, 1940, in Miami.

LONGEST PLAY

The Packers were well on their way to victory over the Los Angeles Rams on Nov. 18, 1984, in Milwaukee. They led, 24-6, with 4½ minutes remaining in the game.

The Rams' Jeff Kemp had thrown three consecutive incompletions from the Packers' 16. He tried once more and this time he connected—with the Packers' Tim Lewis on the one—and Lewis ran 99 yards for the team's longest interception return. It highlighted Green Bay's 31-6 triumph.

INDIVIDUAL PACKER RECORDS

Rushing

Most Yards Game:	186	Jim Taylor, vs N.Y. Giants, 1961
Season:	1,474	Jim Taylor, 1962
Career:	8,207	Jim Taylor, 1958-66

Passing

Most TD Passes Game:	5	Cecil Isbell, vs Cleveland, 1942
	5	Don Horn, vs St. Louis, 1969
	5	Lynn Dickey, vs New Orleans, 1981
	5	Lynn Dickey, vs Houston, 1983
Season:	32	Lynn Dickey, 1983
Career:	152	Bart Starr, 1956-71

Receiving

Most TD Passes Game:	4	Don Hutson, vs Detroit, 1945
Season:	17	Don Hutson, 1943
Career:	99	Don Hutson, 1935-45

Scoring

Most Points Game:	33	Paul Hornung, vs Baltimore, 1961
Season:	176	Paul Hornung, 1960
Career:	823	Don Hutson, 1935-45
Most TDs Game:	5	Paul Hornung, vs Baltimore, 1961
Season:	19	Jim Taylor, 1962
Career:	105	Don Hutson, 1935-45

LOS ANGELES RAMS

TEAM DIRECTORY: Pres.: Georgia Frontiere; VP-Finance: John Shaw; Dir. Operations: Dick Beam; Adm. Football Operations: Jack Faulkner; Dir. Player Personnel: John Math; Dir. Marketing: Pete Donovan; Dir. Pub. Rel.: John Oswald; Head Coach: John Robinson. Home field: Anaheim Stadium (69,007). Colors: Royal blue, gold and white.

SCOUTING REPORT

OFFENSE: Offensive coordinator Ernie Zampese has had a full season to implement his system and he and head coach John Robinson plan to maximize the talent of coming-of-age quarterback Jim Everett after a 6-9 season.

Only the Saints and Seahawks threw less times last season,

Charles White soared to No. 1 in NFL rushing.

and only the Steelers had a less effective passing game. But that should change this season as Everett is turned loose and picks up where he left off late last season when he was hurt in the Dallas game.

With the Rams expected to expand their passing game, Everett (162 for 302 in '87) will have prime targets in wide receiver Henry Ellard, tight end Damone Johnson and perhaps another tight end being sought.

Robinson is counting on another big season from Charles White, the NFL's leading rusher last year with 1,374 yards, 86 more than runnerup Eric Dickerson, the ex-Ram gone to Indianapolis. The Rams need more depth at running back and a good start in that direction is the arrival of No. 1 pick Gaston Green, an explosive threat from UCLA.

The line, one of the league's strongest, is getting older. Dennis Harrah, one of three Pro Bowlers, retired and the other two, Jackie Slater and Doug Smith, are in their 30s.

DEFENSE: The Rams' takeaway total of 27 tied them for 27th in the league, one reason help is needed. And the secondary has its questions because of the unhappiness of cornerback LeRoy Irvin and the uncertain status of safeties Nolan Cromwell and Johnnie Johnson. The team finished 21st in the NFL in total defense, 26th against the pass.

The team is strongest at outside linebacker with Mel Owens, Mike Wilcher and Kevin Greene. Inside depends on how Mark Jerue comes back from knee surgery. And defensive end Shawn Miller is returning from a knee injury.

Vince Newsome, a healthy Johnson and Michael Stewart figure at safety and Pro Bowler Jerry Gray is solid at cornerback.

KICKING GAME: No problems here. Mike Lansford had his best season, clicking on 17 of 21 field-goal attempts and leading the team in scoring with 87 points. Punter Dale Hatcher finished seventh in the league with a 41.3-yard average. Ellard is always a threat on punt returns.

THE ROOKIES: With five picks in the first two rounds, the Rams filled several needs in the draft. Green, UCLA's all-time rusher, is a breakaway runner who's expected to split time in the backfield with White. LA shored up its passing game by selecting wide receivers Aaron Cox (Arizona State) and Willie Anderson (UCLA) on the first and second rounds. The Rams used the other two second-round picks for defense, taking safety Anthony Newman (Oregon) and linebacker Fred Strickland (Purdue).

RAMS VETERAN ROSTER

HEAD COACH—John Robinson. Assistant Coaches—Dick Coury, Artie Gigantino, Marv Goux, Gil Haskell, Hudson Houck, Steve Shafer, Fritz Shurmur, Norval Turner, Fred Whittingham, Ernie Zampese.

No.	Name	Pos.	Ht.	Wt.	NFL Exp.	College
31	Adams, David	RB	5-6	170	2	Arizona
84	Baty, Greg	TE	6-5	241	3	Stanford
42	Bell, Greg	RB	5-10	210	5	Notre Dame
92	Brown, Richard	LB	6-3	240	2	San Diego State
50	Collins, Jim	LB	6-2	230	7	Syracuse
72	Cox, Robert	T	6-5	258	2	UCLA
21	Cromwell, Nolan	S	6-1	200	12	Kansas
8	Dils, Steve	QB	6-1	191	10	Stanford
55	Ekern, Carl	LB	6-3	222	12	San Jose State
80	Ellard, Henry	WR	5-11	175	6	Fresno State
11	Everett, Jim	QB	6-5	217	3	Purdue
35	Francis, Jon	RB	5-11	207	2	Boise State
19	Gaynor, Doug	QB	6-2	205	2	Long Beach State
25	Gray, Jerry	CB	6-0	185	4	Texas
91	Greene, Kevin	LB	6-3	238	4	Auburn
44	Guman, Mike	RB	6-2	218	9	Penn State
5	Hatcher, Dale	P	6-2	200	4	Clemson
38	Heimuli, Lakei	RB	5-11	219	2	Brigham Young
28	Hicks, Cliff	CB	5-10	188	2	Oregon
83	House, Kevin	WR	6-1	185	9	Southern Illinois
47	Irvin, LeRoy	CB	5-11	184	9	Kansas
59	Jerue, Mark	LB	6-3	232	6	Washington
77	Jeter, Gary	DE	6-4	260	12	Southern California
86	Johnson, Damone	TE	6-4	232	3	Cal Poly-SLO
20	Johnson, Johnnie	S	6-1	183	9	Texas
52	Keim, Larry	LB	6-4	226	2	Texas A&M
1	Lansford, Mike	K	6-0	190	7	Washington
67	Love, Duval	G	6-3	263	4	UCLA
90	McDonald, Mike	LB	6-1	235	4	Southern California
24	McGee, Buford	RB	6-0	206	5	Mississippi
69	Meisner, Greg	NT	6-3	253	8	Pittsburgh
12	Millen, Hugh	QB	6-5	216	2	Washington
98	Miller, Shawn	NT	6-4	255	4	Utah State
45	Moore, Malcolm	TE	6-3	236	2	Southern California
66	Newberry, Tom	G	6-2	279	3	Wisconsin-LaCrosse
22	Newsome, Vince	S	6-1	179	6	Washington
58	Owens, Mel	LB	6-2	235	8	Michigan
75	Pankey, Irv	T	6-4	267	9	Penn State
9	Quarles, Bernard	QB	6-2	215	2	Hawaii
93	Reed, Doug	DE	6-3	262	5	San Diego State
63	Shields, Jon	G	6-5	285	2	Portland State
78	Slater, Jackie	T	6-4	271	13	Jackson State
61	Slaton, Tony	C	6-3	265	4	Southern California
56	Smith, Doug	C	6-3	260	11	Bowling Green
23	Stewart, Michael	S	5-11	195	2	Fresno State
65	Stokes, Fred	DE	6-3	262	2	Georgia Southern
49	Sutton, Mickey	CB	5-8	165	3	Montana
70	Teafatiller, Guy	NT	6-2	185	2	Illinois
68	Tulasosopo, Navy	C	6-2	285	2	Utah State
32	Tyrrell, Tim	RB	6-1	201	5	Northern Illinois
51	Vann, Norwood	LB	6-1	237	5	East Carolina
73	Walker, Jeff	T	6-4	295	2	Memphis State
41	Wattelet, Frank	S	6-0	190	8	Kansas
33	White, Charles	RB	5-10	195	8	Southern California
54	Wilcher, Mike	LB	6-3	240	6	North Carolina
99	Wright, Alvin	NT	6-2	265	3	Jacksonville State
88	Young, Michael	WR	6-1	185	4	UCLA

TOP DRAFT CHOICES

Rd.	Name	Sel. No.	Pos.	Ht.	Wt.	College
1	Green, Gaston	14	RB	5-10	194	UCLA
1	Cox, Aaron	20	WR	5-9	175	Arizona State
2	Newman, Anthony	35	S	6-0	200	Oregon
2	Anderson, Willie	46	WR	5-11	167	UCLA
2	Strickland, Fred	47	LB	6-2	244	Purdue

OUTLOOK: With Everett and White igniting the offense, it's the defense that poses the problems. And the Rams may need all the points they can get.

RAM PROFILES

JIM EVERETT 25 6-5 217   Quarterback

Still not the quarterback the Rams gave up two players, two first-round draft choices and a fifth-rounder for in 1986, but he improved significantly over rookie season . . . Turned in five solid performances after slow start in first four games . . . Best game came against Detroit, his only 300-yard game of the season. Completed 20 of 26 passes for 324 yards (76.9 percent completion) and two touchdowns . . . Season ended when he chipped a bone in his right ankle during Monday night game against Dallas in Week 14 . . . Apparently has convinced coach John Robinson to alter his run-run-run philosophy this season . . . That became apparent when the team released blocking tight end David Hill . . . . . . Everett's rating (68.4) still ranked near bottom of NFL quarterbacks last season . . . Outstanding career at Purdue . . . First-round selection by Houston in 1986 and traded to the Rams after Oilers couldn't sign him to contract . . . Born Jan. 3, 1963, in Emporia, Kan.

CHARLES WHITE 30 5-10 195   Running Back

He took a lot of heat off the Rams' front office by making people quickly forget about Eric Dickerson . . . Led league in rushing with 1,374 yards on 324 carries, an average of 4.2 yards per carry . . . Had five consecutive 100-yard games during his team's 5-0 winning streak . . . Hard runner who doesn't wear down . . . One of John Robinson's biggest supporters . . . Best game came against St. Louis when he carried 34 times for 213 yards . . . Had seven games over 100 yards . . . Has overcome off-the-field problems and is regarded as reliable contributor . . . Won 1979 Heisman Trophy after legendary career at USC . . . Born Jan. 22, 1958, in Los Angeles . . . A first-round draft pick by Cleveland in 1980 . . . Rams signed him as free agent in 1985.

HENRY ELLARD 27 5-11 175   Wide Receiver

Turned in second-best season of his career despite an early, three-game-long bout of the dropsies... Caught 51 passes for 799 yards, eighth-best in the NFC... Best game came against Detroit with seven catches for 171 yards, including an 81-yard TD... His role could jump to the forefront this season if Rams open up offensive attack, as expected... Legitimate deep threat... Can't stand living in Los Angeles. Spent offseason building dream house in Fresno... Will earn $375,000 this season and next... Entering sixth season. Selected in second round of 1983 draft out of Fresno State... Born July 21, 1961, in Fresno, Cal.

DAMONE JOHNSON 26 6-4 232   Tight End

Came back strong after being injured (knee) most of '86 season... His performance a factor in Rams releasing 12-year veteran David Hill during offseason... Hadn't caught a pass in his pro career prior to Week 6 against Cleveland. Grabbed six for 69 yards... Big, cumbersome, but can run and has good hands... Finished with 21 catches for 198 yards... Started six games as the second tight end... Selected in the sixth round out of Cal Poly-San Luis Obispo... Played wide receiver in college for two seasons before switching to tight end... Nicknamed "D.J."... Earned $110,000 in final year of contract... Born March 2, 1962, in Santa Monica, Cal.

DOUG SMITH 31 6-3 260   Center

Made Pro Bowl for fourth consecutive season... Perhaps with the retirement of guard Dennis Harrah he'll start receiving some of the attention that he has missed in recent years because the Rams have so many good offensive linemen... Remains one of the best in the league even though teams are looking for bigger centers because of increasing number of huge nose tackles... Has started every position on the offensive line except left tackle... Will earn $300,000 this season in final year of contract... Born Nov. 25, 1956, in Columbus, Ohio... Was second-round Oiler draft pick in 1984, but played for USFL's Birmingham Americans before signing with Oilers in October 1985.

JACKIE SLATER 34 6-4 271 Tackle

Became Rams' elder statesmen with 160 games played after Dennis Harrah retired in offseason . . . Leader of one of the best lines in pro football . . . Made Pro Bowl for fifth time, fourth in last six years . . . Named Offensive Lineman of the Year in *USA Today* poll of players . . . An offensive captain . . . Became a starter in 1979 . . . Center Doug Smith and Harrah also made the Pro Bowl . . . Will work this season next to Duval Love, Harrah's replacement . . . Selected in the third round of 1976 out of Jackson State . . . Earned $400,000 in final year of contract . . . Deeply religious. Can quote any scripture out of bible . . . Born May 27, 1954, in Jackson, Miss.

JERRY GRAY 25 6-0 185 Cornerback

Second straight Pro Bowl season in second full season at cornerback . . . Tied for team lead with two interceptions . . . Had 20 passes defensed . . . Could be switched to safety, where he started his career three years ago, depending on the development of Cliff Hicks and the status of disenchanted cornerback LeRoy Irvin . . . First-rounder out of Texas in 1985 moved to corner in second season because of neck injury to Gary Green . . . Led Rams in pass interceptions with eight and finished fourth in the NFC averaging 12.6 yards a return in '86 . . . Will earn $200,000 this season . . . Two-time consensus All-American. Born Dec. 16, 1962, in Lubbock, Tex.

MIKE WILCHER 28 6-3 240 Linebacker

Has held off challenge from Kevin Greene the last two seasons and gives Rams three solid outside linebackers along with Greene and Mel Owens . . . Finished second on team with five interceptions . . . Started all 12 non-strike games . . . Scored first NFL touchdown in Monday night game at Washington when he picked up Doug Williams' fumble on first series and returned it 35 yards for Rams' first score. L.A. won, 30-26 . . . Best performance came against Cleveland with six tackles, one sack and an interception of a Bernie Kosar pass . . . Quick, good instincts . . . Second-round draft choice in 1983, he replaced Lawrence Taylor at defensive end his junior year at North Carolina . . . Earned $230,000 in final year of contract . . . Born March 20, 1960, in Washington, D.C.

MEL OWENS 29 6-2 235   Linebacker

Hasn't missed a game since coming into the league in 1981. Has played in 99, started 76 ... One of the most valuable players on the defense even though his statistics don't normally rate at the top ... Plays the strongside and is responsible for jamming the tight end ... Had one interception last season ... Outside linebacker is one of strongest positions on team with Owens, Mike Wilcher and Kevin Greene ... Earned $300,000 in final year of contract ... Played in three Rose Bowls and a Gator Bowl as four-year letterman at Michigan ... Born Dec. 7, 1958, in Detroit ... Moved to Illinois after father was named head baseball coach at Northern Illinois ... Holds black belt in karate.

MIKE LANSFORD 30 6-0 190   Kicker

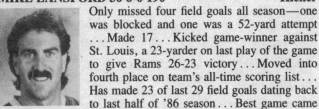

Only missed four field goals all season—one was blocked and one was a 52-yard attempt ... Made 17 ... Kicked game-winner against St. Louis, a 23-yarder on last play of the game to give Rams 26-23 victory ... Moved into fourth place on team's all-time scoring list ... Has made 23 of last 29 field goals dating back to last half of '86 season ... Best game came against Detroit when he made field goals of 47 and 48 yards ... Was seven of nine from 40-49 yards ... Signed with team as free agent in 1982 ... Will earn $195,000 in final year of contract ... Born July 20, 1958, in Monterey Park, Cal ... Kicked at Pasadena City College for two years, then transferred to Washington ... Had a streak of 73 consecutive extra points ... Signed as free agent in 1982.

COACH JOHN ROBINSON: Managed to keep team together despite 24-day players' strike, a 1-7 start, and a highly publicized feud between his star running back, Eric Dickerson, and team management. When Dickerson was traded to the Colts midway through season, Robinson plugged Charles White into his run-oriented offense and the Rams won five straight during one stretch ... Lost quarterback Jim Everett to a bone chip in his ankle before regular-season finale and the team was crushed by San Francisco ... Pro record slipped to 48-26 ...

Missed the playoffs for first time since taking over Rams in 1983 after seven winning seasons at USC (67-14-2)...Coached Charles White and Marcus Allen at USC...Started as Oregon assistant in 1960 after playing end at Oregon...Was an assistant at USC for three years before joining John Madden at Oakland in 1974...Known as conservative, run-oriented coach but style may change with the emergence of Jim Everett...Born July 25, 1935, in Dale City, Cal.

LONGEST PLAY

Bob Waterfield was in his second year as coach of the Rams, running back Jon Arnett was in his fifth season and John F. Kennedy was a rookie President.

It was 1961. On Oct. 22, President Kennedy successfully demanded that the Soviet Union dismantle its missile bases in Cuba. Things went back to normal. A week later, on Oct. 29, Arnett made his own headlines when he ran back a kickoff 105 yards against Detroit, the longest play in team history. It was the Rams' only touchdown in a 28-10 defeat.

INDIVIDUAL RAM RECORDS

Rushing

Most Yards Game:	248	Eric Dickerson, vs Dallas, 1985
Season:	2,105	Eric Dickerson, 1984
Career:	7,245	Eric Dickerson, 1983-87

Passing

Most TD Passes Game:	5	Bob Waterfield, vs N.Y. Bulldogs, 1949
	5	Norm Van Brocklin, vs Detroit, 1950
	5	Norm Van Brocklin, vs N.Y. Yanks, 1951
	5	Roman Gabriel, vs Cleveland, 1965
	5	Vince Ferragamo, vs New Orleans, 1980
	5	Vince Ferragamo, vs San Francisco, 1983
Season:	30	Vince Ferragamo, 1980
Career:	154	Roman Gabriel, 1962-72

Receiving

Most TD Passes Game:	4	Bob Shaw, vs Washington, 1949
	4	Elroy Hirsch, vs N.Y. Yanks, 1951
	4	Harold Jackson, vs Dallas, 1973
Season:	17	Elroy Hirsch, 1951
Career:	53	Elroy Hirsch, 1949-57

Scoring

Most Points Game:	24	Elroy Hirsch, vs N.Y. Yanks, 1951
	24	Bob Shaw, vs Washington, 1949
	24	Harold Jackson, vs Dallas, 1973
Season:	130	David Ray, 1973
Career:	573	Bob Waterfield, 1945-52
Most TDs Game:	4	Elroy Hirsch, vs N.Y. Yanks, 1951
	4	Bob Shaw, vs Washington, 1949
	4	Harold Jackson, vs Dallas, 1973
Season:	20	Eric Dickerson, 1983
Career:	58	Eric Dickerson, 1983-87

MINNESOTA VIKINGS

TEAM DIRECTORY: Chairman: John Skoglurd; Pres.: Wheelock Whitney; Exec. VP/GM: Mike Lynn; Dir. Administration: Harley Peterson; Dir. Football Operations: Jerry Reichow; Dir. Pub. Rel.: Merrill Swanson; Head Coach: Jerry Burns. Home field: Hubert H. Humphrey Metrodome (63,000). Colors: Purple, white and gold.

SCOUTING REPORT

OFFENSE: The offense ranked a mediocre 15th in total yardage in an 8-7 regular season. But it was good enough in the playoffs to score 44 points against New Orleans and 36 more the following week against San Francisco before the 17-10 ousting by Washington for NFC championship.

Anthony Carter was Vikings' pass-reception leader.

Who would have thought the Vikings would have done anything in a season during which quarterback Tommy Kramer spent more time on the bench than he did in the huddle? But while Wade Wilson wasn't always a model of consistency, he proved he could do the job when his team needed him the most. He completed 53 percent of his passes, threw 14 touchdowns in nine starts and riddled defenses with his ability to scramble. So he would seem to have the starting edge going into the new season.

The Vikings appear set everywhere else on offense. They boast a strong nucleous in receivers Anthony Carter, Steve Jordan and Leo Lewis. And No. 1 pick Randall McDaniel of Arizona State will give them offensive depth at guard. They have a set of capable running backs in Darrin Nelson, the team's leading rusher with 642 yards; D.J. Dozier, and Alfred Anderson.

DEFENSE: By the end of the season, the defensive line was considered one of the best in the league. Chris Doleman and Keith Millard were an unbeatable combination on the right side. Doug Martin turned in perhaps his best all-around season and Henry Thomas started as a rookie.

The opportunistic Vikings had 37 takeaways for fourth in the league. Scott Studwell headed an effective group of linebackers and safety Joey Browner stood out in the secondary, the team's weakest unit on defense.

KICKING GAME: Placekicker is one of the team's needs even though Chuck Nelson made all nine of his field goals in the playoffs. His regular-season stats were not as encouraging, making only 13 of 24 field goals. Punter is a different story. Burns will have three to choose among Rich Gannon, Bucky Scribner and Greg Coleman. Leo Lewis ranked fifth in the league in punt returns (12.5-yard average) and Neal Guggemos was fifth in kickoff returns (22.4).

THE ROOKIES: The Vikings expect McDaniel, a 6-3, 258-pounder, will become a standout pulling guard. Secondary help comes from safeties Brad Edwards of South Carolina, the No. 2 pick, and Darrell Fullington, a fifth-rounder from Miami. Defensive end Al Noga of Hawaii (No. 3), a brother of Cardinal LB Niko Noga, adds quickness on the defensive line and guard Todd Kalis of Arizona State (No. 4) provides depth at guard.

OUTLOOK: The Vikes can make a serious bid for the Central Division crown. In fact, if the recent trend continues, Minnesota

VIKINGS VETERAN ROSTER

HEAD COACH—Jerry Burns. Assistant Coaches—Tom Batta, John Brunner, Pete Carroll, Monte Kiffin, John Michels, Floyd Peters, Dick Rehbein, Bob Schnelker, Paul Wiggin.

No.	Name	Pos.	Ht.	Wt.	NFL Exp.	College
46	Anderson, Alfred	RB	6-1	219	5	Baylor
53	Anno, Sam	LB	6-2	230	2	Southern California
58	Ashley, Walker Lee	LB	6-0	240	5	Penn State
50	Berry, Ray	LB	6-2	230	2	Baylor
19	Brim, James	WR	6-3	187	2	Wake Forest
47	Browner, Joey	S-CB	6-2	212	6	Southern California
81	Carter, Anthony	WR	5-11	175	4	Michigan
8	Coleman, Greg	P	6-0	181	12	Florida A&M
56	Doleman, Chris	DE	6-5	250	4	Pittsburgh
42	Dozier, D.J.	RB	6-1	210	2	Penn State
31	Fenney, Rick	RB	6-1	240	2	Washington
62	Foote, Chris	C	6-4	265	6	Southern California
22	Freeman, Steve	S	5-11	185	14	Mississippi State
16	Gannon, Rich	QB	6-3	197	2	Delaware
41	Guggemos, Neal	S	6-0	187	3	St. Thomas
80	Gustafson, Jim	WR	6-1	181	3	St. Thomas
44	Harris, John	S	6-2	198	11	Arizona State
24	Henderson, Wymon	SB-S	5-10	186	2	Nevada-Las Vegas
82	Hilton, Carl	TE	6-3	232	3	Houston
30	Holt, Issiac	CB	6-1	197	4	Alcorn State
51	Howard, David	LB	6-2	228	4	Long Beach State
72	Huffman, David	G	6-6	283	9	Notre Dame
76	Irwin, Tim	T	6-6	289	8	Tennessee
84	Jones, Hassan	WR	6-0	195	3	Florida State
83	Jordan, Steve	TE	6-4	230	7	Brown
68	Koch, Greg	T	6-4	276	12	Arkansas
9	Kramer, Tommy	QB	6-2	207	12	Rice
39	Lee, Carl	CB	5-11	184	6	Marshall
87	Lewis, Leo	WR	5-8	171	8	Missouri
63	Lowdermilk, Kirk	C	6-3	263	4	Ohio State
71	MacDonald, Mark	G	6-4	267	4	Boston College
56	Martin, Chris	LB	6-2	233	6	Auburn
79	Martin, Doug	DE	6-3	270	9	Washington
73	Mays, Stafford	DE	6-2	264	9	Washington
75	Millard, Keith	DT	6-5	262	4	Washington State
86	Mularkey, Mike	TE	6-4	238	6	Florida
77	Mullaney, Mark	DE	6-6	246	13	Colorado State
1	Nelson, Chuck	K	5-11	172	5	Washington
20	Nelson, Darrin	RB	5-9	189	7	Stanford
96	Newton, Tim	DT	6-0	283	4	Florida
52	Rasmussen, Randy	C-G	6-1	254	5	Minnesota
36	Rice, Allen	RB	5-10	203	5	Baylor
95	Robinson, Gerald	DE	6-3	256	3	Auburn
48	Rutland, Reggie	S	6-1	195	2	Georgia Tech
13	Scribner, Bucky	P	6-0	205	4	Kansas
40	Smith, Wayne	CB	6-0	170	9	Purdue
54	Solomon, Jesse	LB	6-0	235	3	Florida State
55	Studwell, Scott	LB	6-2	230	12	Illinois
67	Swilley, Dennis	C	6-3	257	11	Texas A&M
66	Tausch, Terry	T	6-5	275	7	Texas
97	Thomas, Henry	NT	6-2	268	2	Louisiana State
11	Wilson, Wade	QB	6-3	203	8	East Texas State
65	Zimmerman, Gary	T	6-6	277	3	Oregon

TOP DRAFT CHOICES

Rd.	Name	Sel. No.	Pos.	Ht.	Wt.	College
1	McDaniel, Randall	19	G	6-3	258	Arizona State
2	Edwards, Brad	54	S	6-2	195	South Carolina
3	Noga, Al	71	DE	6-1	245	Hawaii
4	Kalis, Todd	108	G	6-6	277	Arizona State
5	Fullington, Darrell	124	S	6-2	190	Miami

could be going to the Super Bowl. Two of the last three teams to lose the NFC championship game came back to win the Super Bowl the following year.

VIKING PROFILES

WADE WILSON 29 6-3 203   Quarterback

Played in 14 non-strike games and led Vikings to two playoff victories, against New Orleans and San Francisco . . . Played entire game in six of seven he started; relieved Tommy Kramer seven times, including wild-card against Saints . . . Great scrambler. Carried 41 times for 263 yards, a 6.1-yard average . . . Was outstanding in 30-24 loss to Bears when he completed 12 of 19 passes for 211 yards and three TDs . . . NFC Player of the Week for his performance in 21-16 victory over Rams. Completed 17 of 38 passes for 285 yards and three touchdowns, including game-winner with 30 seconds left . . . Had 53.0 percentage completion (140 for 264) . . . Will earn $250,000 this season . . . Selected in eighth round of 1981 draft (No. 210) out of East Texas State . . . Born Feb. 1, 1959, in Greenville, Tex.

ANTHONY CARTER 27 5-11 175   Wide Receiver

"Carter has every talent Jerry Rice has, and more," claims Jerry Burns. "I agree [with Carter] that if we threw the ball to him as often as the 49ers do to Rice, he would even catch more." . . . As it was, Carter caught 38 passes for 922 yards . . . His eight catches for 184 yards vs. Dallas was a career best . . . An additional highlight was his 84-yard punt return in a wild-card game vs. the Saints, an NFL playoff record . . . He arrived late in the NFL (1985) after playing three years in the USFL (Michigan Panthers, Oakland Invaders) . . . This followed an All-American career at Michigan, where he was a four-year starter and set records for receptions (161), reception yards (3,076) and touchdowns (37) . . . Vikings acquired his rights from Miami, which drafted him in the 12th round in 1983 . . . Born Sept. 17, 1960, in Riviera Beach, Fla.

SCOTT STUDWELL 34 6-2 230   Linebacker

Scrappy middle linebacker enters his 12th season and keeps piling up team tackling records ...His career tackles now number 1,579...Led team in tackles for six consecutive years through 1985...Has started 114 games, most among current Vikings... Played at Illinois, where he broke Dick Butkus' season record with 177 tackles as a senior...He weighed 260 pounds as a sophomore and played tackle, but didn't get drafted until the ninth round (No. 250) because his speed was suspect...A lighter and presumably swifter Studwell wound up being selected to the Viking fans' 25th anniversary all-star team in 1985...How strong is he? In 1981 he teamed with Jim Hough to win the NFL arm-wrestling championship...Will earn $300,000 in final year of contract ...Born Aug. 27, 1954, in Evansville, Ind.

DARRIN NELSON 29 5-9 189   Running Back

Led team in rushing for third consecutive season (131 carries for 642 yards)...Like most of Viking backs, he's a good receiver... Caught 26 passes for 5.0-yard average...His 72-yard run vs. Denver was longest non-touchdown run in team history...Moved into fifth place in team career-rushing standings with 3,512 yards...Fourth in total yards (7,516)...First running back and seventh player selected in 1982 draft...Became NCAA all-time all-purpose yardage leader during four years at Stanford—4,033 rushing, 2,368 receiving and 484 returns...Was first rookie running back ever to start in Viking opener...Born Jan. 2, 1959, in Sacramento, Cal.

STEVE JORDAN 27 6-4 230   Tight End

Team's second-leading receiver behind Anthony Carter...Caught 35 passes for 490 yards...His 14.0-yard average was second among NFC tight ends, behind the Giants' Mark Bavaro...Leader among Vikings' tight ends for career receptions (217)...Ninth in career yardage (2,812)...Despite several key drops in the NFC title game, has had three exceptional seasons in a row...Seventh-rounder out of Brown in 1982...Will earn $255,000 this season in final year of contract ...Has a degree in civil engineering...Born Jan. 10, 1961, in Phoenix.

CHRIS DOLEMAN 26 6-5 250   Defensive End

Led team with 11 sacks in regular season, three in playoffs...Became first Viking to force a fumble in four consecutive games... Fell one short of team record when he had quarterback sacks in seven straight games... Pulled a hamstring in first-round playoff game against San Francisco but played following week against Washington in NFC title game
...Pro Bowl selection...Emerged as dominant force on defensive line in first full season at end...Played first season and six games at second at outside linebacker before moving to the line ...Quick, explosive...Hard hitter...First-round choice out of Pittsburgh in 1985...Selected as an All-American as a freshman...Born Oct. 16, 1961, in Indianapolis.

DOUG MARTIN 31 6-3 270   Defensive End

Matched his 1986 sacks total of nine, which was four more than brother George achieved with the Giants...Now entering his ninth season with no letup in sight...He led the league in sacks with 10½ in 1982 and set a career high of 12 in '83..."He had his best camp last year," says Jerry Burns, "and he provided leadership on the defensive line with his attitude and work habits."...Ninth player selected in 1980 draft, out of Washington...Was MVP in 1979 Sun Bowl... Lives in Kirkland, Wash., in offseason and is earning credits toward his degree...Also works as a real-estate agent...Born May 22, 1957, in Fairfield, Cal.

JOEY BROWNER 28 6-2 212   Safety

Led team in tackles for second consecutive season, tying linebacker Jesse Solomon with 121...Special-teams standout, fourth on team with 10 hits...Never quits and always shows up at right place and right time...Led team with six interceptions...Brother Ross is a Bengal and brother Keith a 49er...Has played every position in defensive backfield
...Became the first defensive back in team history to be selected in the first round in 1983...Played strong safety as a freshman at USC, cornerback as a sophomore and junior and free safety as a senior...Born May 15, 1960, in Warren, Ohio...Has played in three consecutive Pro Bowls.

KEITH MILLARD 26 6-5 262   Defensive Tackle

Credited as the key to the defense during the playoffs. Hobbled with injury late in the regular season but he excelled in playoffs . . . Had five tackles, one sack and a forced fumble in wild-card game against New Orleans . . . Vital in team's run defense, which didn't allow an opposing back to gain over 100 yards all season . . . Emotional player who doesn't take defeat well . . . Missed three games—Dallas, Chicago and Green Bay—because of a leg injury . . . One of eight players on roster who played in the USFL . . . Will earn $247,000 in final year of contract . . . Selected in first round of 1984 draft out of Washington State . . . Born March 18, 1962, in Pleasonton, Cal.

D.J. DOZIER 22 6-1 210   Running Back

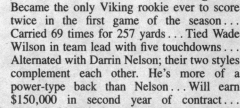

Became the only Viking rookie ever to score twice in the first game of the season . . . Carried 69 times for 257 yards . . . Tied Wade Wilson in team lead with five touchdowns . . . Alternated with Darrin Nelson; their two styles complement each other. He's more of a power-type back than Nelson . . . Will earn $150,000 in second year of contract . . . Selected in the first round of '87 draft, 14th player overall, third running back taken . . . Finished his career at Penn State as school's second all-time leading rusher behind Curt Warner . . . Runs the 40-yard dash in 4.3 seconds . . . Born Sept. 21, 1965, in Norfolk Va. . . . Father known as "Deke," he became "Deke Jr." and now "D.J."

COACH JERRY BURNS: His players look up to him. "Jerry Burns' greatest ability is to communicate exactly what he wants," said veteran guard David Huffman. "He doesn't blow a lot of smoke. He doesn't flower things. He tells you if something is good. He tells you if something is bad." . . . Most of Burns' second season as Vikings' head coach was good . . . In two seasons he has a 19-15 record . . . Minnesota made the playoffs last season for the first time since 1982 . . . In '86 was first Vikings' coach to have a winning record (9-7) his rookie season . . . Served as Vikings' assistant head coach and

offensive coordinator from 1968-85 . . . Played quarterback at Michigan . . . Served as backfield coach at Hawaii in 1951 and Whittier in '52 . . . Coached a year of high-school ball in Detroit before a 12-year stretch (1954-65) at Iowa (last five as head coach) as Hawkeyes won two Big 10 titles . . . Left for Green Bay under Vince Lombardi for two years, then moved to Vikings . . . Credited with originating one-back offense . . . Born Jan. 24, 1927, in Detroit.

Chris Doleman tied for fifth in NFL sacks (11).

LONGEST PLAY

Gary Cuozzo and Lance Rentzel will remember the day, Nov. 14, 1965, for different reasons.

Cuozzo replaced Johnny Unitas as Baltimore quarterback in the first half and threw five touchdown passes to lead the Colts to a 41-21 victory over the Vikings.

Minnesota's Rentzel, who was playing his second season out of Oklahoma, won't forget it because he took Gene Michaels' kickoff a yard deep in his own end zone and ran it back 101 yards for a touchdown, the longest ever by a Viking.

INDIVIDUAL VIKING RECORDS

Rushing

Most Yards Game:	200	Chuck Foreman, vs Philadelphia, 1976
Season:	1,155	Chuck Foreman, 1976
Career:	5,879	Chuck Foreman, 1973-79

Passing

Most TD Passes Game:	7	Joe Kapp, vs Baltimore, 1969
Season:	26	Tommy Kramer, 1981
Career	239	Francis Tarkenton, 1961-66, 1972-78

Receiving

Most TD Passes Game:	4	Ahmad Rashad, vs San Francisco, 1979
Season:	11	Jerry Reichow, 1961
Career:	50	Sammy White, 1976-85

Scoring

Most Points Game:	24	Chuck Foreman, vs Buffalo, 1975
	24	Ahmad Rashad, vs San Francisco, 1979
Season:	132	Chuck Foreman, 1975
Career:	1,365	Fred Cox, 1963-77
Most TDs Game:	4	Chuck Foreman, vs Buffalo, 1975
	4	Ahmad Rashad, vs San Francisco, 1979
Season:	22	Chuck Foreman, 1975
Career:	76	Bill Brown, 1962-74

NEW ORLEANS SAINTS

TEAM DIRECTORY: Owner: Tom Benson; Pres./GM: Jim Finks; VP-Administration: Jim Miller; Bus. Mgr./Controller: Bruce Broussard; Dir. Pub. Rel./Marketing: Greg Suit; Dir. Media Services: Rusty Kasmiersky; Head Coach: Jim Mora. Home field: Superdome (69,551). Colors: Old gold, black and white.

SCOUTING REPORT

OFFENSE: The Saints finished 12-3 in the regular season, second to the 49ers' 13-2 in the Western Division. The defense was the heart of the team, but the offense, relatively unsung, helped get them there with the third-best rushing mark in the league.

Bobby Hebert directed a consistent, controlled attack and completed 164 of 294 passes (55.8 percent), 14 for TDs, and he threw only nine interceptions in contrast to 1986 when he and Dave Wilson combined to throw twice as many interceptions as touchdown passes.

In his second season, Reuben Mayes gained 917 yards for runnerup honors in the NFC, sharing time with Dalton Hilliard, a third-down specialist who added 508 yards rushing and caught 23 passes for 264 yards. The run-oriented Saints could get a charge from their No. 1 pick, 250-pound Pitt fullback Craig (Ironhead) Heyward.

The receivers may not be the swiftest in the league, but they were a factor—Eric Martin, Mike Jones and rookie Lonzell Hill (19 catches for 322 yards) as well as Hilliard.

DEFENSE: Ranked fourth in the NFL—third against the run, sixth against the pass. The Saints' 48 turnovers tied the Eagles for No. 1 in the league. Led by linebackers Pat Swilling (10½) and Rickey Jackson (9½), the pass rush totaled 47 sacks, sixth in the league. Ends Jim Wilks, Bruce Clark and Frank Warren and nose tackle Tony Elliott added pressure and so did linebackers Sam Mills, who made the Pro Bowl, and Vaughn Johnson.

The secondary finished sixth in the league in pass defense. Cornerback Dave Waymer made the Pro Bowl with five interceptions but there were times when he and Van Jakes could have used some help. Safeties Brett Maxie and Antonio Gibson were solid.

KICKING GAME: What more can you say about special teams that blocked seven punts and two field-goal attempts? Placekicker

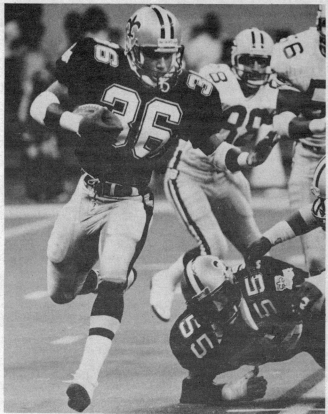

Reuben Mayes expects to crack 1,000-yard mark in '88.

Morten Anderson is the best in the league, and Mel Gray is always a threat on punt and kickoff returns. Punter Brian Hansen didn't have his best season, but he placed 19 punts inside opponents' 20.

THE ROOKIES: When Reuben Mayes had knee surgery after the final game of 1987, the Saints knew they had to find another special back. They got one in Heyward, the mammoth fullback who can also play tailback. Brett Perriman, a swift wide receiver from Miami, selected in the second round, may fill the need for a legitimate deep threat. No. 3 pick Tony Stephens, a 306-pound Clemson nose tackle, adds size and depth on the defensive line.

SAINTS VETERAN ROSTER

HEAD COACH—Jim Mora. Assistant Coaches—Paul Boudreau, Vic Fangio, Joe Marciano, Russell Paternostro, John Pease, Steve Sidwell, Jim Skipper, Carl Smith, Steve Walters.

No.	Name	Pos.	Ht.	Wt.	NFL Exp.	College
40	Adams, Michael	CB	5-10	195	2	Arkansas State
7	Andersen, Morten	K	6-2	200	7	Michigan State
28	Atkins, Gene	CB-S	6-1	200	2	Florida A&M
83	Benson, Cliff	TE	6-4	240	4	Purdue
85	Brenner, Hoby	TE	6-4	240	8	Southern California
67	Brock, Stan	T	6-6	288	9	Colorado
59	Campen, James	C	6-3	260	2	Tulane
75	Clark, Bruce	DE	6-3	275	7	Penn State
89	Clark, Robert	WR	5-11	175	1	North Carolina Central
66	Commiskey, Chuck	G	6-4	290	3	Mississippi
70	Contz, Bill	T	6-5	270	3	Penn State
41	Cook, Toi	S	5-11	188	2	Stanford
26	Dawsey, Stacey	WR	5-9	154	2	Indiana
72	Dombrowski, Jim	T	6-5	298	3	Virginia
63	Edelman, Brad	G	6-6	270	7	Missouri
99	Elliott, Tony	NT	6-2	275	7	North Texas State
11	Fourcade, John	QB	6-1	208	2	Mississippi
97	Geathers, James	DE	6-7	290	4	Wichita State
27	Gibson, Antonio	S	6-3	204	3	Cincinnati
77	Gilbert, Daren	T	6-6	295	4	Cal State-Fullerton
37	Gray, Mel	RB	5-9	166	3	Purdue
10	Hansen, Brian	P	6-3	209	5	Sioux Falls
—	Harris, Herbert	WR	6-1	206	2	Lamar
92	Haynes, James	LB	6-2	233	5	Mississippi Valley
3	Hebert, Bobby	QB	6-4	215	4	NW Louisiana
61	Hilgenberg, Joel	C-G	6-2	252	5	Iowa
87	Hill, Lonzell	WR	5-11	189	2	Washington
21	Hilliard, Dalton	RB	5-8	204	3	Louisiana State
57	Jackson, Rickey	LB	6-2	243	8	Pittsburgh
22	Jakes, Van	CB	6-0	190	5	Kent State
53	Johnson, Vaughan	LB	6-3	235	3	North Carolina State
86	Jones, Mike	WR	5-11	183	6	Tennessee State
23	Jordan, Buford	RB	6-0	223	3	McNeese State
71	Kaplan, Ken	T	6-5	270	4	New Hampshire
78	Knight, Shawn	DE	6-6	288	2	Brigham Young
55	Kohlbrand, Joe	LB	6-4	242	4	Miami
60	Korte, Steve	C	6-2	260	6	Arkansas
24	Mack, Milton	CB	5-11	182	2	Alcorn State
84	Martin, Eric	WR	6-1	195	4	Louisiana State
39	Maxie, Brett	S	6-2	194	4	Texas Southern
36	Mayes, Rueben	RB	5-11	201	3	Washington State
51	Mills, Sam	LB	5-9	225	3	Montclair State
88	Pattison, Mark	WR	6-2	190	3	Washington
56	Swilling, Pat	LB	6-3	242	3	Georgia Tech
69	Swoopes, Patrick	NT	6-4	280	2	Mississippi State
82	Tice, John	TE	6-5	249	6	Maryland
54	Toles, Alvin	LB	6-1	227	4	Tennessee
65	Trapilo, Steve	G	6-5	281	2	Boston College
73	Warren, Frank	DE	6-4	290	8	Auburn
33	Waters, Mike	TE	6-2	230	3	San Diego State
44	Waymer, Dave	CB	6-1	188	8	Notre Dame
94	Wilks, Jim	DE	6-5	266	8	San Diego State
18	Wilson, Dave	QB	6-3	206	7	Illinois
34	Word, Barry	RB	6-2	220	2	Virginia

TOP DRAFT CHOICES

Rd.	Name	Sel. No.	Pos.	Ht.	Wt.	College
1	Heyward, Craig	24	RB	6-2	250	Pittsburgh
2	Perriman, Brett	52	WR	5-9	180	Miami
3	Stephens, Tony	81	NT	6-3	306	Clemson
4	Carr, Lydell	106	RB	6-0	221	Oklahoma
5	Scales, Greg	112	TE	6-3	250	Wake Forest
5	Taylor, Keith	134	DB	5-11	193	Illinois

OUTLOOK: It's not going to be an easy season for coach Jim Mora because now his team will be expected to finish 12-3 again. It may be too much to expect, but they're a playoff contender.

SAINT PROFILES

REUBEN MAYES 25 5-11 201   **Running Back**

Second-leading rusher in NFC in '87 behind Rams' Charles White . . . Gained 917 on 243 carries while sharing time with Dalton Hilliard . . . Opponents knew what they were in for after he surprised the NFL as a third-round rookie, rushing for the league's fourth-highest total and earning Rookie of the Year honors . . . Underwent offseason knee surgery for ligament damage last winter . . . A rarity in the NFL, he was born in Canada, June 16, 1963, in North Battleford, Saskatchewan . . . Wound up at Washington State, where he set all-time rushing records galore and was Pac-10 rushing champion in his last two years . . . New Orleans made him a third-round selection in 1986 . . . Scheduled to earn $175,000 in base salary unless contract is renegotiated.

BOBBY HEBERT 28 6-4 215   **Quarterback**

Characterized the Saints' offense last season . . . He played well enough to win, until the playoffs, but he wasn't spectacular . . . Didn't make many mistakes while running a controlled offense. Tied Cleveland quarterback Bernie Kosar for the fewest interceptions (9) among starters . . . Had knee arthroscoped in offseason and is expected to be ready . . . Critics claimed he wasn't good enough to get Saints through the playoffs even though he finished the season with the best passing rating (82.9) of any quarterback in team history . . . Will earn $550,000 this season in second year of three-year deal . . . Enters fourth year with the Saints . . . Played three seasons in the USFL and led the Michigan Panthers to league title in 1983 . . . Born Aug. 19, 1960, in Galliano, La. . . . Is a product of Northwest Lousiana State.

SAM MILLS 29 5-9 225   Linebacker

Played only on first downs much of the time but played well enough to earn his first trip to the Pro Bowl...League's shortest linebacker doesn't give an inch against the run...Grew into leadership role in his second season as a Saint...Came out for extra defensive back in passing situations...Aggressive, quick and intelligent...Been with coach Jim Mora for three seasons in the USFL and two in New Orleans...Earned $160,000 in last year of contract...Has come a long way since being released by the Browns in 1981...Division II All-American at Montclair State in 1980...Born June 3, 1959, in Neptune, N.J.

RICKEY JACKSON 30 6-2 239   Linebacker

He missed the Pro Bowl for the first time in five years but his coaches believe he had his best season ever...Had 9½ sacks, tied for 10th in the league...Hardest hitter on punishing defense and was a major reason why Saints ranked fourth in the league in total defense...In the class of his good friend, Giants' Lawrence Taylor...Has started every game he's played as a pro...Will earn $600,000 in base salary this season and again next season...Picked off two passes, the most in any one season of his seven-year career...Played defensive end at Pitt and didn't receive the attention he deserved because Hugh Green was on the other side...Born March 20, 1958, in Pahokee, Fla.

PAT SWILLING 23 6-3 242   Linebacker

Getting better with each season...Couples with Rickey Jackson to give Saints one of most lethal one-two outside linebacker punches in the league...Had 10½ sacks. Combined with Jackson for 20 of the Saints' 47 sacks...Finished as fifth-leading tackler on team...Entering his third year, he seems to know his team's defensive system as well as anybody. Seldom makes the same mistake twice...Like Jackson, he played defensive end in college...Third-round choice out of Georgia Tech...Enters final year of contract. Will earn $175,000 this year...Born Oct. 25, 1964, in Toccoa, Ga.

MORTEN ANDERSEN 28 6-2 200   Placekicker

Most accurate all-time kicker in the NFL... Made 28 of 36 attempts last season and has made a remarkable 125 of 157 in six-year career... Led the league in field goals attempted and made... Leading scorer among kickers, 121, 24 points ahead of closest competitor, Cincinnati's Jim Breech... Made 26 of 30 kicks inside the 50 and made all 37 extra points... Consistently kicked off into opponents' end zones... Made Pro Bowl for third consecutive season... Has scored in 62 consecutive games in which he has played (not counting the strike games)... Will earn $325,000 in last year of contract... Speaks six languages and travels extensively during the off season... Born Aug. 19, 1960, in Struer, Denmark... Played at Michigan State.

DALTON HILLIARD 24 5-8 204   Running Back

Most improved player on the team... Started running like the Saints had hoped he would as a rookie in 1986... Coaches said he appeared more comfortable with the system... Gained 508 yards on 123 carries (4.1-yard average) and caught 23 passes for 264 more... Scored eight touchdowns... Shared time with Rueben Mayes... Designated pass receiver out of backfield... Speed and ability to go outside complements Mayes' power style... The two combined to give the Saints the third-best running attack in the NFL... A hometown favorite since he was a second-round pick out of LSU... Ended college career as the third all-time rusher in the SEC behind Herschel Walker and Bo Jackson... Will earn $205,000 in final year of contract... Born Jan. 21, 1964, in Patterson, La.

TONY ELLIOTT 29 6-2 275   Nose Tackle

Felt he didn't make the Pro Bowl because he crossed the picket line during the strike... Leader in the Saints' rushing defense, which finished third in the league... Played a little heavier than coaches would have liked... Hard to move out of the middle... Good athletic ability for his size... Enters final year of two-year contract and will earn $275,000... Joined Saints in 1982 as fifth-round draft choice... Attended North Texas State... Born April 23, 1959, in New York, N.Y.

STAN BROCK 30 6-6 288   Tackle

Started every game, not including the strike, the past three seasons... Successfully came back after having ruptured disc removed during offseason... He's where the Saints look for short yardage... Chuck Fairbanks called him the "best pass blocker in college football" his senior year at Colorado... Voted Pro Bowl alternate... Left guard Brad Edelman made the Pro Bowl... Saints' line regarded as one of best in the league... Signed three-year contract beginning next season. Will earn $250,000 this year... Brother Pete was No. 1 draft choice of Patriots in 1976... Stan was a first-round pick of the Saints in 1980... Father is a retired riverboat fireman... Born June 8, 1958, in Beaverton, Ore.

ERIC MARTIN 26 6-1 195   Wide Receiver

Had his best season last year... Caught 44 passes for 778 yards, ranking him 13th among NFC receivers. His 17.7-yard average was seventh-best in the conference... Provided big plays to an offense that didn't get many through the air... Catches against Houston and the Giants earned him game balls... Doesn't have great speed but runs tight patterns... Good hands... Ended career at LSU as SEC all-time career leader in receiving yardage... Holds school record for 100-yard kick return... Seventh-round draft choice in 1985 will earn $180,000 in final year of contract... Born Nov. 8, 1961, in Van Vleck, Tex.

COACH JIM MORA: The only coach from the USFL to take

similar post in the NFL... In two seasons he has moved the Saints from the basement to second place in the NFC West... Only San Francisco's 13-2 record prevented the Saints from winning their first divison title... As it was, they made the playoffs for the first time in team history... In NFL he has a 19-13 mark... He was the most successful coach in

the USFL, taking the Philadelphia Stars to two championships
. . . Started coaching career at Occidental College, where he had
played tight end and roomed with Jack Kemp, the quarterback
who would go on, after a pro career, to the U.S. Congress and
would be a Republican presidential candidate . . . Was an assistant
coach at Stanford, Colorado and Washington before taking on
assistant roles with Seattle and New England prior to becoming a
head coach in the USFL . . . Born May 24, 1935, in Glendale,
Cal.

LONGEST PLAY

Mel Gray, a 5-9, 166-pound gnat out of Purdue, began his pro
career with the USFL's Los Angeles Express. He didn't get to the
NFL and the Saints until 1986, but he didn't take long to flash his
form.

On Sept. 21, 1986, against the 49ers, he got loose for a
club-record 101-yard kickoff return. He finished the day with
186 yards on three returns. That provided at least some solace
in a 26-17 San Francisco victory.

INDIVIDUAL SAINT RECORDS

Rushing

Most Yards Game:	206	George Rogers, vs St. Louis, 1983
Season:	1,674	George Rogers, 1981
Career:	4,267	George Rogers, 1981-84

Passing

Most TD Passes Game:	6	Billy Kilmer, vs St. Louis, 1969
Season:	23	Archie Manning, 1980
Career:	155	Archie Manning, 1971-81

Receiving

Most TD Passes Game:	3	Dan Abramowicz, vs San Francisco, 1971
Season:	9	Henry Childs, 1977
Career:	37	Dan Abramowicz, 1967-72

Scoring

Most Points Game:	18	Walt Roberts, vs Philadelphia, 1967
	18	Dan Abramowicz, vs San Francisco, 1971
	18	Archie Manning, vs Chicago, 1977
	18	Chuck Muncie, vs San Francisco, 1979
	18	George Rogers, vs Los Angeles, 1981
	18	Wayne Wilson, vs Atlanta, 1982
Season:	121	Morten Andersen, 1987
Career:	536	Morten Andersen, 1982-87
Most TDs Game:	3	Walt Roberts, vs Philadelphia, 1967
	3	Dan Abramowicz, vs San Francisco, 1971
	3	Archie Manning, vs Chicago, 1977
	3	Chuck Muncie, vs San Francisco, 1979
	3	George Rogers, vs Los Angeles, 1981
	3	Wayne Wilson, vs Atlanta, 1982
Season:	13	George Rogers, 1981
Career:	37	Dan Abramowicz, 1967-72

NEW YORK GIANTS

TEAM DIRECTORY: Pres.: Wellington Mara; VP/Treasurer: Timothy Mara; VP/GM: George Young; Dir. Pro Personnel: Tom Boisture; Dir. Pub. Rel.: Ed Croke; Head Coach: Bill Parcells. Home field: Giants Stadium (76,891). Colors: Blue, red and white.

SCOUTING REPORT

OFFENSE: From Super Bowl champs in '86 to the cellar (6-9) in the Eastern Division in '87. The offensive line largely contributed to the reversal—especially at tackle. Karl Nelson was out with Hodgkin's disease and is a question, and Brad Benson has retired. So the Giants used their first two draft picks to get about

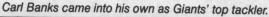

Carl Banks came into his own as Giants' top tackler.

600 pounds worth of tackles with Eric Moore of Indiana and Michigan's John Elliott. Guards Billy Ard and Chris Godfrey and center Bart Oates are solid.

Coach Bill Parcells is hoping Joe Morris, the team's leading rusher with 658 yards on 193 carries, can return to the production that marked the Super Bowl season. The Giants can use bigger rushing contributions from George Adams (169 yards) and anyone else they can muster. Blocking specialist Maurice Carthon will be back at fullback.

Quarterback Phil Simms (163 for 282, 2,230 yards) had a respectable season and Mark Bavaro continues as a premier tight end. The comeback by wide receiver Lionel Manuel was welcome, especially in view of the disappointment over the performance of Mark Ingram, the team's first pick last year.

DEFENSE: Nothing is ever the same after a Super Bowl victory and the defense didn't have a comparable year, but it was seventh in the NFL. Jim Burt played most of the season with a bad back, then had surgery in late December.

Lawrence Taylor tied for fourth in the league with 12 sacks and even appeared human when he sat out a game against Washington as a result of a pulled hamstring. Carl Banks, with a team-leading 113 tackles, had a super season and veteran Leonard Marshall came up with eight sacks.

Free safety Terry Kinard returned to his pre-surgery form, topping the team with five interceptions.

KICKING GAME: The Giants need to improve their field-goal kicking and punt returns. Raul Allegre made a so-so 17 of 27 field-goal attempts while Phil McConkey ranked eighth among NFC punt returners with a modest 9.4-yard average. Sean Landeta ranked fourth in the league with a 42.7-yard average and Lee Rouson was third in the NFC in kickoff returns with a 22.6-yard average.

THE ROOKIES: The Giants figure the only way to deal with the Dexter Manleys and Reggie Whites of the world is with mountain-sized tackles. Moore and Elliott, two massive pro-type pass-blockers from the Big 10, will give vivid meaning to the words "Giant tackles." No. 3 pick Sherman White, a cornerback from Miami (Ohio) could prove an ideal special-teams player.

OUTLOOK: Now that the Giants have all their books behind them, they may be ready to essay another winning chapter on the field. They still have the talent.

GIANTS VETERAN ROSTER

HEAD COACH—Bill Parcells. Assistant Coaches—Bill Belichick, Tom Coughlin, Romeo Crennel, Ron Erhardt, Len Fontes, Ray Handley, Fred Hoaglin, Lamar Leachman, Johnny Parker, Mike Pope, Mike Sweatman.

No.	Name	Pos.	Ht.	Wt.	NFL Exp.	College
—	Abraham, Robert	LB	6-1	236	6	North Carolina State
33	Adams, George	RB	6-1	255	3	Kentucky
2	Allegre, Raul	K	5-10	167	6	Texas
24	Anderson, Ottis	RB	6-2	225	10	Miami
67	Ard, Bill	G	6-3	270	8	Wake Forest
85	Baker, Stephen	WR	5-8	160	2	Fresno State
58	Banks, Carl	LB	6-4	235	5	Michigan State
89	Bavaro, Mark	TE	6-4	245	4	Notre Dame
79	Berthusen, Bill	NT	6-5	285	2	Iowa State
69	Black, Mike	T	6-4	280	2	Cal State-Sacramento
—	Borcky, Dennis	NT	6-3	284	2	Memphis State
47	Brown, Don	CB	5-11	189	3	Maryland
64	Burt, Jim	NT	6-1	260	8	Miami
—	Byrd, Boris	CB-S	6-0	210	2	Austin Peay
53	Carson, Harry	LB	6-2	240	13	South Carolina State
44	Carthon, Maurice	RB	6-1	225	4	Arkansas State
21	Clayton, Harvey	CB	5-9	186	5	Florida State
25	Collins, Mark	CB	5-10	190	3	Cal State-Fullerton
77	Dorsey, Eric	DE	6-5	280	3	Notre Dame
28	Flynn, Tom	S	6-0	195	5	Pittsburgh
30	Galbreath, Tony	RB	6-0	228	13	Missouri
61	Godfrey, Chris	G	6-3	265	6	Michigan
37	Haddix, Wayne	CB	6-1	203	2	Liberty
54	Headen, Andy	LB	6-5	242	6	Clemson
48	Hill, Kenny	S	6-0	195	8	Yale
15	Hostetler, Jeff	QB	6-3	212	4	West Virginia
74	Howard, Erik	NT	6-4	268	3	Washington State
57	Hunt, Byron	LB	6-5	242	8	Southern Methodist
82	Ingram, Mark	WR	5-10	188	2	Michigan State
68	Johnson, Damian	T	6-5	290	3	Kansas State
52	Johnson, Thomas	LB	6-3	248	3	Ohio State
59	Johnston, Brian	C	6-3	275	4	North Carolina
43	Kinard, Terry	S	6-1	200	6	Clemson
5	Landeta, Sean	P	6-0	200	4	Towson State
46	Lasker, Greg	S	6-0	200	3	Arkansas
86	Manuel, Lionel	WR	5-11	180	5	Pacific
70	Marshall, Leonard	DE	6-3	285	6	Louisiana State
75	Martin, George	DE	6-4	255	14	Oregon
80	McConkey, Phil	WR	5-10	170	4	Navy
20	Morris, Joe	RB	5-7	195	7	Syracuse
84	Mowatt, Zeke	TE	6-3	240	5	Florida State
63	Nelson, Karl	T	6-6	285	4	Iowa State
65	Oates, Bart	C	6-3	265	4	Brigham Young
55	Reasons, Gary	LB	6-4	234	5	NW Louisiana
72	Riesenberg, Doug	T	6-5	275	2	California
66	Roberts, William	T	6-5	280	4	Ohio State
81	Robinson, Stacy	WR	-511	186	4	North Dakota State
22	Rouson, Lee	RB	6-1	222	4	Colorado
17	Rutledge, Jeff	QB	6-1	195	10	Alabama
—	Sanders, Charles	RB	6-1	230	2	Slippery Rock
11	Simms, Phil	QB	6-3	215	9	Morehead State
56	Taylor, Lawrence	LB	6-3	243	8	North Carolina
83	Turner, Odessa	WR	6-3	205	2	NW Louisiana
34	Varajon, Michael	RB	6-1	232	2	Toledo
73	Washington, John	DE	6-4	275	3	Oklahoma State
27	Welch, Herb	DB	5-11	180	4	UCLA
36	White, Adrian	S	6-0	200	2	Florida
23	Williams, Perry	CB	6-2	203	5	North Carolina

TOP DRAFT CHOICES

Rd.	Name	Sel. No.	Pos.	Ht.	Wt.	College
1	Moore, Eric	10	T	6-5	280	Indiana
2	Elliott, John	36	T	6-6	305	Michigan
3	White, Sheldon	62	CB	5-11	189	Miami (Ohio)
4	Shaw, Ricky	92	LB	6-4	234	Oklahoma State
5	Carter, Jon	118	DE	6-3	266	Pittsburgh

GIANT PROFILES

CARL BANKS 26 6-4 235　　　　　　　　　Linebacker

Turned in best season ever as he came out of the shadow of Lawrence Taylor...Led team in tackles with 113...Used more as a pass-rusher than he had been in the past. Excellent against the run...Started all 12 games and remained healthy throughout a season in which the Giants' defense was riddled with injuries ...Played out the final year of his contract and said he did not want to play anywhere else besides New York...Considered by some experts the best all-around linebacker in the league...No. 3 overall draft pick in 1984 out of Michigan State, where he was a consensus All-American... Born Aug. 29, 1962, in Flint, Mich....Also played basketball and was a shot-putter at Beecher High.

MARK COLLINS 24 5-10 190　　　　　　　Cornerback

Emerged as best of team's 1986 draft crop... Picked off two passes and finished fourth on the team in tackles with 62...One of the best cover men in the league...Started nine games as rookie and became leader of secondary with departure of Elvis Patterson...Aspires to acting or broadcasting career after football, but that's a long way off...Will earn $175,000 in base salary...Second-round choice out of Cal State-Fullerton ...Stepped into starting slot at left corner when Patterson suffered a groin pull in Week 6 of 1986...Born Jan. 16, 1964, in St. Louis...Won 10 letters in football, basketball and baseball at Pacific High School in San Bernardino, Cal.

LAWRENCE TAYLOR 29 6-3 243　　　　　Linebacker

Despite a dropoff in statistics, coaches say he was as valuable, if not more, to the team than he was the year before when the Giants won the Super Bowl...Seemed to be happy with himself and didn't fall asleep in meetings... Finished third on team in tackles with 62 and second in interceptions with three...Third in NFC with 12 sacks...Played in one strike game, against Buffalo, and took a turn at tight end, coming close to catching a winning touchdown pass...Pulled hamstring in

Week 9 against Philadelphia while tackling Randall Cunningham
... Didn't finish the following game against New Orleans and
missed the next game against Washington... League's MVP in
1986... Seventh straight year in Pro Bowl... No. 2 pick overall
in 1981 out of North Carolina... Born Feb. 4, 1959, in Wil-
liamsburg, Va., where he also played high-school basketball and
baseball... Has become an outstanding golfer, featuring massive
tee-shots... Will earn $1 million in base salary this season.

JIM BURT 29 6-1 260 Nose Tackle

Played through Week 11 against Washington
despite painful, chronic back injury which required surgery... Shared time with Erik Howard and is expected to continue in that role this
season... Inspirational leader of defense...
Was back in weight room two months after
surgery... In Giants' Super Bowl season he
endeared himself to fans by vaulting into
stands to celebrate playoff wins... One of Bill Parcells' favorite
players... Probably the only nose tackle to write a book...
Made Pro Bowl in '86... Joined team as free agent in 1981 out
of University of Miami... Will earn $350,000 in final year of
contract... Born June 7, 1959, in Buffalo.

PHIL SIMMS 31 6-3 215 Quarterback

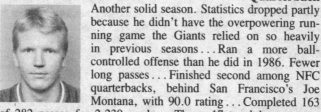

Another solid season. Statistics dropped partly
because he didn't have the overpowering running game the Giants relied on so heavily
in previous seasons... Ran a more ball-
controlled offense than he did in 1986. Fewer
long passes... Finished second among NFC
quarterbacks, behind San Francisco's Joe
Montana, with 90.0 rating... Completed 163
of 282 passes for 2,230 yards... Threw 17 touchdown passes
and nine interceptions... Will earn $750,000 this season...
Favorite target is tight end Mark Bavaro in the clutch...
Highlight of career came in Super Bowl XXI when he was MVP,
setting all-time Super Bowl and playoff record with 88 percent
completion (22 for 25) for 268 yards and three TDs in 39-20
victory over Denver... Has managed to avoid injuries past two
seasons that had plagued him earlier in career... Only second
Morehead State player to make in the NFL... Selected by Giants
in first round of 1979 draft... Born Nov. 3, 1956, in Springfield,
Ky.

JOE MORRIS 27 5-7 195   **Running Back**

Traditionally a slow starter, he really never got untracked after players' strike... Finished seventh in NFC in rushing with 658 yards on 193 carries... Hindered by falloff in performance of offensive line... Was getting tackled frequently in the backfield. He's at his best when he has a chance to explode through the line into the open field... Giants hope he returns to '86 form this season... Will earn $500,000... Born Sept. 15, 1960, in Fort Bragg, N.C..... Set all-time rushing records at Syracuse, erasing marks of former greats such as Jim Brown, Larry Csonka and Floyd Little... Was Giants' second choice in '82 draft behind Butch Woolfolk.

BILLY ARD 29 6-3 270   **Guard**

Voted Pro Bowl alternate for second straight season... Picked up where he left off in 1986 while the rest of the offensive line struggled at times... Excellent run-blocker. Works well with center Bart Oates... Didn't miss a non-strike game and now has played in 95 of last 96 games, not counting the strike... Father Bill Sr. has been a Giants' season-ticket holder for 21 years. The day the team drafted him in the eighth round of the 1981 draft, family members sat in the balcony holding a sign that read: "Let Ard Be Your Guard."... Named first-team All-American as a senior at Wake Forest... Born March 12, 1959, in East Orange, N.J.

LIONEL MANUEL 26 5-11 180   **Wide Receiver**

Silenced critics who kept calling him injury-prone by playing a full season... Finished third on team with 30 receptions for 545 yards... Deep threat... Best per-catch average on team in '87 with 18.5 yards... Only a seventh-round draft pick in 1984 out of Pacific, where he was a wide receiver and running back... Made impact as rookie, finishing year as starter... Led Giant receivers in '85... Missed most of '86 season with knee injury, but recovered in time to make two big catches in NFC championship game against the Redskins and three more in the Super Bowl... Will earn $225,000 this season in final year of contract... Born April 13, 1962, in Los Angeles ... Is talented musician (guitar, drums).

MARK BAVARO 25 6-4 245   Tight End

The best at his position, with only three years' experience... Overcame slow start to finish with 55 catches for 867 yards, seventh in the NFC and tops in the league among tight ends ... His eight touchdowns were a team high and tied for third in the league behind San Francisco's Jerry Rice (22) and Philadelphia's Mike Quick (11)... A human transport for would-be tacklers... Strong, durable... Only does his talking by performance on the field... Played with broken toe and broken jaw in '86... Somehow lasted until the fourth round of the '84 draft... Notre Dame grad... Born April 28, 1963, in East Boston, Mass.... Earned $160,000 in final year of contract... Was outstanding high jumper and hurdler in high school.

TERRY KINARD 29 6-1 200   Free Safety

Couldn't have asked for much more considering he came back after major knee surgery the year before... Started all 12 non-strike games and led team with five interceptions worth 163 yards in returns, including a 70-yarder for a touchdown... Had 55 tackles, tied with strong safety Ken Hill for fifth on the team... Returned stability to safety spot... First-rounder out of Clemson in 1983, he was unanimous choice for All-NFL Rookie team... Was on his way to best season as a pro before tearing knee ligaments Dec. 7, 1986, against the Redskins... Had four interceptions, 59 tackles, a quarterback sack and two fumble recoveries heading into that game... An All-American at Clemson, he played in the Hula Bowl and Senior Bowl (MVP)... Born Nov. 24, 1959, in Bitburg, Germany, where his dad served in the Air Force... Grew up in Sumter, S.C., and had several basketball scholarship offers, but cast his lot in football.

COACH BILL PARCELLS: Endured one of the toughest seasons in his coaching career...No Gatorade baths in '87. Could never find the rhythm that was with his team in '86 and he watched them struggle to 6-9 after winning Super Bowl XXI ...Has record of 47-38-1 over five seasons with Giants...All business. Turned down television offers during Super Bowl week last January because he said he had too much work to do...Best friends include Raiders' owner Al Davis and Indiana basketball coach Bob Knight...Started coaching career at Wichita State. Worked as assistant at Army, Vanderbilt, Florida State and Texas Tech before becoming head coach at Air Force in 1978...Joined Patriots as linebacker coach in 1980...Became Giants' defensive coordinator following season and moved up to head coach when Ray Perkins left in '83...Team missed playoffs for first time in four seasons...Born Aug. 22, 1941, in Englewood, N.J....Was an All-Missouri Valley linebacker at Wichita State.

LONGEST PLAY

There weren't many highlights for the Giants in 1966 as Allie Sherman's team finished 1-12-1. But in the season opener against the Steelers (a 34-34 tie), Earl Morrall connected with Homer Jones for a 98-yard touchdown, the longest via a pass in team history.

Erich Barnes' 102-yard kickoff return against Dallas on Oct. 15, 1961, is the record for longest play, followed by Henry Carr's 101-yard kickoff return against the Rams on Nov. 13, 1966.

INDIVIDUAL GIANT RECORDS
Rushing

Most Yards Game:	218	Gene Roberts, vs Chi. Cardinals, 1950
Season:	1,516	Joe Morris, 1986
Career:	4,638	Alex Webster, 1955-64

Passing

Most TD Passes Game:	7	Y. A. Tittle, vs Washington, 1962
Season:	36	Y. A. Tittle, 1963
Career:	173	Charlie Conerly, 1948-61

Receiving

Most TD Passes Game:	4	Earnest Gray, vs St. Louis, 1980
Season:	13	Homer Jones, 1967
Career:	48	Kyle Rote, 1951-61

Scoring

Most Points Game:	24	Ron Johnson, vs Philadelphia, 1972
	24	Earnest Gray, vs St. Louis, 1980
Season:	127	Ali Haji-Sheikh, 1983
Career:	646	Pete Gogolak, 1966-74
Most TDs Game:	4	Ron Johnson, vs Philadelphia, 1972
	4	Earnest Gray, vs St. Louis, 1980
Season:	21	Joe Morris, 1985
Career:	78	Frank Gifford, 1952-60, 1962-64

PHILADELPHIA EAGLES

TEAM DIRECTORY: Owner: Norman Braman; Pres/CEO: Harry Gamble; VP-Finance: Mimi Box; VP-Marketing: Decker Uhlhorn; VP-Player Personnel: Bill Davis; Dir. Player Personnel: Joe Woolley; Dir. Pub. Rel.: Ron Howard; Head Coach: Buddy Ryan. Home field: Veterans Stadium (65,356). Colors: Kelly green, white and silver.

SCOUTING REPORT

OFFENSE: The Eagles have a dangerous quarterback in Randall Cunningham, a game-breaking receiver in Mike Quick and two promising running backs in Keith Byars and Anthony Toney. They also happen to have one of the most erratic offenses in football. Part of the problem for the NFL's 10th-ranked offense is

QB Randall Cunningham led Eagle rushers with 505 yards.

a still-developing offensive line and, to some extent, Cunningham himself.

Cunningham (223 of 406 for 2,786 yards) can scramble, throw on the run and make plays when it appears there is no play to make, but is as mistake-prone as he is spectacular. While he topped the 1,000-yard rushing mark for his career (three seasons), he also led the NFC in fumbles last season with 12. The good news is that the offensive line is learning to adjust to Cunningham's out-of-pocket ventures as they yielded 72 sacks, down from 104 in '86.

There's good depth at running back, important since Byars (426 yards) has yet to play a full season because of a foot injury. Toney (473 yards) was the Eagles' second-leading receiver with 39 catches, and Junior Tautalatasi, Michael Haddix and Bobby Morse are all-purpose types who all fit into the Eagles' scheme of things.

Besides a late-season knee injury to guard Ron Baker, the only other question mark is at tight end, where aging John Spagnola and Jimmie Giles may give way to No. 1 pick Keith Jackson of Oklahoma.

DEFENSE: Buddy Ryan's swarming "46" defense forced 48 turnovers, tied with New Orleans for tops in the league. Philadelphia has one of the best front fours in the game, featuring sack-master Reggie White at defensive end and DT Jerome Brown, voted NFC Defensive Rookie of the Year by league players. White rushed opposing quarterbacks to the tune of 21 sacks (second-most in NFL history) and the linebackers were adept at stopping the run. The Eagles did not allow over 100 yards on the ground in any of the 12 non-strike games. Veteran Garry Cobb and Seth Joyner, whom Ryan felt should have been a Pro Bowler, are the outside backers while second-year man Byron Evans will battle Mike Reichenbach for the starting inside job.

The secondary is an area of concern. Cornerback Roynell Young never got on track after missing training camp because of a contract dispute, and there was never consistency on the left side, where Elbert Foules and William Frizzell shared starting duties. Strong safety Andre Waters led the team in tackles with 111, and Terry Hoage is an able free safety.

KICKING GAME: Ryan doesn't believe in keeping players just to play special teams, which may be why this area is the team's weakest. In 12 non-strike games, the Eagles finished last in the NFL in both punt and kickoff returns. They ranked 25th in kickoff coverage. Paul McFadden made only 16 of 26 field goals.

EAGLES VETERAN ROSTER

HEAD COACH—Buddy Ryan. Assistant Coaches—Dave Atkins, Jeff Fisher, Dale Haupt, Ronnie Jones, Dan Neal, Wade Phillips, Ted Plumb, Al Roberts, Doug Scovil, Bill Walsh.

No.	Name	Pos.	Ht.	Wt.	NFL Exp.	College
72	Alexander, David	T	6-3	275	2	Tulsa
58	Allert, Ty	LB	6-2	233	3	Texas
87	Bailey, Eric	TE	6-5	240	2	Kansas State
63	Baker, Ron	G	6-4	274	11	Oklahoma State
23	Brown, Cedrick	CB	5-10	182	2	Washington State
99	Brown, Jerome	DT	6-2	292	2	Miami
41	Byars, Keith	RB	6-1	230	3	Ohio State
80	Carter, Cris	WR	6-3	194	2	Ohio State
6	Cavanaugh, Matt	QB	6-2	210	11	Pittsburgh
71	Clarke, Ken	DT	6-2	296	11	Syracuse
27	Clemmons, Topper	RB	5-11	205	2	Wake Forest
50	Cobb, Garry	LB	6-2	230	10	Southern California
79	Conwell, Joe	T	6-5	286	3	North Carolina
21	Cooper, Evan	S	5-11	194	5	Michigan
45	Crawford, Charles	RB	6-2	243	2	Oklahoma State
12	Cunningham, Randall	QB	6-4	192	4	Nevada-Las Vegas
78	Darwin, Matt	T	6-4	275	3	Texas A&M
93	Dumbauld, Jonathan	DE	6-4	259	3	Kentucky
56	Evans, Byron	LB	6-2	225	2	Arizona
67	Feehery, Gerry	C	6-2	270	6	Syracuse
29	Foules, Elbert	CB	5-11	193	6	Alcorn State
33	Frizzell, William	S	6-3	205	5	N. Carolina Central
86	Garrity, Gregg	WR	5-10	169	6	Penn State
38	Gary, Russell	S	5-11	200	8	Nebraska
83	Giles, Jimmie	TE	6-3	240	12	Alcorn State
90	Golic, Mike	DE-DT	6-5	275	3	Notre Dame
26	Haddix, Michael	RB	6-2	227	6	Mississippi State
62	Haden, Nick	G	6-2	270	2	Penn State
34	Hoage, Terry	S	6-3	201	5	Georgia
48	Hopkins, Wes	S	6-1	212	5	Southern Methodist
53	Jiles, Dwayne	LB	6-4	250	4	Texas Tech
54	Johnson, Alonzo	LB	6-3	222	3	Florida
85	Johnson, Ron	WR	6-3	186	4	Long Beach State
59	Joyner, Seth	LB	6-2	241	3	Texas-El Paso
64	Kelley, Mike	G-C	6-5	280	3	Norte Dame
97	Klingel, John	DE	6-3	267	2	Kentucky
65	Landsee, Bob	G-C	6-4	273	2	Wisconsin
89	Little, Dave	TE	6-2	226	5	Middle Tenn. State
8	McFadden, Paul	K	5-11	166	5	Youngstown State
36	Morse, Bobby	RB-KR	5-10	213	2	Michigan State
74	Pitts, Mike	DT	6-5	277	6	Alabama
82	Quick, Mike	WR	6-2	190	7	North Carolina State
66	Reeves, Ken	T-G	6-5	270	4	Texas A&M
55	Reichenbach, Mike	LB	6-2	230	5	East Stroudsburg
76	Schreiber, Adam	G	6-4	277	5	Texas
95	Schulz, Jody	LB	6-3	235	5	East Carolina
96	Simmons, Clyde	DE	6-6	276	3	Western Carolina
68	Singletary, Reggie	G	6-3	280	3	North Carolina State
88	Spagnola, John	TE	6-4	242	9	Yale
37	Tautalatasi, Junior	RB	5-10	210	3	Washington State
10	Teltschik, John	P	6-2	209	3	Texas
25	Toney, Anthony	RB	6-0	227	3	Texas A&M
20	Waters, Andre	S	5-11	185	5	Cheyney
92	White, Reggie	DE	6-5	285	4	Tennessee
43	Young, Roynell	CB	6-1	185	9	Alcorn State

TOP DRAFT CHOICES

Rd.	Name	Sel. No.	Pos.	Ht.	Wt.	College
1	Jackson, Keith		13	TE	6-2	242	Oklahoma
2	Allen, Eric		30	CB	5-9	185	Arizona State
3	Patchan, Matt		65	T	6-3	274	Miami
5	Everett, Eric		122	CB	5-10	161	Texas Tech
6	McPherson, Don		149	QB	6-1	181	Syracuse

Punter John Teltschik punted a league-leading 82 times but finished with only a 38.2-yard average.

THE ROOKIES: Better pass protection is on the way for the Eagles. Jackson, a consensus All-American despite catching only 13 passes in the wishbone, is an excellent blocker. So is tackle Matt Patchan, No. 3 pick from Miami, which uses a pro-style passing game. No. 2 Eric Allen of Arizona State will get a chance to start at cornerback. Quarterback Don McPherson of Syracuse, the Heisman runnerup selected on round six, should fit in the Eagle system.

OUTLOOK: Ryan has predicted the Eagles (7-8 in '87) would make the playoffs in each of his first two seasons, but they still appear a few players away. If the offensive line keeps improving and injuries stay at a minimum, they'll challenge for a wild-card berth.

EAGLE PROFILES

RANDALL CUNNINGHAM 25 6-4 192   Quarterback

Threw a touchdown pass in 12 consecutive starts, tying Cardinals' Neil Lomax for longest streak in NFC in '87...Proved to be more than just a one-dimensional, scrambling quarterback. At one point, threw 118 passes without an interception...His 23 touchdown passes an Eagle high since 1981...Rushed for 505 yards...Voted NFC Player of the Week after completing 17 of 32 passes for 291 yards and three touchdowns against St. Louis...Became free agent at end of season...Brother, Sam, starred for USC and the Patriots...Second-round pick in 1985 out of Nevada-Las Vegas, where he became only third quarterback in NCAA history to throw for over 2,500 yards in three consecutive seasons, joining John Elway and Doug Flutie...Born March 27, 1963, in Santa Barbara, Cal. ...Selected as Pro Bowl alternate.

MIKE QUICK 29 6-2 190   Wide Receiver

After only five seasons he is fourth on the team's all-time receiving list with 319 catches for 5,593 yards and 54 touchdowns...Made Pro Bowl for fifth consecutive year, third as a starter...His 11 touchdown receptions tied for second in the league in '87...Assumed more of a leadership role, as coach Buddy Ryan had wanted...Served as alternate player rep . . . Has lived up to his press clippings as first-round choice out of North Carolina State in 1982 . . . Deep threat with good hands . . . Co-owns a New Jersey fitness and racquet club with teammate John Spagnola and former Eagle quarterback Ron Jaworski . . . Runs a summer football camp in North Carolina . . . Born May 14, 1959, in Hamlet, N.C.

ANTHONY TONEY 25 6-0 227   Fullback

One of Buddy Ryan's favorite players . . . Strong, power-type runner . . . Second-leading rusher, behind Randall Cunningham, with 473 yards on 127 carries, and second-leading receiver with 39 catches for 341 yards . . . Started 11 of 12 non-strike games . . . Can play both fullback and tailback although Ryan prefers him at fullback with Keith Byars at tailback . . . Ryan made no secret before the 1986 draft that he wanted Toney . . . Eagles chose the Texas A&M standout on second round (37th overall) . . . Born Sept. 23, 1962, in Salinas, Cal. . . . Scheduled to earn $175,000 in base salary this season.

RON BAKER 33 6-4 274   Guard

"He didn't have a bad game all year," Buddy Ryan said . . . Leader of the offensive line . . . Has started 101 games, 73 more than any other Philadelphia offensive lineman . . . Second-oldest player on the team, only one of four remaining from the team that made the Super Bowl in 1980 . . . Co-offensive captain . . . Missed two games because of a knee injury . . . Has started in 98 of 101 games since coming to the Eagles in trade with the Colts . . . Drafted in 10th round by Baltimore in 1977 . . . Played mostly as a reserve before Philly . . . Played two years at Oklahoma State after transferring from Indian Hills Community College in Centerville, Iowa . . . Born Nov. 19, 1954, in Gary, Ind.

KEITH BYARS 24 6-1 230   Running Back

Another up-and-down year . . . Didn't register first 100-yard game until regular-season finale against Buffalo . . . Bothered most of the season by foot injury that had kept him sidelined half his rookie season . . . Still finished as team's third-leading rusher with 426 yards on 116 carries . . . Ranked 18th in NFC, making Eagles only team to post three players in top

20 of conference rushing statistics . . . A first-round pick in 1986 (10th overall), he broke a metatarsal bone in his left foot during his senior year at Ohio State and reinjured the foot during the Eagles' mini-camp as a rookie . . . Was second-leading rusher in Buckeye history behind two-time Heisman Trophy winner Archie Griffin . . . Born Oct. 14, 1963, in Dayton, Ohio, where he was a star forward on the high-school state basketball champions and a hard-hitting centerfielder in baseball . . . Will earn $300,000 this season.

REGGIE WHITE 26 6-5 285   Defensive End/Tackle

All-Everything in his third season . . . His 21 sacks in 12 games came just one shy of the NFL record set in 16 games by the New York Jets' Mark Gastineau . . . Dating back to 1986 he has registered at least one sack in 15 of the last 16 games in which he has played . . . Pro Bowl starter for second straight season . . . Strong, quick, fierce pass-rusher . . . "When Reggie is left on a back, it's Katie bar the door—your quarterback is going down," Washington's Joe Gibbs said . . . He's a Baptist minister. "Every time we win he credits the Lord, but whenever we lose, everybody blames me," Buddy Ryan said . . . Moves up and down line of scrimmage, playing end most of the time and over center in "46." . . . Has 52 sacks in three seasons, already making him the team's all-time leader in that category . . . Chosen by the Eagles in first round of 1984 supplemental draft . . . Joined Philly after playing two years with Memphis Showboats of the USFL . . . Will earn $400,000 base salary plus $125,000 roster bonus . . . Born Dec. 19, 1961, in Chattanooga, Tenn. . . . Lombardi Award finalist at Tennessee.

SETH JOYNER 23 6-2 241   Linebacker

Played like a Pro Bowl linebacker in the opinion of Buddy Ryan. "He's as good as some of the linebackers I had seen in Chicago," Ryan said . . . Had six games with nine or more tackles. Finished third on the team with 96 . . . Tied for third on team with four sacks behind White (21) and Clyde Simmons (6) . . . Blocked a 50-yard field goal against the Giants in overtime and ran back a fumble 18 yards for a touchdown against the Saints . . . Key member of team's offseason basketball team . . . Ryan calls him "Zeff" . . . Earned $75,000 in final year of contract last season . . . Born Nov. 18, 1964, in Spring Valley, N.Y. . . . An eighth-round pick out of Texas-El Paso in 1986.

ANDRE WATERS 26 5-11 185   Strong Safety

Buddy Ryan's type of player: hard-nosed, not well-liked around the league... Team's leading tackler with 112. Had three interceptions... Plays linebacker in "46"... Had six games with 10 or more tackles... Reduced number of unsportsmanlike conduct penalties from last season... Ran into Redskins' kicker Jess Atkinson in season opener. Atkinson was out for the season with dislocated left ankle... Became a starter in '86 after spending two seasons as special-teams player and reserve back... Will earn $300,000 in final year of contract... Four-year letterman at Cheyney State... Signed with Eagles as free agent in 1984... Born March 10, 1962, in Belle Glade, Fla.

CRIS CARTER 22 6-3 194   Wide Receiver

Should move into departed Kenny Jackson's starting spot... Caught five passes in brief rookie season, two for touchdowns and three for first downs... First pro grab was a 22-yard TD against St. Louis... Could join Mike Quick to give Eagles two deep threats... Chosen in special supplemental draft last summer after he lost last year of eligibility at Ohio State for accepting money from an agent... An All-American as junior, he set all-time Buckeye career record for receptions (158) and marks for TD catches (11) and receiving yardage (1,127)... Nicknamed "Groucho" due to thick eyebrows... Brother Butch played six years in the NBA... Born Nov. 25, 1965, in Middletown, Ohio.

JEROME BROWN 23 6-2 292   Defensive Tackle

Part of three-man rotation at tackle along with Ken Clarke and Mike Pitts... Fulfilled the promise that convinced Eagles to select him as the ninth player in the 1987 draft... Finished with 50 tackles, four sacks, two interceptions and a fumble recovery... Played with bone chips in elbow and underwent arthroscopic surgery during offseason... Typical University of Miami player, confident, bordering on cocky. After game against Dallas in which he ran 37 yards with a fumble before being caught from behind by Herschel Walker, Ryan said: "He must have been looking at himself on the big screen [at the top of

Texas Stadium]." . . . One of top defensive linemen in country at Miami. First-team All-American . . . Had 75 tackles and five quarterback sacks senior season . . . Majored in criminal justice . . . Grandfather and uncle are ministers. Father Willie is a mechanic . . . While in high school, attended a camp where Reggie White was instructor. Has looked up to White since . . . Born Feb. 4, 1965, in Brooksville, Fla. . . . Will earn $240,000 this season.

COACH BUDDY RYAN: Dennis the Menace of NFL coaches . . . Never at a loss for words . . . Has record of 12-18-1 since coming to Philadelphia in 1986, but he doesn't count the three losses during the '87 strike . . . Regarded as one of the sharpest defensive minds in the game . . . Given total control first two seasons in matters of personnel . . . Gave himself an "A-double-plus" for coaching last season . . . Has coached 20 years in NFL . . . Was given job after Bears won Super Bowl in '86 . . . Innovator of "46" defense, which he installed as Chicago's defensive coordinator . . . In eight seasons with Bears, his defenses ranked among top 10 six times . . . Began coaching career at Gainesville High in Texas (1957-59) . . . Moved into college ranks as defensive coordinator for University of Buffalo from 1961-65 . . . Served as defensive line coach under Bud Grant at Minnesota from 1976-77 before going to Chicago . . . Born Feb. 17, 1934, in Frederick, Okla. . . . Was an offensive guard at Oklahoma State and a master sergeant in the Army in Korea.

LONGEST PLAY

Timmy Brown set many records during his eight years with the Eagles, but none were more spectacular than the ones he posted on kickoff returns.

Dropped by Green Bay as a rookie after the 1959 season (Vince Lombardi said he had "bad hands"), Brown signed as a free agent with the Eagles in 1960.

In the 1961 opener against the Browns he returned a kickoff 105 yards in a 27-20 victory. Over his career he had five kickoff returns for TDs, two in one game against the Cowboys in 1966.

INDIVIDUAL EAGLE RECORDS

Rushing

Most Yards Game:	205	Steve Van Buren, vs Pittsburgh, 1949
Season:	1,512	Wilbert Montgomery, 1979
Career:	6,538	Wilbert Montgomery, 1977-84

Passing

Most TD Passes Game:	7	Adrian Burk, vs Washington, 1954
Season:	32	Sonny Jurgensen, 1961
Career:	167	Ron Jaworski, 1977-85

Receiving

Most TD Passes Game:	4	Joe Carter, vs Cincinnati, 1934
	4	Ben Hawkins, vs Pittsburgh, 1969
Season:	13	Tommy McDonald, 1960 and 1961
	13	Mike Quick, 1983
Career:	79	Harold Carmichael, 1971-83

Scoring

Most Points Game:	25	Bobby Walston, vs Washington, 1954
Season:	116	Paul McFadden, 1984
Career:	881	Bobby Walston, 1951-62
Most TDs Game:	4	Joe Carter, vs Cincinnati, 1934
	4	Clarence Peaks, vs St. Louis, 1958
	4	Tommy McDonald, vs N.Y. Giants, 1959
	4	Ben Hawkins, vs Pittsburgh, 1969
	4	Wilbert Montgomery, vs Washington, 1978
	4	Wilbert Montgomery, vs Washington, 1979
Season:	18	Steve Van Buren, 1945
Career:	79	Harold Carmichael, 1971-83

PHOENIX CARDINALS

TEAM DIRECTORY: Chairman: William Bidwill; VP-Administration: Curt Mosher; Dir. Pro Personnel: Larry Wilson; Dir. Pub. Rel.: Bob Rose; Head Coach: Gene Stallings. Home field: Sun Devil Stadium (72,600). Colors: Cardinal red, white and black.

SCOUTING REPORT

OFFENSE: The rejuvenated Neil Lomax made the Pro Bowl for the second time in his seven-year career, completing 275 of 463 (59.4) of his passes for 24 touchdowns and only 12 interceptions. The Cardinals ranked sixth in the NFL in both passing yardage (230.2 per game) and overall yardage (355.1), respectively.

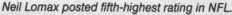

Neil Lomax posted fifth-highest rating in NFL.

Lomax was the most noticeable difference in the Cardinals' offense from a year ago and his receivers were a big reason. All-Pro J.T. Smith led the NFL in catches (91) and receiving yardage (1,117), and Roy Green recovered from an injury-plagued '86 to catch 43 passes for a 17.1-yard average. Tight end Rob Awalt emerged as a pleasant surprise by grabbing 42 passes including six touchdowns and was voted NFL Rookie of the Year by *The Sporting News*.

The Cardinals have a fine running back tandem in versatile Stump Mitchell and fullback Earl Ferrell. Mitchell accounted for 1,178 yards (781 rushing, 397 receiving). Ferrell is a punishing blocker who bulled in for seven touchdowns (second-most in the NFC behind Charles White) despite missing the final four games with a knee injury.

Left tackle Luis Sharpe is a pillar on an improving offensive line that still needs work on its pass protection. The Cardinals allowed 54 sacks in '87.

DEFENSE: Not satisfactory. The Cardinals ranked 25th in both overall yards (358.9) and passing yards (225.5) surrendered. Only Freddie Joe Nunn, who made a successful switch from line-backer to defensive end with 11 sacks, produced any consistent pass-rushing threat. That was particularly vexing to coach Gene Stallings, who switched from the 3-4 to the 4-3 defense primarily to get more pressure on the quarterback. Stallings hopes the return of defensive end David Galloway (out all of '87 with a fractured forearm) will help.

He also hopes a linebacking crew headed by E.J. Junior will continue to mature. Ken Harvey of California, the club's third No. 1 pick in the last four years, will have his share of action behind Niko Noga and Anthony Bell.

The secondary is the big worry. Cardinal defensive backs managed only nine interceptions—and five of those were by sub safety Travis Curtis. Strong safety Leonard Smith led the team in tackles (109) for the third straight season and Lonnie Young is a solid performer at free safety, but the Cardinals seem woefully undermanned at cornerback.

KICKING GAME: Still a continuing headache. Punter Greg Horne (40.5-yard average in the final five games) showed the best among many candidates. The Cardinals have converted less than 50 percent of field-goal tries in the last three years and are still searching for a regular kicker. Vai Sikahema is one of the league's premier kickoff and return men.

CARDINALS VETERAN ROSTER

HEAD COACH—Gene Stallings. Assistant Coaches—Marv Braden, Tom Bresnahan, LeBaron Caruthers, Jim Johnson, Hank Kuhlmann, Leon McLaughlin, Mal Moore, Joe Pascale, Jim Shofner, Dennis Thurman.

No.	Name	Pos.	Ht.	Wt.	NFL Exp.	College
60	Alvord, Steve	DT	6-4	272	2	Washington
80	Awalt, Robert	TE	6-5	248	2	San Diego State
52	Baker, Charlie	LB	6-2	234	9	New Mexico
55	Bell, Anthony	LB	6-3	231	3	Michigan State
71	Bostic, Joe	G	6-3	268	10	Clemson
62	Brown, Ray	G-T	6-5	280	3	Arkansas State
82	Brown, Ron	WR	5-10	186	2	Colorado
41	Carter, Carl	CB	5-11	180	3	Texas Tech
74	Chilton, Gene	T	6-3	271	3	Texas
79	Clasby, Bob	DT	6-5	260	3	Notre Dame
20	Curtis, Travis	S	5-10	180	2	West Virginia
53	Davis, Wayne	LB	6-1	213	2	Alabama
17	Del Greco, Al	K	5-10	191	5	Auburn
73	Duda, Mark	DT	6-3	279	6	Maryland
31	Ferrell, Earl	RB	6-0	240	7	East Tenn. State
13	Gallery, Jim	K	6-1	190	2	Minnesota
65	Galloway, David	DE	6-3	279	7	Florida
76	Garalczyk, Mark	DT	6-5	272	2	Western Michigan
10	Garza, Sammy	QB	6-1	184	2	Texas-El Paso
81	Green, Roy	WR	6-0	195	10	Henderson State
75	Greer, Curtis	DE	6-4	258	8	Michigan
89	Harris, William	TE	6-4	243	2	Texas
82	Holmes, Don	WR	5-10	180	3	Mesa
11	Horne, Greg	P	6-0	188	2	Arkansas
21	Jackson, Mark	CB	5-9	180	2	Abilene Christian
50	Jarostchuk, Ilia	LB	6-3	231	2	New Hampshire
27	Johnson, Greggory	CB-S	6-1	195	6	Oklahoma State
87	Johnson, Troy	WR	6-1	175	3	Southern
54	Junior, E.J.	LB	6-3	235	8	Alabama
70	Kennard, Derek	C	6-3	285	3	Nevada-Reno
15	Lomax, Neil	QB	6-3	215	8	Portland State
47	Mack, Cedric	CB	6-0	194	6	Baylor
33	McAdoo, Derrick	RB	5-10	198	2	Baylor
46	McDonald, Tim	S	6-2	207	2	Southern California
30	Mitchell, Stump	RB	5-9	188	8	Citadel
68	Morris, Michael	G	6-5	275	2	NE Missouri State
57	Noga, Niko	LB	6-1	235	5	Hawaii
85	Novacek, Jay	TE	6-4	235	4	Wyoming
78	Nunn, Freddie Joe	DE	6-4	255	4	Mississippi
64	Peat, Todd	G	6-2	294	2	Northern Illinois
63	Robbins, Tootie	T	6-5	302	7	East Carolina
51	Ruether, Mike	C	6-4	275	3	Texas
72	Saddler, Rod	DE	6-5	276	2	Texas A&M
39	Sargent, Broderick	RB	5-10	215	3	Baylor
69	Scotts, Colin	DT	6-5	263	2	Hawaii
67	Sharpe, Luis	T	6-4	260	7	UCLA
36	Sikahema, Val	RB-KR	5-9	191	3	Brigham Young
84	Smith, J.T.	WR	6-2	185	11	North Texas State
61	Smith, Lance	G	6-2	262	4	Louisiana State
45	Smith, Leonard	S	5-11	202	6	McNeese State
18	Stoudt, Cliff	QB	6-4	215	10	Youngstown State
66	Welter, Tom	T	6-5	280	2	Nebraska
24	Wolfley, Ron	RB	6-0	222	4	West Virginia
43	Young, Lonnie	S	6-1	182	4	Michigan State

TOP DRAFT CHOICES

Rd.	Name	Sel. No.	Pos.	Ht.	Wt.	College
1	Harvey, Ken	12	LB	6-2	224	California
2	Jeffery, Tony	38	RB	5-11	201	Texas Christian
3	Tupa, Tom	68	P/QB	6-4	213	Ohio State
4	Brim, Michael	95	DB	6-0	186	Virginia Union
5	Gaines, Chris	120	LB	6-0	228	Vanderbilt
5	Jordan, Tony	132	RB	6-2	220	Kansas State

THE ROOKIES: The Cardinals look for Harvey, an agile and physical 6-2, 224-pounder, to provide help on the pass rush. Running back Tony Jeffery of Texas Christian has breakaway speed and the Cardinals were fortunate to get him on the second round. Tom Tupa, Ohio State's starting quarterback in 1987, was drafted primarily as a punter in round three. Tupa averaged 41 yards per punt during his collegiate career.

OUTLOOK: Stallings is improving the team year by year, but he still needs defensive help. As the Phoenix in mythology rose from the ashes, perhaps these birds in their new setting in the Southwest can soar beyond their 7-8 mark of last season. That may be expecting too much.

CARDINAL PROFILES

NEIL LOMAX 29 6-3 215   Quarterback

"Comeback Kid" of 1987...Not only did he regain status as one of league's best quarterbacks after a dismal '86 season, he directed the Cardinals to two dramatic come-from-behind victories—against the Buccaneers and the Cowboys...Erased a 28-3 deficit in final period against Tampa and Cardinals won, 31-28...Cardinals rewarded him by renegotiating his contract through 1991. Will earn base of $1.15 million this season, $1.3 million in '89, $1.4 million in '90 and $1.5 million in '91...Contract was announced day after league approved team's move to Phoenix...Made Pro Bowl for second time in career as he passed for 230 or more yards in 10 of 12 starts...Produced second-best season for quarterback in team history, completing 275 of 463 for a league-high 3,387 yards. Threw for 24 touchdowns and only 12 interceptions...Has thrown only 17 interceptions in last 695 attempts...Attended Portland State...Second-round draft pick in 1981...Born Feb. 17, 1959, in Lake Oswego, Ore.

STUMP MITCHELL 29 5-9 188   Running Back

The "Little Big Man" of the NFL, he overcame a slow start in '87 to lead club in rushing for third consecutive season (203 carries for 781 yards)...Combined yards ranked fifth in league (1,178). The team's all-time combined yardage leader with 10,652, he needs only 106 yards to surpass Jim Otis (3,863) and claim second place on club's all-time rushing list.

Tied team record last year for three consecutive 100-yard games—101 vs. Washington, 111 vs. Giants and 101 vs. Tampa Bay—and fell only nine yards shy of the 100-yard mark for a fourth straight game in season finale against Dallas . . . Wore protective shield underneath face mask after suffering a fractured nose against the Giants Oct. 25 . . . Real name is Lyvonia Albert . . . Ninth-round draft choice out of The Citadel in 1981 . . . Born March 15, 1959, in Kingsland, Ga.

ROY GREEN 31 6-0 195   Wide Receiver

The "Jet Steam" hasn't been flowing last two seasons because of injuries. After missing five games in '86 because of ankle surgery, he sat out 4½ games last season because of a sore hamstring. But he finished ninth among NFL receivers in yardage with 731 . . . At 31, he could still do some serious damage to opposing defensive backs if he can remain healthy . . . Needs 13 touchdown catches to break Sonny Randle's team record (60) . . . In 1981 he became the first player since Washington's Eddie Sutton (1957) to catch a TD pass and intercept a pass in the same game (vs. Redskins) . . . Made permanent switch from defensive back to receiver after that season . . . Fourth-round draft choice out of Henderson State (1979) . . . Born June 30, 1957, in Magnolia, Ark.

ROBERT AWALT 24 6-5 248   Tight End

A third-round draft choice out of San Diego State last year, he exceeded all expectations . . . Became a starter at midseason when Jay Novacek was injured and wound up as *The Sporting News* and NFL Players' Association Rookie of the Year . . . Caught nine passes in his debut against the Eagles Nov. 1 and nine more the following week against Tampa Bay, ending the year with 42 receptions for 526 yards and six touchdowns . . . No other NFC rookie caught more passes and only Mark Bavaro of the Giants had more receptions among tight ends . . . He was a star schoolboy quarterback in Sacramento and a freshman quarterback at Nevada-Reno before transferring to San Diego State, where he became a tight end . . . "Sometimes he thinks he is the quarterback," says Neil Lomax. "He's pretty noisy in the huddle suggesting things that might work. I always tell him he's too big to be a quarterback." . . . Born April 9, 1964, in Landsthul, West Germany.

LEONARD SMITH 27 5-11 202   Strong Safety

Crossing the picket line probably cost him a trip to Hawaii last February...That seemed the only logical reason Smith failed to make the Pro Bowl; he was voted an alternate for the second straight season...Finished with a team-high 109 tackles, five sacks, three fumble recoveries, three caused fumbles and one interception...Blocked field goal against Tampa Bay...Has made a total of 344 tackles over last three seasons...A first-round 1983 draft choice out of McNeese State, where he blocked 17 punts as a Division 1-AA All-American...Born Sept. 2, 1960, in New Orleans.

E. J. JUNIOR 28 6-3 235   Linebacker

Injuries have kept him from matching his Pro Bowl years of 1984 and 1985, but he's still a major force...At the Pro Bowl (January 1986) he helped rescue a three-year-old victim in a hit-and-run accident and assisted in capturing the perpetrator...Played during the '87 strike, missed two games because of a strained hamstring and finished fifth on the team in tackles with 53...A return to his old level could give the Cardinals one of the top linebacking corps in the NFC, assuming Niko Noga remains healthy in the middle and Anthony Bell continues to improve...Was an All-American defensive end and shortstop and catcher at Alabama and a first-round draft choice in 1981...Born Dec. 8, 1959, in Nashville, Tenn.

LUIS SHARPE 28 6-4 260   Tackle

Majored in political science but didn't get the votes he deserved for the Pro Bowl until last season...Considered one of the best pass-blockers in the league...Voted second-team All-NFC by UPI. Stood out against Redskins' end Dexter Manley and Giant linebacker Lawrence Taylor...Voted offensive team captain by teammates before the season...Moved with family from Havana, Cuba, to Detroit when he was six...Fluent in two languages, does interviews with Spanish radio stations in a number of NFL cities...First-round draft choice out of UCLA in 1982...Went from St. Louis to Memphis

of USFL in spring of '85, then back to Cardinals in fall of '85.
Didn't miss a game. Born June 16, 1960, in Havana.

FREDDIE JOE NUNN 26 6-4 255 — Defensive End

Started raising havoc at left end after being
moved there from linebacker when team
switched to 4-3 defense... Showed promise,
finishing fourth in NFC with 11 sacks... Total
was highest by a Cardinal since 1984, when
Curtis Greer had 14... Made UPI All-Rookie
team in '85 as a linebacker and stayed at that
spot in '86 before moving back to the position
he played at Ole Miss... Gained approximately 30 pounds last
offseason but maintained his quickness. Somewhat of a Dexter
Manley-type pass-rusher... He and David Galloway could give
Cardinals one of best end tandems in conference. Born April 9,
1962, in Noxubee County, Miss.

DAVID GALLOWAY 29 6-3 279 — Defensive End

Records and quarterbacks are expected to fall
at his feet this season... Expected to be the
Cardinals' best defensive lineman after missing last season with a fractured left forearm
... Gene Stallings admits he switched his
defense to a 4-3 a year ago so that he could
move Galloway from nose tackle to end...
Imagine how he felt in training camp when he
discovered Galloway was out for the year... Played tackle for
first five seasons and still registered 29½ sacks in 59 career
starts... All-American end at Florida and finalist for Lombardi
Trophy in 1981... Second-round choice in '82... Raised by
older sister after father died when he was two and mother died
when he was seven... Standout on Cardinals' offseason basketball team... Born Feb. 16, 1959, in Tampa.

J. T. SMITH 32 6-12 185 — Wide Receiver

After catching only 25 passes his final three
seasons with the Chiefs (1982-84), he has
grabbed 214 for St. Louis since '85... Has
caught more passes in last two seasons (171)
than any other player in the league... Caught
a team-record 91 for 1,117 yards last season
... He and Washington's Art Monk are only
two NFL wide receivers since '64 to catch

more than 90 in one season . . . Still, Smith didn't make the Pro Bowl even though he made 23 more catches than the league's second-leading receiver, the New York Jets' Al Toon . . . Smith and Green could emerge as league's most lethal receiving duo in '88 . . . Played at North Texas State as wide receiver and kick returner . . . Signed with Redskins as free agent in 1978, was released after six games and signed with Chiefs . . . Was a free-agent signee with the Cardinals in '85 . . . Born Oct, 29, 1955, in Leonard, Tex.

COACH GENE STALLINGS: Has gone a long way in two seasons—from 4-11-1 in 1986 to 7-8 and one victory away from making the NFC playoffs as a wild-card team . . . Has learned to be patient under owner Bill Bidwill. Doesn't always get what he wants. Still doesn't have a say in who the team drafts . . . Tom Landry disciple . . . Defensive-minded . . . Disciplined. Knows how he wants to run the team, just a matter of being allowed to do it . . . An All-Southwest Conference receiver at Texas A&M, he began his coaching career as an assistant at Alabama . . . Later became head coach at Texas A&M . . . Fired after '71 season and became defensive back coach at Dallas . . . Turned down offer with Birmingham of the USFL . . . Replaced Jim Hanifan in 1986 . . . Born March 2, 1935, in Paris, Tex.

LONGEST PLAY

Roy Green, a Cardinal rookie out of Henderson State, was six yards in his own end zone when he took a Dallas kickoff on Oct. 21, 1979.

The swift safety was touched only once—by an off-balance arm swipe by Doug Cosbie on the Cardinal 40—as he sped to a touchdown and into the record book. His 106-yard romp tied the NFL mark set by Green Bay's Al Carmichael (1956, vs. Bears) and Kansas City's Noland Smith (1967, vs. Broncos).

INDIVIDUAL CARDINAL RECORDS

Rushing

Most Yards Game:	203	John David Crow, vs Pittsburgh, 1960
Season:	1,605	Ottis Anderson, 1979
Career:	7,999	Ottis Anderson, 1979-86

Passing

Most TD Passes Game:	6	Jim Hardy, vs Baltimore, 1950
	6	Charley Johnson, vs Cleveland, 1965
	6	Charley Johnson, vs New Orleans, 1969
Season:	28	Charley Johnson, 1963
	28	Neil Lomax, 1984
Career:	205	Jim Hart, 1966-82

Receiving

Most TD Passes Game:	5	Bob Shaw, vs Baltimore, 1950
Season:	15	Sonny Randle, 1960
Career:	60	Sonny Randle, 1959-66

Scoring

Most Points Game:	40	Ernie Nevers, vs Chicago, 1929
Season:	117	Jim Bakken, 1967
	117	Neil O'Donoghue, 1984
Career:	1,380	Jim Bakken, 1962-78
Most TDs Game:	6	Ernie Nevers, vs Chicago, 1929
Season:	17	John David Crow, 1962
Career:	60	Sonny Randle, 1959-66

SAN FRANCISCO 49ERS

TEAM DIRECTORY: Owner/Pres.: Edward J. DeBartolo Jr.; Head Coach: Bill Walsh; Administrative VP-GM: John McVay; Dir. Publicity: Jerry Walker. Home field: Candlestick Park (61,499). Colors: 49er gold and scarlet.

SCOUTING REPORT

OFFENSE: The 49ers led the NFL in total offense last year (399.1 yards per game). Joe Montana, who completed 266 of 398 passes for 3,054 yards and a league-leading 31 touchdowns, won the first NFL passing title of his nine-year career. Still, that didn't prevent off-season rumors which had Montana, 32, being traded to make way for Steve Young, 26, who impressed late in '87 when Montana went down with a hamstring injury. Trade Montana? No way, said coach Bill Walsh, who loves the luxury of having two ace quarterbacks.

Montana's favorite target again will be game-breaker Jerry Rice, who led the NFL with 22 touchdown catches—11 more than his nearest competitor, Philadelphia's Mike Quick. The rest of the receiving corps is undergoing changes. With Dwight Clark retired, Mike Wilson and Wes Chandler figure to catch their share. Chandler, the four-time Pro Bowler obtained from San Diego in the trade for center Fred Quillan, is in his 11th NFL season. John Frank replaces Russ Francis at tight end.

The offensive line is also being renovated. Tackles Bubba Paris and Keith Fahnhorst are nearing the end of their careers. Harris Barton, No. 1 draft choice in '87, has already replaced Fahnhorst at right tackle.

While the 49ers could use depth at running back, Walsh can't complain about a running game that finished first in the league (2,237 yards). Roger Craig finished second in the NFC in receptions with 66 and gained 815 yards rushing. He combines with Joe Cribbs (300 yards) and fullback Tom Rathman (257 yards) for a balanced attack.

DEFENSE: Although the 49ers led the NFL in fewest total yards allowed (4,095), they are looking for a stronger pass rush and figure to make good use of first-rounder Dan Stubbs, a 6-3, 253-pound defensive end from Miami. Second-year defensive end Charles Haley led the club in sacks with six. Pro Bowl nose tackle Michael Carter is the prime reason the 49ers had the league's fifth-best run defense.

At linebacker, Michael Walter led the club in tackles with 94. This is an intelligent group, but veterans Riki Ellison, Keena

Joe Montana enters 10th year with first NFL passing title.

Turner and Todd Shell are coming off injuries.

The strongest part of the 49ers' defense has traditionally been the secondary, where Ronnie Lott still terrorizes opposing ball-carriers with his savage hitting. Cornerbacks Tim McKyer and Don Griffin are rising stars.

KICKING GAME: Walsh is looking to replace 10-year punter Max Runager, but Ray Wersching again should be a dependable placekicker. Special-teams star Dana McLemore finished second in the league in punt returns with a 12.6-yard average.

49ERS VETERAN ROSTER

HEAD COACH—Bill Walsh. Assistant Coaches—Jerry Attaway, Dennis Green, Tommy Hart, Mike Holmgren, Sherman Lewis, Bobb McKittrick, Bill McPherson, Ray Rhodes, George Seifert, Lynn Stiles, Fred vonAppen.

No.	Name	Pos.	Ht.	Wt.	NFL Exp.	College
79	Barton, Harris	T	6-4	280	2	North Carolina
76	Board, Dwaine	DE	6-5	248	9	North Carolina A&T
65	Bregel, Jeff	G	6-4	280	2	Southern California
95	Carter, Michael	NT	6-2	285	5	Southern Methodist
—	Chandler, Wes	WR	6-0	188	11	Florida
69	Collie, Bruce	T-G	6-6	275	4	Texas-Arlington
59	Comeaux, Darren	LB	6-1	227	7	Arizona State
52	Cooper, George	LB	6-2	225	2	Michigan State
57	Cousineau, Tom	LB	6-3	225	7	Ohio State
33	Craig, Roger	RB	6-0	224	6	Nebraska
83	Crawford, Derrick	WR-KR	5-10	185	2	Memphis State
21	Cribbs, Joe	RB	5-11	193	8	Auburn
51	Cross, Randy	G	6-3	265	13	UCLA
57	Dean, Kevin	LB	6-1	235	2	Texas Christian
25	DuBose, Doug	RB	5-11	190	1	Nebraska
50	Ellison, Riki	LB	6-2	225	6	Southern California
75	Fagan, Kevin	DE	6-3	260	2	Miami
55	Fahnhorst, Jim	LB	6-4	235	5	Minnesota
32	Flagler, Terrence	RB	6-0	200	2	Clemson
86	Frank, John	TE	6-3	225	5	Ohio State
49	Fuller, Jeff	S-LB	6-2	216	5	Texas A&M
11	Gagliano, Bob	QB	6-3	205	5	Utah State
93	Glover, Clyde	DE	6-6	280	2	Fresno State
29	Griffin, Don	CB	6-0	176	3	Middle Tenn. State
92	Hadley, Ron	LB	6-2	240	2	Washington
94	Haley, Charles	DE-LB	6-5	230	3	James Madison
81	Heller, Ron	TE	6-4	235	2	Oregon State
46	Holmoe, Tom	S	6-2	195	5	Brigham Young
88	Jones, Brent	TE	6-4	230	2	Santa Clara
67	Kugler, Pete	NT-DE	6-4	255	6	Penn State
92	Lilly, Kevin	DE	6-4	265	1	Tulsa
42	Lott, Ronnie	S	6-0	200	8	Southern California
84	Margerum, Ken	WR	6-0	180	6	Stanford
53	McColl, Milt	LB	6-6	230	8	Stanford
62	McIntyre, Guy	G	6-3	264	5	Georgia
22	McKyer, Tim	CB	6-0	174	3	Texas-Arlington
43	McLemore, Dana	CB	5-10	183	7	Hawaii
97	Mikolas, Doug	NT	6-1	270	2	Portland State
16	Montana, Joe	QB	6-2	195	10	Notre Dame
88	Nicholas, Calvin	WR	6-4	208	1	Grambling
20	Nixon, Tory	CB	5-11	186	4	San Diego State
77	Paris, Bubba	T	6-6	299	6	Michigan
15	Paye, John	QB	6-3	205	1	Stanford
44	Rathman, Tom	RB	6-1	232	3	Nebraska
80	Rice, Jerry	WR	6-2	200	4	Miss. Valley State
91	Roberts, Larry	DE	6-3	264	3	Alabama
4	Runager, Max	P	6-1	189	10	South Carolina
61	Sapolu, Jesse	G-C	6-4	260	3	Hawaii
90	Shell, Todd	LB	6-4	225	4	Brigham Young
72	Stover, Jeff	DE	6-5	275	7	Oregon
24	Sydney, Harry	RB	6-0	217	2	Kansas
82	Taylor, John	WR	6-1	185	2	Delaware State
60	Thomas, Chuck	C	6-3	280	3	Oklahoma
41	Thomas, Sean	S-CB	5-11	192	1	Texas Christian
58	Turner, Keena	LB	6-2	222	9	Purdue
74	Wallace, Steve	T	6-5	276	3	Auburn
99	Walter, Michael	LB	6-3	238	6	Oregon
14	Wersching, Ray	K	5-11	215	16	California
27	Williams, Dokie	WR	5-11	180	6	UCLA
27	Williamson, Carlton	S	6-0	204	8	Pittsburgh
85	Wilson, Mike	WR	6-3	215	8	Washington State
21	Wright, Eric	CB	6-1	185	7	Missouri
8	Young, Steve	QB	6-2	200	4	Brigham Young

TOP DRAFT CHOICES

Rd.	Name	Sel. No.	Pos.	Ht.	Wt.	College
2	Stubbs, Daniel	33	DE	6-3	253	Miami
2	Holt, Pierce	39	DT	6-4	274	Angelo State
3	Romanowski, Bill	80	LB	6-3	227	Boston College
4	Helton, Barry	103	P	6-4	190	Colorado
7	Bryant, Kevin	191	LB	6-2	223	Delaware State

THE ROOKIES: A pass rush is what the 49ers said they wanted; that's what they'll get from Stubbs, who holds the all-time Miami record for sacks with 39½. No. 2 pick Pierce Holt, a defensive tackle from Angelo State, was perhaps the top small-college lineman in the draft. Also the oldest (26). Third-rounder Bill Romanowski of Boston College was one of the nation's best inside linebackers.

OUTLOOK: The 49ers (13-2 in '87), NFC Western Division champs five times from 1981-87, will be looking to re-establish their dominance after last season's stunning playoff loss to Minnesota. As long as Walsh is coach and Montana the quarterback, this team will always be capable of beating anybody.

49ER PROFILES

JOE MONTANA 32 6-2 195   Quarterback

Questions arose last March about his future with the team when San Diego coach Al Saunders said the 49ers offered the Chargers Montana for two No. 1 draft choices and line-backer Billy Ray Smith. Chargers declined. Coach Bill Walsh denied the report, saying Montana would start in '88 . . . Sensational season ended on sour note with first-round playoff loss to Minnesota . . . Marked third straight playoff loss for 49ers with Montana at quarterback . . . Made Pro Bowl as starter . . . Set club record for touchdown passes (31) . . . Set NFL record with 22 consecutive completions . . . Purchased apple-red Ferrari worth $127,000 in offseason . . . Will earn $1.1 million in base salary . . . Should be pressed by Steve Young . . . Born June 11, 1956, in New Eagle, Pa.

STEVE YOUNG 26 6-2 200   Quarterback

A quarterback controversy is brewing in the Bay area because of his talents . . . Started three games when Joe Montana was injured and finished as team's fourth-leading rusher . . . Can make things happen with ability to scramble . . . Threw 69 consecutive regular-season passes without an interception . . . Relieved a struggling Montana late in playoff loss to Vikings . . . Is just a matter of time before he takes over the controls... Earned $500,000 as backup and will make $700,000 this season... Southpaw... Signed by Tampa Bay Bucs in 1985 after he was let out of his contract with the Los Angeles Express of the USFL. Played final five games for Bucs that season. Started all but two games in '86 and finished with 363 attempts, 195 completions and eight touchdowns... Traded to 49ers four days before '87 draft... Heisman Trophy runnerup in 1983 to running back Mike Rozier... Shattered BYU records and finished with highest single-season completion percentage in NCAA history his senior year... Born Oct. 11, 1961, in Salt Lake City, Utah.

JERRY RICE 25 6-2 200   Wide Receiver

Won virtually every Most Valuable Player Award there is in NFL... Pro Bowl starter, All-Pro... Had 22 TD passes, caught 65 passes for 1,078 yards... After only three seasons, he is team's 13th all-time scorer and 13th all-time receiver with 200 catches for 3,575 yards... Given the Len Eshmont Award by teammates for being overall best player on team... State of Mississippi declared him the Pro Athlete of the Year for second straight year... "He plays as well as any player in the league regardless of position," coach Bill Walsh said... One of the stars on 49ers' offseason basketball team... First-round draft choice out of Mississippi Valley State in '85... Born Oct. 13, 1962, in Starksville, Miss.

HARRIS BARTON 24 6-4 280   Tackle

Fixture in the weight room... Lifted performance of offensive line after breaking into starting lineup midway through season... Excellent pass blocker. Allowed only one sack... Good feet movement... Made All-Rookie team... Can play center... First-round choice in '87 out of North Carolina... Second lineman chosen behind Missouri's John Clay... Won Atlantic Coast Conference Outstanding Lineman Award in '86... Added 15 pounds during summer prior to senior season... First offensive lineman selected by 49ers in first round since 1968 (Forrest Blue)... Will earn $200,000 this season... Born April 19, 1964, in Atlanta, Ga.

ROGER CRAIG 28 6-0- 224   Running Back

Switch from fullback to tailback seemed to ignite running game midway through season... Could extend career by decreasing wear and tear... Worked well with Tom Rathman at fullback... Led team in rushing for third consecutive year, finishing fifth in NFC with 815 yards on 215 carries... His 66 receptions were second in conference behind J.T. Smith ... Has led team in receiving three of last four years... Moonlights as model for Macy's. His ads appear regularly in San Francisco newspapers... Will earn $600,000 this season... Enters sixth year... Second-round draft choice out of Nebraska in 1983... Born July 10, 1960, in Preston, Miss.

TIM McKYER 24 6-0 174   Cornerback

Started to point his finger back at those who keep pointing at him his rookie season... Quarterbacks didn't pick on him as much as they did the previous season... Finished first in passes defensed. Had two interceptions... Very excitable... Does his share of talking on the field... Should be in secondary for years to come, barring serious injury... Extremely quick... Last player taken out of Texas-Arlington before school dropped football program... Chosen in third round in 1986... One of nine children... Born Sept. 5, 1963, in Orlando, Fla.... Will earn $155,000 this season.

DON GRIFFIN 24 6-0 176   Cornerback

Built on successful rookie season. Had five interceptions, all at crucial times in games... Makes smart decisions for second-year player... Works well with McKyer. The two roomed together as rookies before Griffin married... Older brother James played defensive back for Cincinnati Bengals (1983-85) ... A sixth-round draft choice out of Tennessee State in '86, he made the switch from safety to cornerback... Saw a lot of balls come his way as a rookie... Action was as fierce last season... Should get even better... Will earn $95,000 in final year of three-year contract... Born March 17, 1964, in Pelham, Ga.

MICHAEL CARTER 27 6-2 285   Nose Tackle

Causes havoc in the middle. Not many centers can contain him... Finished with 55 tackles, tied for third on team with Ronnie Lott... Made second-team Pro Bowl... Good explosion off the ball... One of biggest keys to 49ers' defense... Very quiet off the field... Splits time in offseason between San Francisco and Dallas... Silver medalist in shot-put in 1984 Olympics... Holds Texas high-school record for discus throw (204 feet, 8 inches)... Born Oct. 29, 1960, in Dallas... Will earn $450,000 this season.

RONNIE LOTT 29 6-0 200   Safety

Made Pro Bowl as safety for second consecutive year, sixth time overall... Grabbed five interceptions, tying Don Griffin for team lead. Has either led or tied for lead in team interceptions last four seasons... Became second all-time team interception leader (38) behind Jimmy Johnson (47)... One of the hardest hitters in the league... Opened a restaurant, The Sports City Cafe, with four other teammates... Earned $460,000 in final year of contract... Enters eighth season... Selected in first round of 1981 draft, out of USC... Made Pro Bowl as rookie... Played cornerback first four seasons... Born May 8, 1959, in Albuquerque, N.M.

MICHAEL WALTER 27 6-3 238   Linebacker

Most underrated member of the defense... Led team with 94 tackles, 14 more than anyone else... One of most consistent performers on the team... Has started since '85, a year after 49ers claimed him off the waiver list.... Was selected in second round of 1983 by Cowboys, then released a year later after playing special teams and outside on defense... 49ers moved him inside... Three-year starter as defensive end at Oregon... Team captain and Most Valuable Player as a senior... Earned degree in telecommunications... Born Nov. 3, 1960, in Eugene, Ore.

COACH BILL WALSH: His motto in 1987 was "One Heartbeat." He maintained the pulse in one of the most difficult seasons ever for NFL coaches—because of the strike—until the playoffs when the 49ers were upset by Minnesota . . . A great motivator, he—and his players—didn't need incentive from the $10,000 bonus checks offered by owner Edward DeBartolo (ruled illegal by the NFL) . . . Has kept the 49ers in the upper echelon of the NFC since 1981 . . . The 49ers have won 10 or more games in six of last seven seasons and his career mark is 89-56-1 . . . Almost quit in '82 because of "burnout." . . . Coached 49ers to Super Bowl victories in XVI and XIX . . . Played offensive and defensive end at San Jose State . . . Was assistant for Raiders and Bengals. When Bengals snubbed him for head-coaching post he went to Chargers as offensive coordinator in 1977 . . . Spent next two years as head coach at Stanford . . . Finally got pro job he wanted in 1979—with 49ers . . . Born Nov. 30, 1931, in Los Angeles.

LONGEST PLAY

Throughout his career, Steve DeBerg has been known as the perfect backup quarterback. Wherever he goes, he seems to end up No. 2.

But DeBerg and receiver Freddie Solomon have had a No. 1 spot in the 49ers' record book since Sept. 28, 1980, when they combined for the longest pass play in team history. The game was against the Falcons at Candlestick Park.

With the Falcons leading, 20-3, early in the fourth quarter, DeBerg threw from 49er seven to Solomon near midfield and he took the ball home. The 49ers lost, 20-17, but DeBerg and Solomon had made their mark.

INDIVIDUAL 49ER RECORDS
Rushing

Most Yards Game:		194	Delvin Williams, vs St. Louis, 1976
	Season:	1,262	Wendell Tyler, 1984
	Career:	7,344	Joe Perry, 1948-60, 1963

Passing

Most TD Passes Game:		5	Frank Albert, vs Cleveland (AAC), 1949
		5	John Brodie, vs Minnesota, 1965
		5	Steve Spurrier, vs Chicago, 1972
		5	Joe Montana, vs Atlanta, 1985
	Season:	31	Joe Montana, 1987
	Career:	214	John Brodie, 1957-73

Receiving

Most TD Passes Game:		3	Alyn Beals, vs Brooklyn (AAC), 1948
		3	Alyn Beals, vs Chicago (AAC), 1949
		3	Gordy Soltau, vs Los Angeles, 1951
		3	Bernie Casey, vs Minnesota, 1962
		3	Dave Parks, vs Baltimore, 1965
		3	Gene Washington, vs San Diego, 1972
		3	Jerry Rice, vs Indianapolis, 1986
		3	Jerry Rice, vs St. Louis, 1986
		3	Jerry Rice, vs Tampa Bay, 1987
		3	Jerry Rice, vs Cleveland, 1987
		3	Jerry Rice, vs Chicago, 1987
	Season:	22	Jerry Rice, 1987
	Career:	59	Gene Washington, 1969-76

Scoring

Most Points Game:		26	Gordy Soltau, vs Los Angeles, 1951
	Season:	138	Jerry Rice, 1987
	Career:	896	Ray Wersching, 1977-86
Most TDs Game:		4	Bill Kilmer, vs Minnesota, 1961
	Season:	23	Jerry Rice, 1987
	Career:	61	Ken Willard, 1965-73

TAMPA BAY BUCCANEERS

TEAM DIRECTORY: Owner/Chairman: Hugh Culverhouse; VP: Joy Culverhouse; VP/Head Coach: Ray Perkins; VP-Administration: William Klein; Dir. Player Personnel: Jerry Angelo; Dir. Pub. Rel.: Rick Odioso. Home field: Tampa Stadium (74,317). Colors: Florida orange, white and red.

SCOUTING REPORT

OFFENSE: The Bucs seem set with quarterback Vinny Testaverde, who began to justify his No. 1 draft selection in late season. They better be set because Steve DeBerg has gone to KC, and now there is Joe Ferguson as backup.

The Bucs need support on the left side of the line, where tackle Mark Cooper started as a rookie free agent and guard George Yarno will launch his ninth NFL season. They expect big things from Wisconsin offensive lineman Paul Gruber, fourth

His rookie season behind him, Vinny Testaverde takes over.

overall pick in the '88 draft.

For a Ray Perkins team that went 4-11 and was tied with Detroit for last place in the Central Division, additional help will be sought at running back, where James Wilder gained 488 yards on 106 carries (plus 328 yards on 40 catches) and tailback Jeff Smith added 309 yards on 100 carries.

One of the most promising positions is tight end with Calvin Magee, who finished third on the team in receiving with 34 catches for 424 yards. Veteran wide receiver Gerald Carter topped the pass-catchers with 38 for 586 yards and rookie Mark Carrier showed promise with 26 receptions for 423 yards.

But the Bucs finished 27th in offense and had 31 turnovers.

DEFENSE: Tampa's trademark since it entered the league has been defense and although it still was the best unit on the team last season, it was far from dominant. The Bucs needed help in the secondary and on the defensive line. They were virtually helpless against the run, finishing 21st in the league.

Young cornerbacks Ricky Reynolds and Rod Jones proved among the best in the league. But the Bucs didn't strike fear into opposing quarterbacks and could have used help at both safeties. Right inside linebacker Ervin Randle led the team with 108 tackles; Jeff Davis, the other inside linebacker, finished second with 70, and defensive end Ron Holmes led the Bucs in sacks with eight.

On the bright side, the defense improved significantly over the previous season. In 1986, the Bucs' defense finished last in the league in 10 categories. Al least it didn't trail in any category in 1987.

KICKING GAME: Donald Igwebuike (14 of 18) and replacement kicker Van Tiffen (five of six) combined for the best field-goal percentage (79.2) in team history. Punter Frank Garcia, however, finished with only a 38.9-yard average. The Bucs couldn't find a kickoff returner and finished 12th in the NFC with an 18.5-yard average while punt-returner Bobby Futrell finished ninth with an 8.9-yard average.

THE ROOKIES: Ray Perkins had never drafted an offensive lineman as his first pick, so he obviously feels Gruber is special. The 6-4, 293-pounder, the top-rated offensive lineman in the draft, is a versatile blocker who can play anywhere on the line. The Bucs' second-round selection was Georgia running back Lars Tate, the first player in school history to lead the team in rushing (954 yards), receiving (22 catches), and touchdowns (17).

BUCCANEERS VETERAN ROSTER

HEAD COACH—Ray Perkins. Assistant Coaches—Larry Beightol, John Bobo, Sylvester Croom, Mike DuBose, Doug Graber, Kent Johnston, Joe Kines, Herb Paterra, Mike Shula, Rodney Stokes, Richard Williamson.

No.	Name	Pos.	Ht.	Wt.	NFL Exp.	College
20	Austin, Cliff	RB	6-0	190	6	Clemson
42	Bartalo, Steve	RB	5-9	200	2	Colorado State
52	Brantley, Scot	LB	6-1	230	9	Florida
47	Brophy, Jay	LB	6-3	232	5	Miami
78	Cannon, John	DE	6-5	260	7	William & Mary
89	Carrier, Mark	WR	6-0	182	2	Nicholls State
87	Carter, Gerald	WR	6-1	190	9	Texas A&M
71	Cooper, Mark	T	6-5	270	6	Miami
13	Criswell, Ray	P	6-0	189	2	Florida
58	Davis, Jeff	LB	6-0	230	7	Clemson
28	Edwards, Dave	S	5-11	194	4	Illinois
—	Edwards, Randy	DE	6-4	267	5	Alabama
29	Elder, Donnie	CB	5-9	175	3	Memphis State
38	Evans, James	RB	6-0	220	2	Southern
—	Ferguson, Joe	QB	6-1	195	16	Arkansas
81	Freeman, Phil	WR	5-11	185	4	Arizona
36	Futrell, Bobby	CB-S	5-11	190	3	Elizabeth City State
91	Gant, Brian	LB	6-0	235	2	Illinois State
36	Gill, Owen	RB	6-1	240	3	Iowa
79	Goode, Conrad	T-G-C	6-4	285	4	Missouri
31	Gordon, Sonny	S	5-11	192	2	Ohio State
53	Graham, Don	LB	6-2	244	2	Penn State
60	Grimes, Randy	C	6-4	270	6	Baylor
82	Hall, Ron	TE	6-4	238	2	Hawaii
73	Heller, Ron	T	6-6	280	5	Penn State
84	Hill, Bruce	WR	6-0	175	2	Arizona State
90	Holmes, Ron	DE	6-4	255	4	Washington
25	Howard, Bobby	RB	6-0	210	3	Indiana
37	Hunter, Eddie	RB	5-10	195	2	Virginia Tech
1	Igwebuike, Donald	K	5-9	185	4	Clemson
28	Isom, Ray	S	5-9	190	2	Penn State
95	Jarvis, Curt	DT-DE	6-2	266	2	Alabama
22	Jones, Rod	CB	6-0	175	3	Southern Methodist
75	Kellin, Kevin	DE	6-5	250	3	Minnesota
33	Kemp, Bobby	S	6-0	190	8	Cal State-Fullerton
77	Maarleveld, J.D.	T	6-6	300	3	Maryland
86	Magee, Calvin	TE	6-4	240	4	Southern
68	Mallory, Rick	G	6-2	265	4	Washington
99	McHale, Tom	DE	6-4	275	2	Cornell
83	Miller, Solomon	WR	6-1	185	3	Utah State
57	Moss, Winston	LB	6-3	235	2	Miami
59	Murphy, Kevin	LB	6-2	230	3	Oklahoma
54	Randle, Ervin	LB	6-1	250	4	Baylor
29	Reynolds, Ricky	CB	5-11	182	2	Washington State
39	Ricks, Harold	RB	5-10	205	2	Tenn.-Chattanooga
93	Sileo, Dan	NT	6-2	282	2	Miami
35	Smith, Jeff	RB	5-9	204	4	Nebraska
94	Stensrud, Mike	NT	6-5	280	10	Iowa State
70	Swayne, Harry	DE	6-5	268	2	Rutgers
85	Taylor, Gene	WR	6-2	189	2	Fresno State
72	Taylor, Rob	T	6-6	285	3	Northwestern
14	Testaverde, Vinny	QB	6-5	218	2	Miami
24	Tripoli, Paul	S	6-0	197	2	Alabama
50	Turk, Dan	C	6-4	260	3	Wisconsin
56	Walker, Jackie	LB	6-5	245	3	Jackson State
51	Washington, Chris	LB	6-4	230	5	Iowa State
32	Wilder, James	RB	6-3	225	8	Missouri
3	Williams, Keith	RB	5-10	173	2	Southwest Missouri
34	Wright, Adrian	RB	6-1	230	2	Virginia Union
66	Yarno, George	G	6-2	265	9	Washington State

TOP DRAFT CHOICES

Rd.	Name	Sel. No.	Pos.	Ht.	Wt.	College
1	Gruber, Paul	4	T	6-4	293	Wisconsin
2	Tate, Lars	53	RB	6-1	206	Georgia
4	Goff, Robert	83	DT	6-3	262	Auburn
4	Bruhin, John	86	G	6-3	275	Tennessee
4	Robbins, Monte	107	P	6-4	202	Michigan

OUTLOOK: If Testaverde can mature fast enough in his full-time shot and enough of the team's weaknesses are solved, the Bucs should show improvement. But they have a long way to go to challenge for a playoff spot.

BUCCANEER PROFILES

VINNY TESTAVERDE 24 6-5 218   Quarterback

Future of the franchise... Replaced Steve De-Berg in Week 11 and started final four games ... Set rookie record with 369-yard performance against New Orleans in debut... Completed 71 of 165 passes, five touchdowns, six interceptions... Gained 50 yards on 13 carries, a 3.8-yard average... Enters second year of a six-year contract worth $8.2 million. Will earn base of $800,000 this season, $1 million in '89... Projected as one of premium quarterbacks in the league... Heisman Trophy winner in 1986 out of Miami and first player selected in '87 NFL draft... Threw for 6,058 yards as a collegian, surpassing George Mira, Jim Kelly and Bernie Kosar... Also Miami's all-time leader in TD passes with 48... Led Hurricanes to 11-0 regular-season mark in '86... Born Nov. 13, 1963, in Brooklyn, N.Y.... Father is a construction worker... Although right-handed, he writes with his left.

GERALD CARTER 31 6-1 190   Wide Receiver

Came two catches shy of his fifth consecutive, 40-or-more reception season... His 15.4-yard average was career high... Provided experience at a position where the Bucs are injecting plenty of youth... Became valuable as a teacher as well as a player... His five touchdown catches topped the team... Excluding strike, has started every game but one over the last three seasons... Enters final year of contract and will earn $350,000... Bucs selected him in ninth round of 1980 draft, was waived before the season, spent four weeks with the Jets, was waived again in November and re-signed by the Bucs in December... And then was there to stay... Born June 19, 1957, in Bryan, Tex.

MARK CARRIER 22 6-0 182   Wide Receiver

Watch out for this guy. He and quarterback Vinny Testaverde had Buc scouts holding their heads high in Week 12 against the Saints. Testaverde threw for 369 yards and Carrier caught eight passes for 212 of them . . . Finished with 26 catches for 423 yards . . . Has all the qualities of a star: size, speed, and ability to run over the middle . . . Will earn $145,000 this season . . . Holds nearly every receiving record at Nicholls State . . . School's all-time leading receiver with 132 catches for 2,407 yards . . . Has returned punts, although Bucs did not use him in that capacity . . . Entered offseason with 15 credit hours remaining for his degree in engineering . . . Selected 57th overall in '87 draft . . . Hobbies include playing dominoes . . . Spent college summers as a counselor to low-income high-school students . . . Born Oct. 28, 1965, in Lafayette, La.

RANDY GRIMES 28 6-4 270   Center

Without a doubt, the best offensive lineman on the team, according to Ray Perkins . . . Asserted himself more as a leader last season . . . Turned in best all-around performance of five-year NFL career . . . Improved conditioning before '87 season . . . Has started 46 consecutive games, not including strike, since breaking into the starting lineup in Week 15 of '84 season . . . Played out contract last season worth $240,000 in '87 base . . . Recently sold health club he owned in Houston . . . Outdoorsman. Enjoys hunting, fishing and golf . . . Second-round draft choice out of Baylor in 1983 . . . Entered as a freshman weighing 205 pounds and left some 65 pounds heavier . . . Born July 20, 1960, in Tyler, Tex.

CALVIN MAGEE 25 6-3 240   Tight End

When Ray Perkins met him two years ago, he told him he could either be a 280-pound guard or a 240-pound tight end . . . At that time, he looked more like an offensive lineman anyway. He loves to eat. Fortunately for the Bucs, he decided to become a tight end . . . Has caught 79 passes in last two seasons—34 for 424 yards, sixth-best among NFC tight ends last year . . . Signed as free agent in May 1985 . . . Played out contract last season. Earned $95,000 . . . Part of promising young receiving corps that could make it this season with Testaverde throwing . . . Led all Buc receivers in his second season, catching 45 passes for 564 yards . . . Bears' safety Dave Duerson calls him a potential Pro Bowl candidate . . . Played tight end and also kicked at Southern University . . . Works in offseason as a soccer coach for the Tampa Bay recreation department . . . Born April 23, 1963, in New Orleans.

JAMES WILDER 30 6-3 225   Running Back

Moved from tailback to fullback but still held team's best yard-per-carry average at 4.6 . . . Led team in rushing for sixth straight season . . . Carried 106 times for 488 yards . . . Topped team in receptions with 40 . . . Has led Bucs in total offense last seven years, totaling 8,403 yards . . . Played out contract last season, when he earned $500,000 . . . Stayed healthy after missing four games in '86 because of rib and ankle injuries . . . Back to fullback, where he started his career . . . Second-round draft choice out of Missouri in 1981 . . . All-time Missouri rushing leader . . . Sponsors softball team in hometown named "Wilder's Express." . . . Dabbled in modeling . . . Born May 12, 1958, in Sikeston, Mo.

RICKY REYNOLDS 23 5-11 182   Defensive Back

Could argue that he should have made the All-Rookie team . . . Started every game at left cornerback . . . Defended 16 passes and caused two fumbles . . . Finished second on the team in tackles with 70 . . . Will earn $150,000 this season . . . Second-round pick in '86 . . . Quick. Excellent cover man . . . Stood out in Blue-Gray Game . . . Three-year starter for Washington State . . . Blocked two field goals in one game against San Jose State . . . Still looking for his first NFL interception . . . Cousin of baseball's Jerry Royster . . . His fiancee, Pamela Qualls, is a sprinter at Washington State . . . He was a sprinter and footballer in high school . . . Born Jan. 19, 1965, in Sacramento, Cal.

ERVIN RANDLE 25 6-1 250   Linebacker

Ask Bears' running back Neal Anderson how it feels to run into this guy. NFL Films chose a spine-tingling tackle that Randle put on Anderson in Week 2 as its best hit of the season ...Led team in tackles with 108 in only first full season as starter...Entering fourth season...A third-round pick in 1985 draft ...Made switch from outside to inside linebacker in '86 and began seeing extensive duty...Outstanding special-teamer...Played linebacker, defensive end and nose tackle at Baylor...Played out contract last year when he earned $150,000...Born Oct. 12, 1962, in Hearne, Tex.

RON HOLMES 25 6-4 255   Defensive End

Has improved each season since replacing LeeRoy Selmon on the right side three years ago...Registered eight sacks, one more than his 1985-86 total combined...Emerged as Bucs' best all-around lineman...Credits Selmon for much of his development, dating back to his All-American days at University of Washington when he viewed films of his predecessor...Will earn $280,000 in last year of contract... Best game of 1987 came against the St. Louis Cardinals, when he sacked Cardinals' Neal Lomax three times...All-around athlete ...Played on Washington State championship basketball team in high school (1979)...Leading film-goer on team...Born Aug. 26, 1963, in Fort Benning, Ga.....First-round pick in '85.

ROD JONES 24 6-0 175   Defensive Back

Didn't miss a non-strike game despite playing most of the season on a sore ankle...Made 44 tackles, two interceptions and deflected nine passes...Has been a fixture at right cornerback since the Bucs drafted him in the first round in 1986...Nicknamed "K.O." by former SMU teammate and ex-New York Jet Russell Carter because of his numbing tackles ...Combines with Ricky Reynolds to form one of the best young pair of corners in the league...Will earn $165,000 this season ...Talented artist, specializing in caricatures...Born March 31,

1964, in Dallas . . . 400-meter man in high school and also lettered in golf.

COACH RAY PERKINS: When he was in high school, he rel-

ished taking an engine apart and putting it back together. That's what owner Hugh Culverhouse asked him to do when he hired him Dec. 31, 1986 . . . As the Bucs' 4-11 record in '87 indicates, there are still a few parts missing in the Bucs' engine . . . He has total control of football operations . . . Has a good building block for a potent offense in Testaverde . . . A Bear Bryant disciple, he was an All-American receiver at Alabama, under Bryant, and played with quarterback Joe Namath . . . Started coaching at Mississippi State in 1973 and moved to the NFL (New England Patriots) the following year as an assistant to Chuck Fairbanks . . . Moved to San Diego Chargers under Don Coryell in '78 . . . Given head job with New York Giants in 1979 and took team to the playoffs in 1981, the first time in 18 years . . . Left two years later to become Bryant's successor at Alabama . . . Went to three bowl games in four years and won them all. "I don't claim to be a genius," he said. "I work hard, try to make good decisions and surround myself with the right people." . . . Married his high-school teacher in Petal, Miss. . . . Likes to golf . . . Born Nov. 6, 1941, in Mount Olive, Miss.

LONGEST PLAY

The date was Dec. 20, 1981. Tampa Bay vs. Detroit in the Silverdome. At stake was the Central Division title and a playoff berth.

Tampa trailed, 7-3, late in the first half, but Cedric Brown's interception gave the Bucs the ball at their own 16. On second down, quarterback Doug Williams threw a bullet downfield to Kevin House, who completed an 84-yard touchdown play, longest in Tampa history.

It propelled them to a 20-17 victory and they were in the playoffs—until ousted by Dallas, 38-0.

INDIVIDUAL BUCCANEER RECORDS

Rushing

Most Yards Game:	219	James Wilder, vs Minnesota, 1983
Season:	1,544	James Wilder, 1984
Career:	5,370	James Wilder, 1981-87

Passing

Most TD Passes Game:	5	Steve DeBerg, vs Atlanta, 1987
Season:	20	Doug Williams, 1980
Career:	73	Doug Williams, 1978-82

Receiving

Most TD Passes Game:	4	Jimmie Giles, vs Miami, 1985
Season:	9	Kevin House, 1981
Career:	34	Jimmie Giles, 1978-86

Scoring

Most Points Game:	24	Jimmie Giles, vs Miami, 1985
Season:	96	Donald Igwebuike, 1985
Career:	252	James Wilder, 1981-87
Most TDs Game:	4	Jimmie Giles, vs Miami, 1985
Season:	13	James Wilder, 1984
Career:	42	James Wilder, 1981-87

WASHINGTON REDSKINS

TEAM DIRECTORY: Chairman: Jack Kent Cooke; Exec. VP: John Kent Cooke; GM: Bobby Beathard; Dir. Player Personnel: Dick Daniels; VP-Communications: Charlie Dayton; Dir. Information: John Konoza; Dir. Pub. Rel.: Marty Hurney; Head Coach: Joe Gibbs. Home field: Robert F. Kennedy Stadium (55,750). Colors: Burgundy and gold.

SCOUTING REPORT

OFFENSE: It didn't really take off until the playoffs when quarterback Doug Williams had replaced Jay Schroeder, rookie running back Timmy Smith had replaced George Rogers and receiver Ricky Sanders had replaced an injured Art Monk. In all, four key players—the other was center Jeff Bostic—didn't start until late in the season. Smith, a fifth-round draft choice in 1987, made his first start in the Super Bowl and he gained a record-setting 204 yards in the 42-10 blitzing of Denver.

The offensive line, anchored by tackles Joe Jacoby and Mark May, had opened holes all season, but the Redskins' running game sputtered until Smith became an activist in the playoffs. Bostic replaced center Russ Grimm after Grimm tore knee ligaments in Week 8 against Philadelphia and played so well that Grimm never got back into the lineup.

Williams displayed his experience in the playoffs and ran Joe Gibbs' offense to perfection. The only question regarding him this season is whether his knees can hold up over 16 games. Schroeder figures as a backup.

All the other positions have depth. Receiver is solid with Gary Clark, Monk and Sanders. Running back is stable with Smith and third-down specialist Kelvin Bryant and Don Warren leads a solid group at tight end.

DEFENSE: The most consistent unit on the team, the Redskins' defense should only improve with the offseason acquisition of former Bears' linebacker Wilber Marshall. Linebacker was considered the defense's only area of need, considering Neal Olkewicz, Monte Coleman and Rich Milot all are entering their 10th seasons. The line could be the best in the league with ends Charles Mann and Dexter Manley and tackles Darryl Grant and Dave Butz, the league's oldest lineman at 38.

Finding a cornerback to play opposite Darrell Green was a main priority until Barry Wilburn emerged last season and led the league with nine interceptions. Safety is as promising as any spot

Timmy Smith: From fifth round to Super Bowl stardom.

on the team. Free safety Todd Bowles and strong safety Alvin Walton started last season in their second years in the NFL.

KICKING GAME: If consistent kicking is all the Skins lacked in 1987, they may have solved that problem with their first-round selection of Minnesota placekicker Chip Lohmiller. The team is expected to look for serious competition for punter Steve Cox.

THE ROOKIES: The Redskins got the guy they wanted in Lohmiller, whom GM Bobby Beathard called "the top kicker in the country." The Golden Gopher made a 62-yarder in 1986 and converted 16 of 19 field goals as a senior. The Skins went for small, quick, running backs with their next two picks: Puget Sound's Mike Oliphant and Michigan's Jamie Morris, who has the same rushing style as brother Joe with the Giants.

REDSKINS VETERAN ROSTER

HEAD COACH—Joe Gibbs. Assistant Coaches—Chuck Banker, Don Breaux, Joe Bugel, Joe Diange, Dan Henning, Bill Hickman, Paul Lanham, Larry Peccatiello, Richie Petitbon, Dan Riley, Warren Simmons, Charley Taylor, Emmitt Thomas, LaVern Torgeson.

No.	Name	Pos.	Ht.	Wt.	NFL Exp.	College
89	Allen, Anthony	RB	5-11	182	4	Washington
95	Benish, Dan	DT	6-5	275	6	Clemson
53	Bostic, Jeff	C	6-2	260	9	Clemson
23	Bowles, Todd	S	6-2	203	3	Temple
29	Branch, Reggie	RB	5-11	235	3	East Carolina
—	Brilz, Darrick	G	6-3	264	2	Oregon State
24	Bryant, Kelvin	RB	6-2	195	3	North Carolina
50	Butz, Dave	DT	6-7	295	15	Purdue
65	Caldwell, Ravin	LB	6-3	229	2	Arkansas
88	Caravello, Joe	TE	6-3	270	2	Tulane
—	Carlson, Mark	T	6-6	284	2	Southern Conn. State
84	Clark, Gary	WR	5-9	173	4	James Madison
51	Coleman, Monte	LB	6-2	230	10	Central Arkansas
56	Copeland, Anthony	LB	6-2	250	2	Louisville
12	Cox, Steve	P-K	6-4	195	6	Arkansas
—	Coyle, Eric	C	6-3	260	2	Colorado
34	Davis, Brian	CB	6-2	190	2	Nebraska
32	Dean, Vernon	CB	5-11	178	7	San Diego State
86	Didier, Clint	TE	6-5	240	7	Portland State
48	Gage, Steve	S	6-3	210	2	Tulsa
54	Gouveia, Kurt	LB	6-1	227	2	Brigham Young
77	Grant, Darryl	DT	6-1	275	8	Rice
28	Green, Darrell	CB	5-8	170	6	Texas A&I
35	Griffin, Keith	RB	5-8	185	5	Miami
68	Grimm, Russ	C-G	6-3	275	7	Pittsburgh
6	Haji-Sheikh, Ali	K	6-0	172	5	Michigan
78	Hamel, Dean	DT	6-3	290	4	Tulsa
64	Hamilton, Steve	DE-DT	6-4	270	4	East Carolina
—	Hitchcock, Ray	C-G	6-2	289	2	Minnesota
66	Jacoby, Joe	T	6-7	305	8	Louisville
21	Jessie, Tim	RB	5-11	190	2	Auburn
82	Jones, Anthony	TE	6-3	248	5	Wichita State
55	Kaufman, Mel	LB	6-2	230	7	Cal Poly-SLO
61	Kehr, Rick	G	6-3	285	2	Carthage
74	Koch, Markus	DE	6-5	275	3	Boise State
—	Lathrop, Kit	DT	6-5	261	4	Arizona State
72	Manley, Dexter	DE	6-3	257	8	Oklahoma State
71	Mann, Charles	DE	6-6	270	6	Nevada-Reno
58	Marshall, Wilber	LB	6-1	225	5	Florida
73	May, Mark	T	6-6	295	8	Pittsburgh
—	McEwen, Craig	TE	6-1	220	2	Utah
63	McKenzie, Raleigh	G	6-2	275	3	Tennessee
60	McQuaid, Dan	T	6-7	278	3	Nevada-Las Vegas
81	Monk, Art	WR	6-3	209	9	Syracuse
41	Morrison, Tim	CB	6-1	195	3	North Carolina
52	Olkewicz, Neal	LB	6-0	233	10	Maryland
87	Orr, Terry	TE	6-3	227	3	Texas
11	Rypien, Mark	QB	6-4	234	2	Washington State
83	Sanders, Ricky	WR	5-11	180	3	Southwest Texas State
10	Schroeder, Jay	AB	6-4	215	5	UCLA
76	Simmons, Ed	T	6-5	280	2	Eastern Washington
36	Smith, Timmy	RB	5-11	216	2	Texas Tech
69	Thielemann, R.C.	G	6-4	272	12	Arkansas
31	Vaughn, Clarence	S	6-0	202	2	Northern Illinois
90	Verdin, Clarence	WR-KR	5-8	160	3	Southwest Louisiana
40	Walton, Alvin	S	6-0	180	3	Kansas
85	Warren, Don	TE	6-4	242	10	San Diego State
45	Wilburn, Barry	CB	6-3	186	4	Mississippi
17	Williams, Doug	QB	6-4	220	8	Grambling
46	Wilson, Wayne	RB	6-3	220	9	Shepherd
—	Woodberry, Dennis	CB	5-10	183	3	Southern Arkansas
80	Yarber, Eric	WR-KR	5-8	156	2	Idaho

TOP DRAFT CHOICES

Rd.	Name	Sel. No.	Pos.	Ht.	Wt.	College
2	Lohmiller, Chip	55	K	6-2	201	Minnesota
3	Oliphant, Mike	64	RB	5-9	175	Puget Sound
4	Morris, Jamie	109	RB	5-7	185	Michigan
5	Mims, Carl	127	DB	5-9	180	Sam Houston State
6	Humphries, Stan	159	QB	6-3	223	NE Louisiana

OUTLOOK: If Williams stays healthy and Smith matures, the offense could rival the one that broke the league's scoring record in 1983. No reason to think that Richie Petitbon, perhaps the best defensive coordinator in the league, won't work wonders with Marshall and the defense. The Giants seem to have an edge going into the NFC East race because of their schedule, but the Redskins will be right there.

REDSKIN PROFILES

DOUG WILLIAMS 33 6-4 220   Quarterback

The Los Angeles Raiders could have had him for a No. 1 in 1987... Instead, they only offered a second-round draft choice on the day rosters had to be cut to 45 and the Redskins kept the former Tampa Bay quarterback as a backup to Jay Schroeder... When Schroeder sprained his right shoulder nine plays into the season, Williams replaced him and the Redskins went 1-1 before the strike... When Schroeder's poor performances sent him to the bench, Williams relieved him against Detroit and was 1-1 before a back injury sidelined him... Williams' third chance proved the charm. He replaced a struggling Schroeder in the second half of the regular-season finale against the Vikings, then won three straight playoff games, capped by Super Bowl XXII over the Broncos... Voted MVP after directing a record-breaking, 35-point second quarter... Underwent minor arthroscopic surgery in March for sprained left knee... Will earn $500,000 this season unless he renegotiates ... A first-round Tampa Bay draft pick out of Grambling in 1978, he had five years with the Bucs and two in the USFL before signing with the Redskins in '86... Born Aug. 9, 1955, in Baton Rouge, La.

KELVIN BRYANT 27 6-2 195   Running Back

A shining star doesn't come out every night ... That's how Bryant's second season with the Redskins went... At times he was brilliant, at others you couldn't find him... Because of nagging injuries, brought about, the Redskins claim, by Bryant's reluctance to work in the weight room, he was limited mainly to third-down passing situations—not the role the Redskins had in mind when they paid him $3.7 million for four years . . . Despite only 77 carries, Bryant gained 406 yards (5.3 yard average) and finished second on the team in rushing and receiving (43 catches for 490 yards) . . . Tied for third in scoring with 36 points, but yet has to gain over 100 yards rushing in an NFL game . . . The Eagles' seventh-round pick out of North Carolina in the 1983 draft, he came to Washington in '86 after three 1,000-yard seasons with the USFL Stars . . . Born Sept. 26, 1960, in Tarboro, N.C.

DAVE BUTZ 38 6-7 295   Defensive Tackle

Call him the house that George built. Since being signed by George Allen as a veteran free agent in 1975, Butz has become an immovable object at left tackle for Washington . . . Even though he was the oldest defensive lineman in the league last season, he remained the foundation of his team's highly regarded front four . . . Had 50 tackles, 11 quarterback hurries and three sacks . . . Spent the night before the Jets game in the hospital because of a stomach parasite, checked out four hours before gametime and made the play of the game—a fourth-quarter sack that took the Jets out of field-goal range . . . The Redskins won, 17-16, and Butz checked back into the hospital . . . A Purdue grad, he was a first-round pick of the Cardinals in 1973 draft . . . Born June 23, 1950, in Lafayette, Ala.

GARY CLARK 26 5-9 173   Wide Receiver

John Madden's favorite receiver because "his motor is always running." Finished as the team's leader in receptions (56), receiving yards (1,066) and touchdowns (7) . . . Made the Pro Bowl for the second consecutive season and was named to the Associated Press All-Pro team . . . One of the most emotional players on the team, Clark frequently can be seen kicking dirt in disgust, but for the most part he's been all smiles since coming to Washington three years ago from the USFL . . . Washington stole him in the third round of the 1984 supplemental draft . . . Born May 1, 1962, in Dublin, Va., he went to tiny James Madison College. Scheduled to earn $247,000 this season, if he doesn't renegotiate.

DARRELL GREEN 28 5-8 170   Cornerback

He didn't play as well as he did in 1986, but he played well enough to make third trip to Hawaii for the Pro Bowl...NFC Defensive Player of the Week after intercepting three passes against the Lions and was voted by teammates as Special Teams' Player of the Game in the divisional playoff against the Chicago Bears...Green made the play of the game by running back a third-quarter punt 52 yards for a touchdown to key the Redskins' 21-17 victory...He sprained rib cartilage on the play but started the NFC championship game and the Super Bowl and played in great pain...During regular season, he was beaten for nine touchdown passes, the most against him in any one season since the Redskins drafted him No. 1 in 1983 out of Texas A&I. Born Feb. 15, 1960, in Houston.

CHARLES MANN 27 6-6 270   Defensive End

It took him five years to make the Pro Bowl and Redskin coaches say it was his best season of many good ones since his third-round selection out of Nevada-Reno in 1983...As a rookie he made only one start and it was memorable: he sacked Rams' QB Vince Ferragamo for a safety, the team's first in seven years... In '84 he became a starter and he's been majoring in sacks ever since...A product of Valley High School in Sacramento, where he was born April 12, 1961...He's one of most active Redskins in offseason—sells real estate, is continuing his education at George Mason and plays a role in many charities and youth work.

JOE JACOBY 29 6-7 305   Tackle

Can't go over him and it takes too long to go around him. Jacoby probably was the most valuable guy on an excellent offensive line last season...Selected by his coaches as the team's Offensive Player of the Game in Week 8 (vs. the Eagles) and Week 11 (vs. Giants)...In the playoffs, he controlled the Vikings' Chris Doleman and the Bears' Richard Dent and helped the offensive line allow only one sack in those two contests... Figured in paving the way for rookie running back Timmy Smith (202 yards) in the Super Bowl... Jacoby started in all 12 games and was a big reason Washington ranked third in the league in total offense... The price certainly was right; the Redskins signed him a a rookie free agent out of Louisville in 1981 ... He will earn $445,000 in base salary this season... Born July 6, 1959, in Louisville, Ky.

WILBER MARSHALL 26 6-1 225   Linebacker

He made the Pro Bowl, the Super Bowl and a slew of tackles in Chicago, but it took Wahington to help him make history of another sort... He became the first NFL player since Norm Thompson in 1977 to change teams as a free agent; the Redskins offered him a $6-million, five-year contract last March that included $500,000 for signing and a football-related injury guarantee... That was too attractive an offer to turn down for Marshall and too rich for the Bears to match... He will give the Redskins the dominant linebacker they've been searching for the past few years... A Lawrence-Taylor prototype, Marshall can cover receivers, blitz quarterbacks and run over just about anyone... Giants took close look at him when he played at Florida, but chose Carl Banks instead and the Bears made him the 11th choice in the first round in 1984... Interestingly, the Redskins opted for Marshall over Banks, who was also a free agent last spring... Middle name is Buddyhia... Dad is from the Bahamas... Born April 18, 1962, in Titusville, Fla.

TIMMY SMITH 24 5-11 216   Running Back

Teammates call him "Cutback" because he becomes impatient and sometimes takes a detour away from his blockers... But the rookie was patient enough to wait all season for his first start. When he got it—in Super Bowl XXII against the Broncos—he made the most of it ... Smith broke Marcus Allen's Super Bowl rushing record by gaining 202 yards in San Diego. In one afternoon, he ran his way into the starting running back slot for this season, ahead of Kelvin Bryant and George Rogers. "I guess he made me look pretty stupid," said coach Joe

Gibbs, referring to the fact that Smith did not start until the Super Bowl. A fifth-round find by general manager Bobby Beathard, Smith played only six games combined his final two years at Texas Tech because of injuries... Born January 24, 1964, in Hobbs, N.M.

BARRY WILBURN 24 6-3 186   Cornerback

They can't call him Wil-BURNED anymore. Went from the endangered species list in summer camp to an All-Pro in January... Led the league with nine interceptions and returned one—against the Minnesota Vikings in Week 15—100 yards for a touchdown. One of the most frequently booed players his first two seasons in Washington because of his inability to knock down passes, the Mississippi grad started all 12 games after replacing injured Tim Morrison the week before the season opener... He was considered by some team officials as Washington's Defensive Back of the Year... He filled a gap the team had been looking to fill for years—the cornerback slot opposite Darrell Green... Born Dec. 9, 1963, in Memphis, Tenn.... Was Redskins' eighth-round pick (219th overall) in 1985 draft.

COACH JOE GIBBS: Defined as the best coach ever by a rating

system devised by statistician Peter Hirdt... Perhaps last season was Gibbs' best coaching job since taking the helm in Washington in 1981... He assembled a strike team in 10 days and went 3-0, playing two games against division opponents that had 10 or more veterans... Dealt with personnel matters more directly than he had in the past... Changed quarterbacks twice because of reasons other than injury, the last time when he went with Doug Williams in the third quarter of the regular-season finale against the Vikings... Demands that his players do not fire up opponents with words... Direct opposite of Bears' Mike Ditka.... Detail oriented... Nothing falls through the cracks... Career record of 85-33 is top winning percentage among active NFL coaches... Learned offensive philosophy from Don Coryell... Played tight end for Coryell at San

Diego State, later worked for him there as a graduate assistant and at St. Louis as offensive bakfield coach... Assisted John McKay at USC and at Tampa Bay... Played a part in the Bucs' drafting quarterback Doug Williams... Joined Redskins in '81 replacing Jack Pardee, and started 0-5... Won Super Bowl the following season and did it again in 1987 for two Super Bowl Trophies in five seasons... Active in local youth home.... Born Nov. 25, 1940, in Mocksville, N.C.

LONGEST PLAY

During his first two seasons as a Redskin cornerback, Barry Wilburn was knocked for not making the big plays. He was booed by fans, criticized by coaches.

But in 1987 he made plenty of big plays, the most memorable one in the regular-season finale on Dec. 26 at Minnesota. The Redskins trailed, 7-0, in the second quarter, and the Vikings were inside Washington's 20 when Minnesota quarterback Wade Wilson dropped back to pass. He threw to Leo Lewis in the right corner of the end zone, but Wilburn picked it off and, with good blocking, weaved his way 103 yards for a touchdown.

The Super Bowl-bound Skins won, 27-24, and Wilburn owned the longest excursion in team history, topping Larry Jones' 102-yard kickoff return against the Eagles on Nov. 24, 1974.

INDIVIDUAL REDSKIN RECORDS

Rushing

Most Yards Game:	206	George Rogers, vs St. Louis, 1985	
Season:	1,347	John Riggins, 1983	
Career:	7,472	John Riggins, 1976-79, 1981-85	

Passing

Most TD Passes Game:	6	Sam Baugh, vs Brooklyn, 1943	
	6	Sam Baugh, vs St. Louis, 1947	
Season:	31	Sonny Jurgensen, 1967	
Career:	187	Sammy Baugh, 1937-52	

Receiving

Most TD Passes Game:	3	Hugh Taylor (5 times)
	3	Jerry Smith, vs Los Angeles, 1967
	3	Jerry Smith, vs Dallas, 1969
	3	Hal Crisler (once)
	3	Joe Walton (once)
	3	Pat Richter, vs Chicago, 1968
	3	Larry Brown, vs Philadelphia, 1973
	3	Jean Fugett, vs San Francisco, 1976
	3	Alvin Garrett, vs Lions, 1982
	3	Art Monk, vs Indianapolis, 1984
Season:	12	Hugh Taylor, 1952
	12	Charley Taylor, 1966
	12	Jerry Smith, 1967
Career:	79	Charley Taylor, 1964-77

Scoring

Most Points Game:	24	Dick James, vs Dallas, 1961
	24	Larry Brown, vs Philadelphia, 1973
Season:	161	Mark Moseley, 1983
	144	John Riggins, 1983
Career:	1,176	Mark Moseley, 1974-85
Most TDs Game:	4	Dick James, vs Dallas, 1961
	4	Larry Brown, vs Philadelphia, 1973
Season:	24	John Riggins, 1983
Career:	90	Charley Taylor, 1964-77

OFFICIAL 1987 NFL STATISTICS

(Compiled by Elias Sports Bureau)

RUSHING

TOP TEN RUSHERS

	Att	Yards	Avg	Long	TD
White, Charles, Rams	324	1374	4.2	58	11
Dickerson, Eric, Rams-Ind. ...	283	1288	4.6	57	6
Warner, Curt, Sea.	234	985	4.2	t57	8
Rozier, Mike, Hou.	229	957	4.2	41	3
Mayes, Rueben, N.O.	243	917	3.8	38	5
Walker, Herschel, Dall.	209	891	4.3	t60	7
Riggs, Gerald, Atl.	203	875	4.3	44	2
Craig, Roger, S.F.	215	815	3.8	25	3
Mitchell, Stump, St.L.	203	781	3.8	42	3
Allen, Marcus, Raiders	200	754	3.8	44	5

NFC – INDIVIDUAL RUSHERS

	Att	Yards	Avg	Long	TD
White, Charles, Rams	324	1374	4.2	58	11
Mayes, Rueben, N.O.	243	917	3.8	38	5
Walker, Herschel, Dall.	209	891	4.3	t60	7
Riggs, Gerald, Atl.	203	875	4.3	44	2
Craig, Roger, S.F.	215	815	3.8	25	3
Mitchell, Stump, St.L.	203	781	3.8	42	3
Morris, Joe, Giants	193	658	3.4	34	3
Nelson, Darrin, Minn.	131	642	4.9	72	2
Rogers, George, Wash.	163	613	3.8	29	6
Anderson, Neal, Chi.	129	586	4.5	t38	3
Payton, Walter, Chi.	146	533	3.7	17	4
Ferrell, Earl, St.L.	113	512	4.5	t35	7
Hilliard, Dalton, N.O.	123	508	4.1	t30	7
Cunningham, Randall, Phil. ...	76	505	6.6	45	3
Wilder, James, T.B.	106	488	4.6	21	0
Toney, Anthony, Phil.	127	473	3.7	36	5
Dorsett, Tony, Dall.	130	456	3.5	24	1
Byars, Keith, Phil.	116	426	3.7	30	3
Davis, Kenneth, G.B.	109	413	3.8	t39	3

t = Touchdown
Leader based on most yards gained

	Att	Yards	Avg	Long	TD
Bryant, Kelvin, Wash.	77	406	5.3	28	1
Vital, Lionel, Wash.	80	346	4.3	t22	2
Jones, James, Det.	96	342	3.6	19	0
Anderson, Alfred, Minn.	68	319	4.7	27	2
Smith, Jeff, T.B.	100	309	3.1	46	2
Cribbs, Joe, S.F.	70	300	4.3	20	1
Fullwood, Brent, G.B.	84	274	3.3	18	5
James, Garry, Det.	82	270	3.3	17	4
Wilson, Wade, Minn.	41	263	6.4	38	5
Dozier, D.J., Minn.	69	257	3.7	19	5
Rathman, Tom, S.F.	62	257	4.1	35	1
Willhite, Kevin, G.B.	53	251	4.7	61	0
Griffin, Keith, Wash.	62	242	3.9	13	0
McAdoo, Derrick, St.L.	53	230	4.3	17	3
Beverly, Dwight, N.O.	62	217	3.5	25	2
Clark, Jessie, G.B.	56	211	3.8	57	0
Hunter, Eddie, Jets-T.B.	56	210	3.8	23	0
Ellerson, Gary, Det.	47	196	4.2	33	3
Carruth, Paul Ott, G.B.	64	192	3.0	23	3
Young, Steve, S.F.	26	190	7.3	t29	1
Bernard, Karl, Det.	45	187	4.2	14	2
Fenney, Rick, Minn.	42	174	4.1	12	2
Adams, George, Giants	61	169	2.8	14	1
Haddix, Michael, Phil.	59	165	2.8	11	0
Rouson, Lee, Giants	41	155	3.8	14	0
Pelluer, Steve, Dall.	25	142	5.7	21	1
Montana, Joe, S.F.	35	141	4.0	20	1
Francis, Jon, Rams	35	138	3.9	23	0
Brown, Reggie, Phil.	39	136	3.5	23	0
Fourcade, John, N.O.	19	134	7.1	18	0
Word, Barry, N.O.	36	133	3.7	20	2
Rice, Allen, Minn.	51	131	2.6	13	1
Heimuli, Lakei, Chi.	34	128	3.8	12	0
Majkowski, Don, G.B.	15	127	8.5	33	0
Smith, Timmy, Wash.	29	126	4.3	15	0
Blount, Alvin, Dall.	46	125	2.7	15	3
Sydney, Harry, S.F.	29	125	4.3	15	0
Sanders, Thomas, Chi.	23	122	5.3	17	1
Newsome, Tim, Dall.	25	121	4.8	t24	2
Schroeder, Jay, Wash.	26	120	4.6	31	3
Robinson, Jacque, Phil.	24	114	4.8	18	0
Wester, Cleve, Det.	33	113	3.4	14	0
Wright, Adrian, T.B.	37	112	3.0	11	0
Williams, Van, Giants	29	108	3.7	17	0
Lomax, Neil, St.L.	29	107	3.7	19	0
Campbell, Scott, Atl.	21	102	4.9	24	2
Howard, Bobby, T.B.	30	100	3.3	31	1
Guman, Mike, Rams	36	98	2.7	7	1
Hebert, Bobby, N.O.	13	95	7.3	19	0
DiRico, Bob, Giants	25	90	3.6	14	0

	Att	Yards	Avg	Long	TD
Sargent, Broderick, St.L.	18	90	5.0	16	0
McMahon, Jim, Chi.	22	88	4.0	13	2
Thomas, Calvin, Chi.	25	88	3.5	18	0
Badanjek, Rick, Atl.	29	87	3.0	31	1
Wolfley, Ron, St.L.	26	87	3.3	8	1
Bell, Greg, Buff.-Rams	22	86	3.9	13	0
Everett, Jim, Rams	18	83	4.6	16	1
Varajon, Mike, S.F.	18	82	4.6	11	0
Woolfolk, Butch, Det.	12	82	6.8	31	0
Mosley, Anthony, Chi.	18	80	4.4	16	0
Ricks, Harold, T.B.	24	76	3.2	14	1
Galbreath, Tony, Giants	10	74	7.4	17	0
Settle, John, Atl.	19	72	3.8	12	0
Alexander, Vincent, N.O.	21	71	3.4	16	1
Wright, Randy, G.B.	13	70	5.4	27	0
Edwards, Stan, Det.	32	69	2.2	13	0
Hold, Mike, T.B.	7	69	9.9	35	0
Tautalatasi, Junior, Phil. ...	26	69	2.7	17	0
Cherry, Tony, S.F.	13	65	5.0	16	1
Long, Chuck, Det.	22	64	2.9	15	0
Risher, Alan, G.B.	11	64	5.8	15	1
Monk, Art, Wash.	6	63	10.5	26	0
Edwards, Kelvin, Dall.	2	61	30.5	t62	1
Flowers, Kenny, Atl.	14	61	4.4	14	0
Carthon, Maurice, Giants	26	60	2.3	10	0
Hohensee, Mike, Chi.	9	56	6.2	26	0
Brewer, Chris, Chi.	24	55	2.3	16	2
Wilson, Wayne, Wash.	18	55	3.1	11	2
Ross, Alvin, Phil.	14	54	3.9	12	1
Tomczak, Mike, Chi.	18	54	3.0	10	1
Rice, Jerry, S.F.	8	51	6.4	17	1
Testaverde, Vinny, T.B.	13	50	3.8	17	1
Adams, David, Dall.	7	49	7.0	t27	0
Hons, Todd, Det.	5	49	9.8	23	0
Williams, Michael, Atl.	14	49	3.5	9	0
Hardy, Andre, S.F.	7	48	6.9	14	0
Rodgers, Del, S.F.	11	46	4.2	15	1
Stevens, Mark, S.F.	10	45	4.5	16	1
Kramer, Tommy, Minn.	10	44	4.4	15	2
Simms, Phil, Giants	14	44	3.1	20	0
Tyrrell, Tim, Rams	11	44	4.0	13	0
Gentry, Dennis, Chi.	6	41	6.8	12	0
Hargrove, Jimmy, G.B.	11	38	3.5	7	1
Stanley, Walter, G.B.	4	38	9.5	24	0
Gray, Mel, N.O.	8	37	4.6	12	1
Jessie, Tim, Wash.	10	37	3.7	t14	1
Brim, James, Minn.	2	36	18.0	t38	1
Jordan, Buford, N.O.	12	36	3.0	t8	2
Rodenberger, Jeff, N.O.	17	35	2.1	5	0
Green, Roy, St.L.	2	34	17.0	26	0

	Att	Yards	Avg	Long	TD
DuBose, Doug, S.F.	10	33	3.3	11	0
Parker, Freddie, G.B.	8	33	4.1	17	0
Austin, Cliff, T.B.	19	32	1.7	8	1
Teltschik, John, Phil.	3	32	10.7	23	0
Adams, Tony, Minn.	11	31	2.8	12	0
Garza, Sammy, St.L.	8	31	3.9	10	1
Rubbert, Ed, Wash.	9	31	3.4	14	0
Rutledge, Jeff, Giants	15	31	2.1	20	0
Bartalo, Steve, T.B.	9	30	3.3	6	1
Gladman, Charles, T.B.	12	29	2.4	6	0
Williams, Scott, Det.	8	29	3.6	8	0
Payton, Sean, Chi.	1	28	28.0	28	0
Wilson, Ted, Wash.	2	28	14.0	t16	1
Jackson, Kenny, Phil.	6	27	4.5	10	0
Monroe, Carl, S.F.	2	26	13.0	17	0
Weigel, Lee, G.B.	10	26	2.6	7	0
Suhey, Matt, Chi.	7	24	3.4	6	0
Walker, Adam, Minn.	5	24	4.8	11	0
Harris, Frank, Chi.	6	23	3.8	18	0
Beecham, Earl, Giants	5	22	4.4	10	0
Brown, Ron, Rams	2	22	11.0	11	0
Dollinger, Tony, Det.	8	22	2.8	8	0
Miller, Chris, Atl.	4	21	5.3	11	0
Grant, Otis, Phil.	1	20	20.0	20	0
Land, Dan, T.B.	9	20	2.2	6	0
Sterling, John, G.B.	5	20	4.0	9	0
Womack, Jeff, Minn.	9	20	2.2	13	0
Thomas, Lavale, G.B.	5	19	3.8	5	0
Baker, Stephen, Giants	1	18	18.0	18	0
Jean-Batiste, Garland, N.O. ..	8	18	2.3	7	0
Morris, Larry, G.B.	8	18	2.3	10	0
Gault, Willie, Chi.	2	16	8.0	9	0
Wilson, Brett, Minn.	5	16	3.2	6	0
Harbaugh, James, Chi.	4	15	3.8	9	0
Ingram, Kevin, N.O.	2	14	7.0	9	0
Morse, Bobby, Phil.	6	14	2.3	7	0
Verdin, Clarence, Wash.	1	14	14.0	14	0
White, Danny, Dall.	10	14	1.4	8	1
Paige, Tony, Det.	4	13	3.3	6	0
Smith, Jimmy, Minn.	7	13	1.9	5	0
Granger, Norm, Atl.	6	12	2.0	6	0
Clark, Daryl, Chi.	5	11	2.2	5	0
Flagler, Terrence, S.F.	6	11	1.8	5	0
Lovelady, Edwin, Giants	2	11	5.5	8	0
McIntosh, Joe, Atl.	5	11	2.2	5	0
Moore, Leonard, Minn.	4	11	2.8	4	0
Park, Kaulana, Giants	6	11	1.8	4	0
Evans, Donald, Rams	3	10	3.3	5	0
Kramer, Erik, Atl.	2	10	5.0	11	0
Branch, Reggie, Wash.	4	9	2.3	3	1

	Att	Yards	Avg	Long	TD
Brown, Ron, St.L.	1	9	9.0	9	0
Johnson, Troy, St.L.	1	9	9.0	9	0
Williams, Alonzo, Rams	2	9	4.5	7	0
Williams, Doug, Wash.	7	9	1.3	7	1
Archer, David, Atl.	2	8	4.0	7	0
Harrell, Samuel, Minn.	5	8	1.6	4	0
Quarles, Bernard, Rams	1	8	8.0	8	0
Sweeney, Kevin, Dall.	5	8	1.6	5	0
Wolden, Al, Chi.	2	8	4.0	7	0
Holman, Walter, Wash.	2	7	3.5	5	0
Jones, E.J., Dall.	2	7	3.5	5	0
Anderson, Ottis, Giants	2	6	3.0	4	0
McGee, Buford, Rams	3	6	2.0	t2	1
Stamps, Sylvester, Atl.	1	6	6.0	6	0
Van Raaphorst, Jeff, Atl.	1	6	6.0	6	0
Crocicchia, Jim, Giants	4	5	1.3	7	0
DiRenzo, Fred, Giants	1	5	5.0	5	0
Emery, Larry, Atl.	1	5	5.0	5	0
Streater, Eric, T.B.	1	5	5.0	5	0
Ellard, Henry, Rams	1	4	4.0	4	0
Frye, Phil, Minn.	4	4	1.0	2	0
Thomas, Andre, Minn.	6	4	0.7	5	0
Zorn, Jim, T.B.	4	4	1.0	5	0
Cater, Greg, St.L.	2	3	1.5	11	0
Cook, Kelly, G.B.	2	3	1.5	2	0
Harris, Steve, Minn.	4	3	0.8	2	0
Hill, Bruce, T.B.	3	3	1.0	9	0
Mandley, Pete, Det.	1	3	3.0	3	0
Riordan, Tim, N.O.	1	3	3.0	3	0
Boone, Greg, T.B.	1	2	2.0	2	0
Bryant, Cullen, Rams	1	2	2.0	2	0
Frank, John, S.F.	1	2	2.0	2	0
Kowgios, Nick, Det.	1	2	2.0	2	0
Morris, Lee, G.B.	2	2	1.0	4	0
Scott, Patrick, G.B.	1	2	2.0	2	0
Thomas, Derrick, T.B.	1	2	2.0	2	0
Tinsley, Scott, Phil.	4	2	0.5	2	0
Butler, Jerry, Atl.	1	1	1.0	1	0
Freeman, Phil, T.B.	1	1	1.0	1	0
Marshall, Wilber, Chi.	1	1	1.0	1	0
Black, Mike, Det.	1	0	0.0	0	0
Blount, Ed, S.F.	1	0	0.0	0	0
Brown, Kevin, Chi.	1	0	0.0	0	0
Clark, Gary, Wash.	1	0	0.0	0	0
Clemons, Topper, Phil.	3	0	0.0	3	0
Covington, Jamie, Giants	4	0	0.0	2	0
Criswell, Ray, T.B.	1	0	0.0	0	0
Epps, Phillip, G.B.	1	0	0.0	0	0
Horn, Marty, Phil.	1	0	0.0	0	0
Hunter, Tony, G.B.	1	0	0.0	0	0

	Att	Yards	Avg	Long	TD
Neal, Frankie, G.B.	1	0	0.0	0	0
Oliver, Darryl, Atl.	1	0	0.0	0	0
Perry, William, Chi.	1	0	0.0	0	0
Robinson, Tony, Wash.	2	0	0.0	2	0
Snyder, Loren, Dall.	2	0	0.0	0	0
Miller, Larry, Minn.	1	-1	-1.0	-1	0
Cavanaugh, Matt, Phil.	1	-2	-2.0	-2	0
Griffin, Steve B., Atl.	1	-2	-2.0	-2	0
Gustafson, Jim, Minn.	1	-2	-2.0	-2	0
Stoudt, Cliff, St.L.	1	-2	-2.0	-2	0
Bradley, Steve, Chi.	1	-3	-3.0	-3	0
Dixon, Floyd, Atl.	3	-3	-1.0	7	0
Dils, Steve, Rams	7	-4	-0.6	5	0
Matthews, Aubrey, Atl.	1	-4	-4.0	-4	0
Sanders, Ricky, Wash.	1	-4	-4.0	-4	0
White, Gerald, Dall.	1	-4	-4.0	-4	0
Cosbie, Doug, Dall.	1	-5	-5.0	-5	0
Chadwick, Jeff, Det.	1	-6	-6.0	-6	0
Donnelly, Rick, Atl.	3	-6	-2.0	0	0
Hansen, Brian, N.O.	2	-6	-3.0	-3	0
Lewis, Leo, Minn.	5	-7	-1.4	4	0
Scribner, Bucky, Minn.	1	-7	-7.0	-7	0
DeBerg, Steve, T.B.	8	-8	-1.0	0	0
Merkens, Guido, Phil.	3	-8	-2.7	1	0
Awalt, Robert, St.L.	2	-9	-4.5	-1	0
Halloran, Shawn, St.L.	3	-9	-3.0	2	0
Hill, Lonzell, N.O.	1	-9	-9.0	-9	0
Manuel, Lionel, Giants	1	-10	-10.0	-10	0
Barnhardt, Tommy, N.O.	1	-13	-13.0	-13	0
Taylor, Lenny, Atl.	1	-13	-13.0	-13	0

AFC - INDIVIDUAL RUSHERS

	Att	Yards	Avg	Long	TD
Dickerson, Eric, Rams-Ind. ...	283	1288	4.6	57	6
Warner, Curt, Sea.	234	985	4.2	t57	8
Rozier, Mike, Hou.	229	957	4.2	41	3
Allen, Marcus, Raiders	200	754	3.8	44	5
Winder, Sammy, Den.	196	741	3.8	19	6
Mack, Kevin, Clev.	201	735	3.7	t22	5
Jackson, Earnest, Pitt.	180	696	3.9	39	1
Okoye, Christian, K.C.	157	660	4.2	t43	3
Bentley, Albert, Ind.	142	631	4.4	t17	7
Stradford, Troy, Mia.	145	619	4.3	51	6
Kinnebrew, Larry, Cin.	145	570	3.9	52	8
Jackson, Bo, Raiders	81	554	6.8	t91	4
Pollard, Frank, Pitt.	128	536	4.2	33	3
McNeil, Freeman, Jets	121	530	4.4	30	0
Williams, John L., Sea.	113	500	4.4	48	1
Harmon, Ronnie, Buff.	116	485	4.2	21	2

	Att	Yards	Avg	Long	TD
Collins, Tony, N.E.	147	474	3.2	19	3
Heard, Herman, K.C.	82	466	5.7	t64	3
Abercrombie, Walter, Pitt. ...	123	459	3.7	t28	2
Hector, Johnny, Jets	111	435	3.9	t20	11
Byner, Earnest, Clev.	105	432	4.1	21	8
Mueller, Jamie, Buff.	82	354	4.3	20	2
Adams, Curtis, S.D.	90	343	3.8	24	1
Dupard, Reggie, N.E.	94	318	3.4	49	3
Jennings, Stanford, Cin.	70	314	4.5	18	1
Elway, John, Den.	66	304	4.6	29	4
Lang, Gene, Den.	89	303	3.4	28	2
Brooks, James, Cin.	94	290	3.1	18	1
Hampton, Lorenzo, Mia.	75	289	3.9	34	1
Byrum, Carl, Buff.	66	280	4.2	30	0
Anderson, Gary, S.D.	80	260	3.3	25	3
Vick, Roger, Jets	77	257	3.3	14	1
Tatupu, Mosi, N.E.	79	248	3.1	19	0
Banks, Chuck, Ind.	50	245	4.9	35	0
Esiason, Boomer, Cin.	52	241	4.6	19	0
Jackson, Andrew, Hou.	60	232	3.9	t16	1
Spencer, Tim, S.D.	73	228	3.1	16	0
Riddick, Robb, Buff.	59	221	3.7	25	5
Mason, Larry, Clev.	56	207	3.7	22	2
Johnson, Bill, Cin.	39	205	5.3	20	1
Logan, Marc, Cin.	37	203	5.5	51	1
Scott, Ronald, Mia.	47	199	4.2	24	3
Perryman, Bob, N.E.	41	187	4.6	48	0
Porter, Ricky, Buff.	47	177	3.8	13	0
Mueller, Vance, Raiders	37	175	4.7	35	1
LeBlanc, Michael, N.E.	49	170	3.5	42	1
Malone, Mark, Pitt.	34	162	4.8	t42	3
Krieg, Dave, Sea.	36	155	4.3	17	2
Palmer, Paul, K.C.	24	155	6.5	35	0
Dudek, Joe, Den.	35	154	4.4	16	2
Parker, Robert, K.C.	47	150	3.2	10	1
Pinkett, Allen, Hou.	31	149	4.8	22	2
Evans, Vince, Raiders	11	144	13.1	24	1
Hunter, Herman, Hou.	34	144	4.2	21	0
Willhite, Gerald, Den.	26	141	5.4	29	0
Ellis, Craig, Raiders	33	138	4.2	14	2
Stone, Dwight, Pitt.	17	135	7.9	51	0
Kelly, Jim, Buff.	29	133	4.6	24	0
Bligen, Dennis, Jets	31	128	4.1	15	1
Poole, Nathan, Den.	28	126	4.5	15	1
Manoa, Tim, Clev.	23	116	5.0	35	0
Davenport, Ron, Mia.	32	114	3.6	27	1
Smith, Chris, K.C.	26	114	4.4	11	0
Moon, Warren, Hou.	34	112	3.3	20	3
Strachan, Steve, Raiders	28	108	3.9	20	0
Moriarty, Larry, K.C.	30	107	3.6	11	0

	Att	Yards	Avg	Long	TD
Highsmith, Alonzo, Hou.	29	106	3.7	25	1
Bennett, Woody, Mia.	25	102	4.1	18	0
James, Lionel, S.D.	27	102	3.8	t15	2
Wallace, Ray, Hou.	19	102	5.4	19	0
Mackey, Kyle, Mia.	17	98	5.8	17	2
Everett, Major, Clev.	34	95	2.8	16	0
Horton, Ethan, Raiders	31	95	3.1	14	0
McCluskey, David, Cin.	29	94	3.2	12	1
Wilson, Marc, Raiders	17	91	5.4	16	0
Jenkins, Keyvan, S.D.	22	88	4.0	9	0
Brown, Gordon, Ind.	19	85	4.5	t18	1
Sewell, Steve, Den.	19	83	4.4	17	2
Green, Boyce, Sea.	21	77	3.7	17	0
Ramsey, Tom, N.E.	13	75	5.8	19	1
Middleton, Frank, S.D.	28	74	2.6	21	1
Wright, Dana, Cin.	24	74	3.1	10	0
Morris, Randall, Sea.	21	71	3.4	13	0
Wonsley, George, Ind.	18	71	3.9	12	1
Walter, Dave, Cin.	16	70	4.4	16	0
Sanders, Chuck, Pitt.	11	65	5.9	14	1
O'Brien, Ken, Jets	30	61	2.0	11	0
Rice, Dan, Cin.	18	59	3.3	8	0
McLemore, Chris, Ind.	17	58	3.4	9	0
Bailey, Clarence, Mia.	10	55	5.5	13	0
Caldwell, Scott, Den.	16	53	3.3	7	0
Fryar, Irving, N.E.	9	52	5.8	16	0
Morton, Michael, Sea.	19	52	2.7	10	1
Sartin, Martin, S.D.	19	52	2.7	10	1
Harrison, Rob, Raiders	9	49	5.4	13	0
Lacy, Kenneth, K.C.	14	49	3.5	17	0
Konecny, Mark, Mia.	6	46	7.7	19	0
Tagliaferri, John, Mia.	13	45	3.5	7	1
Hansen, Bruce, N.E.	16	44	2.8	7	0
Bell, Ken, Den.	13	43	3.3	11	0
Davis, Elgin, N.E.	9	43	4.8	27	0
Faaola, Nuu, Jets	14	43	3.1	18	2
Flutie, Doug, N.E.	6	43	7.2	13	0
Shepherd, Johnny, Buff.	12	42	3.5	19	0
Christensen, Jeff, Clev.	11	41	3.7	15	0
Isom, Rickey, Mia.	9	41	4.6	8	1
Neuheisel, Rick, S.D.	6	41	6.8	18	1
Lane, Eric, Sea.	13	40	3.1	7	0
Grogan, Steve, N.E.	20	37	1.9	8	2
Burse, Tony, Sea.	7	36	5.1	16	0
Calhoun, Rick, Raiders	7	36	5.1	18	0
Redden, Barry, S.D.	11	36	3.3	7	0
Fontenot, Herman, Clev.	15	33	2.2	14	0
Largent, Steve, Sea.	2	33	16.5	21	0
Pease, Brent, Hou.	15	33	2.2	8	1
Seurer, Frank, K.C.	9	33	3.7	11	0

	Att	Yards	Avg	Long	TD
Parros, Rick, Sea.	13	32	2.5	7	1
Driver, Stacey, Clev.	9	31	3.4	16	0
Kiel, Blair, Ind.	4	30	7.5	16	0
Tillman, Spencer, Hou.	12	29	2.4	13	1
King, Bruce, Buff.	9	28	3.1	8	0
Bono, Steve, Pitt.	8	27	3.4	23	1
Eason, Tony, N.E.	3	25	8.3	13	0
Williams, Leonard, Buff.	9	25	2.8	9	0
Hawkins, Frank, Raiders	4	24	6.0	7	0
Spencer, Todd, S.D.	14	24	1.7	5	0
Cobble, Eric, Hou.	9	23	2.6	12	0
McSwain, Chuck, N.E.	9	23	2.6	9	0
Chirico, John, Jets	12	22	1.8	4	1
Kosar, Bernie, Clev.	15	22	1.5	7	1
Moore, Ricky, Hou.	7	22	3.1	11	0
Blackledge, Todd, K.C.	5	21	4.2	11	0
Collier, Reggie, Pitt.	4	20	5.0	12	0
Nathan, Tony, Mia.	4	20	5.0	8	0
Woods, Carl, N.E.	4	20	5.0	13	1
Meehan, Greg, Cin.	4	19	4.8	17	0
Breen, Adrian, Cin.	6	18	3.0	9	0
Jensen, Jim, Mia.	4	18	4.5	9	0
Smith, Steve, Raiders	5	18	3.6	15	0
Bennett, Ben, Cin.	2	17	8.5	9	0
Harris, Leonard, Hou.	1	17	17.0	17	0
Holland, Jamie, S.D.	1	17	17.0	17	0
Kelley, Mike, S.D.	4	17	4.3	10	0
McNeil, Gerald, Clev.	1	17	17.0	17	0
Goodburn, Kelly, K.C.	1	16	16.0	16	0
Newsome, Harry, Pitt.	2	16	8.0	16	0
Pippens, Woodie, K.C.	3	16	5.3	11	0
Mathison, Bruce, Sea.	5	15	3.0	10	0
Moore, Alvin, Det.	3	15	5.0	13	0
Nattiel, Ricky, Den.	2	13	6.5	10	0
Partridge, Rick, Buff.	1	13	13.0	13	0
Starring, Stephen, N.E.	2	13	6.5	10	0
Carter, Rodney, Pitt.	5	12	2.4	4	0
Totten, Willie, Buff.	12	11	0.9	7	0
Williams, Alphonso, S.D.	1	11	11.0	11	0
James, Craig, N.E.	4	10	2.5	5	0
Roth, Pete, Mia.	3	10	3.3	9	0
Valentine, Ira, Hou.	5	10	2.0	4	0
Bernstine, Rod, S.D.	1	9	9.0	9	0
Foster, Derrick, Jets	1	9	9.0	9	0
Kemp, Jeff, Sea.	5	9	1.8	12	0
Verser, David, Clev.	1	9	9.0	9	0
Clayton, Mark, Mia.	2	8	4.0	4	0
Hilger, Rusty, Raiders	8	8	1.0	6	0
Hoge, Merril, Pitt.	3	8	2.7	5	0
Micho, Bobby, Den.	4	8	2.0	5	0

	Att	Yards	Avg	Long	TD
Reeder, Dan, Pitt.	2	8	4.0	4	0
Boddie, Tony, Den.	3	7	2.3	4	1
Clemons, Michael, K.C.	2	7	3.5	7	0
Davis, Johnny, Clev.	1	7	7.0	7	0
Stevens, Matt, K.C.	3	7	2.3	6	0
Trudeau, Jack, Ind.	15	7	0.5	9	0
Manucci, Dan, Buff.	4	6	1.5	9	0
Espinoza, Alex, K.C.	1	5	5.0	5	0
Jennings, Dave, Jets	2	5	2.5	4	0
Norrie, David, Jets	5	5	1.0	2	0
Ryan, Pat, Jets	4	5	1.3	t8	1
Briggs, Walter, Jets	1	4	4.0	4	0
McClure, Brian, Buff.	2	4	2.0	3	0
Brown, Tom, Mia.	3	3	1.0	3	0
Carver, Mel, Ind.	2	3	1.5	3	0
Hagen, Mike, Sea.	2	3	1.5	4	0
Hogeboom, Gary, Ind.	3	3	1.0	2	0
Karcher, Ken, Den.	9	3	0.3	8	0
Kubiak, Gary, Den.	1	3	3.0	3	0
Steels, Anthony, S.D.	1	3	3.0	3	0
Zachary, Ken, S.D.	1	3	3.0	3	0
Stockemer, Ralph, K.C.	1	2	2.0	2	0
Aikens, Carl, Raiders	1	1	1.0	1	0
Browne, Jim, Raiders	2	1	0.5	2	0
Lofton, James, Raiders	1	1	1.0	1	0
Moffett, Tim, S.D.	1	1	1.0	1	0
Nugent, Terry, Ind.	2	1	0.5	3	0
Reed, Andre, Buff.	1	1	1.0	1	0
Brown, Eddie, Cin.	1	0	0.0	0	0
Camarillo, Rich, N.E.	1	0	0.0	0	0
Danielson, Gary, Clev.	1	0	0.0	0	0
Fouts, Dan, S.D.	12	0	0.0	2	2
Griffith, Russell, Sea.	1	0	0.0	0	0
Hudson, Doug, K.C.	1	0	0.0	0	0
Katolin, Mike, Clev.	1	0	0.0	0	0
Porter, Kerry, Buff.	2	0	0.0	1	0
Roby, Reggie, Mia.	1	0	0.0	0	0
Rodriguez, Ruben, Sea.	1	0	0.0	0	0
Herrmann, Mark, S.D.	4	-1	-0.3	0	0
Brooks, Bill, Ind.	2	-2	-1.0	1	0
Kenney, Bill, K.C.	12	-2	-0.2	6	0
Townsell, JoJo, Jets	1	-2	-2.0	-2	0
May, Dean, Den.	2	-4	-2.0	-2	0
Bleier, Bob, N.E.	5	-5	-1.0	t1	1
Marino, Dan, Mia.	12	-5	-0.4	t5	1
Whitten, Todd, N.E.	2	-6	-3.0	-2	0
Carson, Carlos, K.C.	1	-7	-7.0	-7	0
Johnson, Vance, Den.	1	-8	-8.0	-8	0
McGee, Tim, Cin.	1	-10	-10.0	-10	0
Givins, Ernest, Hou.	1	-13	-13.0	-13	0

Seattle's John L. Williams made all-purpose gains.

James Jones carries a Lion load.

PASSING

TOP TEN PASSERS

	Att	Comp	Pct Comp	Yds
Montana, Joe, S.F.	398	266	66.8	3054
Kosar, Bernie, Clev.	389	241	62.0	3033
Simms, Phil, Giants	282	163	57.8	2230
Marino, Dan, Mia.	444	263	59.2	3245
Lomax, Neil, St.L.	463	275	59.4	3387
Krieg, Dave, Sea.	294	178	60.5	2131
McMahon, Jim, Chi.	210	125	59.5	1639
Kenney, Bill, K.C.	273	154	56.4	2107
DeBerg, Steve, T.B.	275	159	57.8	1891
Wilson, Marc, Raiders	266	152	57.1	2070

NFC - INDIVIDUAL QUALIFIERS

	Att	Comp	Pct Comp	Yds
Montana, Joe, S.F.	398	266	66.8	3054
Simms, Phil, Giants	282	163	57.8	2230
Lomax, Neil, St.L.	463	275	59.4	3387
McMahon, Jim, Chi.	210	125	59.5	1639
DeBerg, Steve, T.B.	275	159	57.8	1891
Cunningham, Randall, Phil. ...	406	223	54.9	2786
Hebert, Bobby, N.O.	294	164	55.8	2119
Wilson, Wade, Minn.	264	140	53.0	2106
White, Danny, Dall.	362	215	59.4	2617
Schroeder, Jay, Wash.	267	129	48.3	1878
Everett, Jim, Rams	302	162	53.6	2064
Campbell, Scott, Atl.	260	136	52.3	1728
Long, Chuck, Det.	416	232	55.8	2598
Wright, Randy, G.B.	247	132	53.4	1507

NFC - NON-QUALIFIERS

	Att	Comp	Pct Comp	Yds
Young, Steve, S.F.	69	37	53.6	570
Wilson, Dave, N.O.	24	13	54.2	243
Sweeney, Kevin, Dall.	28	14	50.0	291
Rubbert, Ed, Wash.	49	26	53.1	532
Williams, Doug, Wash.	143	81	56.6	1156
Hohensee, Mike, Chi.	52	28	53.8	343
Harbaugh, James, Chi.	11	8	72.7	62

t = Touchdown
Leader based on rating points, minimum 210 attempts

Avg Gain	TD	Pct TD	Long	Int	Pct Int	Rating Points
7.67	31	7.8	t57	13	3.3	102.1
7.80	22	5.7	t54	9	2.3	95.4
7.91	17	6.0	t50	9	3.2	90.0
7.31	26	5.9	t59	13	2.9	89.2
7.32	24	5.2	57	12	2.6	88.5
7.25	23	7.8	t75	15	5.1	87.6
7.80	12	5.7	t59	8	3.8	87.4
7.72	15	5.5	t81	9	3.3	85.8
6.88	14	5.1	t64	7	2.5	85.3
7.78	12	4.5	t47	8	3.0	84.6

Avg Gain	TD	Pct TD	Long	Int	Pct Int	Rating Points
7.67	31	7.8	t57	13	3.3	102.1
7.91	17	6.0	t50	9	3.2	90.0
7.32	24	5.2	57	12	2.6	88.5
7.80	12	5.7	t59	8	3.8	87.4
6.88	14	5.1	t64	7	2.5	85.3
6.86	23	5.7	t70	12	3.0	83.0
7.21	15	5.1	67	9	3.1	82.9
7.98	14	5.3	t73	13	4.9	76.7
7.23	12	3.3	43	17	4.7	73.2
7.03	12	4.5	t84	10	3.7	71.0
6.83	10	3.3	t81	13	4.3	68.4
6.65	11	4.2	t44	14	5.4	65.0
6.25	11	2.6	53	20	4.8	63.4
6.10	6	2.4	66	11	4.5	61.6

Avg Gain	TD	Pct TD	Long	Int	Pct Int	Rating Points
8.26	10	14.5	t50	0	0.0	120.8
10.13	2	8.3	38	0	0.0	117.2
10.39	4	14.3	t77	1	3.6	111.8
10.86	4	8.2	t88	1	2.0	110.2
8.08	11	7.7	62	5	3.5	94.0
6.60	4	7.7	28	1	1.9	92.1
5.64	0	0.0	21	0	0.0	86.2

	Att	Comp	Pct Comp	Yds
Crocicchia, Jim, Giants	15	6	40.0	89
Risher, Alan, G.B.	74	44	59.5	564
Gagliano, Bob, S.F.	29	16	55.2	229
Fourcade, John, N.O.	89	48	53.9	597
Reaves, John, T.B.	16	6	37.5	83
Pelluer, Steve, Dall.	101	55	54.5	642
Tinsley, Scott, Phil.	86	48	55.8	637
Majkowski, Don, G.B.	127	55	43.3	875
Kramer, Tommy, Minn.	81	40	49.4	452
Dils, Steve, Rams	114	56	49.1	646
Horn, Marty, Phil.	11	5	45.5	68
Merkens, Guido, Phil.	14	7	50.0	70
Adams, Tony, Minn.	89	49	55.1	607
Garza, Sammy, St.L.	20	11	55.0	183
Tomczak, Mike, Chi.	178	97	54.5	1220
Hold, Mike, T.B.	24	8	33.3	123
Hons, Todd, Det.	92	43	46.7	552
Busch, Mike, Giants	47	17	36.2	278
Testaverde, Vinny, T.B.	165	71	43.0	1081
Kramer, Erik, Atl.	92	45	48.9	559
Halloran, Shawn, St.L.	42	18	42.9	263
Rutledge, Jeff, Giants	155	79	51.0	1048
Van Raaphorst, Jeff, Atl. ...	34	18	52.9	174
Robinson, Tony, Wash.	18	11	61.1	152
Zorn, Jim, T.B.	36	20	55.6	199
Bradley, Steve, Chi.	18	6	33.3	77
Payton, Sean, Chi.	23	8	34.8	79
Miller, Chris, Atl.	92	39	42.4	552
Archer, David, Atl.	23	9	39.1	95
(Fewer than 10 attempts)				
Bartalo, Steve, T.B.	1	0	0.0	0
Bryant, Kelvin, Wash.	1	0	0.0	0
Carruth, Paul Ott, G.B.	1	1	100.0	3
Carter, Cris, Phil.	1	0	0.0	0
Gannon, Rich, Minn.	6	2	33.3	18
Gillus, Willie, G.B.	5	2	40.0	28
Grant, Otis, Phil.	1	0	0.0	0
Hilliard, Dalton, N.O.	1	1	100.0	23
Ingram, Kevin, N.O.	2	1	50.0	5
Jones, James, Det.	1	0	0.0	0
Millen, Hugh, Rams	1	1	100.0	0
Miller, Larry, Minn.	6	1	16.7	2
Mitchell, Stump, St.L.	3	1	33.3	17
Neal, Frankie, G.B.	1	0	0.0	0
Payton, Walter, Chi.	1	0	0.0	0
Quarles, Bernard, Rams	3	1	33.3	40
Riordan, Tim, N.O.	1	0	0.0	0
Snyder, Loren, Dall.	9	4	44.4	44

Avg Gain	TD	Pct TD	Long	Int	Pct Int	Rating Points
5.93	1	6.7	t46	0	0.0	82.4
7.62	3	4.1	t46	3	4.1	80.0
7.90	1	3.4	50	1	3.4	78.1
6.71	4	4.5	t82	3	3.4	75.9
5.19	1	6.3	t26	0	0.0	75.8
6.36	3	3.0	44	2	2.0	75.6
7.41	3	3.5	t62	4	4.7	71.7
6.89	5	3.9	t70	3	2.4	70.2
5.58	4	4.9	t40	3	3.7	67.5
5.67	5	4.4	51	4	3.5	66.6
6.18	0	0.0	23	0	0.0	65.7
5.00	0	0.0	17	0	0.0	64.6
6.82	3	3.4	t63	5	5.6	64.2
9.15	1	5.0	t38	2	10.0	63.1
6.85	5	2.8	t56	10	5.6	62.0
5.13	2	8.3	t61	1	4.2	61.6
6.00	5	5.4	t53	5	5.4	61.5
5.91	3	6.4	t63	2	4.3	60.4
6.55	5	3.0	40	6	3.6	60.2
6.08	4	4.3	33	5	5.4	60.0
6.26	0	0.0	49	1	2.4	54.0
6.76	5	3.2	50	11	7.1	53.9
5.12	1	2.9	24	2	5.9	52.8
8.44	0	0.0	42	2	11.1	48.6
5.53	0	0.0	26	2	5.6	48.3
4.28	2	11.1	t18	3	16.7	45.1
3.43	0	0.0	20	1	4.3	27.3
6.00	1	1.1	57	9	9.8	26.4
4.13	0	0.0	33	2	8.7	15.7
0.00	0	0.0	0	1	100.0	0.0
0.00	0	0.0	0	0	0.0	39.6
3.00	1	100.0	t3	0	0.0	118.8
0.00	0	0.0	0	0	0.0	39.6
3.00	0	0.0	12	1	16.7	2.8
5.60	0	0.0	15	0	0.0	58.8
0.00	0	0.0	0	0	0.0	39.6
23.00	1	100.0	t23	0	0.0	158.3
2.50	1	50.0	t5	0	0.0	95.8
0.00	0	0.0	0	1	100.0	0.0
0.00	0	0.0	0	0	0.0	79.2
0.33	0	0.0	2	1	16.7	0.0
5.67	0	0.0	17	0	0.0	53.5
0.00	0	0.0	0	0	0.0	39.6
0.00	0	0.0	0	1	100.0	0.0
13.33	1	33.3	t40	1	33.3	81.9
0.00	0	0.0	0	0	0.0	39.6
4.89	0	0.0	22	0	0.0	59.5

	Att	Comp	Pct Comp	Yds
Stevens, Mark, S.F.	4	2	50.0	52
Stoudt, Cliff, St.L.	1	0	0.0	0
Sydney, Harry, S.F.	1	1	100.0	50
Teltschik, John, Phil.	0	0	---	0
Toney, Anthony, Phil.	1	0	0.0	0

AFC — INDIVIDUAL QUALIFIERS

	Att	Comp	Pct Comp	Yds
Kosar, Bernie, Clev.	389	241	62.0	3033
Marino, Dan, Mia.	444	263	59.2	3245
Krieg, Dave, Sea.	294	178	60.5	2131
Kenney, Bill, K.C.	273	154	56.4	2107
Wilson, Marc, Raiders	266	152	57.1	2070
Kelly, Jim, Buff.	419	250	59.7	2798
Elway, John, Den.	410	224	54.6	3198
O'Brien, Ken, Jets	393	234	59.5	2696
Trudeau, Jack, Ind.	229	128	55.9	1587
Moon, Warren, Hou.	368	184	50.0	2806
Esiason, Boomer, Cin.	440	240	54.5	3321
Fouts, Dan, S.D.	364	206	56.6	2517
Malone, Mark, Pitt.	336	156	46.4	1896

AFC — NON-QUALIFIERS

	Att	Comp	Pct Comp	Yds
Danielson, Gary, Clev.	33	25	75.8	281
Kemp, Jeff, Sea.	33	23	69.7	396
Kelley, Mike, S.D.	29	17	58.6	305
Flutie, Doug, N.E.	25	15	60.0	199
Ryan, Pat, Jets	53	32	60.4	314
Neuheisel, Rick, S.D.	59	40	67.8	367
Hogeboom, Gary, Ind.	168	99	58.9	1145
Grogan, Steve, N.E.	161	93	57.8	1183
Bono, Steve, Pitt.	74	34	45.9	438
Karcher, Ken, Den.	102	56	54.9	628
Evans, Vince, Raiders	83	39	47.0	630
Eason, Tony, N.E.	79	42	53.2	453
Stevens, Matt, K.C.	57	32	56.1	315
Ramsey, Tom, N.E.	134	71	53.0	898
Walter, Dave, Cin.	21	10	47.6	113
Pease, Brent, Hou.	113	56	49.6	728
Blackledge, Todd, K.C.	31	15	48.4	154
Mackey, Kyle, Mia.	109	57	52.3	604
Hilger, Rusty, Raiders	106	55	51.9	706

Avg Gain	TD	Pct TD	Long	Int	Pct Int	Rating Points
13.00	1	25.0	t39	0	0.0	135.4
0.00	0	0.0	0	0	0.0	39.6
50.00	1	100.0	t50	0	0.0	158.3
----	0	---	0	0	---	0.0
0.00	0	0.0	0	0	0.0	39.6

Avg Gain	TD	Pct TD	Long	Int	Pct Int	Rating Points
7.80	22	5.7	t54	9	2.3	95.4
7.31	26	5.9	t59	13	2.9	89.2
7.25	23	7.8	t75	15	5.1	87.6
7.72	15	5.5	t81	9	3.3	85.8
7.78	12	4.5	t47	8	3.0	84.6
6.68	19	4.5	47	11	2.6	83.8
7.80	19	4.6	t72	12	2.9	83.4
6.86	13	3.3	59	8	2.0	82.8
6.93	6	2.6	55	6	2.6	75.4
7.63	21	5.7	t83	18	4.9	74.2
7.55	16	3.6	t61	19	4.3	73.1
6.91	10	2.7	46	15	4.1	70.0
5.64	6	1.8	63	19	5.7	46.7

Avg Gain	TD	Pct TD	Long	Int	Pct Int	Rating Points
8.52	4	12.1	23	0	0.0	140.3
12.00	5	15.2	55	1	3.0	137.1
10.52	1	3.4	67	0	0.0	106.3
7.96	1	4.0	30	0	0.0	98.6
5.92	4	7.5	t35	2	3.8	86.5
6.22	1	1.7	32	1	1.7	83.1
6.82	9	5.4	t72	5	3.0	85.0
7.35	10	6.2	40	9	5.6	78.2
5.92	5	6.8	57	2	2.7	76.3
6.16	5	4.9	49	4	3.9	73.5
7.59	5	6.0	47	4	4.8	72.9
5.73	3	3.8	45	2	2.5	72.4
5.53	1	1.8	23	1	1.8	70.4
6.70	6	4.5	40	6	4.5	70.4
5.38	0	0.0	35	0	0.0	64.2
6.44	3	2.7	51	5	4.4	60.6
4.97	1	3.2	19	1	3.2	60.4
5.54	3	2.8	30	5	4.6	58.8
6.66	2	1.9	49	6	5.7	55.8

	Att	Comp	Pct Comp	Yds
Herrmann, Mark, S.D.	57	37	64.9	405
Mathison, Bruce, Sea.	76	36	47.4	501
Strock, Don, Mia.	23	13	56.5	114
Totten, Willie, Buff.	33	13	39.4	155
Bleier, Bob, N.E.	39	14	35.9	181
Norrie, David, Jets	68	35	51.5	376
Christensen, Jeff, Clev.	58	24	41.4	297
Kiel, Blair, Ind.	33	17	51.5	195
Salisbury, Sean, Ind.	12	8	66.7	68
Seurer, Frank, K.C.	55	26	47.3	340
Espinoza, Alex, K.C.	14	9	64.3	69
McClure, Brian, Buff.	38	20	52.6	181
Manucci, Dan, Buff.	21	7	33.3	68
Brister, Bubby, Pitt.	12	4	33.3	20
(Fewer than 10 attempts)				
Allen, Marcus, Raiders	2	1	50.0	23
Bennett, Ben, Cin.	6	2	33.3	25
Breen, Adrian, Cin.	8	3	37.5	9
Briggs, Walter, Jets	2	0	0.0	0
Collier, Reggie, Pitt.	7	4	57.1	110
Fontenot, Herman, Clev.	1	1	100.0	14
Hill, Drew, Hou.	1	0	0.0	0
Hillary, Ira, Cin.	0	0	---	0
Hudson, Doug, K.C.	1	0	0.0	0
Jaeger, Jeff, Clev.	1	0	0.0	0
Jennings, Dave, Jets	1	1	100.0	16
Johnson, Vance, Den.	1	0	0.0	0
Jones, Cedric, N.E.	1	0	0.0	0
Kidd, John, Buff.	1	0	0.0	0
Kubiak, Gary, Den.	7	3	42.9	25
Lang, Gene, Den.	1	0	0.0	0
Largent, Steve, Sea.	2	0	0.0	0
May, Dean, Den.	5	0	0.0	0
McGuire, Monte, Den.	3	2	66.7	23
Miller, Mark, Buff.	3	1	33.3	9
Nugent, Terry, Ind.	5	3	60.0	47
Palmer, Paul, K.C.	1	0	0.0	0
Riddick, Robb, Buff.	1	1	100.0	35
Sewell, Steve, Den.	0	0	---	0
Smith, Billy Ray, S.D.	1	0	0.0	0
Stankavage, Scott, Mia.	7	4	57.1	8
Stradford, Troy, Mia.	1	1	100.0	6
Tatupu, Mosi, N.E.	1	1	100.0	15
Vlasic, Mark, S.D.	6	3	50.0	8
Willhite, Gerald, Den.	1	0	0.0	0

Avg Gain	TD	Pct TD	Long	Int	Pct Int	Rating Points
7.11	1	1.8	34	5	8.8	55.1
6.59	3	3.9	47	5	6.6	54.8
4.96	0	0.0	26	1	4.3	51.7
4.70	2	6.1	37	2	6.1	49.4
4.64	1	2.6	35	1	2.6	49.2
5.53	1	1.5	t41	4	5.9	48.4
5.12	1	1.7	34	3	5.2	42.1
5.91	1	3.0	21	3	9.1	41.9
5.67	0	0.0	11	2	16.7	41.7
6.18	0	0.0	33	4	7.3	36.9
4.93	0	0.0	16	2	14.3	36.6
4.76	0	0.0	30	3	7.9	32.9
3.24	0	0.0	15	2	9.5	3.8
1.67	0	0.0	10	3	25.0	2.8
11.50	0	0.0	23	0	0.0	91.7
4.17	0	0.0	18	1	16.7	7.6
1.13	1	12.5	6	0	0.0	85.4
0.00	0	0.0	0	1	50.0	0.0
15.71	2	28.6	49	1	14.3	101.8
14.00	0	0.0	14	0	0.0	118.8
0.00	0	0.0	0	0	0.0	39.6
-----	0	---	0	0	---	0.0
0.00	0	0.0	0	0	0.0	39.6
0.00	0	0.0	0	0	0.0	39.6
16.00	0	0.0	16	0	0.0	118.8
0.00	0	0.0	0	0	0.0	39.6
0.00	0	0.0	0	0	0.0	39.6
0.00	0	0.0	0	0	0.0	39.6
3.57	0	0.0	17	2	28.6	13.1
0.00	0	0.0	0	0	0.0	39.6
0.00	0	0.0	0	0	0.0	39.6
0.00	0	0.0	0	1	20.0	0.0
7.67	0	0.0	13	0	0.0	89.6
3.00	0	0.0	9	1	33.3	2.8
9.40	0	0.0	21	0	0.0	91.3
0.00	0	0.0	0	0	0.0	39.6
35.00	0	0.0	35	0	0.0	118.8
-----	0	---	0	0	---	0.0
0.00	0	0.0	0	1	100.0	0.0
1.14	0	0.0	8	1	14.3	22.6
6.00	0	0.0	6	0	0.0	91.7
15.00	1	100.0	t15	0	0.0	158.3
1.33	0	0.0	7	1	16.7	16.7
0.00	0	0.0	0	0	0.0	39.6

Jim Kelly is ready for the Year of the Buffalo.

Saints' Morten Andersen topped kickers in scoring.

TOP TEN PASS RECEIVERS

	No	Yards	Avg	Long	TD
Smith, J.T., St.L.	91	1117	12.3	38	8
Toon, Al, Jets	68	976	14.4	t58	5
Craig, Roger, S.F.	66	492	7.5	t35	1
Rice, Jerry, S.F.	65	1078	16.6	t57	22
Walker, Herschel, Dall.	60	715	11.9	44	1
Largent, Steve, Sea.	58	912	15.7	55	8
Mandley, Pete, Det.	58	720	12.4	41	7
Reed, Andre, Buff.	57	752	13.2	40	5
Clark, Gary, Wash.	56	1066	19.0	t84	7
Burkett, Chris, Buff.	56	765	13.7	47	4
Harmon, Ronnie, Buff.	56	477	8.5	42	2

TOP TEN RECEIVERS BY YARDS

	Yards	No	Avg	Long	TD
Smith, J.T., St.L.	1117	91	12.3	38	8
Rice, Jerry, S.F.	1078	65	16.6	t57	22
Clark, Gary, Wash.	1066	56	19.0	t84	7
Carson, Carlos, K.C.	1044	55	19.0	t81	7
Hill, Drew, Hou.	989	49	20.2	t52	6
Toon, Al, Jets	976	68	14.4	t58	5
Givins, Ernest, Hou.	933	53	17.6	t83	6
Carter, Anthony, Minn.	922	38	24.3	t73	7
Largent, Steve, Sea.	912	58	15.7	55	8
Lofton, James, Raiders	880	41	21.5	49	5

TOP TEN INTERCEPTORS

	No	Yards	Avg	Long	TD
Wilburn, Barry, Wash.	9	135	15.0	t100	1
Griffin, James, Det.	6	130	21.7	29	0
Browner, Joey, Minn.	6	67	11.2	23	0
Prior, Mike, Ind.	6	57	9.5	38	0
Kelso, Mark, Buff.	6	25	4.2	12	0
Bostic, Keith, Hou.	6	-14	-2.3	7	0
Kinard, Terry, Giants	5	163	32.6	t70	1
Woodruff, Dwayne, Pitt.	5	91	18.2	t33	1
Waymer, Dave, N.O.	5	78	15.6	35	0
Sutton, Reggie, N.O.	5	68	13.6	26	0
Curtis, Travis, St.L.	5	65	13.0	31	0
Lott, Ronnie, S.F.	5	62	12.4	34	0
Walls, Everson, Dall.	5	38	7.6	30	0
Smith, Billy Ray, S.D.	5	28	5.6	12	0
Griffin, Don, S.F.	5	1	0.2	1	0

TOP TEN KICKOFF RETURNERS

	No	Yards	Avg	Long	TD
Stamps, Sylvester, Atl.	24	660	27.5	t97	1
Gentry, Dennis, Chi.	25	621	24.8	t88	1
Palmer, Paul, K.C.	38	923	24.3	t95	2
Bentley, Albert, Ind.	22	500	22.7	45	0
Rouson, Lee, Giants	22	497	22.6	49	0
Lee, Gary, Det.	32	719	22.5	50	0
Guggemos, Neal, Minn.	36	808	22.4	42	0
Sikahema, Vai, St.L.	34	761	22.4	50	0
Clack, Darryl, Dall.	29	635	21.9	48	0
Mueller, Vance, Raiders	27	588	21.8	46	0

TOP TEN PUNT RETURNERS

	No	FC	Yards	Avg	Long	TD
Gray, Mel, N.O.	24	5	352	14.7	80	0
McLemore, Dana, S.F.	21	7	265	12.6	t83	1
Edmonds, Bobby Joe, Sea.	20	4	251	12.6	40	0
James, Lionel, S.D.	32	7	400	12.5	t81	1
Lewis, Leo, Minn.	22	7	275	12.5	t78	1
Sikahema, Vai, St.L.	44	7	550	12.5	t76	1
Townsell, JoJo, Jets	32	11	381	11.9	t91	1
McNeil, Gerald, Clev.	34	9	386	11.4	40	0
Mandley, Pete, Det.	23	6	250	10.9	54	0
McKinnon, Dennis, Chi.	40	4	405	10.1	t94	2

TOP 10 LEADERS - SACKS

	Sacks
White, Reggie, Phil.	21.0
Dent, Richard, Chi.	12.5
Tippett, Andre, N.E.	12.5
Smith, Bruce, Buff.	12.0
Taylor, Lawrence, Giants	12.0
Doleman, Chris, Minn.	11.0
Nunn, Freddie Joe, St.L.	11.0
Swilling, Pat, N.O.	10.5
Jones, Ed L., Dall.	10.0
Green, Jacob, Sea.	9.5
Jackson, Rickey, N.O.	9.5
Mann, Charles, Wash.	9.5

TOP TEN PUNTERS

	No	Yards	Long	Avg
Donnelly, Rick, Atl.	61	2686	62	44.0
Arnold, Jim, Det.	46	2007	60	43.6
Mojsiejenko, Ralf, S.D.	67	2875	57	42.9
Landeta, Sean, Giants	65	2773	64	42.7
Newsome, Harry, Pitt.	64	2678	57	41.8
Fulhage, Scott, Cin.	52	2168	58	41.7
Hatcher, Dale, Rams	76	3140	62	41.3
Horan, Mike, Den.	44	1807	61	41.1
Bracken, Don, G.B.	72	2947	65	40.9
Goodburn, Kelly, K.C.	59	2412	55	40.9

TOP TEN SCORERS — NONKICKERS

	TD	TDR	TDP	TDM	PTS
Rice, Jerry, S.F.	23	1	22	0	138
Hector, Johnny, Jets	11	11	0	0	66
Quick, Mike, Phil.	11	0	11	0	66
White, Charles, Rams	11	11	0	0	66
Byner, Earnest, Clev.	10	8	2	0	60
Warner, Curt, Sea.	10	8	2	0	60
Bentley, Albert, Ind.	9	7	2	0	54
Riddick, Robb, Buff.	8	5	3	0	50
Bavaro, Mark, Giants	8	0	8	0	48
Duper, Mark, Mia.	8	0	8	0	48
Hilliard, Dalton, N.O.	8	7	1	0	48
Kinnebrew, Larry, Cin.	8	8	0	0	48
Largent, Steve, Sea.	8	0	8	0	48
Smith, J.T., St.L.	8	0	8	0	48
Walker, Herschel, Dall.	8	7	1	0	48

Punts	TB	Blk	Ret	Yds	20	Avg
63	8	2	38	501	9	32.1
46	4	0	22	104	17	39.6
67	12	0	37	392	15	33.5
66	6	1	38	606	13	31.0
65	13	1	36	373	8	31.5
52	5	0	31	216	10	35.6
77	4	1	43	317	19	35.6
46	5	2	22	186	11	33.1
73	5	1	45	354	13	34.2
59	5	0	39	403	13	32.4

TOP TEN SCORERS - KICKERS

	XP	XPA	FG	FGA	PTS
Andersen, Morten, N.O.	37	37	28	36	121
Breech, Jim, Cin.	25	27	24	30	97
Biasucci, Dean, Ind.	24	24	24	27	96
Ruzek, Roger, Dall.	26	26	22	25	92
Zendejas, Tony, Hou.	32	33	20	26	92
Karlis, Rich, Den.	37	37	18	25	91
Anderson, Gary, Pitt.	21	21	22	27	87
Lansford, Mike, Rams	36	38	17	21	87
Butler, Kevin, Chi.	28	30	19	28	85
Johnson, Norm, Sea.	40	40	15	20	85
Leahy, Pat, Jets	31	31	18	22	85

NFL STANDINGS
1921-1987

1921

	W	L	T	Pct.
Chicago Staleys	10	1	1	.909
Buffalo All-Americans	9	1	2	.900
Akron, Ohio, Pros	7	2	1	.778
Green Bay Packers	6	2	2	.750
Canton, Ohio, Bulldogs	4	3	3	.571
Dayton Triangles	4	3	1	.571
Rock Island Independents	5	4	1	.556
Chicago Cardinals	2	3	2	.400
Cleveland Indians	2	6	0	.250
Rochester Jeffersons	2	6	0	.250
Detroit Heralds	1	7	1	.125
Columbus Panhandles	0	6	0	.000
Cincinnati Celts	0	8	0	.000

1922

	W	L	T	Pct.
Canton, Ohio, Bulldogs	10	0	2	1.000
Chicago Bears	9	3	0	.750
Chicago Cardinals	8	3	0	.727
Toledo Maroons	5	2	2	.714
Rock Island Independents	4	2	1	.667
Dayton Triangles	4	3	1	.571
Green Bay Packers	4	3	3	.571
Racine, Wis., Legion	5	4	1	.556
Akron, Ohio, Pros	3	4	2	.429
Buffalo All-Americans	3	4	1	.429
Milwaukee Badgers	2	4	3	.333
Marion, O., Oorang Indians	2	6	0	.250
Minneapolis Marines	1	3	0	.250
Evansville Crimson Giants	0	2	0	.000
Louisville Brecks	0	3	0	.000
Rochester Jeffersons	0	3	1	.000
Hammond, Ind., Pros	0	4	1	.000
Columbus Panhandles	0	7	0	.000

1923

	W	L	T	Pct.
Canton, Ohio, Bulldogs	11	0	1	1.000
Chicago Bears	9	2	1	.818
Green Bay Packers	7	2	1	.778
Milwaukee Badgers	7	2	3	.778
Cleveland Indians	3	1	3	.750
Chicago Cardinals	8	4	0	.667
Duluth Kelleys	4	3	0	.571
Buffalo All-Americans	5	4	3	.556
Columbus Tigers	5	4	1	.556
Racine, Wis., Legion	4	4	2	.500
Toledo Maroons	2	3	2	.400
Rock Island Independents	2	3	3	.400

Minneapolis Marines	2	5	2	.286
St. Louis All-Stars	1	4	2	.200
Hammond, Ind., Pros	1	5	1	.167
Dayton Triangles	1	6	1	.143
Akron, Ohio, Indians	1	6	0	.143
Marion, O., Oorang Indians	1	10	0	.091
Rochester Jeffersons	0	2	0	.000
Louisville Brecks	0	3	0	.000

1924

	W	L	T	Pct.
Cleveland Bulldogs	7	1	1	.875
Chicago Bears	6	1	4	.857
Frankford Yellowjackets	11	2	1	.846
Duluth Kelleys	5	1	0	.833
Rock Island Independents	6	2	2	.750
Green Bay Packers	8	4	0	.667
Buffalo Bisons	6	4	0	.600
Racine, Wis., Legion	4	3	3	.571
Chicago Cardinals	5	4	1	.556
Columbus Tigers	4	4	0	.500
Hammond, Ind., Pros	2	2	1	.500
Milwaukee Badgers	5	8	0	.385
Dayton Triangles	2	7	0	.222
Kansas City Cowboys	2	7	0	.222
Akron, Ohio, Indians	1	6	0	.143
Kenosha, Wis., Maroons	0	5	1	.000
Minneapolis Marines	0	6	0	.000
Rochester Jeffersons	0	7	0	.000

1925

	W	L	T	Pct.
Chicago Cardinals	11	2	1	.846
Pottsville, Pa., Maroons	10	2	0	.833
Detroit Panthers	8	2	2	.800
New York Giants	8	4	0	.667
Akron, Ohio, Indians	4	2	2	.667
Frankford Yellowjackets	13	7	0	.650
Chicago Bears	9	5	3	.643
Rock Island Independents	5	3	3	.625
Green Bay Packers	8	5	0	.615
Providence Steamroller	6	5	1	.545
Canton, Ohio, Bulldogs	4	4	0	.500
Cleveland Bulldogs	5	8	1	.385
Kansas City Cowboys	2	5	1	.286
Hammond, Ind., Pros	1	3	0	.250
Buffalo Bisons	1	6	2	.143
Duluth Kelleys	0	3	0	.000
Rochester Jeffersons	0	6	1	.000
Milwaukee Badgers	0	6	0	.000
Dayton Triangles	0	7	1	.000
Columbus Tigers	0	9	0	.000

1926

	W	L	T	Pct.
Frankford Yellowjackets	14	1	1	.933
Chicago Bears	12	1	3	.923
Pottsville, Pa., Maroons	10	2	1	.833
Kansas City Cowboys	8	3	1	.727
Green Bay Packers	7	3	3	.700
Los Angeles Buccaneers	6	3	1	.667
New York Giants	8	4	1	.667
Duluth Eskimos	6	5	2	.545
Buffalo Rangers	4	4	2	.500
Chicago Cardinals	5	6	1	.455
Providence Steamroller	5	7	0	.417
Detroit Panthers	4	6	2	.400
Hartford Blues	3	7	0	.300
Brooklyn Lions	3	8	0	.273
Milwaukee Badgers	2	7	0	.222
Akron, Ohio, Indians	1	4	3	.200
Dayton Triangles	1	4	1	.200
Racine, Wis., Legion	1	4	0	.200
Columbus Tigers	1	6	0	.143
Canton, Ohio, Bulldogs	1	9	3	.100
Hammond, Ind., Pros	0	4	0	.000
Louisville Colonels	0	4	0	.000

1927

	W	L	T	Pct.
New York Giants	11	1	1	.917
Green Bay Packers	7	2	1	.778
Chicago Bears	9	3	2	.750
Cleveland Bulldogs	8	4	1	.667
Providence Steamroller	8	5	1	.615
New York Yankees	7	8	1	.467
Frankford Yellowjackets	6	9	3	.400
Pottsville, Pa., Maroons	5	8	0	.385
Chicago Cardinals	3	7	1	.300
Dayton Triangles	1	6	1	.143
Duluth Eskimos	1	8	0	.111
Buffalo Bisons	0	5	0	.000

1928

	W	L	T	Pct.
Providence Steamroller	8	1	2	.889
Frankford Yellowjackets	11	3	2	.786
Detroit Wolverines	7	2	1	.778
Green Bay Packers	6	4	3	.600
Chicago Bears	7	5	1	.583
New York Giants	4	7	2	.364
New York Yankees	4	8	1	.333
Pottsville, Pa., Maroons	2	8	0	.200
Chicago Cardinals	1	5	0	.167
Dayton Triangles	0	7	0	.000

1929

	W	L	T	Pct.
Green Bay Packers	12	0	1	1.000
New York Giants	13	1	1	.929
Frankford Yellowjackets	9	4	5	.692
Chicago Cardinals	6	6	1	.500
Boston Bulldogs	4	4	0	.500
Orange, N.J., Tornadoes	3	4	4	.429
Stapleton Stapes	3	4	3	.429
Providence Steamroller	4	6	2	.400
Chicago Bears	4	9	2	.308
Buffalo Bisons	1	7	1	.125
Minneapolis Red Jackets	1	9	0	.100
Dayton Triangles	0	6	0	.000

1930

	W	L	T	Pct.
Green Bay Packers	10	3	1	.769
New York Giants	13	4	0	.765
Chicago Bears	9	4	1	.692
Brooklyn Dodgers	7	4	1	.636
Providence Steamroller	6	4	1	.600
Stapleton Stapes	5	5	2	.500
Chicago Cardinals	5	6	2	.455
Portsmouth, O., Spartans	5	6	3	.455
Frankford Yellowjackets	4	14	1	.222
Minneapolis Red Jackets	1	7	1	.125
Newark Tornadoes	1	10	1	.091

1931

	W	L	T	Pct.
Green Bay Packers	12	2	0	.857
Portsmouth, O., Spartans	11	3	0	.786
Chicago Bears	8	5	0	.615
Chicago Cardinals	5	4	0	.556
New York Giants	7	6	1	.538
Providence Steamroller	4	4	3	.500
Stapleton Stapes	4	6	1	.400
Cleveland Indians	2	8	0	.200
Brooklyn Dodgers	2	12	0	.143
Frankford Yellowjackets	1	6	1	.143

1932

	W	L	T	Pct.
Chicago Bears	7	1	6	.875
Green Bay Packers	10	3	1	.769
Portsmouth, O., Spartans	6	2	4	.750
Boston Braves	4	4	2	.500
New York Giants	4	6	2	.400
Brooklyn Dodgers	3	9	0	.250
Chicago Cardinals	2	6	2	.250
Stapleton Stapes	2	7	3	.222

1933

EASTERN DIVISION

	W	L	T	Pct.	Pts.	OP
N.Y. Giants	11	3	0	.786	244	101
Brooklyn	5	4	1	.556	93	54
Boston	5	5	2	.500	103	97
Philadelphia	3	5	1	.375	77	158
Pittsburgh	3	6	2	.333	67	208

WESTERN DIVISION

	W	L	T	Pct.	Pts.	OP
Chi. Bears	10	2	1	.833	133	82
Portsmouth	6	5	0	.545	128	87
Green Bay	5	7	1	.417	170	107
Cincinnati	3	6	1	.333	38	110
Chi. Cardinals	1	9	1	.100	52	101

NFL Championship: Chicago Bears 23, N.Y. Giants 21

1934

EASTERN DIVISION	W	L	T	Pct.	Pts.	OP
N.Y. Giants	8	5	0	.615	147	107
Boston	6	6	0	.500	107	94
Brooklyn	4	7	0	.364	61	153
Philadelphia	4	7	0	.364	127	85
Pittsburgh	2	10	0	.167	51	206

WESTERN DIVISION	W	L	T	Pct.	Pts.	OP
Chi. Bears	13	0	0	1.000	286	86
Detroit	10	3	0	.769	238	59
Green Bay	7	6	0	.538	156	112
Chi. Cardinals	5	6	0	.455	80	84
St. Louis	1	2	0	.333	27	61
Cincinnati	0	8	0	.000	10	243

NFL Championship: N.Y. Giants 30, Chicago Bears 13

1935

EASTERN DIVISION	W	L	T	Pct.	Pts.	OP
N.Y. Giants	9	3	0	.750	180	96
Brooklyn	5	6	1	.455	90	141
Pittsburgh	4	8	0	.333	100	209
Boston	2	8	1	.200	65	123
Philadelphia	2	9	0	.182	60	179

WESTERN DIVISION	W	L	T	Pct.	Pts.	OP
Detroit	7	3	2	.700	191	111
Green Bay	8	4	0	.667	181	96
Chi. Bears	6	4	2	.600	192	106
Chi. Cardinals	6	4	2	.600	99	97

NFL Championship: Detroit 26, N.Y. Giants 7
One game between Boston and Philadelphia was canceled.

1936

EASTERN DIVISION	W	L	T	Pct.	Pts.	OP
Boston	7	5	0	.583	149	110
Pittsburgh	6	6	0	.500	98	187
N.Y. Giants	5	6	1	.455	115	163
Brooklyn	3	8	1	.273	92	161
Philadelphia	1	11	0	.083	51	206

WESTERN DIVISION	W	L	T	Pct.	Pts.	OP
Green Bay	10	1	1	.909	248	118
Chi. Bears	9	3	0	.750	222	94
Detroit	8	4	0	.667	235	102
Chi. Cardinals	3	8	1	.273	74	143

NFL Championship: Green Bay 21, Boston 6

1937

EASTERN DIVISION	W	L	T	Pct.	Pts.	OP
Washington	8	3	0	.727	195	120
N.Y. Giants	6	3	2	.667	128	109
Pittsburgh	4	7	0	.364	122	145
Brooklyn	3	7	1	.300	82	174
Philadelphia	2	8	1	.200	86	177

WESTERN DIVISION	W	L	T	Pct.	Pts.	OP
Chi. Bears	9	1	1	.900	201	100
Green Bay	7	4	0	.636	220	122
Detroit	7	4	0	.636	180	105
Chi. Cardinals	5	5	1	.500	135	165
Cleveland	1	10	0	.091	75	207

NFL Championship: Washington 28, Chicago Bears 21

1938

EASTERN DIVISION	W	L	T	Pct.	Pts.	OP
N.Y Giants	8	2	1	.800	194	79
Washington	6	3	2	.667	148	154
Brooklyn	4	4	3	.500	131	161
Philadelphia	5	6	0	.455	154	164
Pittsburgh	2	9	0	.182	79	169

WESTERN DIVISION	W	L	T	Pct.	Pts.	OP
Green Bay	8	3	0	.727	223	118
Detroit	7	4	0	.636	119	108
Chi. Bears	6	5	0	.545	194	148
Cleveland	4	7	0	.364	131	215
Chi. Cardinals	2	9	0	.182	111	168

NFL Championship: N.Y. Giants 23, Green Bay 17

1939

EASTERN DIVISION	W	L	T	Pct.	Pts.	OP
N.Y. Giants	9	1	1	.900	168	85
Washington	8	2	1	.800	242	94
Brooklyn	4	6	1	.400	108	219
Philadelphia	1	9	1	.100	105	200
Pittsburgh	1	9	1	.100	114	216

WESTERN DIVISION	W	L	T	Pct.	Pts.	OP
Green Bay	9	2	0	.818	233	153
Chi. Bears	8	3	0	.727	298	157
Detroit	6	5	0	.545	145	150
Cleveland	5	5	1	.500	195	164
Chi. Cardinals	1	10	0	.091	84	254

NFL Championship: Green Bay 27, N.Y. Giants 0

1940

EASTERN DIVISION	W	L	T	Pct.	Pts.	OP
Washington	9	2	0	.818	245	142
Brooklyn	8	3	0	.727	186	120
N.Y. Giants	6	4	1	.600	131	133
Pittsburgh	2	7	2	.222	60	178
Philadelphia	1	10	0	.091	111	211

WESTERN DIVISION	W	L	T	Pct.	Pts.	OP
Chi. Bears	8	3	0	.727	238	152
Green Bay	6	4	1	.600	238	155
Detroit	5	5	1	.500	138	153
Cleveland	4	6	1	.400	171	191
Chi. Cardinals	2	7	2	.222	139	222

NFL Championship: Chicago Bears 73, Washington 0

1941

EASTERN DIVISION	W	L	T	Pct.	Pts.	OP
N.Y. Giants	8	3	0	.727	238	114
Brooklyn	7	4	0	.636	158	127
Washington	6	5	0	.545	176	174
Philadelphia	2	8	1	.200	119	218
Pittsburgh	1	9	1	.100	103	276

WESTERN DIVISION	W	L	T	Pct.	Pts.	OP
Chi. Bears	10	1	0	.909	396	147
Green Bay	10	1	0	.909	258	120
Detroit	4	6	1	.400	121	195
Chi. Cardinals	3	7	1	.300	127	197
Cleveland	2	9	0	.182	116	244

Western Division playoff: Chicago Bears 33, Green Bay 14
NFL Championship: Chicago Bears 37, N.Y. Giants 9

1942

EASTERN DIVISION	W	L	T	Pct.	Pts.	OP
Washington	10	1	0	.909	227	102
Pittsburgh	7	4	0	.636	167	119
N.Y. Giants	5	5	1	.500	155	139
Brooklyn	3	8	0	.273	100	168
Philadelphia	2	9	0	.182	134	239

WESTERN DIVISION	W	L	T	Pct.	Pts.	OP
Chi. Bears	11	0	0	1.000	376	84
Green Bay	8	2	1	.800	300	215
Cleveland	5	6	0	.455	150	207
Chi. Cardinals	3	8	0	.273	98	209
Detroit	0	11	0	.000	38	263

NFL Championship: Washington 14, Chicago Bears 6

1943

EASTERN DIVISION	W	L	T	Pct.	Pts.	OP
Washington	6	3	1	.667	229	137
N.Y. Giants	6	3	1	.667	197	170
Phil-Pitt	5	4	1	.556	225	230
Brooklyn	2	8	0	.200	65	234

WESTERN DIVISION	W	L	T	Pct.	Pts.	OP
Chi. Bears	8	1	1	.889	303	157
Green Bay	7	2	1	.778	264	172
Detroit	3	6	1	.333	178	218
Chi. Cardinals	0	10	0	.000	95	238

Eastern Division playoff: Washington 28, N.Y. Giants 0
NFL Championship: Chicago Bears 41, Washington 21

1944

EASTERN DIVISION	W	L	T	Pct.	Pts.	OP
N.Y. Giants	8	1	1	.889	206	75
Philadelphia	7	1	2	.875	267	131
Washington	6	3	0	.667	169	180
Boston	2	8	0	.200	82	233
Brooklyn	0	10	0	.000	69	166

WESTERN DIVISION	W	L	T	Pct.	Pts.	OP
Green Bay	8	2	0	.800	238	141
Chi. Bears	6	3	1	.667	258	172
Detroit	6	3	1	.667	216	151
Cleveland	4	6	0	.400	188	224
Card-Pitt	0	10	0	.000	108	328

NFL Championship: Green Bay 14, N.Y. Giants 7

1945

EASTERN DIVISION	W	L	T	Pct.	Pts.	OP
Washington	8	2	0	.800	209	121
Philadelphia	7	3	0	.700	272	133
N.Y. Giants	3	6	1	.333	179	198
Boston	3	6	1	.333	123	211
Pittsburgh	2	8	0	.200	79	220

WESTERN DIVISION	W	L	T	Pct.	Pts.	OP
Cleveland	9	1	0	.900	244	136
Detroit	7	3	0	.700	195	194
Green Bay	6	4	0	.600	258	173
Chi. Bears	3	7	0	.300	192	235
Chi. Cardinals	1	9	0	.100	98	228

NFL Championship: Cleveland 15, Washington 14

1946

EASTERN DIVISION	W	L	T	Pct.	Pts.	OP	WESTERN DIVISION	W	L	T	Pct.	Pts.	OP
N.Y. Giants	7	3	1	.700	236	162	Chi. Bears	8	2	1	.800	289	193
Philadelphia	6	5	0	.545	231	220	Los Angeles	6	4	1	.600	277	257
Washington	5	5	0	.500	171	191	Green Bay	6	5	0	.545	148	158
Pittsburgh	5	5	1	.500	136	117	Chi. Cardinals	6	5	0	.545	260	198
Boston	2	8	1	.200	189	273	Detroit	1	10	0	.091	142	310

NFL Championship: Chicago Bears 24, N.Y. Giants 14

1947

EASTERN DIVISION	W	L	T	Pct.	Pts.	OP	WESTERN DIVISION	W	L	T	Pct.	Pts.	OP
Philadelphia	8	4	0	.667	308	242	Chi. Cardinals	9	3	0	.750	306	231
Pittsburgh	8	4	0	.667	240	259	Chi. Bears	8	4	0	.667	363	241
Boston	4	7	1	.364	168	256	Green Bay	6	5	1	.545	274	210
Washington	4	8	0	.333	295	367	Los Angeles	6	6	0	.500	259	214
N.Y. Giants	2	8	2	.200	190	309	Detroit	3	9	0	.250	231	305

Eastern Division playoff: Philadelphia 21, Pittsburgh 0
NFL Championship: Chicago Cardinals 28, Philadelphia 21

1948

EASTERN DIVISION	W	L	T	Pct.	Pts.	OP	WESTERN DIVISION	W	L	T	Pct.	Pts.	OP
Philadelphia	9	2	1	.818	376	156	Chi. Cardinals	11	1	0	.917	395	226
Washington	7	5	0	.583	291	287	Chi. Bears	10	2	0	.833	375	151
N.Y. Giants	4	8	0	.333	297	388	Los Angeles	6	5	1	.545	327	269
Pittsburgh	4	8	0	.333	200	243	Green Bay	3	9	0	.250	154	290
Boston	3	9	0	.250	174	372	Detroit	2	10	0	.167	200	407

NFL Championship: Philadelphia 7, Chicago Cardinals 0

1949

EASTERN DIVISION	W	L	T	Pct.	Pts.	OP	WESTERN DIVISION	W	L	T	Pct.	Pts.	OP
Philadelphia	11	1	0	.917	364	134	Los Angeles	8	2	2	.800	360	239
Pittsburgh	6	5	1	.545	224	214	Chi. Bears	9	3	0	.750	332	218
N.Y. Giants	6	6	0	.500	287	298	Chi. Cardinals	6	5	1	.545	360	301
Washington	4	7	1	.364	268	339	Detroit	4	8	0	.333	237	259
N.Y. Bulldogs	1	10	1	.091	153	368	Green Bay	2	10	0	.167	114	329

NFL Championship: Philadelphia 14, Los Angeles 0

1950

AMERICAN CONFERENCE	W	L	T	Pct.	Pts.	OP	NATIONAL CONFERENCE	W	L	T	Pct.	Pts.	OP
Cleveland	10	2	0	.833	310	144	Los Angeles	9	3	0	.750	466	309
N.Y. Giants	10	2	0	.833	268	150	Chi. Bears	9	3	0	.750	279	207
Philadelphia	6	6	0	.500	254	141	N.Y. Yanks	7	5	0	.583	366	367
Pittsburgh	6	6	0	.500	180	195	Detroit	6	6	0	.500	321	285
Chi. Cardinals	5	7	0	.417	233	287	Green Bay	3	9	0	.250	244	406
Washington	3	9	0	.250	232	326	San Francisco	3	9	0	.250	213	300
							Baltimore	1	11	0	.083	213	462

American Conference playoff: Cleveland 8, N.Y. Giants 3
National Conference playoff: Los Angeles 24, Chicago Bears 14
NFL Championship: Cleveland 30, Los Angeles 28

1951

AMERICAN CONFERENCE	W	L	T	Pct.	Pts.	OP	NATIONAL CONFERENCE	W	L	T	Pct.	Pts.	OP
Cleveland	11	1	0	.917	331	152	Los Angeles	8	4	0	.667	392	261
N.Y. Giants	9	2	1	.818	254	161	Detroit	7	4	1	.636	336	259
Washington	5	7	0	.417	183	296	San Francisco	7	4	1	.636	255	205
Pittsburgh	4	7	1	.364	183	235	Chi. Bears	7	5	0	.583	286	282
Philadelphia	4	8	0	.333	234	264	Green Bay	3	9	0	.250	254	375
Chi. Cardinals	3	9	0	.250	210	287	N.Y. Yanks	1	9	2	.100	241	382

NFL Championship: Los Angeles 24, Cleveland 17

1952

AMERICAN CONFERENCE

	W	L	T	Pct.	Pts.	GP
Cleveland	8	4	0	.667	310	213
N.Y. Giants	7	5	0	.583	234	231
Philadelphia	7	5	0	.583	252	271
Pittsburgh	5	7	0	.417	300	273
Chi. Cardinals	4	8	0	.333	172	221
Washington	4	8	0	.333	240	287

NATIONAL CONFERENCE

	W	L	T	Pct.	Pts.	OP
Detroit	9	3	0	.750	344	192
Los Angeles	9	3	0	.750	349	234
San Francisco	7	5	0	.583	285	221
Green Bay	6	6	0	.500	295	312
Chi. Bears	5	7	0	.417	245	326
Dallas	1	11	0	.083	182	427

National Conference playoff: Detroit 31, Los Angeles 21
NFL Championship: Detroit 17, Cleveland 7

1953

EASTERN CONFERENCE

	W	L	T	Pct.	Pts.	OP
Cleveland	11	1	0	.917	348	162
Philadelphia	7	4	1	.636	352	215
Washington	6	5	1	.545	208	215
Pittsburgh	6	6	0	.500	211	263
N.Y. Giants	3	9	0	.250	179	277
Chi. Cardinals	1	10	1	.091	190	337

WESTERN CONFERENCE

	W	L	T	Pct.	Pts.	OP
Detroit	10	2	0	.833	271	205
San Francisco	9	3	0	.750	372	237
Los Angeles	8	3	1	.727	366	236
Chi. Bears	3	8	1	.273	218	262
Baltimore	3	9	0	.250	182	350
Green Bay	2	9	1	.182	200	338

NFL Championship: Detroit 17, Cleveland 16

1954

EASTERN CONFERENCE

	W	L	T	Pct.	Pts.	OP
Cleveland	9	3	0	.750	336	162
Philadelphia	7	4	1	.636	284	230
N.Y. Giants	7	5	0	.583	293	184
Pittsburgh	5	7	0	.417	219	263
Washington	3	9	0	.250	207	432
Chi. Cardinals	2	10	0	.167	183	347

WESTERN CONFERENCE

	W	L	T	Pct.	Pts.	OP
Detroit	9	2	1	.818	337	189
Chi. Bears	8	4	0	.667	301	279
San Francisco	7	4	1	.636	313	251
Los Angeles	6	5	1	.545	314	285
Green Bay	4	8	0	.333	234	251
Baltimore	3	9	0	.250	131	279

NFL Championship: Cleveland 56, Detroit 10

1955

EASTERN CONFERENCE

	W	L	T	Pct.	Pts.	OP
Cleveland	9	2	1	.818	349	218
Washington	8	4	0	.667	246	222
N.Y. Giants	6	5	1	.545	267	223
Chi. Cardinals	4	7	1	.364	224	252
Philadelphia	4	7	1	.364	248	231
Pittsburgh	4	8	0	.333	195	285

WESTERN CONFERENCE

	W	L	T	Pct.	Pts.	OP
Los Angeles	8	3	1	.727	260	231
Chi. Bears	8	4	0	.667	294	251
Green Bay	6	6	0	.500	258	276
Baltimore	5	6	1	.455	214	239
San Francisco	4	8	0	.333	216	298
Detroit	3	9	0	.250	230	275

NFL Championship: Cleveland 38, Los Angeles 14

1956

EASTERN CONFERENCE

	W	L	T	Pct.	Pts.	OP
N.Y. Giants	8	3	1	.727	264	197
Chi. Cardinals	7	5	0	.583	240	182
Washington	6	6	0	.500	183	225
Cleveland	5	7	0	.417	167	177
Pittsburgh	5	7	0	.417	217	250
Philadelphia	3	8	1	.273	143	215

WESTERN CONFERENCE

	W	L	T	Pct.	Pts.	OP
Chi. Bears	9	2	1	.818	363	246
Detroit	9	3	0	.750	300	188
San Francisco	5	6	1	.455	233	284
Baltimore	5	7	0	.417	270	322
Green Bay	4	8	0	.333	264	342
Los Angeles	4	8	0	.333	291	307

NFL Championship: N.Y. Giants 47, Chicago Bears 7

1957

EASTERN CONFERENCE

	W	L	T	Pct.	Pts.	OP
Cleveland	9	2	1	.818	269	172
N.Y. Giants	7	5	0	.583	254	211
Pittsburgh	6	6	0	.500	161	178
Washington	5	6	1	.455	251	230
Philadelphia	4	8	0	.333	173	230
Chi. Cardinals	3	9	0	.250	200	299

WESTERN CONFERENCE

	W	L	T	Pct.	Pts.	OP
Detroit	8	4	0	.667	251	231
San Francisco	8	4	0	.667	260	264
Baltimore	7	5	0	.583	303	235
Los Angeles	6	6	0	.500	307	278
Chi. Bears	5	7	0	.417	203	211
Green Bay	3	9	0	.250	218	311

Western Conference playoff: Detroit 31, San Francisco 27
NFL Championship: Detroit 59, Cleveland 14

1958

EASTERN CONFERENCE

	W	L	T	Pct.	Pts.	OP
N.Y. Giants	9	3	0	.750	246	183
Cleveland	9	3	0	.750	302	217
Pittsburgh	7	4	1	.636	261	230
Washington	4	7	1	.364	214	268
Chi. Cardinals	2	9	1	.182	261	356
Philadelphia	2	9	1	.182	235	306

WESTERN CONFERENCE

	W	L	T	Pct.	Pts.	OP
Baltimore	9	3	0	.750	381	203
Chi. Bears	8	4	0	.667	298	230
Los Angeles	8	4	0	.667	344	278
San Francisco	6	6	0	.500	257	324
Detroit	4	7	1	.364	261	276
Green Bay	1	10	1	.091	193	382

Eastern Conference playoff: N.Y. Giants 10, Cleveland 0
NFL Championship: Baltimore 23, N.Y. Giants 17, sudden-death overtime

1959

EASTERN CONFERENCE

	W	L	T	Pct.	Pts.	OP
N.Y. Giants	10	2	0	.833	284	170
Cleveland	7	5	0	.583	270	214
Philadelphia	7	5	0	.583	268	278
Pittsburgh	6	5	1	.545	257	216
Washington	3	9	0	.250	185	350
Chi. Cardinals	2	10	0	.167	234	324

WESTERN CONFERENCE

	W	L	T	Pct.	Pts.	OP
Baltimore	9	3	0	.750	374	251
Chi. Bears	8	4	0	.667	252	196
Green Bay	7	5	0	.583	248	246
San Francisco	7	5	0	.583	255	237
Detroit	3	8	1	.273	203	275
Los Angeles	2	10	0	.167	242	315

NFL Championship: Baltimore 31, N.Y. Giants 16

1960 AFL

EASTERN DIVISION

	W	L	T	Pct.	Pts.	OP
Houston	10	4	0	.714	379	285
N.Y. Titans	7	7	0	.500	382	399
Buffalo	5	8	1	.385	296	303
Boston	5	9	0	.357	286	349

WESTERN DIVISION

	W	L	T	Pct.	Pts.	OP
L.A. Chargers	10	4	0	.714	373	336
Dall. Texans	8	6	0	.571	362	253
Oakland	6	8	0	.429	319	388
Denver	4	9	1	.308	309	393

AFL Championship: Houston 24, L.A. Chargers 16

1960 NFL

EASTERN CONFERENCE

	W	L	T	Pct.	Pts.	OP
Philadelphia	10	2	0	.833	321	246
Cleveland	8	3	1	.727	362	217
N.Y. Giants	6	4	2	.600	271	261
St. Louis	6	5	1	.545	288	230
Pittsburgh	5	6	1	.455	240	275
Washington	1	9	2	.100	178	309

WESTERN CONFERENCE

	W	L	T	Pct.	Pts.	OP
Green Bay	8	4	0	.667	332	209
Detroit	7	5	0	.583	239	212
San Francisco	7	5	0	.583	208	205
Baltimore	6	6	0	.500	288	234
Chicago	5	6	1	.455	194	299
L.A. Rams	4	7	1	.364	265	297
Dall. Cowboys	0	11	1	.000	177	369

NFL Championship: Philadelphia 17, Green Bay 13

1961 AFL

EASTERN DIVISION	W	L	T	Pct.	Pts.	OP	WESTERN DIVISION	W	L	T	Pct.	Pts.	OP
Houston	10	3	1	.769	513	242	San Diego	12	2	0	.857	396	219
Boston	9	4	1	.692	413	313	Dall. Texans	6	8	0	.429	334	343
N.Y. Titans	7	7	0	.500	301	390	Denver	3	11	0	.214	251	432
Buffalo	6	8	0	.429	294	342	Oakland	2	12	0	.143	237	458

AFL Championship: Houston 10, San Diego 3

1961 NFL

EASTERN CONFERENCE	W	L	T	Pct.	Pts.	OP	WESTERN CONFERENCE	W	L	T	Pct.	Pts.	OP
N.Y. Giants	10	3	1	.769	368	220	Green Bay	11	3	0	.786	391	223
Philadelphia	10	4	0	.714	361	297	Detroit	8	5	1	.615	270	258
Cleveland	8	5	1	.615	319	270	Baltimore	8	6	0	.571	302	307
St. Louis	7	7	0	.500	279	267	Chicago	8	6	0	.571	326	302
Pittsburgh	6	8	0	.429	295	287	San Francisco	7	6	1	.538	346	272
Dall. Cowboys	4	9	1	.308	236	380	Los Angeles	4	10	0	.286	263	333
Washington	1	12	1	.077	174	392	Minnesota	3	11	0	.214	285	407

NFL Championship: Green Bay 37, N.Y. Giants 0

1962 AFL

EASTERN DIVISION	W	L	T	Pct.	Pts.	OP	WESTERN DIVISION	W	L	T	Pct.	Pts.	OP
Houston	11	3	0	.786	387	270	Dall. Texans	11	3	0	.786	389	233
Boston	9	4	1	.692	346	295	Denver	7	7	0	.500	353	334
Buffalo	7	6	1	.538	309	272	San Diego	4	10	0	.286	314	392
N.Y. Titans	5	9	0	.357	278	423	Oakland	1	13	0	.071	213	370

AFL Championship: Dallas Texans 20, Houston 17, sudden-death overtime

1962 NFL

EASTERN CONFERENCE	W	L	T	Pct.	Pts.	OP	WESTERN CONFERENCE	W	L	T	Pct.	Pts.	OP
N.Y. Giants	12	2	0	.857	398	283	Green Bay	13	1	0	.929	415	148
Pittsburgh	9	5	0	.643	312	363	Detroit	11	3	0	.786	315	177
Cleveland	7	6	1	.538	291	257	Chicago	9	5	0	.643	321	287
Washington	5	7	2	.417	305	376	Baltimore	7	7	0	.500	293	288
Dall. Cowboys	5	8	1	.385	398	402	San Francisco	6	8	0	.429	282	331
St. Louis	4	9	1	.308	287	361	Minnesota	2	11	1	.154	254	410
Philadelphia	3	10	1	.231	282	356	Los Angeles	1	12	1	.077	220	334

NFL Championship: Green Bay 16, N.Y. Giants 7

1963 AFL

EASTERN DIVISION	W	L	T	Pct.	Pts.	OP	WESTERN DIVISION	W	L	T	Pct.	Pts.	OP
Boston	7	6	1	.538	317	257	San Diego	11	3	0	.786	399	255
Buffalo	7	6	1	.538	304	291	Oakland	10	4	0	.714	363	282
Houston	6	8	0	.429	302	372	Kansas City	5	7	2	.417	347	263
N.Y. Jets	5	8	1	.385	249	399	Denver	2	11	1	.154	301	473

Eastern Division playoff: Boston 26, Buffalo 8
AFL Championship: San Diego 51, Boston 10

1963 NFL

EASTERN CONFERENCE	W	L	T	Pct.	Pts.	OP	WESTERN CONFERENCE	W	L	T	Pct.	Pts.	OP
N.Y. Giants	11	3	0	.786	448	280	Chicago	11	1	2	.917	301	144
Cleveland	10	4	0	.714	343	262	Green Bay	11	2	1	.846	369	206
St. Louis	9	5	0	.643	341	283	Baltimore	8	6	0	.571	316	285
Pittsburgh	7	4	3	.636	321	295	Detroit	5	8	1	.385	326	265
Dallas	4	10	0	.286	305	378	Minnesota	5	8	1	.385	309	390
Washington	3	11	0	.214	279	398	Los Angeles	5	9	0	.357	210	350
Philadelphia	2	10	2	.167	242	381	San Francisco	2	12	0	.143	198	391

NFL Championship: Chicago 14, N.Y. Giants 10

1964 AFL

EASTERN DIVISION	W	L	T	Pct.	Pts.	OP	WESTERN DIVISION	W	L	T	Pct.	Pts.	OP
Buffalo	12	2	0	.857	400	242	San Diego	8	5	1	.615	341	300
Boston	10	3	1	.769	365	297	Kansas City	7	7	0	.500	366	306
N.Y. Jets	5	8	1	.385	278	315	Oakland	5	7	2	.417	303	350
Houston	4	10	0	.286	310	355	Denver	2	11	1	.154	240	438

AFL Championship: Buffalo 20, San Diego 7

1964 NFL

EASTERN CONFERENCE	W	L	T	Pct.	Pts.	OP	WESTERN CONFERENCE	W	L	T	Pct.	Pts.	OP
Cleveland	10	3	1	.769	415	293	Baltimore	12	2	0	.857	428	225
St. Louis	9	3	2	.750	357	331	Green Bay	8	5	1	.615	342	245
Philadelphia	6	8	0	.429	312	313	Minnesota	8	5	1	.615	355	296
Washington	6	8	0	.429	307	305	Detroit	7	5	2	.583	280	260
Dallas	5	8	1	.385	250	289	Los Angeles	5	7	2	.417	283	339
Pittsburgh	5	9	0	.357	253	315	Chicago	5	9	0	.357	260	379
N.Y. Giants	2	10	2	.167	241	399	San Francisco	4	10	0	.286	236	330

NFL Championship: Cleveland 27, Baltimore 0

1965 AFL

EASTERN DIVISION	W	L	T	Pct.	Pts.	OP	WESTERN DIVISION	W	L	T	Pct.	Pts.	OP
Buffalo	10	3	1	.769	313	226	San Diego	9	2	3	.818	340	227
N.Y. Jets	5	8	1	.385	285	303	Oakland	8	5	1	.615	298	239
Boston	4	8	2	.333	244	302	Kansas City	7	5	2	.583	322	285
Houston	4	10	0	.286	298	429	Denver	4	10	0	.286	303	392

AFL Championship: Buffalo 23, San Diego 0

1965 NFL

EASTERN CONFERENCE	W	L	T	Pct.	Pts.	OP	WESTERN CONFERENCE	W	L	T	Pct.	Pts.	OP
Cleveland	11	3	0	.786	363	325	Green Bay	10	3	1	.769	316	224
Dallas	7	7	0	.500	325	280	Baltimore	10	3	1	.769	389	284
N.Y. Giants	7	7	0	.500	270	338	Chicago	9	5	0	.643	409	275
Washington	6	8	0	.429	257	301	San Francisco	7	6	1	.538	421	402
Philadelphia	5	9	0	.357	363	359	Minnesota	7	7	0	.500	383	403
St. Louis	5	9	0	.357	296	309	Detroit	6	7	1	.462	257	295
Pittsburgh	2	12	0	.143	202	397	Los Angeles	4	10	0	.286	269	328

Western Conference playoff: Green Bay 13, Baltimore 10, sudden-death overtime

NFL Championship: Green Bay 23, Cleveland 12

1966 AFL

EASTERN DIVISION	W	L	T	Pct.	Pts.	OP	WESTERN DIVISION	W	L	T	Pct.	Pts.	OP
Buffalo	9	4	1	.692	358	255	Kansas City	11	2	1	.846	448	276
Boston	8	4	2	.667	315	283	Oakland	8	5	1	.615	315	288
N.Y. Jets	6	6	2	.500	322	312	San Diego	7	6	1	.538	335	284
Houston	3	11	0	.214	335	396	Denver	4	10	0	.286	196	381
Miami	3	11	0	.214	213	362							

AFL Championship: Kansas City 31, Buffalo 7

1966 NFL

EASTERN CONFERENCE	W	L	T	Pct.	Pts.	OP	WESTERN CONFERENCE	W	L	T	Pct.	Pts.	OP
Dallas	10	3	1	.769	445	239	Green Bay	12	2	0	.857	335	163
Cleveland	9	5	0	.643	403	259	Baltimore	9	5	0	.643	314	226
Philadelphia	9	5	0	.643	326	340	Los Angeles	8	6	0	.571	289	212
St. Louis	8	5	1	.615	264	265	San Francisco	6	6	2	.500	320	325
Washington	7	7	0	.500	351	355	Chicago	5	7	2	.417	234	272
Pittsburgh	5	8	1	.385	316	347	Detroit	4	9	1	.308	206	317
Atlanta	3	11	0	.214	204	437	Minnesota	4	9	1	.308	292	304
N.Y. Giants	1	12	1	.077	263	501							

NFL Championship: Green Bay 34, Dallas 27

Super Bowl I: Green Bay (NFL) 35, Kansas City (AFL) 10

1967 AFL

EASTERN DIVISION	W	L	T	Pct.	Pts.	OP	WESTERN DIVISION	W	L	T	Pct.	Pts.	OP
Houston	9	4	1	.692	258	199	Oakland	13	1	0	.929	468	238
N.Y. Jets	8	5	1	.615	371	329	Kansas City	9	5	0	.643	408	254
Buffalo	4	10	0	.286	237	285	San Diego	8	5	1	.615	360	352
Miami	4	10	0	.286	219	407	Denver	3	11	0	.214	256	409
Boston	3	10	1	.231	280	389							

AFL Championship: Oakland 40, Houston 7

1967 NFL

EASTERN CONFERENCE

Capitol Division	W	L	T	Pct.	Pts.	OP
Dallas	9	5	0	.643	342	268
Philadelphia	6	7	1	.462	351	409
Washington	5	6	3	.455	347	353
New Orleans	3	11	0	.214	233	379

Century Division	W	L	T	Pct.	Pts.	OP
Cleveland	9	5	0	.643	334	297
N.Y. Giants	7	7	0	.500	369	379
St. Louis	6	7	1	.462	333	356
Pittsburgh	4	9	1	.308	281	320

WESTERN CONFERENCE

Coastal Division	W	L	T	Pct.	Pts.	OP
Los Angeles	11	1	2	.917	398	196
Baltimore	11	1	2	.917	394	198
San Francisco	7	7	0	.500	273	337
Atlanta	1	12	1	.077	175	422

Central Division	W	L	T	Pct.	Pts.	OP
Green Bay	9	4	1	.692	332	209
Chicago	7	6	1	.538	239	218
Detroit	5	7	2	.417	260	259
Minnesota	3	8	3	.273	233	294

Conference Championships: Dallas 52, Cleveland 14; Green Bay 28, Los Angeles 7
NFL Championship: Green Bay 21, Dallas 17
Super Bowl II: Green Bay (NFL) 33, Oakland (AFL) 14

1968 AFL

EASTERN DIVISION

	W	L	T	Pct.	Pts.	OP
N.Y. Jets	11	3	0	.786	419	280
Houston	7	7	0	.500	303	248
Miami	5	8	1	.385	276	355
Boston	4	10	0	.286	229	406
Buffalo	1	12	1	.077	199	367

WESTERN DIVISION

	W	L	T	Pct.	Pts.	OP
Oakland	12	2	0	.857	453	233
Kansas City	12	2	0	.857	371	170
San Diego	9	5	0	.643	382	310
Denver	5	9	0	.357	255	404
Cincinnati	3	11	0	.214	215	329

Western Division playoff: Oakland 41, Kansas City 6
AFL Championship: N.Y. Jets 27, Oakland 23

1968 NFL

EASTERN CONFERENCE

Capitol Division	W	L	T	Pct.	Pts.	OP
Dallas	12	2	0	.857	431	186
N.Y. Giants	7	7	0	.500	294	325
Washington	5	9	0	.357	249	358
Philadelphia	2	12	0	.143	202	351

Century Division	W	L	T	Pct.	Pts.	OP
Cleveland	10	4	0	.714	394	273
St. Louis	9	4	1	.692	325	289
New Orleans	4	9	1	.308	246	327
Pittsburgh	2	11	1	.154	244	397

WESTERN CONFERENCE

Coastal Division	W	L	T	Pct.	Pts.	OP
Baltimore	13	1	0	.929	402	144
Los Angeles	10	3	1	.769	312	200
San Francisco	7	6	1	.538	303	310
Atlanta	2	12	0	.143	170	389

Central Division	W	L	T	Pct.	Pts.	OP
Minnesota	8	6	0	.571	282	242
Chicago	7	7	0	.500	250	333
Green Bay	6	7	1	.462	281	227
Detroit	4	8	2	.333	207	241

Conference Championships: Cleveland 31, Dallas 20; Baltimore 24, Minnesota 14
NFL Championship: Baltimore 34, Cleveland 0
Super Bowl III: N.Y. Jets (AFL) 16, Baltimore (NFL) 7

1969 AFL

EASTERN DIVISION

	W	L	T	Pct.	Pts.	OP
N.Y. Jets	10	4	0	.714	353	269
Houston	6	6	2	.500	278	279
Boston	4	10	0	.286	266	316
Buffalo	4	10	0	.286	230	359
Miami	3	10	1	.231	233	332

WESTERN DIVISION

	W	L	T	Pct.	Pts.	OP
Oakland	12	1	1	.923	377	242
Kansas City	11	3	0	.786	359	177
San Diego	8	6	0	.571	288	276
Denver	5	8	1	.385	297	344
Cincinnati	4	9	1	.308	280	367

Divisional playoffs: Kansas City 13, N.Y. Jets 6; Oakland 56, Houston 7
AFL Championship: Kansas City 17, Oakland 7

1969 NFL

EASTERN CONFERENCE
Capitol Division

	W	L	T	Pct.	Pts.	OP
Dallas	11	2	1	.846	369	223
Washington	7	5	2	.583	307	319
New Orleans	5	9	0	.357	311	393
Philadelphia	4	9	1	.308	279	377

WESTERN CONFERENCE
Coastal Division

	W	L	T	Pct.	Pts.	OP
Los Angeles	11	3	0	.786	320	243
Baltimore	8	5	1	.615	279	268
Atlanta	6	8	0	.429	276	268
San Francisco	4	8	2	.333	277	319

Century Division

	W	L	T	Pct.	Pts.	OP
Cleveland	10	3	1	.769	351	300
N.Y. Giants	6	8	0	.429	264	298
St. Louis	4	9	1	.308	314	389
Pittsburgh	1	13	0	.071	218	404

Central Division

	W	L	T	Pct.	Pts.	OP
Minnesota	12	2	0	.857	379	133
Detroit	9	4	1	.692	259	188
Green Bay	8	6	0	.571	269	221
Chicago	1	13	0	.071	210	339

Conference Championships: Cleveland 38, Dallas 14; Minnesota 23, Los Angeles 20
NFL Championship: Minnesota 27, Cleveland 7
Super Bowl IV: Kansas City (AFL) 23, Minnesota (NFL) 7

1970

AMERICAN CONFERENCE
Eastern Division

	W	L	T	Pct.	Pts.	OP
Baltimore	11	2	1	.846	321	234
Miami*	10	4	0	.714	297	228
N.Y. Jets	4	10	0	.286	255	286
Buffalo	3	10	1	.231	204	337
Boston	2	12	0	.143	149	361

NATIONAL CONFERENCE
Eastern Division

	W	L	T	Pct.	Pts.	OP
Dallas	10	4	0	.714	299	221
N.Y. Giants	9	5	0	.643	301	270
St. Louis	8	5	1	.615	325	228
Washington	6	8	0	.429	297	314
Philadelphia	3	10	1	.231	241	332

Central Division

	W	L	T	Pct.	Pts.	OP
Cincinnati	8	6	0	.571	312	255
Cleveland	7	7	0	.500	286	265
Pittsburgh	5	9	0	.357	210	272
Houston	3	10	1	.231	217	352

Central Division

	W	L	T	Pct.	Pts.	OP
Minnesota	12	2	0	.857	335	143
Detroit*	10	4	0	.714	347	202
Chicago	6	8	0	.429	256	261
Green Bay	6	8	0	.429	196	293

Western Division

	W	L	T	Pct.	Pts.	OP
Oakland	8	4	2	.667	300	293
Kansas City	7	5	2	.583	272	244
San Diego	5	6	3	.455	282	278
Denver	5	8	1	.385	253	264

Western Division

	W	L	T	Pct.	Pts.	OP
San Francisco	10	3	1	.769	352	267
Los Angeles	9	4	1	.692	325	202
Atlanta	4	8	2	.333	206	261
New Orleans	2	11	1	.154	172	347

*Wild Card qualifier for playoffs
Divisional playoffs: Baltimore 17, Cincinnati 0; Oakland 21, Miami 14
AFC Championship: Baltimore 27, Oakland 17
Divisional playoffs: Dallas 5, Detroit 0; San Francisco 17, Minnesota 14
NFC Championship: Dallas 17, San Francisco 10
Super Bowl V: Baltimore (AFC) 16, Dallas (NFC) 13

1971

AMERICAN CONFERENCE

Eastern Division

	W	L	T	Pct.	Pts.	OP
Miami	10	3	1	.769	315	174
Baltimore*	10	4	0	.714	313	140
New England	6	8	0	.429	238	325
N.Y. Jets	6	8	0	.429	212	299
Buffalo	1	13	0	.071	184	394

Central Division

	W	L	T	Pct.	Pts.	OP
Cleveland	9	5	0	.643	285	273
Pittsburgh	6	8	0	.429	246	292
Houston	4	9	1	.308	251	330
Cincinnati	4	10	0	.286	284	265

Western Division

	W	L	T	Pct.	Pts.	OP
Kansas City	10	3	1	.769	302	208
Oakland	8	4	2	.667	344	278
San Diego	6	8	0	.429	311	341
Denver	4	9	1	.308	203	275

NATIONAL CONFERENCE

Eastern Division

	W	L	T	Pct.	Pts.	OP
Dallas	11	3	0	.786	406	222
Washington*	9	4	1	.692	276	190
Philadelphia	6	7	1	.462	221	302
St. Louis	4	9	1	.308	231	279
N.Y. Giants	4	10	0	.286	228	362

Central Division

	W	L	T	Pct.	Pts.	OP
Minnesota	11	3	0	.786	245	139
Detroit	7	6	1	.538	341	286
Chicago	6	8	0	.429	185	276
Green Bay	4	8	2	.333	274	298

Western Division

	W	L	T	Pct.	Pts.	OP
San Francisco	9	5	0	.643	300	216
Los Angeles	8	5	1	.615	313	260
Atlanta	7	6	1	.538	274	277
New Orleans	4	8	2	.333	266	347

Wild Card qualifier for playoffs

Divisional playoffs: Miami 27, Kansas City 24, sudden-death overtime; Baltimore 20, Cleveland 3

AFC Championship: Miami 21, Baltimore 0

Divisional playoffs: Dallas 20, Minnesota 12; San Francisco 24, Washington 20

NFC Championship: Dallas 14, San Francisco 3

Super Bowl VI: Dallas (NFC) 24, Miami (AFC) 3

1972

AMERICAN CONFERENCE

Eastern Division

	W	L	T	Pct.	Pts.	OP
Miami	14	0	0	1.000	385	171
N.Y. Jets	7	7	0	.500	367	324
Baltimore	5	9	0	.357	235	252
Buffalo	4	9	1	.321	257	377
New England	3	11	0	.214	192	446

Central Division

	W	L	T	Pct.	Pts.	OP
Pittsburgh	11	3	0	.786	343	175
Cleveland*	10	4	0	.714	268	249
Cincinnati	8	6	0	.571	299	229
Houston	1	13	0	.071	164	380

Western Division

	W	L	T	Pct.	Pts.	OP
Oakland	10	3	1	.750	365	248
Kansas City	8	6	0	.571	287	254
Denver	5	9	0	.357	325	350
San Diego	4	9	1	.321	264	344

NATIONAL CONFERENCE

Eastern Division

	W	L	T	Pct.	Pts.	OP
Washington	11	3	0	.786	336	218
Dallas*	10	4	0	.714	319	240
N.Y. Giants	8	6	0	.571	331	247
St. Louis	4	9	1	.321	193	303
Philadelphia	2	11	1	.179	145	352

Central Division

	W	L	T	Pct.	Pts.	OP
Green Bay	10	4	0	.714	304	226
Detroit	8	5	1	.607	339	290
Minnesota	7	7	0	.500	301	252
Chicago	4	9	1	.321	225	275

Western Division

	W	L	T	Pct.	Pts.	OP
San Francisco	8	5	1	.607	353	249
Atlanta	7	7	0	.500	269	274
Los Angeles	6	7	1	.464	291	286
New Orleans	2	11	1	.179	215	361

Wild Card qualifier for playoffs

Divisional playoffs: Pittsburgh 13, Oakland 7; Miami 20, Cleveland 14

AFC Championship: Miami 21, Pittsburgh 17

Divisional playoffs: Dallas 30, San Francisco 28; Washington 16, Green Bay 3

NFC Championship: Washington 26, Dallas 3

Super Bowl VII: Miami (AFC) 14, Washington (NFC) 7

1973

AMERICAN CONFERENCE						NATIONAL CONFERENCE					
Eastern Division						**Eastern Division**					
	W	L	T	Pct.	Pts.	OP	W	L	T	Pct.	Pts.	OP
Miami	12	2	0	.857	343	150	Dallas	10	4	0	.714	382	203
Buffalo	9	5	0	.643	259	230	Washington*	10	4	0	.714	325	198
New England	5	9	0	.357	258	300	Philadelphia	5	8	1	.393	310	393
Baltimore	4	10	0	.286	226	341	St. Louis	4	9	1	.321	286	365
N.Y. Jets	4	10	0	.286	240	306	N.Y. Giants	2	11	1	.179	226	362

Central Division						**Central Division**					
	W	L	T	Pct.	Pts.	OP	W	L	T	Pct.	Pts.	OP
Cincinnati	10	4	0	.714	286	231	Minnesota	12	2	0	.857	296	168
Pittsburgh*	10	4	0	.714	347	210	Detroit	6	7	1	.464	271	247
Cleveland	7	5	2	.571	234	255	Green Bay	5	7	2	.429	202	259
Houston	1	13	0	.071	199	447	Chicago	3	11	0	.214	195	334

Western Division						**Western Division**					
	W	L	T	Pct.	Pts.	OP	W	L	T	Pct.	Pts.	OP
Oakland	9	4	1	.679	292	175	Los Angeles	12	2	0	.857	388	178
Denver	7	5	2	.571	354	296	Atlanta	9	5	0	.643	318	224
Kansas City	7	5	2	.571	231	192	New Orleans	5	9	0	.357	163	312
San Diego	2	11	1	.179	188	386	San Francisco	5	9	0	.357	262	319

*Wild Card qualifier for playoffs
Divisional playoffs: Oakland 33, Pittsburgh 14; Miami 34, Cincinnati 16
AFC Championship: Miami 27, Oakland 10
Divisional playoffs: Minnesota 27, Washington 20; Dallas 27, Los Angeles 16
NFC Championship: Minnesota 27, Dallas 10
Super Bowl VIII: Miami (AFC) 24, Minnesota (NFC) 7

1974

AMERICAN CONFERENCE						NATIONAL CONFERENCE					
Eastern Division						**Eastern Division**					
	W	L	T	Pct.	Pts.	OP	W	L	T	Pct.	Pts.	OP
Miami	11	3	0	.786	327	216	St. Louis	10	4	0	.714	285	218
Buffalo*	9	5	0	.643	264	244	Washington*	10	4	0	.714	320	196
New England	7	7	0	.500	348	289	Dallas	8	6	0	.571	297	235
N.Y. Jets	7	7	0	.500	279	300	Philadelphia	7	7	0	.500	242	217
Baltimore	2	12	0	.143	190	329	N.Y. Giants	2	12	0	.143	195	299

Central Division						**Central Division**					
	W	L	T	Pct.	Pts.	OP	W	L	T	Pct.	Pts.	OP
Pittsburgh	10	3	1	.750	305	189	Minnesota	10	4	0	.714	310	195
Cincinnati	7	7	0	.500	283	259	Detroit	7	7	0	.500	256	270
Houston	7	7	0	.500	236	282	Green Bay	6	8	0	.429	210	206
Cleveland	4	10	0	.286	251	344	Chicago	4	10	0	.286	152	279

Western Division						**Western Division**					
	W	L	T	Pct.	Pts.	OP	W	L	T	Pct.	Pts.	OP
Oakland	12	2	0	.857	355	228	Los Angeles	10	4	0	.714	263	181
Denver	7	6	1	.536	302	294	San Francisco	6	8	0	.429	226	236
Kansas City	5	9	0	.357	233	293	New Orleans	5	9	0	.357	166	263
San Diego	5	9	0	.357	212	285	Atlanta	3	11	0	.214	111	271

*Wild Card qualifier for playoffs
Divisional playoffs: Oakland 28, Miami 26; Pittsburgh 32, Buffalo 14
AFC Championship: Pittsburgh 24, Oakland 13
Divisional playoffs: Minnesota 30, St. Louis 14; Los Angeles 19, Washington 10
NFC Championship: Minnesota 14, Los Angeles 10
Super Bowl IX: Pittsburgh (AFC) 16, Minnesota (NFC) 6

1975

AMERICAN CONFERENCE

Eastern Division

	W	L	T	Pct.	Pts.	OP
Baltimore	10	4	0	.714	395	269
Miami	10	4	0	.714	357	222
Buffalo	8	6	0	.571	420	355
New England	3	11	0	.214	258	358
N.Y. Jets	3	11	0	.214	258	433

Central Division

	W	L	T	Pct.	Pts.	OP
Pittsburgh	12	2	0	.857	373	162
Cincinnati*	11	3	0	.786	340	246
Houston	10	4	0	.714	293	226
Cleveland	3	11	0	.214	218	372

Western Division

	W	L	T	Pct.	Pts.	OP
Oakland	11	3	0	.786	375	255
Denver	6	8	0	.429	254	307
Kansas City	5	9	0	.357	282	341
San Diego	2	12	0	.143	189	345

NATIONAL CONFERENCE

Eastern Division

	W	L	T	Pct.	Pts.	OP
St. Louis	11	3	0	.786	356	276
Dallas*	10	4	0	.714	350	268
Washington	8	6	0	.571	325	276
N.Y. Giants	5	9	0	.357	216	306
Philadelphia	4	10	0	.286	225	302

Central Division

	W	L	T	Pct.	Pts.	OP
Minnesota	12	2	0	.857	377	180
Detroit	7	7	0	.500	245	262
Chicago	4	10	0	.286	191	379
Green Bay	4	10	0	.286	226	285

Western Division

	W	L	T	Pct.	Pts.	OP
Los Angeles	12	2	0	.857	312	135
San Francisco	5	9	0	.357	255	286
Atlanta	4	10	0	.286	240	289
New Orleans	2	12	0	.143	165	360

*Wild Card qualifier for playoffs
Divisional playoffs: Pittsburgh 28, Baltimore 10; Oakland 31, Cincinnati 28
AFC Championship: Pittsburgh 16, Oakland 10
Divisional playoffs: Los Angeles 35, St. Louis 23; Dallas 17, Minnesota 14
NFC Championship: Dallas 37, Los Angeles 7
Super Bowl X: Pittsburgh (AFC) 21, Dallas (NFC) 17

1976

AMERICAN CONFERENCE

Eastern Division

	W	L	T	Pct.	Pts.	OP
Baltimore	11	3	0	.786	417	246
New England*	11	3	0	.786	376	236
Miami	6	8	0	.429	263	264
N.Y. Jets	3	11	0	.214	169	383
Buffalo	2	12	0	.143	245	363

Central Division

	W	L	T	Pct.	Pts.	OP
Pittsburgh	10	4	0	.714	342	138
Cincinnati	10	4	0	.714	335	210
Cleveland	9	5	0	.643	267	287
Houston	5	9	0	.357	222	273

Western Division

	W	L	T	Pct.	Pts.	OP
Oakland	13	1	0	.929	350	237
Denver	9	5	0	.643	315	206
San Diego	6	8	0	.429	248	285
Kansas City	5	9	0	.357	290	376
Tampa Bay	0	14	0	.000	125	412

NATIONAL CONFERENCE

Eastern Division

	W	L	T	Pct.	Pts.	OP
Dallas	11	3	0	.786	296	194
Washington*	10	4	0	.714	291	217
St. Louis	10	4	0	.714	309	267
Philadelphia	4	10	0	.286	165	286
N.Y. Giants	3	11	0	.214	170	250

Central Division

	W	L	T	Pct.	Pts.	OP
Minnesota	11	2	1	.821	305	176
Chicago	7	7	0	.500	253	216
Detroit	6	8	0	.429	262	220
Green Bay	5	9	0	.357	218	299

Western Division

	W	L	T	Pct.	Pts.	OP
Los Angeles	10	3	1	.750	351	190
San Francisco	8	6	0	.571	270	190
Atlanta	4	10	0	.286	172	312
New Orleans	4	10	0	.286	253	346
Seattle	2	12	0	.143	229	429

*Wild Card qualifier for playoffs
Divisional playoffs: Oakland 24, New England 21; Pittsburgh 40, Baltimore 14
AFC Championship: Oakland 24, Pittsburgh 7
Divisional playoffs: Minnesota 35, Washington 20; Los Angeles 14, Dallas 12
NFC Championship: Minnesota 24, Los Angeles 13
Super Bowl XI: Oakland (AFC) 32, Minnesota (NFC) 14

1977

AMERICAN CONFERENCE

Eastern Division

	W	L	T	Pct.	Pts.	OP
Baltimore	10	4	0	.714	295	221
Miami	10	4	0	.714	313	197
New England	9	5	0	.643	278	217
N.Y. Jets	3	11	0	.214	191	300
Buffalo	3	11	0	.214	160	313

Central Division

	W	L	T	Pct.	Pts.	OP
Pittsburgh	9	5	0	.643	283	243
Houston	8	6	0	.571	299	230
Cincinnati	8	6	0	.571	238	235
Cleveland	6	8	0	.429	269	267

Western Division

	W	L	T	Pct.	Pts.	OP
Denver	12	2	0	.857	274	148
Oakland*	11	3	0	.786	351	230
San Diego	7	7	0	.500	222	205
Seattle	5	9	0	.357	282	373
Kansas City	2	12	0	.143	225	349

NATIONAL CONFERENCE

Eastern Division

	W	L	T	Pct.	Pts.	OP
Dallas	12	2	0	.857	345	212
Washington	9	5	0	.643	196	189
St. Louis	7	7	0	.500	272	287
Philadelphia	5	9	0	.357	220	207
N.Y. Giants	5	9	0	.357	181	265

Central Division

	W	L	T	Pct.	Pts.	OP
Minnesota	9	5	0	.643	231	227
Chicago*	9	5	0	.643	255	253
Detroit	6	8	0	.429	183	252
Green Bay	4	10	0	.286	134	219
Tampa Bay	2	12	0	.143	103	223

Western Division

	W	L	T	Pct.	Pts.	OP
Los Angeles	10	4	0	.714	302	146
Atlanta	7	7	0	.500	179	129
San Francisco	5	9	0	.357	220	260
New Orleans	3	11	0	.214	232	336

*Wild Card qualifier for playoffs

Divisional playoffs: Denver 34, Pittsburgh 21; Oakland 37, Baltimore 31, sudden-death overtime

AFC Championship: Denver 20, Oakland 17

Divisional playoffs: Dallas 37, Chicago 7; Minnesota 14, Los Angeles 7

NFC Championship: Dallas 23, Minnesota 6

Super Bowl XII: Dallas (NFC) 27, Denver (AFC) 10

1978

AMERICAN CONFERENCE

Eastern Division

	W	L	T	Pct.	Pts.	OP
New England	11	5	0	.688	358	286
Miami*	11	5	0	.688	372	254
N.Y. Jets	8	8	0	.500	359	364
Buffalo	5	11	0	.313	302	354
Baltimore	5	11	0	.313	239	421

Central Division

	W	L	T	Pct.	Pts.	OP
Pittsburgh	14	2	0	.875	356	195
Houston*	10	6	0	.625	283	298
Cleveland	8	8	0	.500	334	356
Cincinnati	4	12	0	.250	252	284

Western Division

	W	L	T	Pct.	Pts.	OP
Denver	10	6	0	.625	282	198
Oakland	9	7	0	.563	311	283
Seattle	9	7	0	.563	345	358
San Diego	9	7	0	.563	355	309
Kansas City	4	12	0	.250	243	327

NATIONAL CONFERENCE

Eastern Division

	W	L	T	Pct.	Pts.	OP
Dallas	12	4	0	.750	384	208
Philadelphia*	9	7	0	.563	270	250
Washington	8	8	0	.500	273	283
St. Louis	6	10	0	.375	248	296
N.Y. Giants	6	10	0	.375	264	298

Central Division

	W	L	T	Pct.	Pts.	OP
Minnesota	8	7	1	.531	294	306
Green Bay	8	7	1	.531	249	269
Detroit	7	9	0	.438	290	300
Chicago	7	9	0	.438	253	274
Tampa Bay	5	11	0	.313	241	259

Western Division

	W	L	T	Pct.	Pts.	OP
Los Angeles	12	4	0	.750	316	245
Atlanta*	9	7	0	.563	240	290
New Orleans	7	9	0	.438	281	298
San Francisco	2	14	0	.125	219	350

*Wild Card qualifier for playoffs

First-round playoff: Houston 17, Miami 9

Divisional playoffs: Houston 31, New England 14; Pittsburgh 33, Denver 10

AFC Championship: Pittsburgh 34, Houston 5

First-round playoff: Atlanta 14, Philadelphia 13

Divisional playoffs: Dallas 27, Atlanta 20; Los Angeles 34, Minnesota 10

NFC Championship: Dallas 28, Los Angeles 0

Super Bowl XIII: Pittsburgh (AFC) 35, Dallas (NFC) 31

1979

AMERICAN CONFERENCE

Eastern Division

	W	L	T	Pct.	Pts.	OP
Miami	10	6	0	.625	341	257
New England	9	7	0	.563	411	326
N.Y. Jets	8	8	0	.500	337	383
Buffalo	7	9	0	.438	268	279
Baltimore	5	11	0	.313	271	351

Central Division

	W	L	T	Pct.	Pts.	OP
Pittsburgh	12	4	0	.750	416	262
Houston*	11	5	0	.688	362	331
Cleveland	9	7	0	.563	359	352
Cincinnati	4	12	0	.250	337	421

Western Division

	W	L	T	Pct.	Pts.	OP
San Diego	12	4	0	.750	411	246
Denver*	10	6	0	.625	289	262
Seattle	9	7	0	.563	378	372
Oakland	9	7	0	.563	365	337
Kansas City	7	9	0	.438	238	262

NATIONAL CONFERENCE

Eastern Division

	W	L	T	Pct.	Pts.	OP
Dallas	11	5	0	.688	371	313
Philadelphia*	11	5	0	.688	339	282
Washington	10	6	0	.625	348	295
N.Y. Giants	6	10	0	.375	237	323
St. Louis	5	11	0	.313	307	358

Central Division

	W	L	T	Pct.	Pts.	OP
Tampa Bay	10	6	0	.625	273	237
Chicago*	10	6	0	.625	306	249
Minnesota	7	9	0	.438	259	337
Green Bay	5	11	0	.313	246	316
Detroit	2	14	0	.125	219	365

Western Division

	W	L	T	Pct.	Pts.	OP
Los Angeles	9	7	0	.563	323	309
New Orleans	8	8	0	.500	370	360
Atlanta	6	10	0	.375	300	388
San Francisco	2	14	0	.125	308	416

*Wild Card qualifier for playoffs
First-round playoff: Houston 13, Denver 7
Divisional playoffs: Houston 17, San Diego 14; Pittsburgh 34, Miami 14
AFC Championship: Pittsburgh 27, Houston 13
First-round playoff: Philadelphia 27, Chicago 17
Divisional playoffs: Tampa Bay 24, Philadelphia 17; Los Angeles 21, Dallas 19
NFC Championship: Los Angeles 9, Tampa Bay 0
Super Bowl XIV: Pittsburgh (AFC) 31, Los Angeles (NFC) 19

1980

AMERICAN CONFERENCE

Eastern Division

	W	L	T	Pct.	Pts.	OP
Buffalo	11	5	0	.688	320	260
New England	10	6	0	.625	441	325
Miami	8	8	0	.500	266	305
Baltimore	7	9	0	.438	355	387
N.Y. Jets	4	12	0	.250	302	395

Central Division

	W	L	T	Pct.	Pts.	OP
Cleveland	11	5	0	.688	357	310
Houston*	11	5	0	.688	295	251
Pittsburgh	9	7	0	.563	352	313
Cincinnati	6	10	0	.375	244	312

Western Division

	W	L	T	Pct.	Pts.	OP
San Diego	11	5	0	.688	418	327
Oakland*	11	5	0	.688	364	306
Kansas City	8	8	0	.500	319	336
Denver	8	8	0	.500	310	323
Seattle	4	12	0	.250	291	408

NATIONAL CONFERENCE

Eastern Division

	W	L	T	Pct.	Pts.	OP
Philadelphia	12	4	0	.750	384	222
Dallas*	12	4	0	.750	454	311
Washington	6	10	0	.375	261	293
St. Louis	5	11	0	.313	299	350
N.Y. Giants	4	12	0	.250	249	425

Central Division

	W	L	T	Pct.	Pts.	OP
Minnesota	9	7	0	.563	317	308
Detroit	9	7	0	.563	334	272
Chicago	7	9	0	.437	304	264
Tampa Bay	5	10	1	.343	271	341
Green Bay	5	10	1	.343	231	371

Western Division

	W	L	T	Pct.	Pts.	OP
Atlanta	12	4	0	.750	405	272
Los Angeles*	11	5	0	.688	424	289
San Francisco	6	10	0	.375	320	415
New Orleans	1	15	0	.063	291	487

*Wild Card qualifier for playoffs
First-round playoff: Oakland 27, Houston 7
Divisional playoffs: San Diego 20, Buffalo 14; Oakland 14, Cleveland 12
AFC Championship: Oakland 34, San Diego 27
First-round playoff: Dallas 34, Los Angeles 13
Divisional playoffs: Philadelphia 31, Minnesota 16; Dallas 30, Atlanta 27
NFC Championship: Philadelphia 20, Dallas 7
Super Bowl XV: Oakland (AFC) 27, Philadelphia (NFC) 10

1981

AMERICAN CONFERENCE

Eastern Division

	W	L	T	Pct.	Pts.	OP
Miami	11	4	1	.719	345	275
N.Y. Jets*	10	5	1	.656	355	287
Buffalo*	10	6	0	.625	311	276
Baltimore	2	14	0	.125	259	533
New England	2	14	0	.125	322	370

Central Division

	W	L	T	Pct.	Pts.	OP
Cincinnati	12	4	0	.750	421	304
Pittsburgh	8	8	0	.500	356	297
Houston	7	9	0	.438	281	355
Cleveland	5	11	0	.313	276	375

Western Division

	W	L	T	Pct.	Pts.	OP
San Diego	10	6	0	.625	478	390
Denver	10	6	0	.625	321	289
Kansas City	9	7	0	.563	343	290
Oakland	7	9	0	.438	273	343
Seattle	6	10	0	.375	322	388

NATIONAL CONFERENCE

Eastern Division

	W	L	T	Pct.	Pts.	OP
Dallas	12	4	0	.750	367	277
Philadelphia*	10	6	0	.625	368	221
N.Y. Giants*	9	7	0	.563	295	257
Washington	8	8	0	.500	347	349
St. Louis	7	9	0	.438	315	408

Central Division

	W	L	T	Pct.	Pts.	OP
Tampa Bay	9	7	0	.563	315	268
Detroit	8	8	0	.500	397	322
Green Bay	8	8	0	.500	324	361
Minnesota	7	9	0	.438	325	369
Chicago	6	10	0	.375	253	324

Western Division

	W	L	T	Pct.	Pts.	OP
San Francisco	13	3	0	.813	357	250
Atlanta	7	9	0	.438	426	355
Los Angeles	6	10	0	.375	303	351
New Orleans	4	12	0	.250	207	378

*Wild card qualifier for playoffs
First-round playoff: Buffalo 31, N.Y. Jets 27
Divisional playoffs: San Diego 41, Miami 38 (OT); Cincinnati 28, Buffalo 21
AFC Championship: Cincinnati 27, San Diego 7
First-round playoff: N.Y. Giants 27, Philadelphia 21
Divisional playoffs: Dallas 38, Tampa Bay 0; San Francisco 38, N.Y. Giants 24
NFC Championship: San Francisco 28, Dallas 27
Super Bowl XVI: San Francisco (NFC) 26, Cincinnati (AFC) 21

*1982

AMERICAN CONFERENCE

	W	L	T	Pct.	Pts.	OP
L.A. Raiders	8	1	0	.889	260	200
Miami	7	2	0	.778	198	131
Cincinnati	7	2	0	.778	232	177
Pittsburgh	6	3	0	.667	204	146
San Diego	6	3	0	.667	288	221
N.Y. Jets	6	3	0	.667	245	166
New England	5	4	0	.556	143	157
Cleveland	4	5	0	.444	140	182
Buffalo	4	5	0	.444	150	154
Seattle	4	5	0	.444	127	147
Kansas City	3	6	0	.333	176	184
Denver	2	7	0	.222	148	226
Houston	1	8	0	.111	136	245
Baltimore	0	8	1	.063	113	236

NATIONAL CONFERENCE

	W	L	T	Pct.	Pts.	OP
Washington	8	1	0	.889	190	128
Dallas	6	3	0	.667	226	145
Green Bay	5	3	1	.611	226	169
Minnesota	5	4	0	.556	187	198
Atlanta	5	4	0	.556	183	199
St. Louis	5	4	0	.556	135	170
Tampa Bay	5	4	0	.556	158	178
Detroit	4	5	0	.444	181	176
New Orleans	4	5	0	.444	129	160
N.Y. Giants	4	5	0	.444	164	160
San Francisco	3	6	0	.333	209	206
Chicago	3	6	0	.333	141	174
Philadelphia	3	6	0	.333	191	195
L.A. Rams	2	7	0	.222	200	250

*Top eight teams in each Conference qualified for playoffs under format necessitated by strike-shortened season

First-round playoffs: Miami 28, New England 13; L.A. Raiders 27, Cleveland 10; N.Y. Jets 44, Cincinnati 17; San Diego 31, Pittsburgh 28
Second-round playoffs: N.Y. Jets 17, L.A. Raiders 14; Miami 34, San Diego 13
AFC Championship: Miami 14, N.Y. Jets 0
First-round playoffs: Green Bay 41, St. Louis 16; Washington 31, Detroit 7; Minnesota 30, Atlanta 24; Dallas 30, Tampa Bay 17
Second-round playoffs: Washington 21, Minnesota 7; Dallas 37, Green Bay 26
NFC Championship: Washington 31, Dallas 17
Super Bowl XVII: Washington 27, Miami 17

1983

AMERICAN CONFERENCE

Eastern Division

	W	L	T	Pct.	Pts.	OP
Miami	12	4	0	.750	389	250
New England	8	8	0	.500	274	289
Buffalo	8	8	0	.500	283	351
Baltimore	7	9	0	.438	264	354
N.Y. Jets	7	9	0	.438	313	331

Central Division

	W	L	T	Pct.	Pts.	OP
Pittsburgh	10	6	0	.625	355	303
Cleveland	9	7	0	.562	356	342
Cincinnati	7	9	0	.438	346	302
Houston	2	14	0	.125	288	460

Western Division

	W	L	T	Pct.	Pts.	OP
L.A. Raiders	12	4	0	.750	442	338
Seattle*	9	7	0	.562	403	397
Denver*	9	7	0	.562	302	327
San Diego	6	10	0	.375	358	462
Kansas City	6	10	0	.375	386	367

NATIONAL CONFERENCE

Eastern Division

	W	L	T	Pct.	Pts.	OP
Washington	14	2	0	.875	541	332
Dallas*	12	4	0	.750	479	360
St. Louis	8	7	1	.531	374	428
Philadelphia	5	11	0	.313	233	322
N.Y. Giants	3	12	1	.219	267	347

Central Division

	W	L	T	Pct.	Pts.	OP
Detroit	9	7	0	.562	347	286
Green Bay	8	8	0	.500	429	439
Chicago	8	8	0	.500	311	301
Minnesota	8	8	0	.500	316	348
Tampa Bay	2	14	0	.125	241	380

Western Division

	W	L	T	Pct.	Pts.	OP
San Francisco	10	6	0	.625	432	293
L.A. Rams*	9	7	0	.562	361	344
New Orleans	8	8	0	.500	319	337
Atlanta	7	9	0	.438	370	389

*Wild card qualifier for playoffs
First-round playoff: Seattle 31, Denver 7
Divisional playoffs: Seattle 27, Miami 20; L.A. Raiders 38, Pittsburgh 10
AFC Championship: L.A. Raiders 30, Seattle 14
First-round playoff: L.A. Rams 24, Dallas 17
Divisional playoffs: San Francisco 24, Detroit 23; Washington 51, L.A. Rams 7
NFC Championship: Washington 24, San Francisco 21
Super Bowl XVIII: L.A. Raiders 38, Washington 9

1984

NATIONAL CONFERENCE

Eastern Division

	W	L	T	Pct.	Pts.	OP
Washington	11	5	0	.688	426	310
N.Y. Giants*	9	7	0	.563	299	301
St. Louis	9	7	0	.563	423	345
Dallas	9	7	0	.563	308	308
Philadelphia	6	9	1	.406	278	320

Central Division

	W	L	T	Pct.	Pts.	OP
Chicago	10	6	0	.625	325	248
Green Bay	8	8	0	.500	390	309
Tampa Bay	6	10	0	.375	335	380
Detroit	4	11	1	.281	283	408
Minnesota	3	13	0	.188	276	484

Western Division

	W	L	T	Pct.	Pts.	OP
San Francisco	15	1	0	.939	475	227
L.A. Rams*	10	6	0	.625	346	316
New Orleans	7	9	0	.438	298	361
Atlanta	4	12	0	.250	281	382

AMERICAN CONFERENCE

Eastern Division

	W	L	T	Pct.	Pts.	OP
Miami	14	2	0	.875	513	298
New England	9	7	0	.563	362	352
N.Y. Jets	7	9	0	.438	332	364
Indianapolis	4	12	0	.250	239	414
Buffalo	2	14	0	.125	250	454

Central Division

	W	L	T	Pct.	Pts.	OP
Pittsburgh	9	7	0	.563	387	310
Cincinnati	8	8	0	.500	339	339
Cleveland	5	11	0	.313	250	297
Houston	3	13	0	.188	240	437

Western Division

	W	L	T	Pct.	Pts.	OP
Denver	13	3	0	.813	353	241
Seattle*	12	4	0	.750	418	282
L.A. Raiders*	11	5	0	.688	368	278
Kansas City	8	8	0	.500	314	324
San Diego	7	9	0	.438	394	413

*Wild card qualifier for playoffs
Wild Card Game: N.Y. Giants 16, L.A. Rams 13
NFC Divisional playoffs: San Francisco 21, N.Y. Giants 10; Chicago 23, Washington 19
NFC Championship: San Francisco 23, Chicago 0
Wild Card Game: Seattle 13, L.A. Raiders 7
AFC Divisional playoffs: Miami 31, Seattle 10; Pittsburgh 24, Denver 17
AFC Championship: Miami 45, Pittsburgh 28
Super Bowl XIX: San Francisco 38, Miami 16

1985

AMERICAN CONFERENCE

Eastern Division

	W	L	T	Pct.	Pts.	OP
Miami	12	4	0	.750	428	320
N.Y. Jets	11	5	0	.688	393	264
New England	11	5	0	.688	362	290
Indianapolis	5	11	0	.313	320	386
Buffalo	2	14	0	.125	200	381

CENTRAL DIVISION

	W	L	T	Pct.	Pts.	OP
Cleveland	8	8	0	.500	287	294
Cincinnati	7	9	0	.438	441	437
Pittsburgh	7	9	0	.438	379	355
Houston	5	11	0	.313	284	412

WESTERN DIVISION

	W	L	T	Pct.	Pts.	OP
L.A. Raiders	12	4	0	.750	354	308
Denver	11	5	0	.688	380	329
Seattle	8	8	0	.500	349	303
San Diego	8	8	0	.500	467	435
Kansas City	6	10	0	.375	327	360

NATIONAL CONFERENCE

Eastern Division

	W	L	T	Pct.	Pts.	OP
Dallas	10	6	0	.625	357	333
N.Y. Giants	10	6	0	.625	399	283
Washington	10	6	0	.625	298	313
Philadelphia	7	9	0	.438	286	310
St. Louis	5	11	0	.313	279	415

CENTRAL DIVISION

	W	L	T	Pct.	Pts.	OP
Chicago	15	1	0	.938	456	198
Green Bay	8	8	0	.500	337	355
Minnesota	7	9	0	.438	346	359
Detroit	7	9	0	.438	307	366
Tampa Bay	2	14	0	.125	294	448

WESTERN DIVISION

	W	L	T	Pct.	Pts.	OP
L.A. Rams	11	5	0	.688	340	287
San Francisco	10	6	0	.625	411	263
New Orleans	5	11	0	.313	294	401
Atlanta	4	12	0	.250	282	452

Wild Card Game: New England 26, N.Y. Jets 14
AFC Divisional playoffs: Miami 24, Cleveland 21; New England 27, L.A. Raiders 20
AFC Championship: New England 31, Miami 14
Wild Card Game: N.Y. Giants 17, San Francisco 3
NFC Divisional playoffs: L.A. Rams 20, Dallas 0; Chicago 21, N.Y. Giants 0
NFC Championship: Chicago 24, L.A. Rams 0
Super Bowl XX: Chicago 46, New England 10

1986

AMERICAN CONFERENCE

Eastern Division

	W	L	T	Pct.	Pts.	OP
N.Y. Giants	14	2	0	.875	371	236
Washington	12	4	0	.750	368	296
Dallas	7	9	0	.438	346	337
Philadelphia	5	10	1	.344	256	312
St. Louis	4	11	1	.281	218	351

Central Division

	W	L	T	Pct.	Pts.	OP
Chicago	14	2	0	.875	352	187
Minnesota	9	7	0	.563	398	273
Detroit	5	11	0	.313	277	326
Green Bay	4	12	0	.250	254	418
Tampa Bay	2	14	0	.125	239	473

Western Division

	W	L	T	Pct.	Pts.	OP
San Francisco	10	5	1	.656	374	247
L.A. Rams	10	6	0	.625	309	267
Atlanta	7	8	1	.469	280	280
New Orleans	7	9	0	.438	288	287

NATIONAL CONFERENCE

Eastern Division

	W	L	T	Pct.	Pts.	OP
New England	11	5	0	.688	412	307
N.Y. Jets	10	6	0	.625	364	386
Miami	8	8	0	.500	430	405
Buffalo	4	12	0	.250	287	348
Indianapolis	3	13	0	.188	229	400

Central Division

	W	L	T	Pct.	Pts.	OP
Cleveland	12	4	0	.750	391	310
Cincinnati	10	6	0	.625	409	394
Pittsburgh	6	10	0	.375	307	336
Houston	5	11	0	.313	274	329

Western Division

	W	L	T	Pct.	Pts.	OP
Denver	11	5	0	.688	378	327
Kansas City	10	6	0	.625	358	326
Seattle	10	6	0	.625	366	293
L.A. Raiders	8	8	0	.500	323	346
San Diego	4	12	0	.250	335	396

NFC Wild Card Game: Washington 19, L.A. Rams 7
NFC Divisional playoffs: Washington 27, Chicago 13; N.Y. Giants 49, San Francisco 3
NFC Championship: N.Y. Giants 17, Washington 0
AFC Wild Card Game: N.Y. Jets 35, Kansas City 15
AFC Divisional playoffs: Cleveland 23, N.Y. Jets 20 (2 OT); Denver 22, New England 17
AFC Championship: Denver 23, Cleveland 20 (OT)
Super Bowl XXI: N.Y. Giants 39, Denver 20

The down side of Super Bowl XXI for John Elway.

Skins' Ricky Sanders scores on pass in Super Bowl XXII.

1987

NATIONAL CONFERENCE

Eastern Division

	W	L	T	Pct.	Pts.	OP
Washington	11	4	0	.733	379	285
St. Louis	7	8	0	.467	362	368
Dallas	7	8	0	.467	340	348
Philadelphia	7	8	0	.467	337	380
N.Y. Giants	6	9	0	.400	280	312

Central Division

	W	L	T	Pct.	Pts.	OP
Chicago	11	4	0	.733	356	282
Minnesota	8	7	0	.533	336	335
Green Bay	5	9	1	.367	255	300
Tampa Bay	4	11	0	.267	286	360
Detroit	4	11	0	.267	269	384

Western Division

	W	L	T	Pct.	Pts.	OP
San Francisco	13	2	0	.867	459	253
New Orleans	12	3	0	.800	422	283
L.A. Rams	6	9	0	.400	317	361
Atlanta	3	12	0	.200	205	436

AMERICAN CONFERENCE

Eastern Division

	W	L	T	Pct.	Pts.	OP
Indianapolis	9	6	0	.600	300	238
New England	8	7	0	.533	320	293
Miami	8	7	0	.533	362	335
Buffalo	7	8	0	.467	270	305
N.Y. Jets	6	9	0	.400	334	360

Central Division

	W	L	T	Pct.	Pts.	OP
Cleveland	10	5	0	.667	390	239
Houston	9	6	0	.600	345	349
Pittsburgh	8	7	0	.533	285	299
Cincinnati	4	11	0	.267	285	370

Western Division

	W	L	T	Pct.	Pts.	OP
Denver	10	4	1	.700	379	288
Seattle	9	6	0	.600	371	314
San Diego	8	7	0	.533	253	317
L.A. Raiders	5	10	0	.333	301	289
Kansas City	4	11	0	.267	273	388

NFC Wild Card Game: Minnesota 44, New Orleans 10
NFC Divisional playoffs: Minnesota 36, San Francisco 24; Wash. 21, Chicago 17
NFC Championship: Washington 17, Minnesota 10
AFC Wild Card Game: Houston 23, Seattle 20 (OT)
AFC Divisional playoffs: Cleveland 38, Indianapolis 21; Denver 34, Houston 10
AFC Championship: Denver 38, Cleveland 33
Super Bowl XXII: Washington 42, Denver 10

1988 NFL DRAFT

Player	Order No.	Pos.	College	Club	Round
Abdur-Ra'oof, Azizuddin	224	WR	Maryland	Kansas City	9
Alexander, Mike	199	WR	Penn State	Los Angeles Raiders	8
Allen, Eric	30	DB	Arizona State	Philadelphia	2
Allen, Marvin	294	RB	Tulane	New England	11
Alston, O'Brien	270	LB	Maryland	Indianapolis	10
Ambrose, J.R.	96	WR	Mississippi	Kansas City	4
Anderson, Willie	46	WR	UCLA	Los Angeles Rams	2
Andolsek, Eric	111	G	Louisiana State	Detroit	5
Bailey, Carlton	235	NT	North Carolina	Buffalo	9
Ball, Michael	104	DB	Southern U.	Indianapolis	4
Baylor, John	129	DB	So. Mississippi	Indianapolis	5
Beathard, Jeff	333	WR	Southern Oregon	Los Angeles Rams	12
Beckman, Brad	183	TE	Nebraska-Omaha	Minnesota	7
Bedford, Brian	232	WR	California	Dallas	9
Bell, Kerwin	180	QB	Florida	Miami	7
Birden, J.J.	216	WR	Oregon	Cleveland	8
Blades, Bennie	3	DB	Miami	Detroit	1
Blades, Brian	49	WR	Miami	Seattle	2
Blaylock, Anthony	103	DB	Winston-Salem	Cleveland	4
Bolton, Scott	312	WR	Auburn	Green Bay	12
Bonner, Brian	247	LB	Minnesota	San Francisco	9
Booty, John	257	DB	Texas Christian	New York Jets	10
Borcky, Tim	177	T	Memphis State	Buffalo	7
Brantley, John	325	LB	Georgia	Houston	12
Bratton, Melvin	153	RB	Miami	Miami	6
Brim, Michael	95	DB	Virginia Union	Phoenix	4
Brooks, Chet	303	DB	Texas A&M	San Francisco	11
Brown, Henry	277	T	Ohio State	Washington	10
Brown, Phillip	194	LB	Alabama	Atlanta	8
Brown, Tim	6	WR	Notre Dame	Los Angeles Raiders	1
Brown, Vincent	43	LB	Mississippi Valley	New England	2
Bruce, Aundray	1	LB	Auburn	Atlanta	1
Bruhin, John	86	G	Tennessee	Tampa Bay	4
Bryant, Kevin	191	LB	Delaware State	San Francisco	7
Cadigan, Dave	8	T	Southern California	New York Jets	1
Cain, Joe	210	LB	Oregon Tech	Minnesota	8
Calvin, Richard	304	RB	Washington State	Denver	11
Campbell, Joe	91	DE	New Mexico State	San Diego	4
Carr, Lydell	106	RB	Oklahoma	New Orleans	4
Carrier, Chris	318	DB	Louisiana State	Phoenix	12
Carter, Johnny	332	NT	Grambling	Denver	12
Carter, Jon	118	DE	Pittsburgh	New York Giants	5
Carter, Pat	32	TE	Florida State	Detroit	2
Cecil, Chuck	89	DB	Arizona	Green Bay	4
Chandler, Chris	76	QB	Washington	Indianapolis	3
Charlton, Clifford	21	LB	Florida	Cleveland	1
Cheek, Louis	220	T	Texas A&M	Miami	8
Clark, Greg	329	LB	Arizona State	Chicago	12
Clarkson, Larry	219	T	Montana	San Francisco	8
Clayton, Stan	250	T	Penn State	Atlanta	10

Falcons made Auburn LB Aundray Bruce No. 1 in draft.

Player	Order No.	Pos.	College	Club	Round
Collins, Patrick	200	RB	Oklahoma	Green Bay	8
Cooper, George	156	RB	Ohio State	Miami	6
Copeland, Danny	244	DB	Eastern Kentucky	Cleveland	9
Corrington, Kip	223	DB	Texas A&M	Detroit	9
Cotton, Marcus	28	LB	Southern California	Atlanta	2
Couch, Gary	302	WR	Minnesota	New Orleans	11
Cox, Aaron	20	WR	Arizona State	Los Angeles Rams	1

Notre Dame WR Tim Brown was Raider pick (No. 6).

Player	Order No.	Pos.	College	Club	Round
Craig, Paco	254	WR	UCLA	Detroit	10
Crain, Kurt	157	LB	Auburn	Houston	6
Cross, Jeff	239	DE	Missouri	Miami	9
Crudup, Derrick	171	DB	Oklahoma	Los Angeles Raiders	7
Curkendall, Pete	289	NT	Penn State	Buffalo	11
Davis, Reuben	225	DT	North Carolina	Tampa Bay	9
Davis, Scott	25	DE	Illinois	Los Angeles Raiders	1
Davis, Wendell	27	WR	Louisiana State	Chicago	1
Dawson, Bobby	295	DB	Illinois	Pittsburgh	11
Dawson, Dermontti	44	G	Kentucky	Pittsburgh	2
Dee, Donnie	297	TE	Tulsa	Indianapolis	11
Delpino, Robert	117	RB	Missouri	Los Angeles Rams	5
Derby, Glenn	218	T	Wisconsin	New Orleans	8
Des Rochers, Dave	326	T	San Diego State	Seattle	12
Dill, Scott	233	G	Memphis State	Phoenix	9
Dillahunt, Ellis	253	DB	East Carolina	Cincinnati	10
Dimry, Charles	110	DB	Nevada-Las Vegas	Atlanta	5
Dishman, Cris	125	DB	Purdue	Houston	5
Dixon, Rickey	5	DB	Oklahoma	Cincinnati	1
Driscoll, John	309	T	New Hampshire	Buffalo	12
Earle, James	322	LB	Clemson	Pittsburgh	12
Early, Quinn	60	WR	Iowa	San Diego	3
Eaton, Tracey	187	DB	Portland State	Houston	7
Edmunds, Ferrell	73	TE	Maryland	Miami	3
Edwards, Brad	54	DB	South Carolina	Minnesota	2
Elliott, John	36	T	Michigan	New York Giants	2
Erlandson, Tom	316	LB	Washington	Buffalo	12
Ervin, Corris	136	DB	Central Florida	Denver	5
Everett, Eric	122	DB	Texas Tech	Philadelphia	5
Farr, Mel	248	RB	UCLA	Denver	9
Figaro, Cedric	152	LB	Notre Dame	San Diego	6
Fizer, Vincent	276	LB	Southern U.	New Orleans	10
Floyd, Norman	296	DB	South Carolina	Minnesota	11
Foley, Tim	275	K	Georgia Southern	San Francisco	10
Forch, Steve	301	LB	Nebraska	Chicago	11
Ford, Bernard	65	WR	Central Florida	Buffalo	3
Forde, Brian	190	LB	Washington State	New Orleans	7
Foster, Pat	231	DT	Montana	Los Angeles Rams	9
Frank, Garry	192	G	Mississippi State	Denver	7
Franklin, Darryl	201	WR	Washington	Los Angeles Rams	8
Franklin, Jethro	298	DE	Fresno State	Houston	11
Frase, Paul	146	DE	Syracuse	New York Jets	6
Fullington, Darrell	124	DB	Miami	Minnesota	5
Futrell, David	313	NT	Brigham Young	New York Giants	12
Gadson, Ezekial	123	DB	Pittsburgh	Buffalo	5
Gaines, Chris	120	LB	Vanderbilt	Phoenix	5
Galbraith, Neil	240	DB	Central State (Okla.)	New England	9
Galbreath, Harry	212	G	Tennessee	Miami	8
Galvin, John	287	LB	Boston College	New York Jets	11
Gamble, Kenny	251	RB	Colgate	Kansas City	10
Garcia, Teddy	100	K	N.E. Louisiana	New England	4
Gash, Thane	188	DB	East Tennessee State	Cleveland	7
Goad, Tim	87	NT	North Carolina	New England	4
Goff, Robert	83	DT	Auburn	Tampa Bay	4
Goode, Kerry	167	RB	Alabama	Tampa Bay	7
Goss, Albert	314	NT	Jackson State	New York Jets	12
Grabisna, Erwin	143	LB	Case Western	Los Angeles Raiders	6

Packers got South Carolina WR Sterling Sharpe (No. 7).

Rams went for UCLA RB Gaston Green (No. 14).

Jets' top pick (No. 8) was USC OT Dave Cadigan.

Player	Order No.	Pos.	College	Club	Round
Grant, David	84	NT	West Virginia	Cincinnati	4
Green, Gaston	14	RB	UCLA	Los Angeles Rams	1
Gregory, Ted	26	NT	Syracuse	Denver	1
Gruber, Paul	4	T	Wisconsin	Tampa Bay	1
Guidry, Kevin	79	DB	Louisiana State	Denver	3
Habib, Brian	264	DT	Washington	Minnesota	10
Hadd, Gary	196	DE	Minnesota	Detroit	8
Hagy, John	204	DB	Texas	Buffalo	8
Harmon, Kevin	101	RB	Iowa	Seattle	4
Harper, Dwayne	299	DB	South Carolina State	Seattle	11
Harrell, Newt	255	T	West Texas State	Los Angeles Raiders	10
Harris, Greg	286	WR	Troy State	New York Giants	11
Hart, Roy	158	NT	South Carolina	Seattle	6
Harvey, Ken	12	LB	California	Phoenix	1
Hasty, James	74	DB	Washington State	New York Jets	3
Hawkins, Hendley	300	WR	Nebraska	Cleveland	11
Haynes, Michael	166	WR	Northern Arizona	Atlanta	7
Helton, Barry	102	P	Colorado	San Francisco	4
Hennings, Chad	290	DE	Air Force	Dallas	11
Herrod, Jeff	243	LB	Mississippi	Indianapolis	9
Heyward, Craig	24	RB	Pittsburgh	New Orleans	1
Hickerson, Eric	259	DB	Indiana	New York Giants	10
Hickert, Paul	280	K	Murray State	Cincinnati	11
Hicks, Harold	193	DB	San Diego State	Washington	7
Higdon, Alex	56	TE	Ohio State	Atlanta	3
Higgs, Mark	205	RB	Kentucky	Dallas	8
Hill, Nate	144	DE	Auburn	Green Bay	6
Hinkle, George	293	NT	Arizona	San Diego	11
Hinnant, Mike	211	TE	Temple	Pittsburgh	8
Holt, Pierce	39	DT	Angelo State	San Francisco	2
Hooven, Owen	178	T	Oregon State	Dallas	7
Hoover, Houston	140	G	Jackson State	Atlanta	6
Houle, David	145	G	Michigan State	New York Giants	6
Howard, Joey	238	T	Tennessee	San Diego	9
Howard, William	113	RB	Tennessee	Tampa Bay	5
Hummel, Ben	317	LB	UCLA	Dallas	12
Humphries, Stan	159	QB	N.E. Louisiana	Washington	6
Hutson, Mark	67	G	Oklahoma	Dallas	3
Irvin, Michael	11	WR	Miami	Dallas	1
Irvin, Todd	234	T	Mississippi	Detroit	9
Jackson, Artis	266	NT	Texas Tech	Miami	10
Jackson, John	252	T	Eastern Kentucky	Pittsburgh	10
Jackson, Keith	13	TE	Oklahoma	Philadelphia	1
Jackson, Ray	185	DB	Ohio State	Seattle	7
James, Jeff	169	WR	Stanford	Detroit	7
Jarvis, Ralph	78	DE	Temple	Chicago	3
Jeffery, Tony	38	RB	Texas Christian	Phoenix	2
Jenkins, Izel	288	DB	North Carolina State	Philadelphia	11
Jetton, Paul	141	G	Texas	Cincinnati	6
Johnson, Greg	99	T	Oklahoma	Miami	4
Johnson, Marco	271	WR	Hawaii	Houston	10
Johnson, Steve	154	TE	Virginia Tech	New England	6
Johnson, Troy	133	LB	Oklahoma	Chicago	5
Jones, Aaron	18	DE	Eastern Kentucky	Pittsburgh	1
Jones, Dante	51	LB	Oklahoma	Chicago	2
Jones, Derwin	269	DE	Miami	Seattle	10
Jones, Ernie	179	WR	Indiana	Phoenix	7
Jones, Keith	147	RB	Nebraska	Los Angeles Rams	6

Oilers tabbed Michigan State RB Lorenzo White (No. 22).

Denver chose Syracuse NT Ted Gregory (No. 26).

Player	Order No.	Pos.	College	Club	Round
Jones, Quintin	48	DB	Pittsburgh	Houston	2
Jones, Victor	310	LB	Virginia Tech	Tampa Bay	12
Jordan, Darin	121	LB	Northeastern	Pittsburgh	5
Jordan, Tony	132	RB	Kansas State	Phoenix	5
Jurgensen, Paul	330	DE	Georgia Tech	New Orleans	12
Kalis, Todd	108	G	Arizona State	Minnesota	4
Kane, Tommy	75	WR	Syracuse	Seattle	3
Kaufusi, Steve	319	DE	Brigham Young	Philadelphia	12
Kelleher, Tom	292	RB	Holy Cross	Miami	11
Kelly, Pat	174	TE	Syracuse	Denver	7
Kenney, Aatron	308	WR	Stevens Point (Wis.)	Indianapolis	12
Keyes, Bud	256	QB	Wisconsin	Green Bay	10
Kinchen, Brian	320	TE	Louisiana State	Miami	12
Knapton, Jeff	165	DT	Wyoming	Los Angeles Rams	6
Koch, Curt	305	DE	Colorado	Washington	11
Kumerow, Eric	16	DE	Ohio State	Miami	1
Kunkel, Greg	311	G	Kentucky	Los Angeles Raiders	12
Lanza, Chuck	70	C	Notre Dame	Pittsburgh	3
Lee, Shawn	163	DT	North Alabama	Tampa Bay	6
Lilly, Sammy	202	DB	Georgia Tech	New York Giants	8
Lockbaum, Gordie	236	RB	Holy Cross	Pittsburgh	9
Lohmiller, Chip	55	K	Minnesota	Washington	2
Lossow, Rodney	267	C	Wisconsin	New England	10
Magee, Rogie	245	WR	Louisiana State	Chicago	9
Martin, Sammy	97	WR	Louisiana State	New England	4
Maxey, Curtis	195	NT	Grambling	Cincinnati	8
Mayhew, Martin	262	DB	Florida State	Buffalo	10
McCoin, Danny	281	QB	Cincinnati	Detroit	11
McCormack, Brendan	323	DT	South Carolina	New York Giants	12
McCoy, Keith	291	DB	Fresno State	Phoenix	11
McDaniel, Randall	19	G	Arizona State	Minnesota	1
McDaniel, Terry	9	DB	Tennessee	Los Angeles Raiders	1
McGill, Darryl	221	RB	Wake Forest	Washington	8
McGowan, Paul	237	LB	Florida State	Minnesota	9
McLeod, Rick	284	T	Washington	Seattle	11
McManus, Danny	282	QB	Florida State	Kansas City	11
McMillan, Erik	63	DB	Missouri	New York Jets	3
McPherson, Don	149	QB	Syracuse	Philadelphia	6
Miller, Anthony	15	WR	Tennessee	San Diego	1
Miller, Ed	285	C	Pittsburgh	San Diego	11
Milling, James	278	WR	Maryland	Atlanta	11
Mims, Carl	127	DB	Sam Houston State	Washington	5
Mira, George	331	LB	Miami	San Francisco	12
Montgomery, Greg	72	P	Michigan State	Houston	3
Moore, Eric	10	T	Indiana	New York Giants	1
Moore, Tim	206	LB	Michigan State	Phoenix	8
Morris, Jamie	109	RB	Michigan	Washington	4
Mullin, R.C.	258	T	S.W. Louisiana	Los Angeles Rams	10
Murray, Dan	150	LB	E. Stroudsburg	Buffalo	6
Muster, Brad	23	RB	Stanford	Chicago	1
Neubert, Keith	203	TE	Nebraska	New York Jets	8
Newman, Anthony	35	DB	Oregon	Los Angeles Rams	2
Nichols, Mark	209	NT	Michigan State	Pittsburgh	8
Noga, Al	71	DT	Hawaii	Minnesota	3
Norton, Ken	41	LB	UCLA	Dallas	2
Nugent, Dave	321	NT	Boston College	New England	12
Nunn, Clarence	246	DB	San Diego State	New Orleans	9

Pittsburgh RB Craig Heyward (No. 24) is a Saint.

Michigan's John Elliott got second-round Giant call.

Player	Order No.	Pos.	College	Club	Round
Oliphant, Mike	66	KR	Puget Sound	Washington	3
Owens, Billy	263	DB	Pittsburgh	Dallas	10
Painter, Carl	142	RB	Hampton	Detroit	6
Parker, Carl	307	WR	Vanderbilt	Cincinnati	12
Patchan, Matt	64	T	Miami	Philadelphia	3
Patterson, Shawn	34	DT	Arizona State	Green Bay	2
Patton, Gary	172	RB	Eastern Michigan	New York Jets	7
Perez, Mike	175	QB	San Jose State	New York Giants	7
Perriman, Brett	52	WR	Miami	New Orleans	2
Perry, Gerald	45	T	Southern U.	Denver	2
Perry, Michael Dean	50	DT	Clemson	Cleveland	2
Peterson, Blake	249	LB	Mesa, Colo.	Washington	9
Phillips, Jon	148	G	Oklahoma	Phoenix	6
Phillips, Wendell	324	DB	North Alabama	San Diego	12
Piel, Mike	82	DT	Illinois	Los Angeles Rams	3
Pillow, Frank	279	WR	Tennessee State	Tampa Bay	11
Porter, Joel	273	G	Baylor	Chicago	10
Porter, Kevin	59	DB	Auburn	Kansas City	3
Price, Dennis	131	DB	UCLA	Los Angeles Raiders	5
Primus, James	222	RB	UCLA	Atlanta	9
Putzier, Rollin	88	DT	Oregon	Green Bay	4
Reed, Darrell	116	LB	Oklahoma	Green Bay	5
Reed, Harvey	217	RB	Howard	Chicago	8
Reese, Jerry	128	NT	Kentucky	Pittsburgh	5
Rehder, Tom	69	T	Notre Dame	New England	3
Rentie, Caesar	189	T	Oklahoma	Chicago	7
Richard, Gary	173	DB	Pittsburgh	Green Bay	7
Richards, David	98	T	UCLA	San Diego	4
Roach, Kirk	135	K	Western Carolina	Buffalo	5
Robbins, Monte	107	P	Michigan	Tampa Bay	4
Roberts, Alfredo	197	TE	Miami	Kansas City	8
Romanowski, Bill	80	LB	Boston College	San Francisco	3
Romer, Rich	168	LB	Union (N.Y.)	Cincinnati	7
Ross, Wayne	315	P	San Diego State	Washington	12
Rother, Tim	90	DT	Nebraska	Los Angeles Raiders	4
Roundtree, Ray	58	WR	Penn State	Detroit	3
Santos, Todd	274	QB	San Diego State	New Orleans	10
Saxon, James	139	RB	San Jose State	Kansas City	6
Scales, Greg	112	TE	Wake Forest	New Orleans	5
Schillinger, Andy	260	WR	Miami (Ohio)	Phoenix	10
Schuster, Joe	261	DT	Iowa	Philadelphia	10
Searels, Stacy	93	T	Auburn	San Diego	4
Secules, Scott	151	QB	Virginia	Dallas	6
Sharpe, Sterling	7	WR	South Carolina	Green Bay	1
Shaw, Ricky	92	LB	Oklahoma State	New York Giants	4
Simpson, Anthony	198	RB	East Carolina	Tampa Bay	8
Sims, Bob	162	G	Florida	New Orleans	6
Slayden, Steve	328	QB	Duke	Cleveland	12
Smith, David	207	RB	Western Kentucky	Philadelphia	8
Smith, Neil	2	DE	Nebraska	Kansas City	1
Spielman, Chris	29	LB	Ohio State	Detroit	2
Spradlin, David	241	LB	Texas Christian	Houston	9
Stedman, Troy	170	LB	Washburn	Kansas City	7
Stephens, John	17	RB	N.W. Louisiana	New England	1
Stephens, Tony	81	NT	Clemson	New Orleans	3
Sterling, Rob	160	DB	Maine	Philadelphia	6
Stinson, Lemuel	161	DB	Texas Tech	Chicago	6
Strickland, Fred	47	LB	Purdue	Los Angeles Rams	2
Stubbs, Danny	33	DE	Miami	San Francisco	2

Eagles liked Syracuse QB Don McPherson for backup.

Player	Order No.	Pos.	College	Club	Round
Tabor, Scott	229	P	California	Los Angeles Raiders	9
Tamm, Ralph	230	G	West Chester (Pa.)	New York Jets	9
Tate, David	208	DB	Colorado	Chicago	8
Tate, Lars	53	RB	Georgia	Tampa Bay	2
Taylor, Keith	134	DB	Illinois	New Orleans	5
Thomas, George	138	WR	Nevada-Las Vegas	Atlanta	6
Thomas, Rodney	126	DB	Brigham Young	Miami	5
Thomas, Thurman	40	RB	Oklahoma State	Buffalo	2
Thornton, Jim	105	TE	Cal State-Fullerton	Chicago	4
Tupa, Tom	68	P	Ohio State	Phoenix	3
Tyler, Robert	215	TE	South Carolina State	Seattle	8
Usher, Darryl	181	WR	Illinois	New England	7
Verhulst, Chris	130	TE	Cal State-Chico	Houston	5
Vesling, Tim	327	K	Syracuse	Indianapolis	12
Viaene, Dave	214	C	Minnesota-Duluth	Houston	8
Waiters, Van	77	LB	Indiana	Cleveland	3
Walker, Kevin	57	LB	Maryland	Cincinnati	3
Ware, Reggie	227	RB	Auburn	Los Angeles Raiders	9
Washington, Brian	272	DB	Nebraska	Cleveland	10
Washington, James	137	DB	UCLA	Los Angeles Rams	5
Weber, David	283	QB	Carroll (Wis.)	Los Angeles Raiders	9
Wells, Brandy	226	DB	Notre Dame	Cincinnati	9
Wester, Herb	114	T	Iowa	Cincinnati	5
Whitaker, Danta	186	TE	Mississippi Valley	New York Giants	7
White, Derrick	164	DB	Oklahoma	Minnesota	6
White, Lorenzo	22	RB	Michigan State	Houston	1
White, Sheldon	62	DB	Miami (Ohio)	New York Giants	3
White, Todd	176	WR	Cal State-Fullerton	Philadelphia	7
White, William	85	DB	Ohio State	Detroit	4
Widell, Dave	94	T	Boston College	Dallas	4
Wiley, Carter	306	DB	Virginia Tech	Atlanta	12
Wilkes, Steve	265	TE	Appalachian State	New York Giants	10
Wilkinson, Neal	228	TE	James Madison	Green Bay	9
Williams, Channing	268	RB	Arizona State	Denver	10
Williams, Jarvis	42	DB	Florida	Miami	2
Williams, Terry	37	DB	Bethune-Cookman	New York Jets	2
Williams, Warren	155	RB	Miami	Pittsburgh	6
Wise, Deatrich	242	NT	Jackson State	Seattle	9
Withycombe, Mike	119	T	Fresno State	New York Jets	5
Wolkow, Troy	115	G	Minnesota	New England	5
Woods, Ickey	31	RB	Nevada-Las Vegas	Cincinnati	2
Woodside, Keith	61	RB	Texas A&M	Green Bay	3
Wright, Bo	184	RB	Alabama	Buffalo	7
Wright, Jeff	213	NT	Central Missouri	Buffalo	8

1988
NFL SCHEDULE

*NIGHT GAME

SUNDAY, SEPT. 4
Atlanta at Detroit
Cleveland at Kansas City
Dallas at Pittsburgh
Houston at Indianapolis
Los Angeles Rams at Green Bay
Miami at Chicago
Minnesota at Buffalo
New York Jets at New England
Philadelphia at Tampa Bay
Phoenix at Cincinnati
San Diego at Los Angeles Raiders
San Francisco at New Orleans
Seattle at Denver

MONDAY, SEPT. 5
*Washington at New York Giants

SUNDAY, SEPT. 11
Chicago at Indianapolis
Cincinnati at Philadelphia
Detroit at Los Angeles Rams
Kansas City at Seattle
Los Angeles Raiders at Houston
Miami at Buffalo
New England at Minnesota
New Orleans at Atlanta
New York Jets at Cleveland
Pittsburgh at Washington
San Diego at Denver
San Francisco at New York Giants
Tampa Bay at Green Bay

MONDAY, SEPT. 12
*Dallas at Phoenix

SUNDAY, SEPT. 18
Atlanta at San Francisco
Buffalo at New England
Cincinnati at Pittsburgh
Denver at Kansas City
Los Angeles Rams at LA Raiders

Minnesota at Chicago
New Orleans at Detroit
New York Giants at Dallas
Philadelphia at Washington
Phoenix at Tampa Bay
Seattle at San Diego

MONDAY, SEPT. 19
*Indianapolis at Cleveland

SUNDAY, SEPT. 25
Atlanta at Dallas
Chicago at Green Bay
Cleveland at Cincinnati
LA Rams at New York Giants
Miami at Indianapolis
New England at Houston
New York Jets at Detroit
Philadelphia at Minnesota
Pittsburgh at Buffalo
San Diego at Kansas City
San Francisco at Seattle
Tampa Bay at New Orleans
Washington at Phoenix

MONDAY, SEPT. 26
*Los Angeles Raiders at Denver

SUNDAY, OCT. 2
Buffalo at Chicago
Cincinnati at Los Angeles Raiders
Cleveland at Pittsburgh
Denver at San Diego
Detroit at San Francisco
Green Bay at Tampa Bay
Houston at Philadelphia
Indianapolis at New England
Kansas City at New York Jets
Minnesota at Miami
New York Giants at Washington
Phoenix at Los Angeles Rams
Seattle at Atlanta

Pats' Andre Tippett was players' pick as LB of the Year.

MONDAY, OCT. 3
*Dallas at New Orleans

SUNDAY, OCT. 9
Chicago at Detroit
Denver at San Francisco
Indianapolis at Buffalo
Kansas City at Houston
Los Angeles Rams at Atlanta
Miami at Los Angeles Raiders
New England vs. Green Bay
　at Milwaukee
New Orleans at San Diego
New York Jets at Cincinnati
Pittsburgh at Phoenix
Seattle at Cleveland
Tampa Bay at Minnesota
Washington at Dallas

MONDAY, OCT. 10
*New York Giants at Philadelphia

SUNDAY, OCT. 16
Atlanta at Denver
Cincinnati at New England
Dallas at Chicago
Detroit at New York Giants
Green Bay at Minnesota
Houston at Pittsburgh
Los Angeles Raiders at Kansas City
New Orleans at Seattle
Philadelphia at Cleveland
Phoenix at Washington
San Diego at Miami
San Francisco at Los Angeles Rams
Tampa Bay at Indianapolis

MONDAY, OCT. 17
*Buffalo at New York Jets

SUNDAY, OCT. 23
Cleveland at Phoenix
Dallas at Philadelphia
Denver at Pittsburgh
Detroit at Kansas City
Houston at Cincinnati
Indianapolis at San Diego
Los Angeles Raiders at New Orleans
Minnesota at Tampa Bay
New England at Buffalo
New York Giants at Atlanta
New York Jets at Miami

Seattle at Los Angeles Rams
Washington vs. Green Bay
　at Milwaukee

MONDAY, OCT. 24
*San Francisco at Chicago

SUNDAY, OCT. 30
Atlanta at Philadelphia
Chicago at New England
Cincinnati at Cleveland
Green Bay at Buffalo
Kansas City at Los Angeles Raiders
Los Angeles Rams at New Orleans
Miami at Tampa Bay
Minnesota at San Francisco
New York Giants at Detroit
Phoenix at Dallas
Pittsburgh at New York Jets
San Diego at Seattle
*Washington at Houston

MONDAY, OCT. 31
*Denver at Indianapolis

SUNDAY, NOV. 6
Buffalo at Seattle
Dallas at New York Giants
Detroit at Minnesota
Green Bay at Atlanta
Kansas City at Denver
Los Angeles Rams at Philadelphia
Miami at New England
New Orleans at Washington
New York Jets at Indianapolis
Pittsburgh at Cincinnati
San Francisco at Phoenix
Tampa Bay at Chicago
*Los Angeles Raiders at San Diego

MONDAY, NOV. 7
*Cleveland at Houston

SUNDAY, NOV. 13
Chicago at Washington
Cincinnati at Kansas City
Cleveland at Denver
Houston at Seattle
Indianapolis at Green Bay
Los Angeles Raiders at San Francisco
New England at New York Jets
New Orleans at Los Angeles Rams
New York Giants at Phoenix

Philadelphia at Pittsburgh
San Diego at Atlanta
Tampa Bay at Detroit
*Minnesota at Dallas

MONDAY, NOV. 14
*Buffalo at Miami

SUNDAY, NOV. 20
Atlanta at Los Angeles Raiders
Chicago at Tampa Bay
Cincinnati at Dallas
Denver at New Orleans
Detroit vs. Green Bay
  at Milwaukee
Indianapolis at Minnesota
New York Jets at Buffalo
Philadelphia at New York Giants
Phoenix at Houston
Pittsburgh at Cleveland
San Diego at Los Angeles Rams
Seattle at Kansas City
*New England at Miami

MONDAY, NOV. 21
*Washington at San Francisco

THURSDAY, NOV. 24
Minnesota at Detroit
Houston at Dallas

SUNDAY, NOV. 27
Buffalo at Cincinnati
Cleveland at Washington
Green Bay at Chicago
Kansas City at Pittsburgh
Los Angeles Rams at Denver
Miami at New York Jets
New England at Indianapolis
Phoenix at Philadelphia
San Francisco at San Diego
Tampa Bay at Atlanta
*New York Giants at New Orleans

MONDAY, NOV. 28
*Los Angeles Raiders at Seattle

SUNDAY, DEC. 14
Buffalo at Tampa Bay
Dallas at Cleveland
Denver at Los Angeles Raiders
Green Bay at Detroit

Indianapolis at Miami
New Orleans at Minnesota
New York Jets at Kansas City
Phoenix at New York Giants
San Diego at Cincinnati
San Francisco at Atlanta
Seattle at New England
Washington at Philadelphia
*Pittsburgh at Houston

MONDAY, DEC. 5
*Chicago at Los Angeles Rams

SATURDAY, DEC. 10
Indianapolis at New York Jets
Philadelphia at Phoenix

SUNDAY, DEC. 11
Atlanta at Los Angeles Rams
Cincinnati at Houston
Dallas at Washington
Detroit at Chicago
Kansas City at New York Giants
Los Angeles Raiders at Buffalo
Minnesota at Green Bay
New Orleans at San Francisco
Pittsburgh at San Diego
Tampa Bay at New England
*Denver at Seattle

MONDAY, DEC. 12
*Cleveland at Miami

SATURDAY, DEC. 17
New England at Denver
Washington at Cincinnati

SUNDAY, DEC. 18
Atlanta at New Orleans
Buffalo at Indianapolis
Detroit at Tampa Bay
Green Bay at Phoenix
Houston at Cleveland
Kansas City at San Diego
Miami at Pittsburgh
New York Giants at New York Jets
Philadelphia at Dallas
Seattle at Los Angeles Raiders
*Los Angeles Rams at San Francisco

MONDAY, DEC. 19
*Chicago at Minnesota

Jets' Ken O'Brien revs up for a better season.

Nationally Televised Games

(All games carried on CBS Radio Network)

REGULAR SEASON

Monday, Sept. 5–Washington at New York Giants (night, ABC)
Monday, Sept. 12–Dallas at Phoenix (night, ABC)
Monday, Sept. 19–Indianapolis at Cleveland (night, ABC)
Monday, Sept. 26–Los Angeles Raiders at Denver (night, ABC)
Monday, Oct. 3–Dallas at New Orleans (night, ABC)
Monday, Oct. 10–New York Giants at Philadelphia (night, ABC)
Monday, Oct. 17–Buffalo at New York Jets (night, ABC)
Monday, Oct. 24–San Francisco at Chicago (night, ABC)
Sunday, Oct. 30–Washington at Houston (night, ESPN)
Monday, Oct. 31–Denver at Indianapolis (night, ABC)
Sunday, Nov. 6–Los Angeles Raiders at San Diego (night, ESPN)
Monday, Nov. 7–Cleveland at Houston (night, ABC)
Sunday, Nov. 13–Minnesota at Dallas (night, ESPN)
Monday, Nov. 14–Buffalo at Miami (night, ABC)
Sunday, Nov. 20–New England at Miami (night, ESPN)
Monday, Nov. 21–Washington at San Francisco (night, ABC)
Thursday, Nov. 24–(Thanksgiving) Minnesota at Detroit (day, CBS)
                                     Houston at Dallas (day, NBC)
Sunday, Nov. 27–New York Giants at New Orleans (night, ESPN)
Monday, Nov. 28–Los Angeles Raiders at Seattle (night, ABC)
Sunday, Dec. 4–Pittsburgh at Houston (night, ESPN)
Monday, Dec. 5–Chicago at Los Angeles Rams (night, ABC)
Saturday, Dec. 10– Indianapolis at New York Jets (day, NBC)
                                     Philadelphia at Phoenix (day, CBS)
Sunday, Dec. 11–Denver at Seattle (night, ESPN)
Monday, Dec. 12–Cleveland at Miami (night, ABC)
Saturday, Dec. 17– Washington at Cincinnati (day, CBS)
                                     New England at Denver (day, NBC)
Sunday, Dec. 18–Los Angeles Rams at San Francisco (night, ESPN)
Monday, Dec. 19–Chicago at Minnesota (night, ABC)

POSTSEASON

Saturday, Dec. 24–AFC First–Round Playoff (NBC)
Monday, Dec. 26–NFC First–Round Playoff (CBS)
Saturday, Dec. 31–AFC and NFC Divisional Playoffs (NBC and CBS)
Sunday, Jan. 1–AFC and NFC Divisional Playoffs (NBC and CBS)
Sunday, Jan. 8–AFC and NFC Championship Games (NBC and CBS)
Sunday, Jan. 22–Super Bowl XXIII, Joe Robbie Stadium, Miami (NBC)
Sunday, Jan. 29–AFC–NFC Pro Bowl, Honolulu (ESPN)

Revised and updated with over 75 all
new sports records and photographs!

THE ILLUSTRATED
SPORTS RECORD BOOK
Zander Hollander and David Schulz

Here in a single book are more than 350
all-time sports records with stories and
photos so vivid it's like "being there." All the
sports classics are here: Babe Ruth, Wilt
Chamberlain, Muhammad Ali ... plus the
stories of such active stars as Dwight Gooden
and Wayne Gretzky. This is the authoritative
book on what the great records are, and
who set them—an engrossing, fun-filled
reference guide filled with anecdotes of
hundreds of renowned athletes whose
remarkable records remain as fresh as when
they were set.
